IT SHINED

The Saga of The Ozark Mountain Daredevils

by

MICHAEL SUPE GRANDA

authorHOUSE

AuthorHouse™
1663 Liberty Drive, Suite 200
Bloomington, IN 47403
www.authorhouse.com
Phone: 1-800-839-8640

This book is a work of non-fiction. Unless otherwise noted, the author and the publisher make no explicit guarantees as to the accuracy of the information contained in this book and in some cases, names of people and places have been altered to protect their privacy.

© 2008 Michael Supe Granda. All rights reserved.

No part of this book may be reproduced, stored in a retrieval system, or transmitted by any means without the written permission of the author.

First published by AuthorHouse 8/13/2008

ISBN: 978-1-4343-9166-7 (sc)
ISBN: 978-1-4343-9165-0 (hc)

Library of Congress Control Number: 2008905410

Printed in the United States of America
Bloomington, Indiana

This book is printed on acid-free paper.

Dedicated to my dear mother, Ellen, who, four years ago—as she was taking her final breaths—taught me several things about life. She helped me realize that life is fragile, time is short, and there isn't a lot of it to just fool around and not get things done. It was her inspiration that sat me down. It took four years to write this story.

ACKNOWLEDGMENTS

I would be remiss if I didn't the time to thank a few people who were instrumental in the process of this story.

To Michael Kuelker, who transcribed the very acorn of this book, while helping send me on my way.

To Ron Bowles, for persistently pursuing and encouraging this tale's fruition.

To Joel Pierson, for helping me get over my addiction to commas.

To Jim Huff, who not only helped with the final touches, but over the years, has helped out everyone in a pinch.

To Hey Bill Haines, who researched and answered every crazy rock 'n' roll question I shot at him—no matter how stupid. Without him, many of the details in this book would not have been as anatomically correct.

To (in no certain order) Mark Marymont, Mike O'Brien, Mike O'Dell, Suze Dunville, Curt Hargus, Joe Bidewell, Wayne Carson, Dave Marsh, Paul Peterson, Stan Plesser, Bob Garcia, Bill Lloyd, Donald Bromage, David Mattacks, Michael Brewer, Tom Shipley, Chris Albert, Ken McMahan, Jay Orr, Dawn Oberg, Tom & Pam Pierson, Scott McEwen, Maple Byrne, Dennis Pratt, David Coonrod, John Einarson, Mike Robertson, Lee Roy Parnell, Rob Rains, Carl Tatz, Jerry Hoover, Jim Mayfield, and Billy Higgins for their input, cooperation, and time.

Most of all, I'd like to thank my partners, which consists of every musician who, over the years, I've stepped onto the stage with as a Daredevil. They all played their roles—as well as their instruments—very, very well.

All shined.

PROLOGUE

Greetings, friend. It's nice to see you. I'm glad, as well as thankful, you've picked up this book. The story you're about to dig into is an odd one, filled with many twists and turns. This long and winding road will NOT fit into Reader's Digest or People magazine. It'd be quite hard to fit a thirty-hrmphhh-year career into anything but a healthy tome.

Not only is it the tale of a little hillbilly rock-n-roll band, who just happened to be in the right place at the right time, but a story of the love affair I've maintained with my adopted home of Springfield, Missouri.

Unlike many of the characters you're about to meet, I did not grow up in Springfield, Missouri. My formative years were spent learning to play guitar in the shadow of Mel Bay's south St. Louis music store. By the time I got to Springfield, I was already a stoned-out hippie square peg with one thing—and one thing only—on my mind. That was making music and finding other people who liked making it too.

The Ozarks have always had a very rich musical tradition, from its mysterious hill lilts to the frisky country music of the Ozark Jubilee. (For you history buffs, the first syndicated country music television show emanated from Springfield, Missouri.) When the Jubilee closed its doors and headed for Nashville, many wonderful musicians decided not to go—opting to stay snug as a bug in the wonderful Ozark hills. The musical proficiency of the area is and has always been very high—something I really enjoyed.

I had the best of both worlds. Not only was I able to experience remnants of the Jubilee, I was able to bring along the lively spirit of one of St. Louis's own traditions: Gaslight Square. Though Gaslight was in its waning hours and I was only a seventeen-year-old kid and it was only a one-night stand, this is where I canceled my subscription to Boys' Life. It's also where I learned to administer the frisky nature of rock 'n' roll, St. Louis style. This is the element I tried to bring to the table when the Ducks convened.

Though the Ducks—which you will soon learn to be the nickname we used when we didn't want to refer to ourselves with our cumbersome, seven-syllable name—gained notoriety as being from Springfield, I was always the kid from St. Louis.

Much of this book is written for the fans of Springfield music. This is done by design—a gesture to thank them for welcoming me into their community of art, music, sociology, and botany. It contains names and places that won't mean much to the outside world. But to Springfieldians, they mean the world.

I realize I'm one of the lucky ones. I've been afforded a wonderfully adventurous life, doing the only thing I've ever wanted to do—a life many wish for and don't attain. Just to be in a position to write this book about that life is an absolute privilege. Dreams can come true.

This is how I remember it—from the stage, looking out. If you ask other Ducks to verify various occurrences, they may not be able to—for two reasons. One, they may not have been there when a certain scene was unfolding, or two, they just can't remember either. As I researched this story, each man sat for long periods of time, recollecting how things unfolded. All were completely cooperative, for which I'm completely grateful. After listening to their variations on a theme, I'm confident I was able to glean the real story—or close to it.

Pull up a chair and get comfortable beside this wood stove. I'll grab us a couple beers and roll one up. If you want to read about my early musical days (before I even got to Springfield), you can start with the epilogue. For those who don't care about that, here comes chapter 1.

As I recall …

CHAPTER 1

It was the beat. There it was. I could hear it. I could hear it coming through the glass of my father's behemoth, faded-red '67 Ford station wagon. Actually, it wasn't coming through the glass. You see, all of the windows of our very un-air-conditioned family sedan were already rolled down. That beat was pounding through the open windows.

The Ozark summer was in full sweat. Late August, 1969 was as muggy as muggy can be, as we pulled our red tank up to the front doors of Fruedenberger Hall—one of the two men's dormitories on the campus of Southwest Missouri State University in Springfield, Missouri. This small, state school may have been one of the only facilities our family could afford. But that did not matter to me. Today was my *bon voyage* and I couldn't wait to get out of the car.

This was the first time anyone in my family had moved outside the small, blue-collar around the south side of St. Louis. This would mean I would no longer be able to pick up Grandma, get her to the store, get her to the bakery, and make it in time for Sunday afternoon family barbecue/beer fest/wiffleball games.

Springfield, Missouri? I'd never heard of it. But, it sounded good to me. It didn't matter where I was going. The important thing was that I was going somewhere, scared like any red-blooded American kid off to college for the first time. I couldn't wait to get on with it.

The four-hour drive from St. Louis to Springfield along Route 66 was a long one for a car with seven people crammed into it. My brother, Mark sat in front between my parents. I squeezed into the back seat with my three younger sisters, Pat, Penny, and Pam. As you can see, my folks had a real fifties approach to naming kids. Pick a letter and run with it.

When I stepped out of the car, that thud of bass and drums remained in the air.

Check-in proceedings began, at once. Page after page of applications were filled out, line after line signed. Still, all I could do was remain transfixed on the rock 'n' roll band I could hear off in the distance.

I knew that sound. Everyone knows that sound. There's no mistaking the distant sound of strange boys of all ages, making strange noises of all kinds.

You see, I am one of those strange boys, for packed into the back of our car, along with all of the basic necessities one takes to college (alarm clock, toothbrush, underwear), was my Harmony guitar, my Kingston bass, my Hilgen bass amp with its semi-shredded fifteen-inch speaker, a record player, and two boxes of records.

Space was cramped, but I was not about to leave this music behind. Clothes? Don't need many. Boxes of assorted knickknacks? Don't need any. Chalk this one up as a classic example of priorities. These musical instruments were wreaking havoc on my young mind and soul, while instilling a sense of pleasure that would never leave my bones.

Fortunately—or unfortunately—they also bestowed upon me a sense of tunnel vision I have also never been able to shake.

The metamorphosis—much to my father's chagrin—had been taking place over the last few years of my middle-class, suburban, high school days. My love of sports and mathematics had been displaced by a burning desire to play guitar, grow my hair, drink beer, smoke cigarettes, and sing at the top of my lungs (whether it was good, or not). Oh yeah, and chase girls. Yay adolescence!

Now, here I was. But where was I, and what *was* this place named Springfield? I didn't know and I didn't care. I was out of the car and there was music in the air.

It took no time to carry what little stuff I had in the car up to the second floor, where it was just piled into my empty room. An eerie calm hung in the cool, quiet linoleum hallways.

With teary good-byes, we parted ways. As the Granda clan headed back to St. Louis, Mama Ellen cried. Papa Bob muttered to himself, "Phew. One down, four to go." Brother Mark was elated, about to inherit the cramped bedroom we'd shared for the past fifteen years. My sisters—just glad to reclaim any kind of space in the back of the car—could only look out the back window, wave and whisper to each other, "He's weird."

All I heard was the distant thudding.

Before unpacking one thing out of one box, the very first moment of my new life was spent in search of the noisy grail. I located the building that contained all the racket and walked in on a student welcoming concert. As a band of young guys flailed away with renditions of David Bowie (who I've never been a fan of) and "Yummy, yummy, yummy, I've got love in my tummy" (which made me sick to mine), my enthusiasm quickly waned.

The first thing I noticed was "The Bubble" neatly painted on the bass drum head. The name was appropriate—a nice, clean-cut group of bubbly, well-dressed, well-mannered, rosy-cheeked lads. The next thing I noticed was their equipment—nice, new, shiny, and abundant. Then, I couldn't help but hear their British accents. Now, I love listening to John Lennon and Paul McCartney sing as much as the next guy. But I've always had a hard time swallowing a bunch of suburban American guys trying to sound like they're from Liverpool. They were less than convincing. I left, disappointed.

While taking the long way back to my room, I slowly meandered through my second hour of college life. Among the myriad of notes plastered across the campus bulletin boards, my eye was caught by a poster for another gig that evening. Maybe nightfall would bring a better band to the table.

My dorm room was silent and—because I had no roommate yet—half-filled. The rest of the day was spent lolling about, reading, staring out the window, and trying to figure out where in the hell I was. Basically, I was just biding my time until show time.

When evening rolled around, the distant pounding started and once again, I was drawn to it. It was a beautiful evening, as I walked over the crest of the hill and saw the large gathering sprawled across the lawn in front of Craig Hall, home of the school's vaunted theater department.

I could tell, right off the bat, that this was a bigger band than the Bubble. These guys had a nice big PA, lots of lights, and a large trailer with their name scrawled on the side. The stage looked like the showroom floor of a damned music store. There were guitars and amps and keyboards and drums and shit everywhere.

Plus, one of the guys had a beard, which I took as a good sign. By this time, my beard was almost twelve hours old. Things were looking up. But, as the Lavender Hill Mob began to play, David Bowie songs were replaced by Three Dog Night songs and "Yummy, yummy, yummy …" turned into "Jeremiah was a bullfrog …"

I quickly realized that I wasn't in St. Louis anymore, Toto.

Though I was too young to have made any kind of an impact on the St. Louis music scene, it had made a gigantic impression on me. Its rich musical history was heaven for the musical sponge I had become over the past five years. I also feel privileged to have acquired its diverse musical palette. I loved being able to hear the Rolling Stones and the Kinks one night, then hear James Brown and Otis Redding the next, then attend a dance where local icons Ike Turner, Oliver Sain and Bob Kuban were rocking houses with their bands.

Within the past few months, I'd been to Kiel Auditorium (where I'd just seen Jimi Hendrix), the Fox Theater (where I'd just seen the Grateful Dead) and the Mississippi River Festival (where I'd just seen Bob Dylan sit in with my all-time favorite musical entity—the Band).

Now, here I was in this place called Springfield, Missouri, alone for the first time in my life, listening to some guy, who looked like he had been selling insurance all day, trying to be One Dog Night.

I stayed to see if the music would get any better. But it didn't. Still, it was the only rock 'n' roll band in town—at least as far as I knew. But then, what did I know? I hadn't even been in town for a day.

Once again, I left disappointed—batting 0 for 2, musically. When I returned to my room, it was still empty. After an evening of loud music, the quiet of the dorm was deafening. The bright sunlight, which had streamed through my large windows all day, was replaced by a dappled light, trickling in from the lamppost on the corner of Madison and Lombard.

Where was I, and what was this place called Springfield? As I began to drift off to sleep, thoughts of the eventful day danced in my head. Then thoughts of the two signs I had earlier seen rolled in. These two giant signs would turn out to be two giant clues to where I was.

The first appeared before I even got to town. As the large exit sign on the highway came into view, emblazoned with the words Springfield/Buffalo, I had to chuckle at the coincidence of getting off the highway, two hundred miles from home, in a place that shared the names of another one of my favorite bands—Buffalo Springfield. The green sign shone through the windshield of the red car like a beacon of light, a ray of hope, a breath of fresh air

When we pulled off the highway (Route 66) onto Glenstone Avenue (Route 65), things shifted down several gears and back several years. Complete with the mandatory glut of burger joints, gas stations, car lots and churches, Glenstone (which connects the two burgs of Buffalo and Springfield) can only be described as the quintessential main drag of the quintessential American town.

As we pulled off the highway and into the first gas station we could find, I saw the second sign.

Bob lifted the hood of the car to check the oil and water, as my sisters ran for the restroom. I strolled across the parking lot, just to stretch and get some feeling back into my legs.

The church that sat at the far end of the lot displayed the large, ornate sign declaring its denomination and numeric value (First or Second or Third Church of the Blessed Whatever). But as I got closer, it was the smaller sign that hung underneath that caught my attention. This subtler message bellowed, loudly. Under the hours of worship and the witty proverb, the small placard read—RICH WHITE, PASTOR.

I couldn't believe my eyes. My quiet astonishment slowly faded into startled realization. Could this guy's name actually be Richard White, or was this some kind of subliminal message about this place called Springfield, Missouri?

I sighed with relief at the sign on the highway.

I gasped in disbelief at the sign on the church.

Signs. Signs. Everywhere signs. These two would begin my love affair with this small American town, its rich, white pastors (whom I would pay no attention to) and its rich musical heritage (which I would pay plenty of attention to). I'd found a place to hang my hat.

Day two of college life, and I woke up in a still unshared dorm room. As I looked out my window at the scene below, it looked like an ant colony—people scurrying about, unloading cars and carrying boxes up steps. Outside my door, I could hear the hustle and bustle in the hall. My door remained closed.

I'd like to say that the first thing I did was pull my guitar out of its case. But that wasn't the case. It did not have a case. I hauled it around—carefully, mind you—by its neck. I WILL say the first thing I did was pick it up and start playing it.

Then, the second thing I did was plug in my record player and start playing it. While the collegiate world rushed by outside, I spent my day settling into my new home, two hundred miles away from a tumultuous Lindbergh High School and their scrict 'length of hair' policies.

Boxes eventually got unpacked. What few possessions I did have got put away into drawers and closets. The airwaves were immediately filled with the sounds of Fats and the Beatles, the Coasters and Stones, Spike, the Mothers, and Chuck.

When lunchtime rolled around, I strolled to the cafeteria. On my way, I saw yet another poster on yet another bulletin board for yet another gig. This time, the band's name really grabbed me. I stood there and laughed out loud. I've always enjoyed hearing off-the-wall band names. This was a good one. The gig was later that afternoon. I had to check out the guys who decided to call their band "Granny's Bathwater."

After the two I heard yesterday, expectations weren't high. But when Granny's weighed in with "Milk Cow Blues", "Sweet Root Man" and "What's the Matter with the Mill?" along with a handful of Jimmy Reed and Bo Diddley songs, I was had. I did *not* leave early.

The driving force was a tall, lanky guitarist by the name of Mike Bunge, who stood center stage and led the proceedings. Drummer Lloyd Hicks—who would go on to play with everyone from Martha Reeves to Dave Alvin—attacked his drums in a very un-Three Dog Night-like manner. Alongside bassist Dave Pease, the two provided a very solid rhythm section.

The fourth member was lead singer and rhythm guitarist John Dillon.

While each member had his own personality, they really played well together—the same way the good St. Louis bands I was used to hearing, did. Their song list was made up of old rock 'n' roll and R&B tunes, many of which I was familiar with. Plus, I enjoyed the fact that they looked like they were having a great time, singing in their natural voices—instead of trying to feign British accents.

This time, the third time was the charm. I finally found some musicians I could sit and listen to. I became an immediate Granny's fan. I couldn't wait to hear them again. Afterward, when I approached them to let them know just how much I enjoyed them, I learned they were playing at a place on the outskirts of town called the Half-a-Hill Club. Though I had no mode of transportation, I was going to be there.

Dave Concors had a motorcycle—and two helmets.

As I sat in my room, listening to Paul Butterfield's "East, West" (another musician I'd also just seen in St. Louis), a head of fuzzy hair stuck itself in my door. Introducing himself as Dave, he observed that we were probably the only two people in the entire place who knew who Paul Butterfield was. As I invited him in, he asked if I'd heard of Magic Dick.

When I told him that I hadn't, he was off to his room, down the hall, to retrieve a record. Along with it, he brought a copy of an album by a guy from his home town of Atlantic City. The rest of the afternoon was spent listening to Butterfield, J. Geils, and Bruce Springsteen.

We hit it off immediately, as he talked as proudly of Springsteen as I did about Chuck Berry. When dinnertime rolled around, talk turned to Viet Nam and this small, Ozark town, no one in the outside world seemed to be paying much attention to.

In his high school days, he had played in local bands around Atlantic City, the same way I had around St. Louis. When he picked up my bass and started playing it, I asked, "Do you sing?"

"No. Not really," came his hesitant reply.

"Okay. Then you'll be the bass player and I'll be the singer."

Thus, a friendship was struck between two guys with identical tastes in music.

As we spent the next few days hanging out, playing music and listening to records, another knock on the door came. Rick Montgomery, who had heard the racket, introduced himself as another guitar player from St. Louis. In less than a week, we had the makings of a band.

Because we all just lived down the hall from each other, getting together was not a problem. And because no one had ever moved into the other side of my room, it became our makeshift practice hall. Of course, we couldn't play very loud. After all, we were still in a college dormitory and I did not want to draw a whole lot of attention to my single room.

Practices basically consisted of just sitting around, listening to records (at "dorm room" volume) and trying to figure out how to play them on our guitars. These sessions became our source of escape from the glut of David Bowie and Three Dog Night cover bands that Springfield seemed to be saturated with.

I told Dave he needed to hear this cool band I'd heard called Granny's Bathwater. We jumped on his bike and headed to the Half-a-Hill. I loved the place. When we got to the club, no one checked to see if we were twenty-one. It also seemed to be filled with locals instead of college students. This was more to my liking.

During breaks, everyone just headed outside into the quiet evening, where joints were freely passed among friends, scattered through the shadows of the tall sycamore trees. It was on the Half-a-Hill parking lot where we met Chris Albert, who had just moved to Springfield from Dallas. In Dallas, he spent his time singing and playing guitar. In Springfield, he was just another new guy in town.

As we walked back inside and bellied up to the bar, when Dave and I told him we had the makings of a band, he lit up like a Christmas tree. When he let us know he had a drummer he could bring to the table, in the snap of a bottle cap, we became a band.

Chris knew the owner of the Warehouse Experience, a dark, seedy club right in the heart of downtown Springfield. Complete with blacklight posters of Jimi Hendrix and Bob Dylan, peanut shells all over the floor, parachutes hung from the ceiling, and a well-stocked jukebox, we took up residence in the damp, aromatic basement of the building.

If the club was seedy, the basement was even seedier, smelling of stale beer and musty cardboard boxes. We didn't care. We knew the guy who ran the club upstairs. We could play as loudly as we wanted in the basement.

When we assembled, we were introduced to Mike Schwartz, yet another St. Louisan, who played a double bass drum kit in a very manic style. This suited me fine. Keith Moon was and still is, my favorite rock star. Rick and Chris manned the guitars. Dave played bass. I became the lead singer. I have never been a very good singer, but I wasn't going to let a small detail like that get in my way.

Dave remembers, "So, let's see now. Here's a new teen power group for ya. It's 1969 and we put together a ragged East Coast Jew, a madman that wears a Superman shirt, a half-baked Chicano-cum-Italiano and a GQ, hairpiece-wearing, pre-law drummer named Schwartz. Why didn't we make it?

"Let's not forget our beautiful equipment, my Thunderbass amp, which had two settings—'distortion' and 'more distortion'. A Vox PA that consisted of eight transistor radio speakers in a column that also met our distortion criteria."

As we began to run through the Chuck Berry, Buffalo Springfield, Grateful Dead, and Cream songs we'd been working on in my dorm room, Chris threw in songs from his acoustic sets.

That Halloween, just two months after I'd moved to town (and three months after Woodstock shook the nation), we were added to the lineup of the Springfield Pop Festival. Held at the Four Star Opry House on Commercial Street, the place was one of the last musical bastions trying to fill the void left by the recently departed and dearly missed Ozark Jubilee. The Four Star was set up nicely, with a small stage, facing an auditorium full of comfortable seats, heavy curtains and thick aisle carpets. The place bulged around the eighty or ninety mark.

In those days, there were no ad campaigns, marketing plans, or video clips to advertise. All we really had was posters nailed to telephone poles, and of course friends, who called friends, who called friends, who called friends.

When the gig came around, we still hadn't decided on a name. In a classic example of "nothing spurs creativity like a deadline," it wasn't until right before we stepped on stage that we deemed ourselves the Grate Sloth. When we began, the Sloth blasted away as hard as we did in the basement. I was terrified. I had played lots of gigs and had been the main singer in my high school bands for years. The only difference was, I had always worn a bass. Tonight, when Dave put on his, I put on my best Roger Daltrey routine, jumping around like a monkey on a hot tin stage, two tambourines ablaze, two eyes afire, two vocal cords abused.

That night of October 31, 1969, when we loaded our gear out of the Four Star Opry House and back into the basement of the Warehouse, I played my first gig in Springfield.

Having worn a Superman T-shirt for the gig, the next few weeks were filled with people walking by, saying, "Hey, you're that guy in that band—that guy in the Superman shirt." After the Pop Festival (which was a huge success at eighty-five attendees), several gigs on campus, and a plethora of nights at the Warehouse Experience, I became "Supe" to those around me.

It was all an adventure for a kid who, until now, had never hit a lick outside the St. Louis area.

We became the house band at the Warehouse Experience for the rest of the school year, constantly dragging our gear up and down those creaky basement stairs. If the club had a last-minute cancellation, we were the automatic, last-minute replacement. The Sloth developed a very odd following of students, downtown characters, street people, local misfits, wayward stoners, and an amoeba-like circle of friends.

Before I went back to St. Louis for the summer of '70, we held a business meeting. Deciding we needed to make a demo tape to help us get gigs next year, Chris suggested we head over to Wayne Carson's Top Talent Studio. I was all ears. I had never been in a studio. But if we could record a couple of songs, we could press up an actual 45-rpm record for fall—when we returned to school and started gigging again.

Sitting in a small, cinder-block building at the corner of Glenstone and Elm, Top Talent was owned and operated by Carson, who had just written "The Letter." Along with publisher/partner, Si Siman (Earl Barton Music), the two had begun cashing the large publishing checks that had started to trickle in from the Box Tops' version of the song. Wayne and Si put this money right back into the studio. It became The House "The Letter" Built.

Though, I had never been in a recording studio, I'd seen pictures. I completely understood the theory of multi-track recording. When Chris suggested we stop by and check out a session his friends were playing on, I was all antennae.

When we walked in, the place was jumping. Wayne and Bunge sat at the mixing console, a long guitar cable reaching from Mike's guitar in his lap to his amp in the other room. The rest of Granny's—John Dillon,

Lloyd Hicks, and Dave Pease—were providing the backing tracks. Horn man, Bill Jones and singer, Larry Lee were also lending a hand. Though only a sixteen-track studio, it sounded like a million bucks to me. Wayne's songs, with Granny's funky sound, felt like 10 million.

Give me a ticket for an aeroplane.

When the band finished the take, everyone re-entered the control room for the playback. Handshakes went around, as did joints and beer. As the session enlivened, I became the new guy/quiet guy in the back of the room.

I *kind of* knew these guys. But, not really.

These guys *kind of* knew me. But, not really.

They didn't mind us hanging around. So, we did.

As the session continued, Chris, Dave and I took Wayne off to the side. When we told him that we wanted to come in and record a couple of songs, he got out his appointment book. The Grate Sloth booked their first recording session. Bunge agreed to be "engineer on the spot."

Snap your fingers.

By the time we walked into Top Talent, we had two songs worked up, nicely. Rehearsals were spirited. But when the day of the session rolled around, Schwartz was unexpectedly summoned to St. Louis. When he called with the bad news, we were left without a drummer. The house kit sat quietly in the drum booth.

Chris recalls, "When we realized Schwartz wasn't going to make it, we just looked at each other and wondered, 'What are we going to do? Who else knows these songs? Supe, can you play drums?'"

It was this or cancel the session. That was out of the question. I said, "Gimme those sticks," and started setting up the drums the same way I used to set up my mom's kitchen chairs into a makeshift set. Instead of thumping on her stuffed cushions, I was going to do some serious banging on some real drums.

The Sloth became an instant quartet, as I morphed from Mick into Ringo. With Chris, Dave and Rick, we pulled the session off. Luckily, rock 'n' roll beats aren't too difficult. Though, they weren't the smoothest tracks, I was able to macho my way through them and get them on tape.

Then it came time to add my vocals.

We all know how much we hate our voice when we hear it played back. I am the worst. I realize I'm not a gifted singer—and don't pretend to be. But I WAS the singer and it WAS time for the singer to step up to the microphone, which Bunge set up and adjusted to my height. I was stone cold petrified.

When the time came, everybody gathered in the control room. Once we got started and my squawking began, Mike—recognizing how nervous I was—stopped the tape and walked into the studio with a joint, pretending to re-adjust the microphone. He basically came in to hang around for a couple of minutes, have a couple of tokes, crack a couple of jokes, and loosen me up.

It was a wonderful gesture—one I'll never forget. Though I didn't know him that well, he broke the ice, calmed me down, fired me up, and allowed me to deliver a couple of those stunningly average vocals I've become so famous for. It was my first recording session. He helped me through it.

The songs were cut. The Sloth was captured. Shortly afterward, Rick informed us that he wouldn't be returning to school in the fall. Therefore, he would be leaving the band, effective immediately. After vanishing into thin air, Schwartz was never heard from again.

The three remaining members bid each other adieu for the summer. Chris stayed in Springfield. Dave returned to Atlantic City. I packed my bags and hitchhiked to St. Louis, returning as a guy in a band that had just made a record. Well, technically, the band wasn't really together and technically, the record wasn't really pressed up yet. But, what are a few minor details and a mere ninety days among friends?

Though I was only going to be gone three months, when I left, I immediately began counting the days until I could get back to Springfield. I had fallen completely in love with the place.

CHAPTER 2

As the summer of '70 slowly finished in St. Louis, a radio spot on K-SHE caught my ear. When the words "Finley River Memorial Festival" and "Springfield, Missouri" jumped out of the speakers, they hit me in the face like a ton of rolling stones. A rock festival? In Springfield? Count me in.

A phone call to Chris the next day informed me that somehow he was involved in the festival, and if I could somehow make it back in time, the Grate Sloth could garner a slot somewhere over the course of the weekend. Plans were immediately put into action to get back down to the Ozarks earlier than I had intended.

Held on a small farm just outside the city limits, security for the festival was tight. The three days of Woodstock in August, 1969 scared the "Good Old Boy" network of Christian County to death. These zealots just *knew* the hippies were going to descend on their town like locusts and a festival would surely drag everyone into eternal damnation. The end WAS near!

Suspicion, combined with small-town politicians, purposely clogged things up, bogged things down, and turned the whole ordeal into a long, complicated affair. Local authorities made things very difficult every step of the way. Sheriff L.E. "Buff" Lamb was having none of this rock festival nonsense. "I said there was no way they were going to hold that thing in my county," said Lamb. "They wanted to hold it at the old drag strip north of Ozark. I wouldn't allow it."

When the *Christian County Headliner* further reported that a county official had said, "No intoxicants of any kind would be permitted inside the gates. This is to be a concert, not a free-for-all," last-ditch efforts were made by Lamb and other Christian County authorities to squelch any kind of anything. This forced promoters to switch venues at the last minute.

Lamb's hopes and dreams of complete annihilation of the event were dashed when Mickey Owen, sheriff of adjoining Greene County, stepped up to the plate.

Owen, a one-time catcher for the St. Louis Cardinals and Brooklyn Dodgers (1937-1954), had a nice career in baseball. Unfortunately, he will always be remembered as the man who dropped Hugh Casey's last strike in the 1941 World Series, insuring the Dodgers' all-but-certain championship would be delivered to the Yankees. After retiring from baseball, he retired to his home in Greene County, where he opened his Mickey Owen Baseball Camp in Hollister—and ran for sheriff.

Owen knew Lamb was a bozo and a bigger threat than the music fans who were going to bring their tents—as well as their wallets—to town. The *Headliner*, covering the latest twist in the story, reported, "The Greene County Sheriff and prosecutor had voiced no opposition to the festival. One source said: 'This attitude of Sheriff Owen, again displays the sound judgment and understanding that has earned him an enviable reputation as an enforcement officer throughout the entire area.'"

The Christian County citizenry was saved from the plight of the hippies. The gig was switched to a 550-acre farm, 12 miles east of Springfield, which was leased for the occasion from local veterinarian, Dr. Walter Love.

Love recalled, "I just leased them 100 acres and, as I recall, I got it back in good shape. I was out there during the festival and I saw no problems. The media called it my concert. I didn't have anything to do with it."

When Owen invited law enforcement officials from other counties to help him police the event, Buff and his boys were first in line. Making his presence felt, Lamb knocked a few heads, maintaining, "There was no good that came out of that festival, none whatsoever. No good ever comes out of a rock festival. Where you've got kids and drugs, nothing good will come of it."

Owen knew there wouldn't be a lot of trouble. The show went on. Everybody showed.

Amid a lineup that included the James Gang, Pacific Gas & Electric, Sugarloaf, Crow, and the Ides of March, the Sloth was given an early Sunday morning "local band" slot. After a rainy Saturday night, when people began to stir the next morning, emerge from their tents, coffee up, and slowly migrate to the stage, we got the bad news.

We already knew Rick would not be there and because we still hadn't seen hide nor hair of Schwartz, drummer John Lipscomb was lined up to play. When we learned Dave was not going to be able to make it back from Atlantic City in time, we were without a bass player.

Then I realized, "Hey, wait a minute. I'm a bass player."

Though I didn't have my bass with me, I was not about to let this opportunity pass me by. I went on a frantic search for an axe. It happened to belong to Don Shipps, Granny's new bass player. Scheduled to hit the stage shortly after us, they waited in the wings. Don gladly consented to let me play his old Fender Jazz bass.

I will always be grateful for his generosity—a trait many musicians in the Ozarks have. When I was in a jam, Don was there to help. We bonded as bass players, though we were never able to play at the same time—a band doesn't need two bass players. Years later, when I assembled Supe & the Sandwiches, Don was the one I entrusted with bass and groove duties. We became dear friends, sharing a zeal for bass, as well as baseball.

Even though we were scheduled to play at 10:00 on Sunday morning, Chris and I were not going to let opportunity's knock slip away. Last year, the Sloth had slimmed from a quintet to a quartet. This morning, it went on stage as a trio. Trying to re-create the havoc we were used to wreaking with more guys, we played and sang our hearts out.

Details of the show, as well as the song list, are cloudy, probably consisting of me doing Stephen Stills's "Bluebird" and Chris doing the Airplane's "Volunteers." Though we turned in an unmemorable set, I can proudly say that I played the First Annual Finley River Memorial

Festival. Here, I excitedly stepped back into my place among the musicians and artists of the Ozarks.

A footnote to this story—there was no Second Annual Finley River Memorial Festival.

The new year produced a couple of Sloth recruits, as guitarist John Barnes and drummer John Mitchell joined ranks. But, gigs were few and far between. We played a couple of times at the Warehouse Experience before it (ahem) mysteriously closed its doors. Details were (ahem) mysteriously withheld. The Sloth napped.

Chris, in the process of forming a new band with guitarist and fellow SMS classmate Randy Chowning, was losing interest in the Sloth—and to be honest with you, so had I. Let me rephrase that: I no longer had a desire to be a lead singer. I missed playing bass.

There were absolutely no hard feelings when we disbanded and, for the first time, I became a component in a long line of Springfield bands biting the dust. It didn't matter. The Warehouse Experience was just another in a long line of Springfield clubs biting the dust. As the fall of 1970 began, not only did I have no place to play, I had no band.

Grate Sloth at the Finley River Memorial Festival, 1970. Left to right: Chris Albert, John Lipscomb, me (photo by Mike O'Dell)

Grate Sloth at the Warehouse Experience, 1970. Left to right: Chris Albert, Dave Concors, me, John Mitchell, John Barnes. (photo by Marc Barag)

Though I had only been gone for a few months, everywhere I looked, the landscape of the music scene had shifted. Even when Granny's took the stage at the festival, they were in a radical state of change. Bunge was the only face I recognized as a constant. Don Shipps, a large black man—instead of Dave Pease, a large white man—was playing bass. It was John Dillon's last gig, as they were turning from a small, blues band into a large, horn band. They used two drummers—Lloyd, who was phasing out and Larry Lee, who was playing his first gig. The two banged away, side by side.

The funky little quartet I remembered from last year had ballooned to a ten-piece outfit this year. I still liked what I heard, but things sure were different. The repertoire, as well as the sound, swelled mightily, as Memphis Slim mushroomed into the Tower of Power.

This, I learned, would be a common occurrence and an interesting characteristic of the Springfield music scene. Everywhere I looked, things were different. The faces were the same, though the combinations of them weren't. Bands changed—not only personnel, but names. Those who kept their old name had new faces. New faces kept popping up in old places. Old faces kept popping up anew. I enjoyed this a great deal.

The year slowly passed, as I attended classes, bided my time and continued my search for guys to play music with. As the Sloth played the occasional fraternity party at Be-Bops and I got the occasional pick-up gig, I began to feel more comfortable navigating my way around town.

This helped me notice another characteristic of the Springfield music scene. Most of the musicians were local guys who, when putting a band together, remained loyal to their childhood buddies. I was still the kid from St. Louis.

I did get my first chance at infiltration when I was asked to meet with Bob Filbert, head of the local booking agency and percussionist for the Lavender Hill Mob. Their bass player would be leaving soon. The search had begun for his replacement.

The meeting proved fruitless as, during our talk, Bob noticed the absence of a car in front of his office. When I informed him this was because I didn't own a car, he seemed amused. When I told him I had borrowed a friend's bicycle, he was even less amused.

Then, when I informed him that I only had a little-bitty shitty bass amp and a plastic guitar, painted like an American flag, the interview came to a semi-screeching halt. I jumped on my bike and rode off. The Mob's search for a bass player continued. I wasn't too bummed out. It would've been nice to have had a gig, but I didn't miss having to learn all those Three Dog Night and K.C. & the Sunshine Band songs that peppered their song list.

The fall semester proceeded at a snail's pace—my interest in school fading fast. My focus, as well as every male student's, remained on Viet Nam, our student deferments and the new lottery system the Selective Service had just installed.

We all convened in the dormitory lounge for the first year's drawing. It was an uneasy evening as we all sat, nervously listening to Nixon call out numbers, as if he was playing bingo. Tensions weren't eased much either, when my birthday, December 24, was assigned number ninety-five. This wasn't a bad number, nor was it a good number. Still, it was in the lower third percentile of eligibility—well within reach. This made my deferment more valuable than ever.

A couple of weeks of dorm life was all I could take. On a quest for another abode, a handful of us dormitory hippies stumbled upon a large, vacant two-story house, a short hike from campus. Though the place had no glass in the windows, we were so anxious to move in, we took immediate residence. Windows eventually got installed—just in time for the first snow.

When friendly vandals in the middle of the night, attached a four-by-eight sheet of plywood to the front of the house, adorned with spray-paint penmanship, the place was christened the "House of Nutz & Loonies." The place became a hangout for the hippies, musicians, drug users, drug dealers, rubes, and curiosity seekers.

Anything went at any time of the day or night. Occasionally, our Civil War enthusiast landlord would burst in the door with a handful of his friends in full regalia, fresh from battle re-enactments. How odd it was—to sit around, drink beer, and smoke pot with a bunch of guys dressed up like Union and Confederate soldiers.

Three of the four initial Nutz and Loonies were musicians. The fourth was a photographer. This meant Marc Barag was able to convert the basement into a darkroom, while Bob Berman, John Lauritzen and I converted the big dining room into a music room. Here, we combined all of our equipment—Bob's drums, my bass, and John's trombone.

Though the Sloth was dwindling, I was having a great time. Whoever felt like playing music, day or night, had free access to the room. Friends came by to rehearse their bands. (In the years to come, the Daredevils would even hold a handful of rehearsals at the House) Others would convene for impromptu, psychedelic-laced Grateful Dead blues jams that would roll through the night. Other times, the sound of a drum, a bass and a trombone made for some interesting music.

Experimentation was encouraged; open-mindedness essential.

My "undecided" major was switched to mathematics. Most of the year was spent working and playing with numbers, statistics and the eight notes of the musical scale. Odd jobs were taken to make ends meet, as much of the year was spent painting lines on empty mall parking lots in the middle of the night.

Astride the math, I also kept my fingers in the theater department, finding the strict grid of mathematics to be just as entertaining as the free flow of the arts. Though I never made it onto the stage of SMS's renowned Tent Theater, roles in several smaller student productions, as well as a role in my modern dance class instructor's master thesis presentation, came my way. Funny little student films were made. Art was in the air.

Because the Warehouse was closed, I was forced to find other musical venues and avenues, which I did as often as I could. Everywhere I went, I continued to be pleasantly surprised with everyone's very high level of musicianship.

I continued to frequent the Half-a-Hill Club. Here, I became a fan of Benny Mahan, Zachary Beau, and never missed Clark Pike's crazy version of the popular *Gong Show*. As Clark crossbred the spirits of Little Richard and Chuck Barris, each week was a study in silly people acting silly, just for the sake of being silly. Granny's was the house band. Everyone banged a gong. The circus was in town.

Though I enjoyed Half-a-Hill, which sat among the more affluent south side neighborhoods, my favorite club sat outside the city limits on the north side. Be-Bop's, a funky little joint run by local piano player, Be-Bop Brown, stood back in the woods, well off the road.

Attracting the smaller black community who resided on the north side of Springfield, the smell of Smitty's bar-b-que shack would waft through the place to the beat of Granny's, Dallas Bartley, Eddie Eugene, Dave Bedell & the Flames, and any other incarnation of Bedell brothers that could be assembled.

Martha Reeves, after hearing one of Granny's tapes, came to town, scooping up the whole band for her first solo tour after the Vandellas. Rehearsals were conducted at Be-Bop's. Several of their rehearsals turned into late-night jam sessions.

Not only did I love playing Be-Bop's, I loved just going to Be-Bop's. I loved the way the musicians, as well as the crowd, mixed musically as well as racially. The place was further up my St. Louis alley than its white-bread south side counterpart. The beer was colder, the bar-b-que funkier, the music greasier, the lights lower, and the air smokier—my description of heaven.

When I was in the mood to honky-tonk, it was off to the west side of town, the Ritz Club and the Flamingo Room, a couple of well-worn roadhouses on old Route 66. As the famous highway began its westward fade into the sunset, I had little trouble getting in to listen to the honkytonkers kick up dust. I had a fake ID, but no one seemed to be the least bit interested in asking me for it. It quietly remained in my pocket.

Another favorite haunt was the Rendezvous Club. Sitting directly off the lobby of the Colonial Hotel, Buddy Stoops sat at his Hammond B-3 organ, a guitar in his lap. As he pounded the keys or strummed the strings, his feet continued to stomp the bass pedals. Red candles flickered in the dark to the downtown beat. Hotel residents and transients came and went.

I spent the year really enjoying the diversity of the Springfield music scene, old and young. This small town had a real scene and I was starting to become part of it. I enjoyed our new attitudes, as we interacted with stragglers from the Jubilee. I joined in, whenever and wherever I could.

Before I knew it, the school year had come and gone. I had met my grades, had the summer off, and opted to spend it hitchhiking to Cambridge, Massachusetts. I felt very comfortable here, enacting chapters of *On the Road*, while hanging around its coffee shops, nightclubs, and crash pads. I really dug the place, as well as its views on current events and Nam—viewpoints that differed greatly from the rich, white pastors of Springfield. Plus, I LOVE clam chowder.

After a month of couches and sleeping bags, though, I was anxious to get back to the craziness of the House and the calm of Springfield.

Plus, my twenty-first birthday was in a few months.

The trip was planned, so as to return just in time to unpack bags and enroll for another school year. As I walked into the marbled registration office, the enrollment process began with a small manila envelope filled with computer cards. Male students were issued one extra card—from the Selective Service System. Viet Nam may have been losing steam in the headlines, but fear and dread of the jungle still raged in the back of my adolescent mind. My suitcase to Canada remained packed by the door.

After coordinating a schedule of classes, I walked to the registration desk to turn in my envelope. Here, I realized that I did not have my draft card in my pocket. I knew right where it was. I had simply forgotten it.

I nervously approached the desk, apologizing profusely for my absent-mindedness. After explaining my situation to the frail woman behind the desk, I promised to return in the morning with my pertinent info.

Reluctantly, she bent a rule and enrolled me. I was relieved as I walked out of the building.

Here, I ran into close friend and fellow student, Clarence Brewer—a meeting that would change the rest of my life. Clarence, a wonderful photographer and sculptor, had also just gone through the enrollment process and just happened to be on his way to Nutz & Loonies' darkroom.

When he offered a ride, I accepted. In return, I bartered with herbs and spices. The rest of the day was spent in the basement—I mean *darkroom*. While Marc and Clarence developed film, mixed chemicals and made prints, my role was to play guitar and roll joints. It was good to be back in the Nest of Nutz & Loonies.

The year began fine, except for the fact that I completely forgot about returning that next morning to the registration office with my draft board information. I have no excuse. I just got stoned and forgot. The semester started. So did my samba with the Selective Service System.

Ramifications of my absent-mindedness didn't manifest until I returned to St. Louis for Thanksgiving dinner. Here, I found a 1-A draft card sitting on my mom's kitchen table. She was horrified. I was petrified.

Because I'd never delivered my info to the registration office, they hadn't sent it to my draft board. The draft board, with no other reason than to think I was no longer in school, rescinded my deferment. My worst fears stared me right in the face.

I immediately called a draft counselor and set up an appointment. Though, the war was waning, it was still happening. By the end of November, lottery picks had reached the lower fifties. Ninety-five may have been a ways off, but I wasn't going to take any chances.

When I sat down at the counselor's desk, my knees were shaking, my brow beaded with sweat. As I began filling him in on the details, the scenario quickly came clear. After listening to my tale, he leaned back in his chair, grinned and said, "You may be one of the lucky ones."

Then, he explained. The current Selective Service Act, which had been in place since 1954, had just expired. In the fall of '71, while Congress remained in the process of enacting a new bill, the following guidelines were posted.

The first three months of 1972 were to be tacked on, an extension of the 1971 calendar year—and compensation for the three months everyone went without a bill. This same ninety-day period would also mark the beginning of the new year—lottery-wise. Those particular people who held 1-A status on or before December 31, 1971, only had to make it until the end of March to fulfill their year's eligibility—and re-classification. On January 1, 1972, they would call number one.

Thus, our strategy. New Year's was right around the corner and I had a 1-A draft card in my hand. My counselor informed me that if I wanted, with the simple stroke of a pen, re-obtaining a deferment could easily be done. Then, he explained Plan B.

Plan B was nerve-wracking, calling for me to not seek another deferment, keep my 1-A status, and try to make it under the April 1 wire. If I could make it through March before Tricky Dick could call out, "Number ninety-five—BINGO," my year's eligibility would be fulfilled.

It was the most unnerving four-month period I'd ever spent. Every night, I prayed for additional numbers not to be called. Every morning, I grabbed the newspaper to see if my prayers had been answered.

While many of my friends were traveling to Kansas City to take their physicals and inductions, I remained crouched under the radar. While some took drastic measures—i.e. shooting off toes, faking mental illnesses, ingesting massive amounts of drugs, and shitting in their pants—I quietly watched Plan B unfold.

When Nixon only reached the mid-thirties by the end of March, I called my counselor to confirm my status with the draft board. When he informed me that my prayers had been answered and the new draft card that I would soon be getting was not an April Fool's joke, the Nutz & Loonies went into wild celebration. I unpacked my bags.

I shall always credit Clarence and marijuana with setting Plan B into motion. If he hadn't offered a ride and I hadn't bartered with a joint, I might have remembered to return to the registration office that next morning. Thank you, Mother Nature. Thank you, Clarence.

This isn't the only reason the fall of '71 was monumental. I was about to help put together another band.

CHAPTER 3

That fall, things began innocently enough with a commercial on the radio for a new nightclub in town. I had become accustomed to hearing radio commercials for new nightclubs in town. This one, though, had a different ring to it.

After a couple of years of listening to Springfield radio, I realized that it was basically a wasteland of Top 40 hits and farm reports—both of which I had little use for. That is, except for local disc jockey, Mark Marymont, who tried to convince the powers that be at KWTO-FM that the times actually were a-changing.

He convinced them—well, sort of.

Marymont, under the watchful eye of partner Les Sweckert, was allowed to take over the airwaves for a nightly show called "Campus '71." With his smooth FM voice, as well as the music he played, his show was more suited to my tastes. His seven-to-midnight time slot was more suited to my hours.

Marymont, who would move on to be a respected journalist and Sweckert, who would change his surname to Garland and move on to start MTV, recognized the changing musical sands. Breathing new life into the station's call letters—"Keep Watching The Ozarks"—the nightly show was actual music to my ears.

Marymont recalls, "Every night, after the station ran Garner Ted Armstong's 'The World Tomorrow' at 6:30, the old guard would leave and I was given free rein to play whatever I wanted until midnight—when the station would sign off. The first couple hours I remained somewhat low-key and under the radar. But after about nine, I figured all of those old guys had probably already gone to bed and weren't listening anyway. Then, I was able to open up my playlist a bit. I played anything I wanted and everything I could get my hands on.

"I also knew how much local talent there was in the Ozarks. So, in between album cuts, ranging from Parliament/Funkadelic to the Who, I played 45s by Ronnie Self, Brenda Lee, Porter Wagoner, and a young Wayne Carson. I even threw some of Granny's demo tapes they'd made at Top Talent into the mix. They were actually reel-to-reel tapes."

It was on Marymont's Campus show that I heard the radio spot. I couldn't believe my ears when the words "Harvey Mandel" came blaring from my speakers.

"What? Could it be THE Harvey Mandel? Coming to Springfield? Nahhhhh," I muttered. I knew about Harvey Mandel. I didn't know about this new club. I liked what I heard, though. I had to find this place they were calling the New Bijou Theater.

"It was the reason I stayed in Springfield," recalls Steve Cash, just back from a two-and-a-half-year residency in Berkeley, California, where he spent his time writing poetry, working for the post office, and listening exclusively to rural blues. He explains, "My mom had just died. So when I came back to town for her, I ran into Curt [Hargus] and Steve [Canaday], who told me what they were going to do with the Bijou.

"I had to hang around, just to see what was going to happen. I knew I could hang out there because I knew the bartenders and I could get free beer."

"We were excited," recalls Curt Hargus, co-manager of the Bijou. "Nobody had ever done anything like this before. We were just kids. It was a shared interest. Everybody pitched in. Everybody did everything.

"It was no big deal. Just a bar and a stage. It was a BIG building, so the first thing we had to do was build a block wall down the middle to partition off our sixty-foot by one hundred-foot half. We painted it black so it looked like night in there. For the acoustics, we hung plywood and covered everything with different colors of diamond-tucked burlap.

"We handmade everything. We handmade the bar. We handmade the cooler. We had a guy named Fuzzy, who could build anything. He told us what to do. We just helped him do it. Plus, he drank beer all damn day long.

"The stage was in the corner, about thirty-five to forty feet across, three feet tall. The drum riser was another foot and a half taller. Right next to the stage, Fuzzy built a little building—inside our big building—that would serve as a control room/dressing room. Mike [Bunge] helped with what really sounds right, because he was a genius about what sounded good. We got it really sounding nice."

Though not huge, the room was well designed and musician-friendly. With enough size to comfortably accommodate a couple hundred people, the place was quite versatile. When Fuzzy's little room—with its glass window that looked directly onto the stage—wasn't being used to record, it could be used to hang out in and smoke pot. We liked that. So did the national acts who began to come through. Though the recording equipment wasn't very sophisticated, some wonderful music began to take place on that stage.

Along with partner Steve Canaday, who had just returned from Viet Nam with his bride and new baby, Curt sites, "we sat down and on a yellow legal pad, outlined what we thought would be happening, what we could expect to be happening, and get our minds right about just what we were trying to accomplish."

Canway, who, as Hargus describes, "just had a way about him that knew how to go about getting something done. He took care of bringing in talent. I took care of the everyday logistics of the bar." The two, with a $10,000 loan from Steve's father Paul, were up and running.

Steve called old friend and West Coast promoter, Skip Taylor. When he laid out his plan about what he was trying to do, Taylor became Steve's Under Assistant West Coast Promo man. The Bijou began booking many of Taylor's acts as they passed through the St. Louis/Kansas City/Tulsa triangle, including not only Mandel, but Sugarcane Harris, who quickly returned in a package with Mandel as the Pure Food & Drug Act, Canned Heat, and War.

One week, Dan Hick & His Hot Licks brought in their cool brand of swinging humor. The next, Sonny Terry and Brownie McGehee brought in the blues. The musical spectrum was quite broad. So was the clientele. I still wasn't old enough to legally be in the place. But if they weren't going to ask me about it, I sure as hell wasn't about to bring it up. I couldn't get enough of the place.

"Tuesday night was movie night. After all, the place was called the New Bijou Theater," Curt recalls. "We had a giant screen on stage and set up a movie projector on a table in the middle of the room. Wednesday was kind of a practice night. Granny's was the house band and most everybody who showed up would get up and jam. Sometimes, they'd play two or three nights a week if we didn't have anyone booked.

"We'd get these lists of bands passing through town every month, but I didn't know who they were. Canway did. We didn't know what these guys sounded like. Demo tapes weren't in the picture then. Word of mouth was."

It was this word of mouth that also attracted the local music community.

It was here that I met Larry Lee again. Not only had he been a member of Fuzzy's construction crew, he was the daytime bartender.

It was here that I met Steve Cash, who was just hanging around the bar, drinking beer with Larry.

It was here that I ran back into John Dillon, who informed me of a weekly solo gig he was doing at Tim's Pizza on the south side of town. Though I was still a fan of the new Granny's, I missed John's funky presence in the old version. This seemed like a good reason to hear him play again. Plus, there was pizza and beer.

"I grew up in Southern Arkansas," the Stuttgart native recalls, "in a home where music was part of what people were interested in. My mother played guitar and was a wonderful country harp player. My dad, when he was younger, played drums. Music was a thing that was done after all the work was done.

"The first music I heard was by people playing 'live.' My mom and dad would go to square dances where people were playing and just having a ball. Then, I remember hearing Hank Williams do 'Jambalaya' on the radio. I thought it was a kids' song—kinda like 'Chicken Train.' It spoke to me and I became interested in the whole idea about where that came from and what that was all about.

"Growing up in that part of the world, there were all these great places to go to listen to music … and they were all bad places. You're not supposed to go there. So I went to all of them… and had a great time. I was influenced by these old Appalachian guys like Roscoe Holcomb and even guys from around Arkansas. Then, Bob Dylan came along and I realized that music had stuff to say."

Sitting in the corner of the quiet pizzeria, he played his Gibson Hummingbird acoustic guitar, oftentimes accompanied by girlfriend Elizabeth Anderson. Occasionally, he'd invite Steve to join in on harmonica. The two had written a handful of songs, which I found to be much more interesting than anything else I'd heard being played around town.

"My influences were all over the place," Steve cites. "I was just a kid growing up in the '50s. I didn't play music and I didn't play in any bands. At one point, I said, 'I'm tired of just listening. I want to play.' Once I started, I was influenced by everything. Then, when we started playing, we all just started influencing each other."

What I found to be even more interesting was the radio jingle the two had written for Stinger Sam's, a local auto parts store, owned by high school pal Ronnie Stenger. After hearing the commercial on the radio during the day, I really enjoyed the fact that, at night, Steve would sing the same melody over the same two-chord riff—with different lyrics. By night, "It's Stinger Sam for your automobile" turned into, "It's a black sky forming on the ridge."

"He [Steve] ripped himself off," Dillon laughs. "We were living in a cabin on the James River for free. Had no money. Steve walked in one day and said, 'Man, I got us a commercial and I've already got the lyrics. I need some music.' It was just a little harp riff and a two-chord guitar thing. We figured out how to get it recorded at Top Talent. Remember, Bunge had a key? So, we went in to do it. Then, we sold it to Stinger Sam for $600.

"This was the most money we'd seen in years. It was huuuge money. I lived off that three hundred bucks for about six months. So, we recorded a few more. We did one for Bottom's Up ('Go Down to Bottom's Up'), and something for Friendly Ford. All of a sudden, we had this little jingle business, where we'd do a jingle once every six or seven months.

"In the meantime, I was playing at Tim's Pizza on Wednesday nights for all the pizza I could eat all week and all the beer I could drink all week and twenty bucks. Steve would come by, we would write songs on the spot and showcase new material. That's when we started writing songs together."

"I met him [Cash] through some mutual friends," John recalls. "When I first saw him, he was getting out of a car. He was just back from San Francisco. He had hair down to his waist and boots—kind of a moccasin—that came up to his knees. I'd never seen anyone like him. I just saw him and said, 'Oh shit,' 'cause he looked so weird. You didn't see a whole lot of people around here looking like that.

"When we met, we discovered that we had a lot of the same interests—especially poetry and music. We began hanging out and became friends. He was living with Jim Marshall in a little hovel on the north side, paying forty bucks or something a month for this complete dump.

"I'd go over there every night. We'd get high and listen to music, and just have a great time. One day, Steve showed up with this harp and said, 'You know what? I think I can play this harp. How do you play harp?'

"I said, 'Here's how you hold it.' I showed him how to hold it and said, 'I'll teach you the way my mom taught me how to play. She said, *Take this harmonica, and put it in your pocket. Always have it in your pocket and you'll learn how to play.* That's how she taught me. I didn't know what she was talking about for a couple of weeks. Then, all of a sudden, I realized that I could play a little bit—just because I kept it in my pocket. Keep it in your pocket. You'll learn how to play it.'"

Steve took it from there.

There seemed to be music everywhere in the fall of '71. I formed a band called Stone County with Mark McCann, fresh into town from Southern California and a stint as guitarist with West Coast psychedelic band, the Count Five. We hit it off, sharing a penchant for really loud rock 'n' roll music, as well as a penchant for smoking a whole lot of pot right before we played this really loud rock 'n' roll. The air was filled with smoke. The music was filled with life. I'd played "Psychotic Reaction" on Gaslight Square with my high school band, the Coachmen Four.

We fronted one of the area's first power rock bands—a Missouri version of Blue Cheer—raucous, raunchy and really, really, REALLY loud. Mark had tons of gear, outfitting everyone with a gaudy display of speaker cabinets and decibels. When Stone County played, my plastic Hagstrom bass thundered through a tall, silver pleated Kustom bass amp—a hillbilly wall of sound.

I really enjoyed another local group at the time—Shorty Dunn. As they drew from the subtler repertoire of Young, as well as Nash, Crosby, Stills, Joplin, and Slick, they were fronted by St. Louis singer/pianist Sherry Peters and included Sloth alums Chris Albert on guitar and John Mitchell on drums. But it was guitarist Randy Chowning who stood out.

"I moved to Springfield from Mt. View, Missouri—the south central Missouri outback," Randy recounts. "What first motivated me about music was my mother. She never sang professionally, but she sang around the house all the time. I'm sure that listening to her sing is what made me want to do it, too. Plus, I remember hearing [brother] Rusty sing on the 'Amateur Hour' in West Plains. I remember the song, too: 'Your Love is Everything.'

"In the '50s, my dad was a radio guy—a tech sergeant with Patton in North Africa. When he came home, he put up this huge aerial on the house and aimed it at Memphis. I remember me and Rusty dialing in Memphis radio with a good, clear signal and hearing the black music before Elvis. I was five or six years old and that stuff was really scary. It was like hearing stuff from another planet. It was exciting, but really scary. Then, the '60s came along, and I got swept up in the Beatles thing, like everybody else."

I made sure Wednesday nights with Granny's at the Bijou were part of my weekly itinerary. I enjoyed Larry's drumming and singing, as well as his contribution to the evening's overall vibe. "I played drums in grade school and high school," he recalls, "and got a classical guitar when I was about sixteen. I lived a block and a half from KWTO. Michael [Bunge] and I were in high school and somehow, he knew Si, who was working with this young songwriter named Wayne Carson.

"Wayne used to go play these little hootenannies in little towns like Pierce City, Monett and other places in Kansas, Oklahoma and Arkansas. Bunge was playing bass and Bobby Threadgill was playing drums. When Bobby couldn't do it anymore, Michael told Wayne that he should hire me to play drums. So I went to Si's office and met Wayne.

"He played me some of the songs he was writing and I was thinking, 'Man, this guy is good. I want to be in a band with him.' We'd do these shows where we'd play fifteen to twenty minutes as part of a revue. Then, I started to cut a lot of demos with him at the KWTO studios.

"My first summer after high school, Louie Taylor, who was Bunge's cousin, came to town. We started rehearsing, and I played with them until I went into the navy the following September. I had done a USO tour in the summer of '66 for the State Department with Louie & the Seven Days. Si booked the tour and we went to Viet Nam.

"When we got back, my draft notice had come. After just coming back from there, and having all those guys my age or a little older telling me, 'Do whatever you have to do. Do NOT come back to this place,' one option was to join a safer service. So I thought, if nothing else, I'll be on a boat instead of in the jungle.

"I didn't start writing songs until I was in the navy. I used to go to the chapel, because no one was ever there. They had an old, upright piano by the altar. I started just throwing my hands down on the keyboard until I came across things I liked. I'd remember what the notes were, then I'd go find another chord I liked.

"When I got out, one of the first places I went was the studio [Top Talent]. Si owned it, Wayne was usually there and they always had Bunge working with them. Mike would end up with the keys to the joint.

"Because I was hanging with Mike so much in the studio, that's where I met John [Dillon], who was coming in to do his demos."

From week to week, you never knew who was going to show up at the Bijou and jump into the Wednesday night fray. Wayne would stop in and do the new tunes he, Larry, Bunge, and Bill Jones had been working on that day in the studio. Any number of Bedell brothers would show and blow. Local legend, Benny Mahan became Granny's official lead singer—and a Wednesday night staple. As they caromed off into funky town, when Larry stepped up to the microphone, their sound swayed even more than it already did.

I enjoyed Larry's voice. I enjoyed Bunge's voice. I enjoyed Benny's voice. Come to think of it, I enjoyed everything about Wednesdays. That's just the way it was. The Bijou was the flame. We were the moths.

As the fall semester wore on, I continued to run into Randy around campus. Daily conversations about music pre-empted any kind of talk about any kind of class. When he informed me that he had gotten together with John and Larry at the Bijou, I was intrigued. When he mentioned the idea of trying to gather some guys to play nothing but original material—and no "hits of the day"—I offered a bass-playing hand.

There were many bass players around town. Granny's had a bass player. Shorty Dunn had a bass player. The Lavender Hill Mob had a bass player. I could tell, though, that this cast of characters didn't call for just another Springfield bass player from another Springfield high school. This was not going be just another Springfield band.

I agreed to attend a rehearsal to see what, if anything, would happen. I was itching to keep playing bass anyway. I knew I could bring cool ideas to the table, along with my St. Louis rock 'n' roll shoes that paid absolutely no attention to whether or not Jeremiah was a bullfrog.

Then, I informed Randy that I had no car. This time, this wasn't an issue. He'd been to Nutz & Loonies on several occasions. He heard the music we were listening to and making. After an early December morning of classes, he swung by the House, we loaded up our amps, and we headed to the Bijou.

It was a very interesting cast of characters, as Larry, Steve, Randy, John, Elizabeth, and I began using the Bijou stage on quiet weekdays, when the place was inhabited by nothing but beer and potato chip delivery men.

In, what the local newspaper would refer to as a "hillbilly approach to the Woodstock Nation," we began playing, singing, writing and interacting, musically. With no overblown aspirations of fame and fortune—or even being a formal band—we were more interested in making each song sound as good as it possibly could. We were also interested in the free beer that could be delivered to the stage in a matter of seconds from Fuzzy's handmade cooler.

Hair was long and shaggy, as the six of us spent that first afternoon just having a ball. Not only did we enjoy each other's music, we enjoyed each other's company. Springfield's hippie community in the early '70s was still minuscule.

Once we set up and tuned up, we broke the ice with an extended version of "Bo Diddley," a song that would remain a staple of our shows for decades. I knew how to administer the simple, lazy qualities the Bo Diddley beat requires. I relate easily to both: simple and lazy. When we finished, I remember thinking, "Wow, that was good. That was really good. This is going to go places."

I took this same swampy approach when Steve started the Stinger Sam commercial—I mean "Black Sky," turning it from a thirty-second radio ad into a three-minute song, complete with bass, drums, verses, choruses, and a harmonica solo.

When a customer walked in, Larry would have to get up and serve them a beer. This didn't bother anyone. If things got busy, Canaday, who'd played drums around town for years with David Kerr & the Playboys, would jump on Larry's kit. (You'll learn more about David Kerr later.) The music would continue. We never missed a beat. Canway became—and will remain—a very integral part of this story in the days, months, years, and chapters to come.

In between songs, instruments were swapped. John played guitar, mouth bow, piano, and fiddle. Randy played guitar, banjo, lap steel, and harmonica. When Larry would get up from the drums to play piano—and Canway wasn't around—John would pick up the drumsticks.

When Steve wasn't playing harmonica, he joined Elizabeth at a table they had hauled onstage. Laden with a plethora of percussion instruments Liz carried around in a large tote bag, each song got the appropriate banging, clanging, shaking, or jangling it needed. Plus, "the percussion table" doubled as a good place to set pitchers of beer and ashtrays. A resourceful lot, we were.

Some songs were loud and raucous. Others, soft and subtle. All were played back to back to back. Each was given the proper amount of attention it deserved. None was homogenized.

Time did not exist in the Bijou that day, as we threw ourselves headlong into the creative process. As the afternoon came to an end, the Sons of Champlain blasted from the PA system and Happy Hour began. The empty room transformed into a nightclub.

The Sons were a favorite at the Bijou. If their records weren't playing on the PA, Granny's was covering their songs onstage. If you ever wonder how Granny's sounded, grab any Sons record.

I went absolutely crazy for them, more than all of the other San Francisco bands I was already crazy about—even the Dead. I enjoyed what they were saying and the sound they made while saying it. In St. Louis, they made no splash. In Springfield, they were a smash.

Their music came to the town as a by-product of the path beaten between doors in Southwest Missouri and doors in Northern California. Though not exactly a pot-smuggling route, it was a seed-smuggling route—kind of a "cultural exchange program."

As farmers in both areas traded seeds, they also traded music. When friends in the Bay Area insisted we listen to this band that sounded like Granny's, Sons of Champlain records rang through the Ozarks.

As we cleared what little equipment we had off the stage and convened at the bar for beer, discussion of when to do it all again flowed. The overwhelming consensus was, "Soon."

I headed back to the House of Nutz & Loonies, charged out of my mind about the day of music I'd just had and the days that lay ahead. I knew this combination of people was going to be successful from the very first day. Hell, I knew it after the very first song. Excitedly, I called St. Louis.

My mother listened politely, softly saying, "That's nice, Michael."

My father grumbled, "Great. Just what you need. Another fucking band. Have you gotten a haircut yet?"

In addition to gathering at the Bijou, we began to gather at each other's houses. Here, mellower songs could be concentrated upon, without the blare and glare of electronics, or the bang and clang of beer kegs. We strummed acoustic guitars. I played through a small amp at a low volume. Harmonies were worked on. Soon, an entire set of acoustic material was worked up.

Though we didn't try to bring our electric songs into our living rooms, we were determined to take our acoustic songs to the stage. Both worked well together, as a rock 'n' roll blaster blended seamlessly into a country lilt, which bled into a hoedown, which trod comfortably through a ballad, a swing, a swamp, and a stomp. We knew it would work. We knew we were tilling fertile fields.

When Larry sat at the piano, his chords sounded great. Unfortunately, they didn't resemble anything close to the simple G-C-D chord patterns we were accustomed to. Much time was spent around the piano, as he would hold down and call out the single notes of the chord he was playing. John, Randy and I hunted and pecked around our guitar necks like two-fingered typists.

No one, Larry included, knew what the name of the chord was. It just sounded cool. Then, it was on to the next chord. Here, the process started all over again, until we finally got everything together and sounding nice. Because several of his songs were instrumentals, there wasn't a lyrical hook to grab on to. Some were given appropriate names. "Wild Parrots" was a nice fit for the samba tune, featuring charted melody lines, sax solos and an a capella vocal bridge. Others were given completely absurd names that had absolutely nothing to do with the music. From this category, we played "Nouveau-Tubular Relapse."

When played correctly, Larry's songs went places the others didn't. His songs may have taken a little more time to learn, but time was not an object. We had time. We had lots of time. None of us had anything else to do—or anywhere else to go.

When we were through making Larry's song sound like he wanted, we did the same with one of Randy's. The tapestry spun where the weave got wove.

When the topic of adding an actual piano player arose, I suggested my friend, Rick Campanelli—thought to be one of the better piano players around town. Not only was he a frequent visitor to the House's late-night jams, Campy was already a veteran of the local music scene.

Though he'd played in several of Springfield's top Top 40 bands, his personal tastes leaned more into jazz. On occasion, he would join Bob Berman on drums and myself on bass, informally playing as an unnamed House of Nutz & Loonies jam band. Resembling the Jimmy Smith Trio more than a rock band, we played twelve-bar blues, freeform jams in odd time signatures, Brubeck and Beefheart riffs, and whatever other grooves and standards we could find.

When the three of us were slated to begin a Sunday afternoon of music at Lake Springfield, we smoothed along as people began to gather on the banks. As other bands began arriving with their gear, Bob, Campy and I began catching ears with a song list that included the aforementioned Smith, Monk, the Captain, and our favorite, Booker T.

As Shorty Dunn began setting up, the scene around the stage burst into hearty rounds of handshakes and back slaps. When Randy and I asked Campy if he would like to stop by the Bijou that week, he consented. The next time we met, Campy joined in, fattening the sound as only a piano can. Along with Granny's horn man, Bill Jones, they immediately became the two best musicians in the band. As the rest of us clopped along in our usual lumpy style, these two provided an actual sense of virtuosity.

Plus, when Bill showed up, he was able to teach us Larry's chords a lot faster. This saved pecking time and made for more picking time. Bill's presence was completely embraced, as he was issued a "free pass" to join in, whenever and wherever he could. Along with his wailing saxes, he brought along his flutes and oboes.

We started utilizing all of these tools—immediately.

This may be a good spot to take a second and point out just how close we were with Granny's. Both, John and Larry had been members. To fill out our sets, several cover songs were thrown into the mix. When John would bust into "What's the Matter with the Mill?" and "Sweet Root Man," this provided the funky element I dug so much with the old Granny's.

When Larry did one of his smoother tunes, we would capture the feel of the new Granny's. He had been their drummer. Bill was still their horn man.

Randy would take off on long versions of Donovan Leitch's "Season of the Witch," complete with extended jams from whoever was there and ready. Campy played piano. Bill played flute. Everybody joined in.

Steve, who I'd just met at an SMS student film festival (where we both appeared on screen), provided his funny, funky songs, with more emphasis being placed on lyrical content than musical virtuosity. I found their simplicity to be soothing. Plus, he played a mean Jerome Green when we blasted into "Who Do You Love?" and "Bo Diddley."

His role in *Life at Smackout*, Carol Burke's account of a small, communally run farm in the rural Missouri mountains of Ava, was simple. The sixteen-millimeter film chronicled a day in the life of Smackout's residents—of which, Steve was one—as they skinny-dipped in the pond by day and hung out in the middle of nowhere by night.

The role I played in Michael Dali's film, *Let's Hear It for the Good Guys* was even simpler. Set to Country Joe and the Fish's "Good Guys/Bad Guys Cheer," when Country Joe McDonald yelled, "Let's hear it for the good guys," I was one of a handful of carefree hippies, joyously dancing on the screen, throwing our hands into the air. The Fish cheered.

When CJ reciprocated with, "Let's hear it for the bad guys," a handful of friends, dressed up like cops and Republicans, would barge into the frame and knock all the hippies down like bowling pins.

Then, Joe would yell, "Let's hear it for the good guys," the cops would leave the frame and the hippies would get back up and start skipping around again. This Mobius strip continued throughout the film.

Having just returned from San Francisco, Steve knew all about the Good Guys/ Bad Guys cheer, Country Joe, the Fish, the Dead, the Sons, and the Airplane. We shared an affinity for the sociologies of San Francisco, as well as its music. He experienced it firsthand. I had to settle for it when it passed through St. Louis.

When we began gathering at the Bijou, I didn't realize that he had just started playing harp and had never been in a band before. I found his simple grooves unique and very enjoyable. When he offered his songs, I easily comprehended "Black Sky" and "Rhythm of Joy." The funkier, the better. The lazier, the funkier.

As rehearsals spilled over into '72 with Bill, Campy, Canway and Bunge stopping by, the cast of characters came through an ever-revolving door. Still, the music was always first, foremost and original.

This regimen—one day at the Bijou and another at one of our houses—became the focus of my life. I continued to attend classes, but by this point, I was consumed by this music. When my Plan B took effect on April 1, 1972, I was completely consumed.

At this point of the story, my wonderful grandmother, Ethel Cromer needs to stand up and take a bow. The sophisticated woman, with her wonderfully wicked wit, was a fixture on the St. Louis social scene. Not only had she observed my passion for music, she'd observed my father's disdain for it.

When she and I found time alone, she would endlessly sit and tirelessly listen to me babble about music and how, one day, I was going to be successful at it. Unlike her boy, she encouraged me every step and every conversation of the way.

When I expressed displeasure with my inferior equipment, she drew me close, whispering, "Do you need a guitar, Mike? If you need a guitar, you go get a guitar. We'll find the money."

When I sheepishly asked about an amplifier, her response was a resounding, "Whatever you need." When I asked for her confidentiality, a wink of her eye assured me that her lips were sealed.

When my crazy uncle Don would stop by, I was able to share my tales with him, too. He laughed when he heard the silly stories of his silly nephew. He also reassured me that the money would be there. Hands were shaken. Cheeks were kissed. It would take numerous $30 and $40 payments over the next few years. But, the deal got done.

It was apparent that, if I was going to be serious about this music thang, I had to get serious about this equipment thang. I'd already lost one gig due to the fact that I had an $80 bass amp and a $40 plastic bass painted like an American flag.

I could not wait to get to Springfield and get to shopping. Heading straight downtown to the pawn shops that populate Boonville Street, I found an old cream-colored Fender Telecaster Bass and a Fender Bassman amp with two fifteen-inch speakers.

As I began to explain my situation to the broker, he stopped me in mid-sentence, informing me that he'd heard about what we were doing at the Bijou. News travels fast in a small town. The deal was easily struck. The phone call to St. Louis was easily made. When assured that the check was in the mail, I became the proud owner of a nice rig designed by Leo Fender.

Now, I would be able to do my low-end duties in tall cotton. Now, I could provide a solid bottom, played on a real bass through a real amp. The artists of Nutz & Loonies immediately upholstered it with a tie-dyed speaker cloth.

Though I owned a nice big amp, I still did not own a car. This made lugging the thing around town a problem. Every time I needed to go somewhere, I had to scavenge a ride. Thank goodness for the Nutz & Loonies Cab Company.

As we continued to rehearse into '72, we worked up enough songs to do a gig. Oddly enough, this didn't happen at the Bijou. It happened in the psychiatric ward of St. John's Hospital.

It was a quiet afternoon, as we sat and played in Larry's living room. When his phone rang, old friend—and future road crew member—David Trask was on the other end. Informing Larry that the patients' entertainment for the evening had canceled at the last minute, he asked if we'd bail him out of his predicament.

With an amused look on his face, Larry walked back into the living room, where he laid out David's offer. All we could do was look at each other, shrug our collective shoulders, chuckle and say, "Psych ward? Why not?"

We knew we would be helping out a friend, Larry only lived a few blocks from the hospital and we already had our instruments in our laps. On the spot, we dubbed ourselves the Emergency Band and headed to the rescue.

Here, we set up in their linoleumed recreation room the same way we'd been setting up in our carpeted living rooms. When the patients came in, we sat smack dab in the middle of them. As we played, they sang and clapped along. Elizabeth's percussion instruments were handed out.

We had been playing these songs among ourselves for a few months. We figured it'd do them some good to see the light of day. Plus, it was a low-pressure environment—so low-pressure that in a later interview, Steve would describe the scene: "They kept wanting to hear 'Rudolph, the Red-nosed Reindeer.' The gig was in July."

St. John's may have been our first gig. But, it wasn't our first public performance. *That* was at the Bijou.

This was very easily arranged, as Thursday nights at the Bijou were already being billed as "John Dillon and Friends." Having recently agreed to move his pizza-house gig to the nightclub, so as to accommodate electric guitars and drums, all we had to do was schedule a Thursday afternoon rehearsal.

Then, all we had to do was leave our gear set up, head home, eat dinner, relax, refresh, call as many friends as we could, and return to play that night. After having spent the entire day making the place sound nice, we left all the knobs set right where they were, to make it sound just as nice that evening.

Because the lineup of the band came from so many different circles, we drew from everywhere. Locals, young and old, rubbed elbows with hippies, bikers, itinerants, and students from St. Louis and Kansas City. The Nutz & Loonies had perfect attendance. The place filled with friends, the lights came up, and we took the stage for the first time.

I know I already said that our first gig was at St. John's. It was. There wasn't a stage in the psych ward.

That night, the Bijou transformed into a Bay Area nightclub, complete with incense, peppermints, alcohol, and plenty of marijuana. As we tuned up on stage, Canaday prepared the tape recorder in Fuzzy's control room. When we hit our first note, Steve hit the red button. Though the quality of these tapes will never get mentioned in any kind of *Studio Today* magazine, they captured the music, as well as the feeling in the room. They would soon play an important role.

The interaction between band and crowd was electric—the difference, negligible. Everyone was loud when it was appropriate, and quiet when need be. It was the first public performances of Randy's "Road to Glory" and "Country Girl," John's "Walking Down the Road" and "Standing on the Rock," Larry's "You Know Like I Know" and "Homemade Wine" and Steve's "Black Sky" and "Rhythm of Joy."

Everyone had a great time. After that first gig, it became apparent that we were capturing something substantial. It also became apparent that we needed a name—a minor detail we'd never paid much attention to. The Emergency Band was rightfully dismissed.

After several suggestions, Family Tree was unceremoniously settled upon. It was a nice name. We were all deriving nourishment from musical roots and branches, spreading in many different directions—all spawned from the same acorn of creativity. We looked at each other and said, "Yeah. Sure. Family Tree sounds good." It was much better than the other nominees, "Buffalo Chips," "Burlap Socks" and "Those Guys & That Girl."

Because we continued to practice on a sporadic basis, a mid-January gig was parlayed into a mid-February gig. As fate would soon have it, these would be the only two times we would play at this marvelous venue.

After the first night, when Campy got a real gig, making real money with a real band, he made a sudden exit. Canway suggested we fill the hole with his friend, Buddy Brayfield. The call was made. The hole was filled. The piano was played.

The soft-spoken Springfield native recalls, "All through high school, Charlie [McCall] and I played in a band called Pure Sunshine. Charlie sang and I played a Vox Continental organ. He smoked a lot, which gave him this great, raspy R&B voice—which was what I was into. We played every Friday and Saturday night. In those days, there was a party somewhere, or a dance going on every weekend. I was rich. I was making forty or fifty bucks every weekend, playing everywhere around town.

"I'd seen you guys play at the Bijou, due to the fact that Canaday and I were such good friends. I'd gone with him out to John's house, where everyone was just sitting around, singing. Afterwards, John called and asked if I'd be interested in playing piano.

"The first time I got together and sat down with you guys was a rehearsal at the BIjou. There was an old upright piano there, and the first song we did was 'Leatherwood,' which was in the key of F-sharp. I don't know how it is on bass. But, on the piano, man, all I could say was, 'Fucking F-sharp? Wait a minute.' Then, I just figured, Okay, let's go."

As the Bijou circles grew, new limbs began to sprout on my own musical tree. One evening, while the Nutz and Loonies lounged, a panicked phone call came from the club. Dillway was on the other end of the line, frantically pleading with me to get there as soon as I could. Jimmy Reed had come to town, but his bass player hadn't. Steve had a room full of paying customers and the show was being held up. He pleaded with me to hurry.

He didn't have to plead long, as, before even hanging up the phone, I grabbed my bass, my amp, my roommate, and his car.

When we pulled up to the front door, ambulance style, Steve was pacing out in front—a nervous wreck. From here, we quickly elbowed our way through the crowd, pleading, "Excuse me, excuse me." When

I got to the stage, Reed's band was ready to go and nervously milling about. I set up as quickly as I could. Canway kept the beer coming.

When Jimmy walked onstage, he offered a simple "Hey, man. How ya doing?" and the gig was on. Already enfeebling by this time of his life and already drunk by this time of the night, when his guitar needed tuning, his road manager grabbed it, tuned it and handed it back.

When the guitar returned to Jimmy's lap, Jimmy took over. His second, much younger guitar player looked flustered, embarrassed and very glad to see me. As we shook hands, he leaned over and whispered, "Follow me, not him." I had no trouble following either.

I didn't know why Reed's bass player wasn't there. I didn't care. I didn't ask. I was having the time of my life. I was playing with THE Jimmy Reed. When I looked about the stage, realizing that I was the only white kid in a sea of old black guys, the place felt like Gaslight Square.

Straight out of a scene from *Reefer Madness*, his piano player flailed away at the same piano Larry and Buddy played during the day. With a microphone stuffed into the sound board, he attacked the keys, blasting the hammers off the thing.

The drummer, at least thirty years my senior, cast an eyebrow as I stepped on stage. But once we started playing, he quickly loosened up. It took a song or two, but I had no trouble locking in with these guys. The Jimmy Reed groove is as simple and primitive as the Bo Diddley groove. I understand both well.

I was never given the title of the next song. But that didn't matter. All the information I needed was the key and the opening chord sequence. After that, it was smooth sailing and extra-smooth grooving. On occasion, Jimmy would inadvertently add a thirteenth bar to "Big Boss Man" or drop one from "Hush, Hush."

I had no trouble, as I've always believed that the ability to listen, anticipate and adjust quickly are more valued assets to a bass player than a million fancy licks. Over the years, I've often told interviewers that I play my bass with my ears—not my fingers.

The joke: All bass players can play guitar. But all guitar players can't play bass. Why?

The punch line: They'd have to know the song. (rim shot)

If the bass player gets lost, everyone gets lost. If the guitar player gets lost, he can just stop playing and light up a cigarette. That night, no one got lost, as I had no problem playing Reed's songs. I was already familiar with them. I'd played them with the Coachmen Four. I'd played them with the Grate Sloth. I was honored just to be on the same stage with the man.

By the end of the night, his band of fifty-year-old black men from Detroit enthusiastically shook the hand of a skinny, twenty-year-old white kid from St. Louis.

This feeling of artistic interaction was what the Bijou prided itself in. It was a very exciting time. The schedule they kept was an ambitious one, as Canaday and Hargus wanted to keep the artists on this stage, where they belonged and the fraternity beer bands in the fraternity houses, where *they* belonged.

In a nutshell, the place had integrity, class, and very good taste.

It was a very sad morning, when the March 11, 1972 headline of the *Springfield News-Leader* read, "Overnight Fire Claims Night Club." A fire, starting in the welding shop that occupied the other half of the unoccupied building, savagely spread in the middle of the night, catching everyone by surprise and everything on fire.

There was nothing the fire department could do. They were helpless, as both halves of the building went up like a tinder box. The place was beyond hope before anyone could even get there. Nothing was salvageable, including Larry's drums. Dreams went up in smoke.

I heard the news that day, oh boy. I could not believe my ears. I hopped on my bike to see if what they said had happened, had really happened. When I arrived on the scene, I sadly found out that it had really happened. I could not believe my eyes. The smoldering scene filled our nostrils with stench and our hearts with sadness. The place may have only been open less than a year. But it was, definitely the end of an era.

The Family Tree was homeless.

CHAPTER 4

With the embers of the Bijou still smoldering, we were forced to shift our focus elsewhere. This took place in two other venues around town—one large, one small: the 754-seat Landers Theatre and the 54-seat Trilogy.

Built in 1909, the Landers Theater, a National Historic Site and host to one of Missouri's oldest and largest civic theatres, still sits on East Walnut Street in downtown Springfield—one block south of old Route 66. The brick and terra cotta building, built by John and D.J. Landers, houses the plush, acoustically blessed theater house.

After opening with *The Golden Girl* in September, 1909, the Landers stage has remained open, a vibrant part of the Springfield performing arts community. Playing host to touring acts and Vaudeville, ranging from Lillian Russell to John Philip Sousa and Fanny Brice, '09 also marked the year the Landers became only the thirty-fifth facility in the world to acquire "talkies." It is a grand old theater and a perfect setting for our music.

That spring, we phoned the box office, inquiring if the place was rentable and, if it was, could we rent it? The initial reaction was a stammering, "Uh … yeah. Well, I guess. We've never had a band ask us about doing anything like that. We guess it'd be okay."

Thursday, April 20, 1972 was booked as "The Celebration"—a co-bill with the Family Tree and Granny's Bathwater. Along with a sense of melancholy about the club burning was an excitement about the coming of spring. We were very excited about the prospect of playing music on this stage.

Thursdays were "off nights" for the Landers. But it had been our regular night at the Bijou. Tickets were one dollar in advance—one dollar at the door. That night, the place filled with friends, each paying a dollar to

Family Tree poster, 1973

help each other get over the burning of the Bijou and celebrate spring at this wonderful theater. Mother Nature was getting her green coat out of mothballs. Everyone donned their "Thursday, go-to-meeting" clothes.

That afternoon, both bands set up at the same time, for—as was usually the case—there would be liberal doses of "sitting in" between the two. We set all of our gear up, among and around each other.

Then, directly in front of all the amps and drums, the Family Tree set up a semi-circle of chairs. Amplifiers were clicked onto "stand by," acoustic instruments miked up. We would come out, sit down and play a set of our acoustic songs, then strip away the chairs, plug in our electric guitars and let 'er rip. Bill Jones played horns, Buddy played piano. The percussion table jangled.

The combination of acoustic and electric instruments—which would become our trademark—sparkled that night. So did the songs. So did the theater's brass and chandeliered dome, warmly embracing everyone with her plush seats and deep, robe-like curtains. We all danced in the carpeted aisles. The music sounded wonderful in that place.

Spring was springing outside, as we became Springfield's official band of hippies and weirdoes and kooks, oh my.

The Trilogy, run by relocated St. Louisans Bruce Rader, Chuck Dunville and his soon-to-be wife, Suze, sat at the corner of Clay and Monroe, directly across the street from the ROTC field that occupies the northwest corner of the SMS campus. The plain brick-and-stone building had occupied the corner for years, once operating as the neighborhood grocery store. It now fed the counterculture of Springfield bean sprouts, pizza and beer.

Oftentimes, the view out the large front windows was funny. As soldiers marched in straight lines on their side of Monroe, a cafe full of longhairs marched in less-than-straight lines on theirs.

The Trilogy became the place to meet, eat, drink, visit with friends, and make the scene—the epicenter of Springfield's burgeoning—though still small—hippie community. Suze recalls, "We were open when we wanted. Sometimes, we'd close for the summer. Sometimes, we'd close for the sunset. We did what we wanted."

The day it opened, I fell in love with the place. Becoming a regular, I stopped in every afternoon. After a morning of mathematics and bowling classes, I would step in and head straight to the kitchen, where I would attack the piles of dirty dishes left from the lunch crowd. When I finished, in a fine example of the barter system, I helped myself to a big bowl of chili, a ham sandwich and a fistful of beers. Then, I was on my merry way to the House—with a full stomach and a smile on my face.

Because they served food, once a month, they were able to stay open—and serve beer—on Sunday. The place would transform from a small restaurant into a small music club. Of course, it could only hold fifty people. But it was a perfect size for the Family Tree to play, acoustically.

Drums and electric guitars were left at home. A small PA system was set up on the upright piano in the corner, near the door. Tables were rearranged, as we sat in chairs around the piano. Here, we were able to nicely blend our voices. It was easy to sing Porter Wagoner's "A Satisfied Mind" for a hushed and attentive group of friends. Everyone in the place knew we wouldn't be doing the loud rock 'n' roll they'd heard us play at the Bijou.

Larry, sans drums, would play the piano and his guitar. John would play guitar, fiddle and mouth bow. Randy would play guitar, lap steel and banjo. Steve would play harmonica and tambourine, joining Elizabeth at a smaller, but still functional, percussion table. Bill Jones played flute. Both he and Buddy played oboe. I played bass and toy xylophone.

The atmosphere was very relaxed. Our friends knew what we were trying to do with this music. They also knew what we could—and could not—do in this little place. The air was light, the room was packed. Toes tapped. Here, our acoustic songs got their finishing touches before being etched into vinyl. Voices were blended. Everyone sang. Everyone listened.

It was at the Trilogy where "Chicken Train" received its final plumage. Originally written as a modal stomp—thus its original name, "Chicken Train Stomp"—when John began twanging on the mouth bow and Steve began his harp riff, everyone in the room started stomping along.

As the in-tune and in-time crowd picked up the beat, Elizabeth's percussion instruments scattered. Others began clanging water glasses with their silverware. Salt and pepper shakers thumped tables. The whole room pulsed to the one-chord song. One-chord songs are really hard to fuck up. They're also a hell of a lot of fun.

We had only done it a few times. But it was here where the warmth

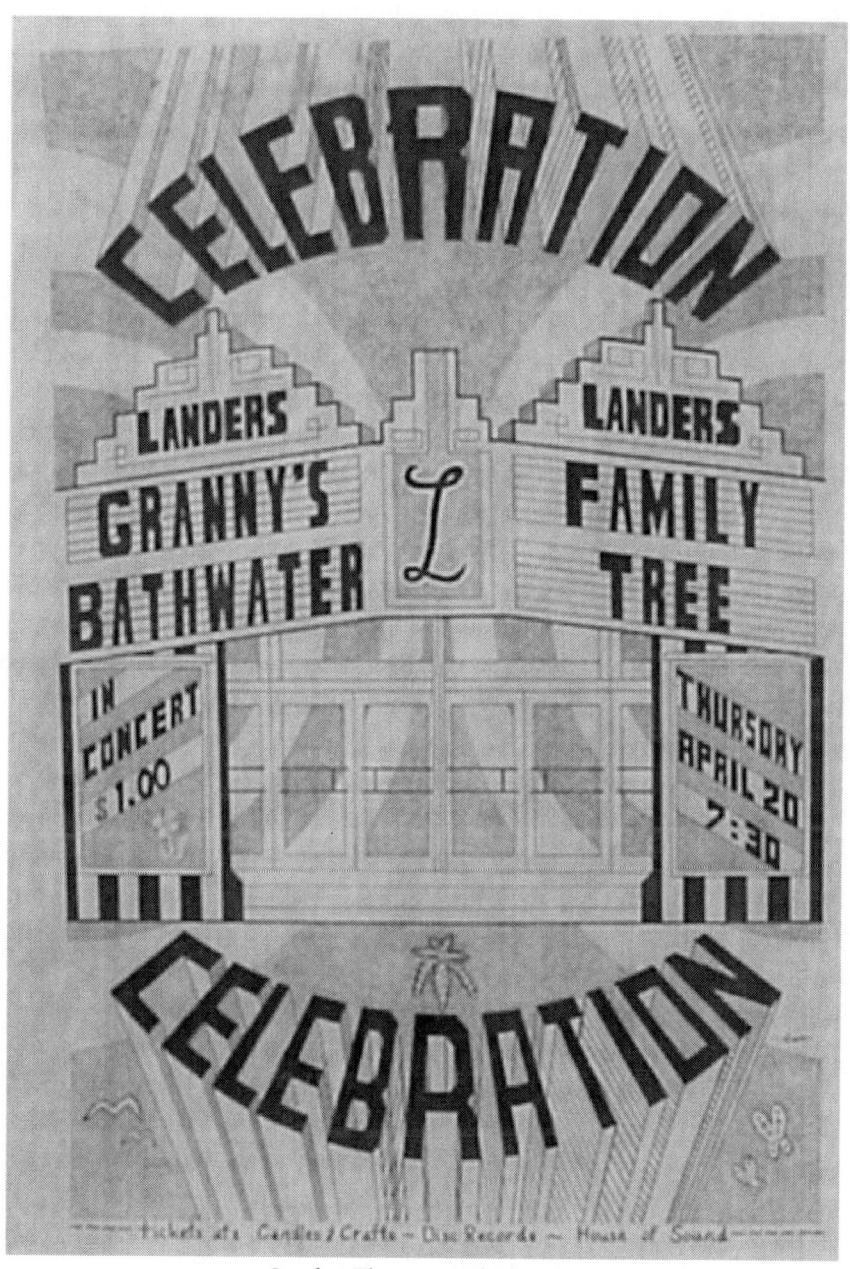

Landers Theater, April 20, 1973

of the heartbeat—as well as the warmth of the beer—slung me into fits of rhythmic squawking in the middle of the song. When I started the clamor, every corner of the room joined in, turning the place into a virtual barnyard.

What started as an impromptu joke, would become an integral part of the song—a trait it carries to this day. The tune, as you will find out, will have a very interesting life of its own. At the Trilogy, it obtained its chicken solo.

It was at the Trilogy that I found a toy xylophone laying in the bottom of Elizabeth's "Bag-O-Percussion." You know the one—straight out of the Milton Bradley catalogue. The one with eight brightly colored keys and two little red-and-white plastic mallets. I felt it should also be utilized.

Because you can't really tune a toy xylophone, everyone was forced to play in the key dictated by the three-dollar piece of plastic—G-sharp. As John, Larry and Randy launched into a simple, twelve-bar blues shuffle, I would pick out little melodies on the keys. As the song built and crescendoed, I would cap it off with a rock'n' roll grimace, a simple sweep up the keyboard and a bow to the audience.

Lionel Hampton would've loved the "Xylophone Boogie." Liberace would've loved the "Xylophone Boogie." It never failed to bring the Trilogy laughing to its feet. Unfortunately, after a few gigs, Little Toy Xylophone was crushed by Big Heavy Amplifier. The gag was retired.

Sundays at the Trilogy were wonderfully elastic evenings, filled with music of all kinds. Anything went. Elizabeth would join John on acoustic guitars for a couple of duets. Larry sang "You Know Like I Know" and "Wild Parrots" from the piano. Randy sang "Country Girl" and "Leatherwood." We all slugged our way through Steve's "Hey, Muhammad"—another one-chord rant.

In between sets, everyone congregated outside, transforming the corner of Clay and Monroe into a small-town version of the corner of Haight and Ashbury. Oftentimes, the merriment would spill across the street and onto the darkened ROTC field—now devoid of soldiers. It became a popular place to wander off to, for some (ahem) fresh air.

There was always plenty of food, music, people, laughter, beer, and merriment when the Family Tree played the Trilogy. As the entire community gathered from the surrounding neighborhoods, our black friends stopped by. In a town of rich, white pastors, they were as much of an outcast as the hippies. It was still the early '70s. Plus, we all liked to smoke pot.

Nourished from a lunchbox of BLT's (Bijou, Landers, Trilogy), we marched into the summer of '72, ready to conquer the world.

CHAPTER 5

Dr. Irene Ruedi headed the sociology department of Southwest Missouri State. Any student who came to SMS to study sociology could not avoid a class with Dr. Ruedi. A frail, diminutive presence in the classroom, she was a stalwart of the faculty, a pillar of the academic community.

The department's senior professor was quite popular among her younger, liberal-thinking students. Her tolerance of the rampant opposition to the Viet Nam War was in direct opposition to that of fellow professor and future secretary of state John Ashcroft, who was teaching political science in the next building.

If you came to SMS to study the science of politics, you could not avoid Ashcroft.

If you came to SMS to study the science of sociology, you could not avoid Ruedi.

If you came to SMS to goof off and drink beer, you could not avoid Ashcroft or Ruedi.

It was a gray day as Ruedi entered her classroom, troubled with her father's deteriorating health and consequential move from the family farm in Aldrich, Missouri. As she quietly talked about her dad, the house and the farm, a handful of students heard her tale—one of whom

Ruedi-Valley mailbox, Aldrich, MO. (photo by Billy Higgins)

was Randy Chowning. He saw this as an opportunity to turn a negative into a positive.

When asked if she'd be interested in renting out the place, Ruedi thought it was a great idea. Randy, along with older brother Rusty, had been actively searching for a place to live. A 12-room, pre-Civil War mansion on 550 acres, out in the middle of nowhere seemed ideal.

"I asked her for directions and posed the question whether she'd be interested in letting us rent it," Randy recalls. "She told us how to get there. But she didn't want to charge us any rent. We voluntarily drew up this little contract for $20.00 a month. And they didn't have to move the dog [Prince], who came with the place. They moved out. We moved in. Simple as that. Rusty wanted to buy it, but just couldn't get it together."

Heading north from Springfield on Highway 13, the half-hour drive seemed like an eternity. When a turn onto Highway U was made, the road got smaller. When the next turn dumped you onto Highway UU, the houses got fewer and farther between. As Highway UU ended, turning into a dirt road, houses disappeared altogether.

The large, stately black mailbox marked the driveway that took you another quarter mile farther off the dirt road and into the woods. As the tree-lined lane led through the front gate, opening onto a gently sloping

Ruedi-Valley front porch (photo by Billy Higgins)

two-acre glade, you couldn't help but have your breath taken away by the majesty of the white mansion on the hill at the far end.

Though the six-bedroom stead was more than one hundred years old, it was built well and still in pretty good shape. Once used as a stopover on the Underground Railroad, massive oak and sycamore trees shrouded the house, regally providing shade in the summer, as well as shelter from the winter winds. A large barn and root cellar told silent, but vivid stories of colorful days gone by.

The place provided an ideal setting for those who had passed through over the years. It would provide an ideal setting for the Family Tree.

Even though the Bijou burned, we were all still intrigued by this music we were making. We were also faced with the dilemma of not having a place to gather to make it. After a couple of, brief get-togethers at Nutz & Loonies, we settled into this magical place in the middle of the woods. There was no more perfect spot on the planet for this music to nestle and flourish than the Ruedi-Valley Ranch.

Because the thirty-minute trek to the ranch was a long way for a bunch of guys without cars, when we got there, we stayed—for days. And because the house was so big, everyone had a bedroom. What little gear we had easily fit into one of the front living rooms, affording us space to set up Buddy's upright piano in one corner and our small PA system on the fireplace mantle.

As had always been the case, we took great care to make the room sound as good as it could. The drums were deadened just right to create a thumping—instead of a blasting—beat. The amplifiers were turned down a couple of notches, as vocals blended through a PA that did not have to strain to be heard.

The entire room, as well as the entire house, was made of seasoned wood. Curtains hung from the windows, the floors were covered with the thick, heavy rugs and sofas left behind by the Ruedi family. The air may have worn the musty cloak of an old house, but it sure sounded good.

When the weather turned cold, fires were built in the fireplaces. When spring rolled around, windows were thrown wide open. There was no way we were going to disturb anybody, due to the fact that the closest neighbor was a mile and a half away. We were completely—and I mean, completely—alone with the music.

Designated weekends found Larry, Steve, Buddy, John, Elizabeth, and me heading from the Springfield city limits to Aldrich. With guitars, drums, sleeping bags, groceries, beer, whiskey, drugs, and other assorted sundries, we would arrive in time to set up our stuff, watch the sunset, eat dinner, get stoned, and play music into the evening, before heading off to our respective rooms.

Mornings at the Ranch were even more mystical than the evenings. Beginning slowly and quietly, fog would engulf the low-lying areas that surrounded the house. Dew turned the huge lawn into a sparkling emerald carpet. As the morning progressed, we huddled around the kitchen, drinking coffee, eating breakfast, laughing, and talking about everything under the sun.

Then, we would slowly filter into the rehearsal room for some daytime music, which usually consisted of our less-raucous material.

On nice evenings, the scene would oftentimes spill out onto the front porch—the same front porch that would be featured on the back cover of our first album. Here, we were accompanied by crickets—the same crickets that would be featured on our second album. Under the huge trees that surrounded the house, every square inch of the place was idyllic. Every square inch was utilized.

At times, we'd strike up the band in the kitchen. Songs were being written, worked on and worked up in every corner of the place. Then, we'd bring them into the room and play them for each other. Then, we'd play the shit out of all of them. Ideas flew freely. Some were accepted. Others were rejected. All were considered. The flood gates were open.

When breaks were taken, football and Frisbee games broke out across the lawn. Prince, the epitome of "old farm dog," enjoyed the company, jumping around like a puppy.

Randy recalls the days as "…relaxed and very casually playing, never playing more than a couple of hours or so at a stretch. Someone was always leaving the room, or coming or going, which was kind of neat in a way. It didn't matter if you were there when the song was going by or not. We knew you weren't going anywhere, because there was nowhere to go. We said, 'He'll be back.'"

Oftentimes, not everyone was needed to get the work done. As Larry would be teaching John, Buddy and me one of his songs, Randy and Steve sat in the kitchen, writing another. Songs were rifling, fast and furious.

Saturday would pass slowly with these bursts of music. A break was taken for those who wanted to walk up the hill and watch the sun go down. Sunsets at the Ranch were spectacular—well worth the hike. As a meal was prepared and libations broken out, Saturday night kicked in. At this point, attention to formal arrangements was redirected into a party of ranting, ne'er-do-wells.

As the night wore on, the songs got more outrageous, more free-form and much, much funnier. As we hunkered down on the music, Rusty would sit on the windowsill, a small tray of freshly grown marijuana at his side. His job was to keep drinks, joints and the party rolling.

Though he didn't play an instrument, he became an essential part of things. His thoughts and opinions—many of which were very good—were considered a seventh of the equation. This seven-way split would soon be reflected when we entered negotiations about how to set up Lost Cabin Music.

When Sunday morning rolled around, things started slower and later, the coffee brewed darker and stronger. Those songs with arrange-

It Shined

ments and harmonies would get run over, refined, roughly recorded, and cemented into our memory bank.

Tapes of last night's bash were also listened to and laughed at. It was these late-night sessions that spawned Steve's "Hey, Muhammad" and Rusty's "Mau-Mau"—both testaments to drunken, one-chord throw-downs. This "bombs away" approach also found its way onto "River to the Sun" and the "Ruedi-Valley Boogie." Everybody must—and did—get stoned.

Sunday afternoon passed. We watched the sunset. Then, we loaded up and headed back into town. Randy, Rusty and Prince stayed behind.

This was to become our regular regimen, as we all looked forward to getting away from Springfield and into the seclusion Ruedi-Valley provided. The place would become our musical home for the next few years.

Gigs weren't rolling in. But that didn't bother us. We weren't that anxious about playing many, anyway. We did, however, agree to do an opening slot for Southwest Baptist College's 1972 homecoming concert.

Ruedi-Valley, 1974. Left to right: Larry Lee, Steve Cash, me, John Dillon, Randy Chowning, Buddy Brayfield (photo by Jim Mayfield)

Located just a few miles away in nearby Bolivar, we knew it would be easy to get to. We also knew that playing at a Baptist college would be real weird. But, they were going to pay us $250, which worked out to $40 a man (Elizabeth couldn't make the gig). The extra ten dollars went into our gas tanks.

Local favorites, Uncle Wally—which featured trumpeter and future booking agent, Randy Erwin—headlined the show. Erwin knew that we had a band and knew we were close by. He and Rusty took care of business. The $250 gig was booked.

As we lumbered into town and onto campus, we loaded our gear into the gymnasium, to the roar of the homecoming football game being played nearby. That evening, when it came time for the concert, the students filled the field house with a sea of rented tuxedos, corsages and posture.

You could hear their collective gasp when we walked on stage to open the show. They were there to be dazzled by Uncle Wally, the sound of their shiny horns, the sight of their flashy disco suits, and their happy, snappy choreography. We provided them with a lethal dose of flannel, denim and facial hair. They stared at the Family Tree like we were from Mars.

Unlike the next time we tried to play for a fraternity crowd, this one didn't try to fight us. (You'll learn about that gig in a few minutes) These rich, white pastors weren't hostile at all. They weren't anything at all, sitting motionless and emotionless, staring at us like they were watching a movie that they weren't understanding. We played well. We sang well. Their applause was polite. But it was clear that these people had absolutely no idea what we were doing.

We kept our set upbeat and forty-five minutes long. Still, we were no match for Uncle Wally, who immediately brought the crowd screaming to its feet with some fancy footwork of their own. While Rusty collected the money in the basketball coach's office, we quickly packed up, leaving the auditorium to the strains of "Shake, shake, shake. Shake, shake, shake. Shake your booty." The Baptists had come alive, finally getting the chance to shake their booty.

The Family Tree left the building as fast as we could. After a short stop at the liquor store on the Bolivar city limits, we were back at the

Ranch by the time Uncle Wally were hitting the last strains of "That's the way, uh-huh, uh-huh, I like it."

We all had hearty laughs at the absurdity of the evening, as well as the twenty-dollar bills in our pockets. It was an exciting weekend.

We didn't care that the crowd didn't go crazy. We had our sights set on a completely different set of priorities. Making a crowd rise to their feet wasn't one of them. Making a record was. It was the only thing on our collective mind. We tailored our songs, as well as our rehearsals, to this end.

The Band had their Big Pink. We had our Ruedi-Valley Ranch.

CHAPTER 6

The ringing telephone shattered the quiet morning at John and Elizabeth's cabin on the Finley River. Like most phone calls, it started with your typical RINGGGGGGG, followed by your typical "Hello?"

"John?" came the voice on the other end.

"Yeah."

"It's Canway."

"Hey, Steve. How ya doin'?"

"Great."

"Where ya been?"

"You're NOT going to believe what just happened."

"What just happened?"

"I just met with John Hammond."

"Bullshit."

"No, man. I just walked out of his office. I'm in New York on the street, at a payphone, right outside his building."

After an extremely pregnant pause, Steve broke the silence. "You still there?"

"Yeah."

"John, I'm not kidding. I just came from John Hammond's office. I played him one of those tapes from the Bijou. He loved it and he wants to talk to you guys about it."

"What the …? How …? What? How'd you do that?"
"Man, it was just a magic thing. Wait until you hear this."

The secretary behind the reception desk at the offices of Columbia Records looked as old and stoic as the granite that comprised the Manhattan skyscraper. Unannounced, Steve walked in, approaching her desk with a gentlemanly, "Good morning. Is John Hammond here?"

"Yes, he is," came the startled reply. "Who wants to see him?"

"Steve Canaday."

"What's the purpose?"

"I have a tape I want him to hear."

"He's not going to see you," she leerily continued. "Nobody gets in to see Mr. Hammond," finishing her thought with, "Plus, he doesn't listen to tapes."

"Could you please give him a call?"

"I'll call him, but he's not going to see you. Have a seat."

The quiet in the lobby was deafening as Steve sat down. After what probably seemed like an eternity—but was probably only a few minutes—she returned and said, "You're not going to believe this, but he wants to see you."

As Steve walked in, Hammond sat with his back to the door, reading the paper, staring out the window, his feet up on the desk. Without turning around, he instructed Steve to, "Sit down. I'll be with you in a minute."

When he turned around, with "Who are you?," "Steeeve Canaday" was the confident reply.

"Whatcha got?"

"I've got this group of musicians back in Springfield, Missouri."

"Yeah, Springfield. I've heard of Springfield. That's where the Jubilee used to be."

"These guys got original material, they're really good and they're really unique. I'd like for you to hear them."

"Okay. Give me the tape."

As Hammond plugged our cassette into his machine and turned back to the window, our "live," two-track version of "Black Sky" tumbled from the speakers. As the song began, Steve noticed Hammond starting to move. As the song slunk along, so did both men. When the song finished,

Steve Canaday (photo by Jim Mayfield)

Hammond slowly turned back around, and with a deep breath, said, "I discovered Sonny Terry."

"Yes, sir. I know that," was Steve's reply.

"This reminds me of Sonny Terry."

As the conversation progressed, Steve mentioned the rough recording, rough playing and rough singing. Hammond curtly cut him off with, "Hey, Woody Guthrie couldn't sing either."

Steve ended the call with, "John. He played two or three other things and said, 'I like this. Have one of the boys call me and we'll set something up.' Get a pencil. Here's his number."

John picks up the story. "A couple days later, when I called the number, it was his secretary who picked up the line. When I told her who I was, she said, 'This is your lucky day. Mr. Hammond won't quit listening to that tape. He wants to set up a meeting with you and Epic Records and send someone down there to see you guys. I'll let you know when I have more details. I'll be calling within a week, or ten days.'"

Phone receivers returned to their hooks. Quiet settled back onto the banks of the Finley River. As the summer of '72 began, it was one filled with relative inactivity. It would not end that way.

If you're making any sense out of this jumbled mess, you're probably asking yourself, "What was Canaday doing in New York in the first place?" The tale continues.

All you have to do is look back to the burning of his club. Though we continued to rehearse, the Family Tree no longer had anywhere to just hang out and play. The entire Bijou family began to drift off into individual Plan B's.

One of Steve's Plan B's was to utilize his pilot's license, flying late-night, low-altitude marijuana runs into and out of Mexico. Without the club to occupy his time, he had lots of it on his hands. What he didn't have lots of, was the revenue the club generated.

Jumping back and forth across the border, numerous trips were made, well under the radar. Though he didn't let any of us know what he was up to when he was up to it, you can hear the melancholy in his song, "Rescue Me."

> That old, Mexican flatland desert
> Reaches out to a yellow sky
> And the hills to the north cast a purple shadow
> On the corner of my eye
> And I long to be in Missouri
> With the ones that I left behind
> But the times are hard down at the railroad yard
> And I've got to make the bills on time
>
> Rescue me
> Won't you take me into the sky
> Fly me over the mountains
> Let the teardrops fill my eye
> Rescue me
> Won't you take me into the sky
> And drop me off in Missouri

On one such trip, when suspicion got the best of him, he was unable to shake the feeling that he was being followed. An impromptu, middle-of-the-night landing was made at a small airport near Boulder, Colorado.

After landing the plane and nervously heading to the end of the dark runway, he quickly gathered his thoughts, as well as his things. Without even bothering to taxi back in to the small terminal, he shut the engine off and jumped from the plane, leaving it to sit on the far end of the runway, its cargo intact.

Reaching the first payphone he could find, he hurriedly called Springfield, informing his wife Terry to, "Get Holly, pack up all my things and meet me at your mom's in Jersey." Here, he would lay low and wait for things to cool off back in the Ozarks. After several weeks of laying low, he decided to head into the city with one of our tapes in his pocket, to see if he could track down John Hammond.

He did.

My Plan B was much less eventful. With my new draft card, officially declaring me free of military obligation, and the House of Nutz & Loonies partying like it was 1972, I was no longer forced to go to school. So, I didn't.

The choice was simple—get up early and go to class or stay up late and play music. One final semester of a 'B', a 'C', a 'D' and an 'I' (Incomplete) brought an uncelebrated end to my unspectacular college career.

Larry lays out his Plan B: "Two weeks before the club burned down, Dean [Billingsley] called me from San Francisco and said, 'What are you doing?' I told him I was just tending bar and playing music with some friends. He said, 'Man, you've got to come out here.'

"I didn't have any money, but Benny [Mahan] said, 'I've got some. I'll pay for our trips out there, but I want to stop in Las Vegas to see this chick.' I thought, cool. If we're going to be that far south, could we swing through L.A.? I might want to just stay there, because I've got these songs. They're pop songs, and I might want to see what's going on out there.

"This friend of mine gave me a phone number of a friend of hers and said, 'Why don't you call this guy when you get to L.A.? Maybe you can stay there.' It was eleven o'clock or so on a Sunday night when we hit town, and I called somebody I'd never heard of before from a payphone on Sunset Strip.

"This person said, 'I don't know who you are and, no, you're not going to stay here.' I got cold feet, trying to tell my friends, who were just sitting there in the car, good-bye. So I jumped back in and we drove to San Francisco. I stayed there for a couple weeks and fell in love with the place.

"Dean offered, 'Come on back out. I'm playing a lot, and you can play with me.' I said, 'Fine. I'm going to go home and get my drums. I'll be right back.' The night before I got home, the club burned down. My drums burned up. My piano got burned up. I never made it back to San Francisco. If that fire had not happened, I might not have been in the band."

Larry found some new drums, but there just wasn't much going on. Just as the closing down of the Warehouse Experience left me without a place to play in the summer of '71, the burning down of the Bijou left us all without a place to play in the summer of '72.

Though another gig at the Landers, a couple of Sundays at the Trilogy and a week at the Peppermint Lounge were all fine, it was an ill-fated fraternity party that best describes the bottom of the barrel we were scraping.

Playing the Landers was great. But, we knew we could only do that once a year. We'd begun to outgrow the Trilogy. The week at the Peppermint Lounge just turned into a nightly tequila fest to keep the songs tight. When we were hired to play a Delta Kappa Shithead party, we actually entered the Twilight Zone.

We were just as leery about the fact that we played absolutely no songs of the day as we were astounded at the amount of money they were going to pay us. The chairman of the "hiring the band committee" reassured everyone that our oddball song list would not be an issue. He'd heard us at the Landers. He caught the buzz, picturing himself as some kind of visionary who was going to enlighten all of his fraternal brothers and their fraternal dates, by introducing them to this new band called the Family Tree.

Just to even make the ninety-mile trek to the Bagnell Dam Holiday Inn, located in the middle of central Missouri's resort district, we had to wrangle our way any way we could. We crammed all our shit—as well as ourselves—into several cars, wondering what we were about to get ourselves into and wondering if it was going to be as weird as our gig at the Baptist college.

As we set up in the ballroom and began playing, the chairman who had hired us showed up—completely smashed out of his ever-loving mind. He and his brethren had spent the entire afternoon drinking on the lake. When we started, without him able to explain to his cohorts what we were doing, the entire crowd stared at us as if we were from Jupiter. Their backs remained to the walls. Their dates remained in the lobby.

After a very unsettling first set, we took our break and retreated to the parking lot for some fresh air. Here, we saw our employer completely passed out. Unfortunately, he had done this before he paid us.

This left us with his brethren, who, by this time, were REALLY smashed and REALLY not amused at our inability—as well as our unwillingness—to even attempt a Kool & the Gang song. Their dates wanted to dance and didn't have a clue what to do with "Nouveau-Tubular Relapse."

We played harder and louder, hoping that that would do the trick. But, it didn't. We played "Bo Diddley," "River to the Sun," "Ruedi-Valley Boogie," and "Nadine" as fast and furious as we could. That didn't help either. "Chicken Train," which had never failed to elicit spontaneous fits of dancing, may as well have been Chinese arithmetic.

As the evening wore on, the harder we tried, the worse the situation got. By the end of the night, we had one eye on the clock, one eye on the drunks, one eye on the door, and one eye on each other's back.

We immediately packed up and headed out the door as fast as we could. Here, our liaison was still out cold, his henchmen out of their minds. Things got quite tense, as they belligerently threatened to not only not pay us (because they hated our music), but kick our ass (because they could). We were outnumbered—twenty drunken fraternity brutes to seven scrawny hippies.

Cooler heads prevailed before fisticuffs, when a couple of their more level-headed dates stepped in, realizing they HAD to pay us. We needed the money just for the gas to get home. We let out a large, collective sigh of relief when we finally left the Bagnell Dam city limits. We vowed it would be the last fraternity party we would ever attempt to play.

The volatile episode didn't depress us at all when we got home. Nor, did it deter us from our objective. We knew John Hammond liked our tape and was going to send someone to see us.

Michael Sunday, staff producer for Epic Records, was assigned the task of coming to Springfield to see who in the hell was making this strange music Hammond couldn't get enough of. A day of rehearsal at the Ranch was scheduled, along with three days in the studio. The time had come. We were going to play our music for someone from a record company—and we were ready.

Sunday had no idea what was about to hit him.

As we assembled at the Ranch, like we were accustomed to, Cash and Canaday met the New York producer at the airport. Cash recalls, "I went with Steve to pick him [Sunday] up in that great big, old limousine he had for a while and drove him out to the Ranch. We were all nervous.

"That drive from the airport to the Ranch is where the song 'Lost Cabin' came from. 'Riding in the back of our old limousine. Wondering if we'd pass or we'd fail.' He was hipper than thou, talking all this New York jive. We were still intrigued, because this might be a break."

"I don't remember him being very dictatorial, thinking he was a producer," Larry recalls. "And now that I know what a producer does, I don't remember him doing anything."

As he drove up the lane and through the Ruedi-Valley gate, the setting made his eyes widen.

When he walked into the house and heard the music, his ears widened.

As the orientation process began, he tried to explain why he was here. We already knew why he was here. Then, he played his latest production, the self-titled album from Texas rock group, Bang. We'd never heard of them. Nor, were we interested in hearing them.

We were here for one reason. When we convened in the rehearsal room, though everyone was nervous, things proceeded nicely. As we began playing song after song after song, Rusty proceeded to roll joint after joint after joint. Somewhere in the purple haze, Sunday ceded control of the proceedings, opting just to sit back and watch what we were doing.

Expecting to find a group of undisciplined hillbilly musicians with a handful of rough song ideas in a brown paper bag, he instead found a band of focused hillbilly musicians with well-written, well-arranged and well-thought-out songs.

"We were all nervous," Steve adds. "We didn't know what was going on. But, he gave us those $500."

When Sunday walked in to check out the studio, he took one look at the place, handed us our check and caught the next flight back to New York. This, pretty much left us alone to record our songs the way we wanted. That was fine with us. That's what we wanted to do in the first place.

Though local engineer Joe Higgins had just bought Top Talent from Si and Wayne, changing its name to American Artists, we were all familiar with the place. He may have given it a new name and a new paint job, but it was the same old studio—and we knew how to make it sound nice.

As we lumbered in with our arsenal of instruments, Higgins slid behind the board with Canway on one side and Rusty on the other. We just huddled up, set up, miked up, and ripped it up.

Years later, Paul Peterson, who would soon become part of our managerial team, offered these observations: "The cool thing is that these songs were recorded without any pressure or without anybody looking over their shoulder. It's a real, honest rendering of the material."

With three days of studio time, Sunday thought, surely this would be adequate to record the handful of songs he would need to decide whether we were worth signing. As we began laying down track after track, work progressed so smoothly that, by day's end, we'd cut twenty-three songs. The next day, overdubs and well-rehearsed vocals were added. Everything got mixed the third day.

Steve sums the session up with, "I remember we had only so much money, we had to get things done fast. When we first went in to make that demo for Epic, we had $500 to work with. They expected two or three songs. We did twenty-three."

A small, production deal was agreed to, stipulating that Epic would have first shot at the tape. If Sunday deemed them worthy of further pursuit, an actual recording contract would be drawn up. On our end, we demanded that, if this didn't happen, we would retain control of the master tapes as well as the songs.

Sunday may have been impressed with our music. He was not impressed with our lack of a manager or any kind of business acumen. It didn't take him long to pass on the Family Tree. We may not have procured a record deal, but we had nice demo tapes of a couple dozen songs. The summer of '72 marched on.

So did the weekly series of Sunday afternoon concerts on the banks of Lake Springfield. The gatherings had become quite popular, drawing nice crowds. Alongside Granny's and Zachary Beau, the Family Tree (with a fresh demo under our arm), was booked. Even though Epic had passed on us, word about the big-time record producer put an extra buzz into the air.

That morning, as we met at Larry's house to head out to the lake, when John pulled up, Elizabeth was not with him. When he informed us that she and Randy had fallen for each other and would be coming to the gig together, the craziness began.

In a pre-Fleetwood Mac-like manner, the Family Tree took to the stage—which wasn't really a stage, but just a patch of level ground under the trees right outside one of the pavilions. Our friends from the Bijou showed up. Our friends from the Landers showed up. Our friends from the Trilogy showed up.

As the air was thick with anticipation, the members of the band were filled with unease. As we charged on anyway, laying down "Black Sky," "Outside My Country Home," "Standing on the Rock" and "Sheriff's Coming," focus on the music remained distracted by the soap opera being played out behind the scenes.

Liz played a much smaller role as we played our usual set, oftentimes not even being near. In her absence, the percussion table shrunk to a tambourine and some maracas laying around. The air was thicker than thick. That day, it was a good thing our two guitarists stood on opposite sides of the stage.

Though no one in the crowd knew what was going on, I did. So did Steve and Larry, as we formed an informal three-man buffer zone down the middle of the stage. Pots never boiled over. Nor, did they ever settle into any kind of groove. Though we played all right, it was not a pleasant day.

Even though we solidified our position as the hippest band in town, all we could say to our friends was, "Yeah, he came to town," and "No, we didn't get a record deal." The air was tense. The water in the lake, still.

If our set wasn't crazy enough, as the day progressed, one of the local dealers, and frequent visitor to the House (let's just call him Rudy), walked up to the blanket of Nutz & Loonies with a six-pack of ice-cold soda pop in his hand. Let me rephrase that: He walked up with five bottles of ice-cold soda pop in a six-pack container. In his other hand, he held the sixth bottle.

As the parched gathering began to pass around the cold beverages, Rudy made sure the bottle in his hand was guzzled by the actual tenants of the House. I took the first large gulp and passed it on to Marc, who did the same. He passed it to John, who took a healthy swig and handed it to Clarence, who finished off the laced contents.

After the sun-filled afternoon of music, many of the sun-drenched music lovers were coming back to the House for one of our infamous fish fries. Lauritzen, whose father was a commercial fisherman on the Missouri River, had received his monthly allotment of "catch of the day"—and he was going to fry it all up for whoever came over hungry.

When we got home, our exhilaration of the music was replaced with the hallucinations of the acid. All four of us had been royally dosed, courtesy of Rudy. As the world began to melt in front of our very eyes, the fireworks began.

The House of Nutz & Loonies became a house of *extremely* nutty loonies. Wild Man Fisher records blared from the stereo. People danced everywhere. All we could do was stand there and laugh at the fish.

Somehow, the fish got fried.

Somehow, the music played on.

Somehow, Canaday found his way into John Hammond's office.

Somehow, the Family Tree would hold on.

The summer of '72 continued. As it slowly turned into fall, we rehearsed. But not much. Even though we had a nice demo tape, the band began to fall apart as informally as it had fallen together.

CHAPTER 7

The corner of 43rd & Main was jumping in the fall of '72.

Sitting on the northern edge of Kansas City's fountain-laden Plaza, the busy intersection was home to noted coffeehouse, the Vanguard. Opened in 1963, the converted art gallery was an integral stop on the folk music circuit of the '60s. As acts worked their way across the country from the Cellar Door in Washington, D.C. to the Ice House in Pasadena, frequent stops were made in Kansas City.

Owner and operator, Stan Plesser explains, "I went in one day just to look at the artwork. On the other side of the space was a little coffeehouse. It was just a lot of kids hanging around on the weekend. I was intrigued." The transplanted Brooklynite would soon buy the place and begin presenting music.

San Francisco singers, Mort & Linda became early regulars. Dan Moriarty, along with partner, Linda King, knew many of the singers traveling the folk highways. When Mort offered to help Stan book the club, Stan took him up on his offer.

Thus, began a decade-long parade of entertainers across the Vanguard stage. As Loudon Wainwright III, Steve Gillette, Josh White, Jr., Bill Moss, the Nitty Gritty Dirt Band, Steve Goodman, Corky Siegel, and Jim Schwall frequented the place, all enjoyed its mellow Midwest atmosphere.

Comedian, Steve Martin brought his banjo and his arrow through his head to the Vanguard. Pat Paulsen brought his quadrennial campaign for vice-president to the Vanguard. All brought the house down.

It was here that L.A. folk scene veterans, Michael Brewer and Tom Shipley met. After several Kansas City appearances, performing as solo acts, they began to return as a duo. Brewer & Shipley liked the club, the city and the people so much, they moved to town and acquired Plesser as their manager.

Talent showcases, dubbed the "New Faces Series," attracted college representatives from all over the Midwest. "We had sixty colleges come to town," Stan recalls. "My job was to find employment for my artists. We held these showcases for all these schools and they bought our acts. Out of that, we formed a nice, little coffeehouse circuit around the Midwest.

"The Vanguard was only open Thursday through Sunday. We had jazz on Sunday nights. The jazz people in town—and Kansas City has always been known for its jazz—were looking for something to do. Most of the folk music kids that were there on Friday and Saturday weren't around. On Sunday, they were at home, getting ready to go to school. The jazz people were looking for somewhere to play. Many of them had gigs on Friday and Saturday and were just looking for a place to hang out on Sunday.

"I always loved jazz, so I said, 'Let's have some.' Lots of local players, like Groove Holmes and the Pete Eye Trio, came in. I never had a problem with booze. But, on Sundays, when everyone cleared out, there were always at least a dozen empty bottles stashed away under the tables."

Like its barbecue, Kansas City likes its jazz.

The corner of 43rd & Main was rocking.

On the opposite corner of Main Street stood the large, two-story house Stan had bought to accommodate the artists who were coming to town to play his club. Day-to-day operations of the club were run from the basement of the house.

As the '60s began to fade into the '70s, America's shifting musical landscape impelled Stan to shift his focus from the Vanguard (Kansas City's answer to the Cellar Door), to Cowtown Ballroom (Kansas City's answer to the Fillmore). The Vanguard was transformed into an art movie house and sold.

Along with partner, Paul Peterson, the two formed a team, combining Stan's New York business sensibilities with Paul's California demeanor. Though they worked together well, they could not have looked any more different when standing side by side.

At a stubby five foot five, Stan lived in the suburbs with his wife Carole and their three young sons. Paul, who packed 150 soaking-wet pounds onto his lanky five-foot-nine-inch frame, preferred living in the Westport district, a few short blocks from the office.

When Stan had a business idea, Paul listened. When Paul heard something interesting musically, Stan listened.

Together, they ran Good Karma Productions. Not only did they book most of the acts that passed through Cowtown Ballroom, they managed the careers of Brewer & Shipley, who had just had a hit with "One Toke Over the Line"; Ted Anderson, who had just written "Seems Like a Long Time" for Rod Stewart; Kansas City actor and singer, Danny Cox, whose angelic voice boomed from his 260-pound, linebacker-like body; Chicago-born singer-songwriter Chet Nichols, and White Eyes, a local rock 'n' roll band that featured the raspy voice of Kathy Helmich.

Though unassuming from the outside, the two-story building—dubbed the Good Karma House—had been restored to its original condition, complete with high ceilings, hardwood floors, chandeliered foyers, and ornate wooden staircases. Stained-glass windows cast prisms of sunlight everywhere.

Standing tall at 4218 Main, the house was soon to become "home away from home" for the Family Tree.

It was the address we'd seen on the back of Brewer & Shipley's album. It was the address Rusty mailed our press kit to—a press kit that basically consisted of the cassette tape we'd made for Sunday, wrapped with a rubber band. We thought it'd be a good idea to contact these people.

The man on the receiving end of the package was Cowtown Ballroom manager, Frank Polte, a figure of the '60s San Francisco music scene who had recently moved to town. Bringing his Bay Area attitudes with him—and having basked in several "summers of love"—he became part of the Good Karma team.

As Cowtown's nightly emcee, it was Frank's laid-back voice that got everyone relaxed and ready for the show. It was Frank who fielded and opened the odd-looking package from the Ruedi-Valley Ranch. After a brief listen, he passed it on to Paul with a simple, "I think you need to hear this."

As Peterson plugged the tape in, he knew he was hearing something unique and something genuine. "It was one of those experiences you feel—like your whole body's metabolism changes. I remember thinking, 'Gee, this is going to be important.' The tape had 'Rhythm of Joy' handwritten on the front and a bunch of song titles. I listened to side A twice before I realized side B was also filled with songs."

Enjoying what he heard, he walked it across the hall to Plesser's office. The two sat down for a listen. Stan recognized the originality and, more importantly, the marketability. Could a bunch of hillbillies from Missouri be marketed and sold like shoes in Brooklyn?

The corner of 43rd & Main was rocking.

The definite kings of the hill, though, were Mike and Tom. The lanky pair, fleeing the Los Angeles music scene they'd been entrenched in for the past several years, moved to Kansas City in search of mellower pastures in which to raise their families.

After having met on the mid-'60s folk circuit, the two joined forces. They would soon relocate to California. Mike recalls, "At the time, if you were serious about being in the music business, there were only two places to go, New York or L.A. We started hanging around with John Boylan, who was working with [Dan] Fogelberg and the Eagles guys.

"Tom and I lived around the corner from each other in El Segundo. I was right next door to Jim Messina, who was living in Lenny Bruce's old house. This is where Buffalo Springfield were hanging out and rehearsing. All I had to do to hear Buffalo Springfield was walk outside my house.

"Some of our first gigs out there were warming up for the Byrds. Our band was drummer, Billy Mundi [Mothers of Invention, Little Feat] and bass player, Jim Fielder [Blood, Sweat, and Tears]. We were, basically just a bunch of musicians hanging out and stealing groceries together."

Shipley continues, "Mike and I both got gigs as staff writers with this new company started by Herb Alpert and Jerry Moss. Then, they approached us and said, 'Why don't you guys cut your own songs?'"

The resulting tapes became "Down in L.A.," Brewer & Shipley's initial A&M album (1968). Mike chuckles, "Then, we moved to Kansas City."

No longer interested in the fast lane of the West Coast, they opted for the dirt roads of the heartland. Over the next few years, the duo began to visit San Francisco, where "we cut three records for Kama Sutra at Wally Heider's. Nick Gravenites, who we'd met when he played solo at the Vanguard, produced a couple of our records. He helped by pulling in some of the guys from his band, The Electric Flag—Michael Bloomfield and Mark Naftalin."

The resulting *Weeds* (1969) and *Tarkio* (1970) hit the airwaves, establishing the duo as legitimate singer/songwriters. *Weeds* contained their minor hit, "Whitchi-Tai-To," which featured Nicky Hopkins on piano. *Tarkio* contained major hit, "One Toke Over the Line," which featured Jerry Garcia on pedal steel.

In the summer of '71, everyone's radio blasted the controversial "One Toke." Not only was it burning up the radio airwaves, it was heating up the walls of Congress. Filling the nightly news, as well as the *Westport Trucker*, (KC's alternative, weekly entertainment magazine) with political rhetoric, the song became an anthem for a generation.

"We made Nixon's 'Enemies List,' which we hold as a badge of honor to this day," proudly claims Brewer. "Vice-president, Spiro Agnew personally named us—on national TV one night—as subversives to American youth. We never considered ourselves political at all. We were just a couple of singers.

"This is how weird it got with 'One Toke.' As Agnew was coming down on us, Lawrence Welk played it on his show, introducing it as a gospel song. Sweet Jesus. The FCC was threatening radio stations with their licenses if they didn't edit lyrics. They were also trying to ban 'Puff, the Magic Dragon,' for God's sake."

"We were doing a lot of TV. We did the *Tonight Show*, when it was still in New York. But Johnny wasn't there. We got Joey Bishop as guest host. We did the *Dick Cavett Show*, the *David Frost Show* and a whole slew of others, when lip-synching was still okay. At least we didn't have to worry about the sound. We got real good at lip-synching 'One Toke.'"

Another thing they forbade was visiting the host's couch. "'One Toke' was why we were on TV, because it was a hit—and it was controversial. But, we had no doubt in our minds what they wanted to talk about. So, we passed at sitting on the couch. We were fed up with dealing with it.

We didn't want to make it a bigger deal than it already was. It was just a song and we were saying, 'You people are taking this far too seriously.'"

Not only did the Family Tree agree with the politics of their records, we enjoyed the sound of their records—acoustic-based, with a strong bass and drum track that gives the music a little nudge.

It's that little nudge that makes people happy.

It's that little nudge that makes people peppy.

It's that little nudge that makes people dance.

It's that little nudge that, when I deem necessary, I feel comfortable administering—St. Louis style.

Copies of the *Rhythm of Joy* tape got passed around the office, as other members of the Good Karma stables gave a listen—and liked what they heard. Mike and Tom loved it, immediately plucking "Black Sky" for inclusion on their subsequent record, *Rural Space*.

All concurred about the music's substantiality. A phone call to the number on the tape rang through to the Ranch. Rusty picked up the other end of the line. A brief phone conversation garnered a meeting and an invitation for a visit.

Rusty Chowning at the wheel (photo by Billy Higgins)

"It was Rusty who kept it going," Stan points out. "He wouldn't let this go. He really wanted to make this thing happen between us and you guys. He was the energy that kept this thing cooking—to bring you to Good Karma and make sure Good Karma was feeling good about what was happening. We decided 'Let's go down and see what this is all about.' Plus, we wanted to meet the people who were making the music on this tape."

A trip to the Ozarks made an impression on the Good Karma team. Stan and Paul were not only impressed with the Ranch itself, but were impressed when the Family Tree gathered to play. An afternoon of music and Frisbee was followed by visits to our individual homes. By the end of the trip, impressions were deep.

Plesser recalls, "The one thing that got me the most, when I went down there, was when nobody talked about their own songs. Larry would say, 'Hey, Steve, play them this,' or John would say to Larry, 'Why don't you play him that song?' Nobody was saying, 'HEY. Listen to me.'

"Everybody was pulling for the other guy. They weren't just pulling for themselves. In the end, when guys did start pulling for themselves, it disappointed me. But, that's not what I saw there in the beginning. I saw more of a real democratic group."

A reciprocal invitation was extended, as guests of Good Karma, for an upcoming Poco concert at Cowtown. We all liked Poco, jumping at the chance to go to Kansas City, go out to eat and continue talks with a prospective and soon-to-be manager.

As we walked up the steps that delivered us from the hustle and bustle of Main Street to the hushed quiet of the Good Karma house, I was slapped in the face with a deja vu. As I stepped inside, the ambience of the large foyer flashed me back into those pleasant old houses in St. Louis's Central West End.

As soon as you walked in the front door, concert posters from Cowtown were plastered everywhere. Receptionist, Bambi greeted everyone with big eyes and a big smile. Along with Bonnie Harney, the two comprised the secretarial staff—both wonderful people, valuable assets and completely in love with what they were doing.

Directly across the foyer, the formal living room had been converted into a conference room, complete with a long antique wooden table and a bay window overlooking Main Street. Large, sliding oak doors opened back into the dining room, which was filled with filing cabinets and stacks of merchandise from the stable of Good Karma artists.

At the top of a winding staircase, the second floor housed Stan's office, which looked out over Main Street and Paul's office, which looked out back, over Westport.

A smaller set of stairs took you from the second to the third floor, nicely remodeled with couches, chairs, a TV, a stereo system for listening to music, and a couple of small amps for playing music.

A brief meet-and-greet with Stan and Paul started the evening. As the Vanguard faded, Plesser's focus had shifted several blocks to the larger Cowtown.

"The place had been a ballroom years ago for big bands," Stan recalls. "Red Skelton even played there. Then, it became a skating rink because of the smooth, wooden floors. Then, it just turned into a warehouse for a printing company. I'd been to San Francisco to see what was going on. When I walked in and saw the place, I said, 'This is perfect.' So, we started putting concerts together."

The place became the premier venue for rock 'n' roll bands passing through Kansas City. Even though Plesser was now booking bigger acts into a bigger venue, he continued his allegiance to the Vanguard veterans, many of whom still passed through town. Many were given opening slots on the Cowtown stage before bigger bands.

This made for wonderfully interesting combinations. No one seemed to mind when Steve Goodman opened the show with his acoustic guitar before Humble Pie blew the roof off the place, or when Steve Martin was booked alongside B.B. King. When we began to play here, one of our first appearances at the place was on a co-bill with Loudon Wainwright III, riding high on the charts with *Dead Skunk in the Middle of the Road*. We opened the show, electrically. He followed us with his acoustic guitar.

Word of Cowtown had already spread throughout the area. Springfield was no exception. I had already made several trips to hear artists who I knew would never make it down to us. It was on the Cowtown stage that I saw the Firesign Theater. It was on the Cowtown stage that I saw Frank and his Mothers—for four dollars.

I fell in love with the place. I had walked through the front door several times as a paying customer. Now, I was walking in the back door. I was thrilled.

The corner of 31st & Gillham was rocking.

After a spirited dinner, we all headed to 31st & Gillham, where we were handed blue, Cowtown backstage passes. They weren't really needed, as security wasn't much of an issue. A couple hundred mellowed hippies didn't get out of line very often.

We were introduced to the guys in Poco, who were nice enough to allow us to mingle freely throughout the evening. My turntable had spun Rusty Young, Jim Messina, Richie Furay, George Grantham and Timothy B. Schmidt—often.

Schmidt explained how detuning their guitars a half step allowed them to hit their trademark, high harmonies. This process allowed them to play normal "E" chords on their guitars, but only have to reach "E flat" with their voices.

The show was slick and impressive—and after having been let in on their little tuning trick, even more impressive. The playing was tight, the harmonies tighter. But what really struck me was the dynamics of their strong, diverse personalities. Hell, they kind of reminded us of us.

It wasn't until their second show, when discord would rear its ugly head in our camp. When the lights came up, Poco started with the same song they started the first show with. At this point, they clicked into autopilot. For the duration of the second show, they played the exact same song list, complete with the exact same, "C'mon, everybody, clap your hands" banter in the exact same places.

The crowd, not realizing this, ate up it. They hadn't seen the first show. It did, however, affect members of our entourage. As both shows elicited the same reaction, discussion among our ranks over the next few hours, days and weeks was "testy." In a fine example of "Is the glass half-empty or half-full?" Steve grumbled about how sterile and unadventurous they were. Randy, on the other hand, countered with how well-rehearsed and efficient they were.

When alcohol was thrown into the mix, frazzled nerves turned to loud discussions. Occasionally, they turned into really loud discussions.

I had no preference. I saw both sides of the story, neither bothering me enough to argue about. I enjoy spontaneity. I also like band practice. Band practice should not be a chore. Band practice should be fun. Oftentimes, band practice is more fun than the gigs.

I saw how Poco prepared. I saw how they tuned their guitars down and warmed their voices up. I saw the robotic execution of their shows, as well as the Siamese standing ovations they received. What I didn't see was the need for all the fussing that accompanied our drive back to Springfield.

Animated discussions will be a recurring theme throughout the next few chapters, as Randy would insist on rehearsing a song over and over, until rote execution kicked in. Steve liked to play a song, then play another song. These polarized views will be a sore spot and, in several cases, a stumbling block. Plus, Elizabeth had had a change of heart, returning to John's side.

Oftentimes, Larry and I would be arbiters between the two camps. Neither he, nor I really cared who was—or who wasn't—doing what. We both felt that, if we were playing well and singing well, arguing about shit like this didn't matter.

I love spontaneity. I also like rehearsing. I like knowing what I'm doing when I walk onstage. I also have enough confidence in my abilities to spot a musical curve ball and be light enough on my feet to handle it—and handle it well.

Negotiations continued on the Good Karma/Family Tree/Rhythm of Joy front over the next couple of months, which, as Larry simply states, "was good because it was, at least, something positive going on—something that wasn't going on before."

With this growing interest, as well as a desire to see us play "live," we were invited to participate in a late summer, Sunday afternoon of music in Kansas City's Penn Valley Park. This was good. We knew how to play music on Sunday afternoons. This also reinstated a zip into our step, as we crammed in a couple of extra rehearsals for our "big city" debut.

In another ragtag caravan of vans, cars and trucks, we found our way north and into the park. After acoustic sets from Chet Nichols and Danny Cox, we set up our tattered gear in front of White Eyes' mountain of equipment.

Because, it was the first time we'd ever played for an audience that didn't just consist of a bunch of our Springfield friends, we were scared shitless. This different crowd in this different city was intimidating for a bunch of guys from Springfield.

Our set, though upbeat and well-played, was met with less than jubilation. Though we may not have won over the throngs that afternoon, we did catch the eye of local scenesters. These folks may not have danced while we played, but they sat up and took note of what we were doing—and the sound we were making.

After what we thought to be an unspectacular set, we quietly left the stage and packed our gear back into our trucks and trunks. As we headed south, with our tails between our legs, little did we know that the phones at the Good Karma house would start ringing the next morning with inquiries about those guys and that girl.

We had caught the ear of Herb Palmer, who booked Cowtown. We also caught the ear of the Kansas City Art Institute, who wanted us to play their Halloween party. Negotiations between Stan and us picked up a notch. He knew he had something. *We* knew we had something. We also knew that if something didn't happen soon, there was the distinct possibility that the something we had just might disintegrate into nothing.

Stan and Paul made another trip south to the Ranch and a management deal was placed on the table. I knew we had nothing to lose. Anything would be better than not playing gigs in Springfield. Most of us figured, "What the hell? Let's go for it."

Stan figured, "There was nobody else on the horizon that was coming to you. You saw what we did. We were from the area. I could throw a Frisbee. What else do you need?"

Others weren't so sure, as Dillon recalls, "I was just real nervous and wary about anybody—everybody. I was just paranoid about managers. I thought Stan was aggressive and pushy. He scared me a little bit. At the same time, he kept talking about getting us a record deal. I liked that. But in order for him to go to work for us and get a deal, we had to sign a management contract with him and Good Karma. I had misgivings about signing my life away to a manager.

"I was concerned about publishing because of all the things Si had told me. In the end, it just came down to Stan and Paul convincing Steve and myself that we could actually have a career based on our music. I remember being completely worn out by his talk, by the negotiations ... and I also remember just saying, 'Gimme a pen.'"

With a gleam, he finishes with, "... and, I'm really, really, really, really, really glad we signed with them."

It Shined

On October 18, 1972, a one-year contract was inked between Good Karma Productions and "artist," giving Stan the authority to head out into the world on our behalf. I would say he hit the ground running, but that would be a gross understatement. His short legs hit the ground in a full sprint.

Our contract read "artist" for the following reason—an acoustic folk group from New England already held the rights to "Family Tree." They owned the name. They had records out. Our first piece of business was to change the name of our band. Simple as that. End of story.

While this process was taking place, we did several gigs under several names, playing as Leatherwood (after one of Randy's songs) and Rhythm of Joy (after one of Steve's). They're both wonderful songs. Neither, is a very good name for a band.

Discussions continued. Around Springfield, we were still the Family Tree.

Nothing was hitting the spot, until a case of beer and a late night "name the band" party broke out at the Good Karma House. As the party geared, the beer disappeared. As the beer disappeared, names flew through the air. As the beer began to take effect, the names got funnier. Friends, who just stopped by for the party, were immediately sucked into the fray. At one point, there were a dozen folks, spewing away.

At one point, amid the spewings, Cash bellowed, "How about this? Cosmic Corncob and his Amazing Ozark Mountain Daredevils."

That evening, many of the names made us laugh. This one made the entire room howl. We moved on, taking it about as seriously as we'd taken the first 280 suggestions. The party raged on.

As the evening began to wind down, everyone and everything kept gravitating back to the word *Ozark*. It is a very sturdy word, steeped in mystery and phonics. It was not to be ignored. It wasn't.

Plus, we were living in the times of long-haired hippie bands with long, hippie names like the New Riders of the Purple Sage, the Pure Prairie League, the Goose Creek Symphony, the Amazing Rhythm Aces, and Commander Cody & His Lost Planet Airmen. We weren't trying to beat them. So, we joined them.

No one was thrilled with the Daredevil part, but Stan and Paul knew it when they heard it—and, when they heard it, they let us hear about it. Our general consensus was, "It is kind of catchy. What the hell?"

First, we knew we would have to drop the word "amazing," so as to not step on any toes in the Rhythm Aces' camp. No problem. It was deleted at once.

George Frain may have become Commander Cody. Joe McDonald may have become Country Joe. But, no one in our camp wanted to step up to the plate and become Cosmic Corncob. Therefore, the whole "Cosmic Corncob & the Something Somethings" approach was scrapped and the name got shortened to the three words it is today. The party was over.

From the very first moment, though, the name change sat awkwardly with us. It was hard for us—as well as our friends—to refer to ourselves as the Ozark Mountain Daredevils. We'd never been anything but the Family Tree. Family Tree was short, pleasant, easy to remember, and easier to say. Our new name was long and cumbersome, with way too many syllables. Not only did it take too long to say, none of us was really interested in being daredevilish on a daily basis.

What Stan saw, though, was the marketability.

The second piece of business we conducted was a new promo picture. We didn't even have an old promo picture. The only poster we had was a grainy, black-and-white photograph of a bare woman standing alone on a gray day under the bare branches of a large tree. With "Family Tree" scripted in small letters in the lower right hand corner, it was very simple, very unassuming, and very un-Ozark Mountain Daredevil-like.

New publicity photo? No problem. Nutz & Loonies roommate, Marc Barag was a photographer. The Atlantic City native was majoring in photography. He had a nice camera. We picked a nice day and met at the pavilion in Phelp's Grove Park.

Here, we gathered a couple of park benches and sat down. Let me put that another way: We walked over to an area where there already were some park benches ... and sat down. Preparation consisted of pushing a couple of these benches together—wide enough for six guys. A third bench, that just happened to be sitting in front of us, became a footstool.

"Okay. Everybody, sit down and let's get this over with," was the common sentiment, a sentiment that permeated many of our early dealings—especially photographs. That suited us, just fine.

We sat there. But not for long. We knew it had to be done. So, it got done. Nothing fancy—a simple, black-and-white photo of denim and whiskers. For years, it was the only picture of us there was. For years, everyone had to look at my big feet sticking up in the air. Still, they weren't as big as the smile on my face or the heart, pounding behind that smile.

We bought a heavy-duty blue Ford van from Cowtown business manager, Mike Waggoner. This would eliminate the need to scramble for rides every time we had a gig. Plastered on the front doors, just below the windows, were decals of ducks. It immediately became the Duck Truck. Then, figuring that the band that climbed in and out of the Duck Truck must be the Ducks, we became the Ducks.

As we began to flutter around the Midwest, we began to see Ducks Unlimited literature all over the truck stops and gas stations we were using. Though none of us were duck hunters ... yet (you'll learn about our duck-hunting escapade soon), we bought handfuls of their colorful patches, which were sown onto tattered jeans, jackets, and hats.

Those of us—friends included—who weren't adjusting well to our new, eight-syllable name began to refer to us as the Ducks. While the Ozark Mountain Daredevils began climbing on and off stages, the Ducks

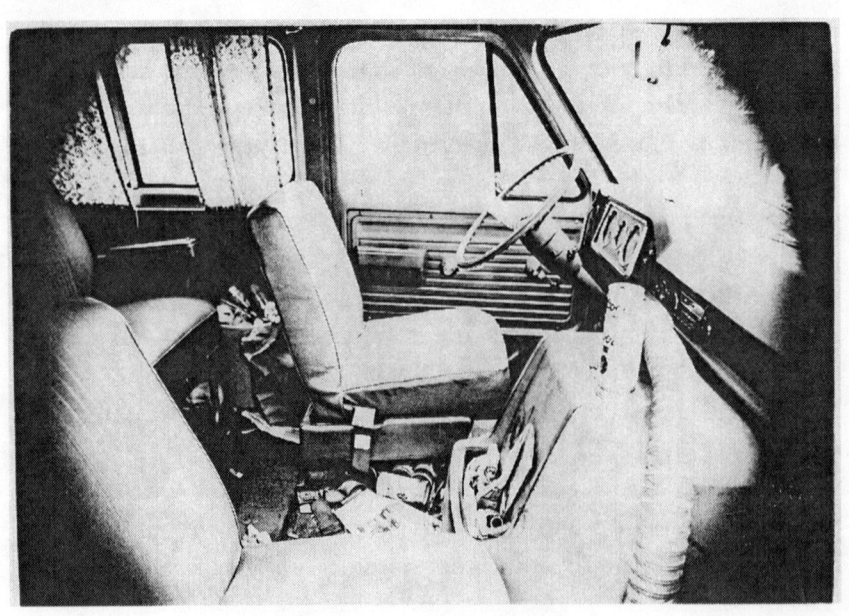

Duck Truck (photo by Billy Higgins)

began climbing in and out of the van. There are those, who still refer to us as such.

The driving duties were relegated to whoever was awake, sober, or able. With seven guys, we were usually able to find someone to fit one of these criteria. Steve claimed the back bench, which was deemed the Troll Seat. The Troll Seat became the place where the least awake, least sober, or least able would go.

Beer flowed in the Troll Seat. Smoke emanated from the Troll Seat. Songs were written in the Troll Seat. Sermons were delivered from the Troll Seat.

Everyone had his role. Steve's role was "Song List Man," which is self-explanatory. Mine was "Packing Man"—the guy who packs all the gear into the trailer after everyone else has carried it out of the club. I have a knack for being able to see which amp or drum will fit into which open space with the least amount of jostling.

Many nights, right after Packing Man finished packing, the Ducks would make tracks. Most of these overnight trips were fine. Others weren't. It's "duck-hunting time."

The gas gauge read *empty* as we pulled into the small-town gas station. The sign in the window read *Closed*. After having played a small run of gigs, ending at Grinnell College in Grinnell, Iowa, we were all anxious to get home. As mile after mile of dark, rural space roared past our windshield, Rusty began to realize we weren't going to make it to a town of any size without running out of gas. Running out of gas in the middle of nowhere was just that—nowhere. He had to think fast.

Though we were sitting right next to a gas pump, it was the middle of the night and every light in town was off. Not wanting to wait six hours for the gas station to open, Rusty turned around with an emphatic, "Don't anybody get out of the van."

A quarter was dropped into the slot of the payphone in the parking lot. The sheriff's department was called—a risky move, due to the fact that we probably had enough drugs and alcohol in the van to warrant every one of us jail time.

"I'm sorry to bother you, sir. But, my name is Kenneth Chowning and I'm in a bind," claimed Ken (Rusty's real name). "I'm out of gas and I'm sitting at a gas station here in your town. I know it's late and I wouldn't bother you, except for the fact that I'm part of a group of doctors. We've been up here in Iowa, duck hunting all weekend and every one of us has a full slate of patients to tend to, first thing in the morning. We've just got to get back to Springfield, Missouri tonight. Do you know the owner of the gas station?

"You do? Great.

"You will? Great.

"You'll phone him right away? Fantastic. Thank you, sir. Thank you very much."

When he climbed back into the van, he turned around and reiterated, "Do NOT get out of the van. Everybody stay down. You are all asleep. Understood?" Shortly afterward, the owner of the station and the police chief pulled up. Rusty thanked them profusely, showing them the duck decals on the van and our trailer, with all of our duck-hunting equipment in it. While recounting tales of the sleeping doctors' Iowa weekend, the pumps got turned on. The Duck Truck got filled with gas. The Ozark Mountain Duck Hunting Doctors made it home that night.

Stan booked a couple of shows in the Kansas City area that fall. Halloween was booked at the Kansas City Art Institute and a gig at Cowtown was booked, two days before Thanksgiving. We had an automatic "in" in both instances. Stan helped Herb book the ballroom and the Art Institute was five blocks from the Good Karma house. The holiday spirit was in the air.

Sitting directly behind the Nelson Art Gallery, the Art Institute lures innovative artists from all over the world. The institute was—and still is—renowned for its freeform methods of teaching, as well as its electric Kool-Aid Halloween parties.

When we played, we found an audience much more receptive to our deal than the one that had gathered in Penn Valley Park just a couple of months ago. Elaborate scenery turned the large student gallery into a castle. The small, student body embraced us into their inner circles of performance, art and drugs. It was our first official gig as the Ozark Mountain Daredevils. But, nobody gave a shit. That night, we were just the band. Everyone howled at the moon.

As the evening progressed, the instruments on the percussion table found their way into the hands of the students. This was not a problem. As Frankenstein played cowbell and his genie dance partner played tambourine, this provided large and funky percussion tracks. Stan, caught up in the moment, played maracas on the side of the stage—like Louis Prima on acid. Paul mingled with crowd. The atmosphere became so elastic and relaxed, I broke out a taped-up toy xylophone.

Afterward, it was a good thing the Duck Truck only had a couple of blocks to go up the hill. That night, the Good Karma House became the Good Karma Hotel. As the Ducks roosted, we knew Kansas City was going to be a lot of fun.

On November 22, 1972, Cowtown Ballroom presented Hot Tuna with special guests, the Ozark Mountain Daredevils—for two shows. With Thanksgiving just a few days away, the holiday season was gearing up. We really geared up.

Hot Tuna was also already in heavy rotation. Right before he moved back to Springfield, Steve had seen one of their first Berkeley gigs. We were both big fans of the music from San Francisco in general. I was a fan of Jack Cassady's bass playing in particular. I was excited as hell.

When we hit the stage and charged into "Absolute Zero"—our adaptation of "She'll Be Coming around the Mountain"—years of anticipation and focus were unleashed in an avalanche of stomping. Buddy's squawking, oboe mouthpiece solo brought the crowd to their feet. By the end of the very first song, the ice was completely broken.

As we condensed an entire evening at the Bijou into a tight, forty-minute set, the audience enjoyed the diversity of the songs. When Randy sang "Country Girl" and Larry sang "You Know Like I Know," they swayed to the beat. When Buddy reassembled his oboe, his hypnotic solo on "Mountain Range" hit a very deep groove. When we finished the set with our seven-minute rave-up of "River to the Sun," the crowd rose to their feet and stayed there. Each time we turned the harp riff around, they cheered louder and danced wilder. When we finished, a standing ovation was already underway.

As pride of the Ozarks rose up that night, many friends accompanied us on the long drive up from Springfield. So many so, that they found their way into the photo essay that accompanied the *Trucker's* review of our gig. There was not one review—but two—by world-renowned journalists, Luther Goose and Uncle Bubbles.

It will be helpful at this point, if I can talk for a minute to the journal-

It Shined

Cowtown Ballroom, Kansas City 1972.

ists who have covered us over the years. Your job has not been easy. Many of you have tried to put into words what you heard with your ears and saw with your eyes. But you've been frustrated at our lack of a distinctive genre that would enable you to use clichéd fountains of, "Their unique brand of (genre here) diametrically reaffirms their views of sociopolitical blah, blah, blah with poignant songs about the repression of man in a modern world filled with injustice, as blah, blah, blah, blah, blah, blah, blah."

On several occasions, though, attentive, talented writers have been able to understand what we were trying to do—and put it into words. When they do, I will credit them. Over the years, I've enjoyed reading attempts to describe a band who plays "Chicken Train" and "Jackie Blue" in the same set. We thank all of you who "got it" and tried to help others "get it."

Both Kansas City pundits started their reviews not talking about Hot Tuna—but talking about us. Goose wrote, "What a pleasant surprise the Ozark Mountain Daredevils were. Completely honest and sincere, they have their style down pat, with traces of a lot of different influences—nicely blended elements of country, mountain, rock, and western. They even manage to slip in a highly classical oboe solo, which earned them a round of applause.

"Although none of them were outstanding musicians, the bass player was quite good and an interesting departure from the average. His tone was mellow and full; and he stayed in the lower registers, where the bass player belongs, creating a nice, deep bottom.

"Their harmonies were not forced at all and, thank God, did not sound like Crosby, Stills and Nash. It was readily apparent that the Daredevils have their own unique roots and their own original interpretations of what they've heard. Their rock and roll was played more like Buck Owens than Chuck Berry. Their songs were very well written. They know how to build songs very effectively, often repeating the same riff. I hope to see them again in the future."

Uncle Bubbles added, "Fucking Jesus, when I staggered out of Cowtown Wednesday night my jaw was slack. With the concert rumbling in my skull, I could only recall two things: One, the Ozark Mountain Daredevils mellowed this old, city critter out more than he thought ever possible and Two, Hot Tuna sits on the right hand of whatever cosmic creature's running the universe.

"The Ozark Mountain Daredevils were introduced as being direct from Springfield, Missouri: and are sure as hell going to go much farther. Showing amazing musical versatility (they opened as a jug band, switched to an acoustic format, moved on to electric guitars and even had an oboe for one number), songwriting ability and being some of the most real people ever to walk on the Cowtown stage, the Daredevils have incredible potential.

"The stage act was, in spots, a little unprofessional, but can easily be excused, since we were told that this was their first gig in front of 'this many people.' The band plays sweet country ballads, such as 'Leatherwood,' or knee slapper 'Chicken Train,' or straight rock and roll in a way that makes an audience relax and breathe easy for a while. Two encores from these folks, and hopefully more to come."

There was Jorma's picture at the top of the page. There was Jack's picture. There was my picture. There was John and Steve doing "Chicken Train." There were the pictures of the kimonoed dancers from the Ozarks.

Not everyone in town read Goose, Bubbles, or the *Trucker*. Nancy Ball (a regular name), covering the concert for the *Kansas City Star* (a regular newspaper), introduced us to mainstream Kansas City with "The warm up act was provided by the Ozark Mountain Daredevils, a 6-piece group from Springfield, Mo. The group started off with various backwoods instruments such as violin, mouth bow and spoons, and moved gradually into rock. Even the harder rock numbers took on a velvety surface quality due to the tastefully muffled drums and the smooth blend of acoustic and electric instruments.

"They captured the down-home spirit of the crowd with 'Chicken Train Stomp,' featuring Supe duJour's ridiculously appropriate chicken squawking. If any band is to break out of the Midwest soon, this will be the one to do it. Maybe there is an Ozark Renaissance in the making."

Though, Hot Tuna were louder than God and blew everyone's mind, those Cowtown shows put us on the musical map. We returned home, this time as conquering heroes. We just played Cowtown Ballroom and, maaaan, we were good!

Our focus shifted up Highway 13.

CHAPTER 8

The year 1973 was ushered in with a return appearance on a New Year's Eve gig at Cowtown, featuring the entire stable of Good Karma artists. As the evening wore on, though the atmosphere was festive, the anxious crowd was not present. Nor, did the folk music do much to bring about anything different.

Short acoustic sets by Ted Anderson and Chet Nichols were followed by another acoustic set from Danny Cox. Headliners, Brewer & Shipley were pleasant enough, but hardly the kind of music to incite any kind of jingle-bell rocking. This, along with the fact that everyone in Kansas City had already seen these guys many times, didn't do much for the evening's panache.

As the proceedings plodded toward midnight, the crowd politely waded through a sea of folk singers for some New Year's Eve dancing. We came out and delivered. We played a smoking set, but had to cut it short, to make sure Mike & Tom were on stage at midnight for the countdown.

We had no problem with that, except for the fact that the crowd was really into what we were doing. Everyone was ready to rock and roll. Mike and Tom sat them back down.

When asked to join in for a New Year's jam, I climbed back on stage to join the cast of "Anyone Even Remotely Connected to Anyone Who

Had Anything to Do with Good Karma." Plesser played the maracas like it was 1973—until they exploded in his hand, sending clouds of maraca dust into the air.

I dove right in with a handful of bass and a bellyful of champagne—ready to fire it up and let it rip. Once on stage, though, I realized that a "Mau-Mau Jam" would be just an extended version of Mike and Tom's "50 States of Freedom," followed by one song each from Chet, Danny and Ted.

I like all of these guys and I like their music. But, this was New Year's Eve and I was disappointed how things never really busted loose. I said nothing, due to the fact that I was still one of the new kids on the block. I was ready to rip into some old, Chuck Berry songs, but quickly realized that this was not St. Louis.

After the show, the party, once again shifted back to the Good Karma house, where we became much better acquainted with a wider circle of local music makers. The new year ushered in new hopes.

As 1973 began, The Good Karma house became "command central" for our musical assault on the Midwest. All roads led to—and from—Kansas City. This is where we would eat, sleep, read, play music, listen to music, hang out, watch TV, and pass the time between gigs.

The third floor became the Duck Room—our own personal clubhouse. During the day, as business took place downstairs, we lounged around upstairs. At night, we would venture out to do a gig. Afterward, we returned to the roost.

Late-night bashes took place here, as our new Kansas City friends would stop by, bringing ... shall we say ... botanical efforts from the area. The place became notorious. The locals knew that, when the Ducks were in town, there'd be smokin' in the boys' room.

Out of this, the Coughing Dogs were born. Consisting of nothing more than group drinking, group smoking, group singing, and group songwriting, the theme of the evening was *absurdity*. Songs like "I've Got My Eye on an Ion, and I Own an Island (So Fuck You)" brought the house down with laughter. Loud renditions of, "You're a Horrible Person" greeted party-comers as they walked in the door. After being serenaded, cocktails were placed into their hands and their presence inserted into the party.

As we howled through the nights, we found that these Kansas City folks liked to have a good time the same way we did. Many became—and remain—good friends. Soon, we would start hiring them as our road crew.

In this manner, we began to frequent the Kansas City area, playing as many gigs and wreaking as much havoc as we could in the shortest amount of time. Extended stays were spent in sleeping bags and on the couches of the Good Karma house. When extra housing was needed, we spilled over onto the couches of Paul's.

Still, Mike and Tom were the biggest act in town. While Stan was dealing with their label (Buddha Records) in Los Angeles, the small Good Karma staff kept their finger on the local pulse, concentrating on booking their acts into regional colleges, state fairs, county fairs, coffeehouses and nightclubs throughout the area. We began to attack this list.

We would play somewhere every day—sometimes, twice a day—oftentimes at the same college. It was an effective approach. The routine was simple: Set up in the student union during lunch hour and play as the students passed through. Wondering why a band was playing at this time of day, many stopped to listen.

As we played, Rusty made sure everyone in the room was aware that we would be playing in the coffeehouse that evening. After an afternoon to travel through the campus grapevine, our evening gigs became happenings. It was a strategy that worked like a charm.

Afterward, we'd hightail it back to the Good Karma house, where we would sleep, regroup and do the same thing the next day at a different college in a different town. Many of these runs were made into Kansas, where we could easily play for days in an area that included Topeka, Manhattan, Wichita, Hutchison, Hays and our favorite, Lawrence.

Then, it was off to Nebraska and Iowa, where we played Omaha and Lincoln, before scooting over to Des Moines and Ames. Stops in between—like St. Joe and Columbia, Missouri-were frequent. These guerrilla runs would last for a week, after which we'd haul ass back down to Springfield.

A maximum ten-day "away from home" period was set. We would adhere to this policy for years. This gave us two weekends, with the week in between. That was enough time to get some work done—and more than enough time to start getting on each other's nerves.

As Good Karma began to book up the calendar, we put ourselves on a weekly salary of $50.00. Every Friday, a check for fifty bucks would arrive in our mailboxes. We could open checking accounts. We were in tall cotton.

After a few days off, we'd head right back up Highway 13, where we'd hit another handful of colleges, clubs, coffeehouses and fairs. This craggy, 200-mile stretch of road became our two-lane lifeline between Springfield and Kansas City. We got to know every bump in the road.

We made the trip in the summer.

We made it in the winter.

We made it in the bright sunlight.

We made it in the dead of night.

We made it laughing all the way.

We made it by the skin of our teeth—as one night in the winter of '73 almost put us out of business.

As the gray, Sunday afternoon began to turn into an ominous winter evening, the weather forecast was not good. With a major blast of ice and snow looming on the northern horizon, we were scheduled to get to Kansas City the next day.

If we waited until morning, there would be a good chance we would not even be able to make it out of town. Deciding to make a run for it, we gathered and drove into the dark, into the snow and into the large expanses of open space between Springfield and Kansas City. We knew it'd be hairy. We also knew we had to do it. We'd done it before. We could do it again. No big deal. Off we went.

After an hour, driving conditions went from bad to worse to worst. As we hit the exact middle of nowhere, Highway 13 became nothing but two frozen ruts in the snow, stretching off into the dark distance. No one in their right mind would be out on a night like this. No one was—except us.

The driving snow filled our headlights as we headed right into the jowls of winter. Progress was slow but sure. Then, we heard the clunk. As the timing chain of the Duck Truck snapped, things came to a standstill. Rusty pulled over as best he could.

Night was upon us and there was no traffic. Nor, were there any prospects of any. Nor, was there any way to get out to check under the hood—or try to walk somewhere. We were stuck inside the van as winter raged outside. When the first pair of headlights finally appeared over the hill, Rusty jumped out to flag them down. Once into the next town, he would contact the highway patrol about the rest of us.

John and Larry jumped right up, grabbed their grips and said, "We're going, too". The driver couldn't fit seven guys into the cab of his small truck. He could fit three. Rusty turned to the rest of us with, "Stay here." Like we were going to be going somewhere!

As the taillights faded into the snow, darkness re-descended on Buddy, Randy, Steve and me. Deeming ourselves the Frozen Bros (rhymes with 'toes'), we had no other choice than to sit in the van, pass the time and talk. As it got later, it got darker. As it got darker, the snow continued to softly pelt the windows.

Things were fine. Things were warm. That is, until the engine stalled and we couldn't get it to turn back over. The lights and heater stopped working, as things became completely dark. Even if we had wanted to, where were we going to go? We were miles from any kind of house. Drifts mounted. Talk slowed. Here comes the night.

How long it took the highway patrolman to finally pull up isn't clear. But the classic symptoms of freezing to death had begun to set in. When people are found frozen, oftentimes they're found naked and in the fetal position—to preserve body heat. All four of us had already become silent and sluggish, curled up in our sleeping bags with our shoes and socks off.

"Except for a few times we flew around thunderstorms in those little planes," recalls Buddy, "that night was the most perilous travel experience we had. We very easily could've died that night."

We scrambled to get dressed, then quickly climbed into the patrol car, where the temperature was set on "super thaw." Never has sitting in the back of a police car felt so good! We crammed in and the patrolman made it into Clinton. We piled into a motel and took hot showers.

The next morning, though the storm had passed, huge amounts of snow still lay on the ground. While a local farmer with a Jeep was hailed to tow the van somewhere to be fixed, we made it into Kansas City.

Thankfully, most trips weren't this eventful.

On many of our visits, we'd swing by the office, where there was a built-in cast of Good Karma characters. We would pick up Danny, Chet, or Ted, who'd jump right into the Duck Truck with their guitar and become our opening act. Instant show. No assembly required. Just add beer.

Most of the bigger bills were shared with Brewer & Shipley, though for the longest time, we remained their opening act. They had hit records. They were nationwide. They'd been on the Smothers Brothers' show. We hadn't been anywhere.

As we traveled the Midwest together, we would begin the evening with our set—half acoustic, half electric. Mike and Tom would come out and play their set. Then, we'd join them on stage for their encore and one final rave-up.

As time wore on—and we switched places on the charts—we switched places on the marquee. It was still basically the same show. Other than re-adjusting the height of a couple of microphones, nothing else had to be moved. When they finished, they just unplugged their two guitars and walked off stage. Our amps were flipped on and we began without having to make many changes—or take much time. It was a very smooth and simple show.

The official change would take place in Seattle a couple of years later—and can be directly blamed on their Buddha Record Company man, who produced some very potent Thai Stick for the Northwest leg of their/our tour. When we walked off stage after our set, Mike handed me a small joint, saying, "Hey, man. Try this before you guys come back out to play." After immediately consuming it in the dressing room, Rusty walked in with an enthusiastic, "Hey, look what Shipley gave me."

That pot sent us all into cartoon land. When we heard, "One Toke Over the Line, Sweet Jesus," that was our cue. But by this time, we were so stoned, Steve had all of his clothes on backwards, playing harmonica through a hole he'd ripped into the brown paper bag he wore on his head. I donned a cardboard mask of a grizzled, seafaring captain (the kind they give little kids at seafood restaurants). Larry and John turned into greaseballs, complete with sunglasses and slicked-back pompadours. Buddy found some Groucho Marx nose glasses and Randy crawled on stage through the legs of the piano, with a stocking cap pulled over his head. We were stoned in Seattle.

I do know that, when Mike and Tom started "50 States of Freedom" and we began to meander to our positions, all the two could do was look around and mutter, "What the …?" We came on and played like our sideburns were on fire. The crowd went crazy. We dubbed ourselves the Notes.

Ever since then, Seattle—as well as the entire Pacific Northwest—has supported us very well, not only understanding what we were trying to do, but filling the venues when we arrived.

As our jaunts around the Midwest began to expand to other parts of the country, the Ozark Mountain Daredevils with special guests, Brewer & Shipley, became a hot ticket. We'd all become great friends. The show was well paced, though I could never understand Mike and Tom's aversion to using a drummer.

When their situation and budget allowed, they would bring along Springfield guitarist, Donnie Thompson and Kansas City bassist, Steve Baker. But never a drummer. Mike and Tom's sound was pleasant—and Donnie and Steve made it a little beefier. But, it still didn't have that "oomph." One night, in the middle of South Dakota, I decided to "oomph" it up.

While they were playing their set in the field house, we were eating and drinking at a restaurant across town. The daily routine was not to arrive at the venue until after they had started. This way, the crowd would already be inside the building, meaning less traffic and hassle outside.

On this night, the Duck party hit "warp speed" early, spilling over from the restaurant to the field house. In my case, this meant spilling from the field house onto the stage. I'd threatened Donnie many times. One night, I was going to sneak up onto Larry's drums and join in on "Witchi-Ti-To." I could play the song's beat, the same way I used to bang it out on my mother's kitchen chairs. They closed every show with it.

As they unsuspectingly began the song, I quietly climbed onto the drum stool and waited for my cue. During the first verse, I made eye contact with Donnie, who muttered under his breath, "What took you so long?"

When the song launched into the second verse, it did so with a full band. Instead of bashing in like Keith Moon, I slithered in like Levon. Even though I was tipsy, I knew I could play the song's simple 4/4 beat.

It Shined

Once again, Mike and Tom turned around with startled looks. When they realized it was me and I was actually going to play the song—and play it well—they rolled with the nudges.

They're pros. They weren't about stop in the middle of the song, turn around and say, "Oh, c'mon Supe, what the hell you trying to do? Get down from there. You trying to ruin our set?" The beat went on. The oomph of the drums brought the South Dakotans to their feet.

When word got back to the dressing room that my party cup was runnething over, the wings of the stage filled with laughing ducks and coughing dogs. The crowd laughed and clapped along. Mike and Tom laughed and shook their heads.

Afterward, though I only played the one song, I immediately found my way to their dressing room, which was basically our dressing room. I was hoping that I hadn't overstepped my bounds. Paul reassured me that I hadn't. Stan was going nuts, trying to convince the two of them that they needed a drummer. I tuned my bass and got ready for our set, which also had a heaping helping of "oomph."

Wonderfully silly things began to happen out there on that prairie, like the night in Manhattan, Kansas when someone yelled, "Hey, Supe, come here. Look as this." We had come to play on the same stage where, just a month earlier, the Kansas State University theater department had staged their production of *Superman*. While we waited in our dressing room—which was their converted wardrobe department—we were allowed to wander through row after row of costumes.

In a far corner, there it was—cape and all. Complete with a padded undershirt that provided abs, pecs and all of the Superman-like muscles I've never had, the suit fit me to a "T"—or an "S."

While everyone else was getting ready for the show on one side of the dressing room, a dark, secluded corner became my phone booth. Never having been one to shy away from any kind of juvenile sight gag, I had to put it on. Afterward, the theatrical authorities were approached and a deal was struck. The play was over. They didn't need a Superman suit any more.

Actually, it mysteriously found its way into the bottom of my amp case—and out the door.

And so the stories go. In 1973, everyone wanted to see what this crazy little traveling hillbilly consortium was all about.

We took advantage of our residency at Cowtown by being able to take part in a series of recorded concerts, sponsored by Lee Jeans. Under the production guidance of Harvey Bruce, *Lee Jeans Presents, Live at Cowtown'* (a precursor to the King Biscuit Hour and Westwood One) was captured on tape. Under the engineering guidance of John Stronack

Washington University, St. Louis, 1974 (photo by Jim Mayfield)

and Stephen Barncard, the Record Plant's mobile recording truck was driven in from Los Angeles and pulled alongside the ballroom for an entire month.

Numerous artists were booked and recorded, their sets mixed and spliced into broadcast-ready radio shows. Over the month, B.B. King, Freddy King, the Byrds, Paul Butterfield, Commander Cody and his gang, Poco, the Nitty Gritty Dirt Band, as well as everyone in the Good Karma stable, took the stage and hit the red button.

As word spread, even the Kansas City Symphony jumped on board— sans tuxedos. Stan recalled, "To be able to play in casual clothes for a room full of kids, sitting around on the floor, really getting into what they were doing. Those were some of their favorite gigs."

We recorded a two-night stand, which gave us a very high-quality tape of our shows. At the end of the month, when the truck pulled out

It Shined

of town, it swung through St. Louis to capture an evening with Mike and Tom and John Mayall at the Kiel Opera House. I was thrilled beyond belief. I was going to play Kiel—a place where, just a few short years ago, I'd spent many nights in the audience.

The sound in the Opera House (unlike the adjoining Kiel Auditorium) was magnificent. I was in an absolute dream world. I'd arranged for my entire family to have seats right down front. But, when the lights went down and the crowd fired up, my father (who would eventually become more tolerant of smoking pot) stood his family right up and marched them right out the door.

Red tape and cold feet slowed *Live at Cowtown*, as several of the artists who had initially agreed to participate, heard their shows and forbade them to ever see the light of day. The tapes sounded great. Unfortunately, performances didn't. An abbreviated series ran that summer in a few cities, but to little fanfare.

Then, our master tapes were put away into a vault (actually, Paul's closet) for nearly twenty-five years. When Navarre Records licensed them as part of their 1995 "Archive Alive" series, we—as well as Mike & Tom—released our Cowtown shows.

Those who hear the recordings are treated to the frisky nature of our sets, as we rambled through Cash's comical "Commercial Success," along with the squawking "Absolute Zero." Also included are three of our quirkier songs which, for some unexplained reason, would never make it onto vinyl—"Sonora," "(I Threw Away) the Chains" and "Reudi Valley Boogie"—a twelve-bar blues song we would blast into on occasion, when we would get over-amped and over-served. The Kiel Opera House was one of those occasions.

Many who hear the recordings comment on the absence of "If You Want to Get to Heaven" and "Jackie Blue." There is a very good reason for this, my friend: Neither had been written, yet.

Over the years, several of the artists have let their recordings trickle out to the public. If you can ever find one of them, it is a testament not only to the music but to the good times everyone was having at the Cowtown Ballroom.

As we took up residency in Kansas City, we also visited the St. Louis area. With the same strategy, gigs were played in the student unions of St.

Louis University, the University of Missouri at St. Louis, the University of Illinois at Champaign and the two campuses of Southern Illinois University—Carbondale and Edwardsville, site of the Mississippi River Festival, which was in full swing.

Washington University, though, became our favorite. Not only were we embraced by academia for our literate approach toward songwriting, we were embraced by the counterculture for our idiotic approach toward our shows.

Our very first appearance was an evening in Graham Chapel, one of the oldest and most hallowed halls on campus. A curious crowd braved a torrential rainstorm as they filed into the stained-glassed chapel. Because there was no way to step outside without getting completely soaked, no one did.

While we played, everyone inside the building—ourselves included—was treated to a terrific lightning storm that lit up the whole chapel with brilliant bursts of stained-glass light. With each flash, gasps of delight rippled across the stage and through the pews. Completely inspired, we played and sang our asses off, garnering a return engagement for the school's spring fling in its quadrangle.

The aged, ivied quadrangle of Washington University encompasses a beautifully manicured half-acre lawn. Not only providing a quiet, serene environment for its student body, its ivy created a nice sound baffle for the performers who took to the stage on its north end.

The Saturday slate of performers built slowly. Stuck right in the middle of five slots, we were preceded by Furry Lewis and John Hammond, Jr., while followed by Captain Beefheart and Weather Report, featuring Joe Zawinul, Wayne Shorter and Jaco Pastorius.

The entire Granda clan attended en masse, including my two elderly grandmothers, who were ill-equipped for any late-night activity. This mid-afternoon gig was more to their liking. They sat comfortably in their lawn chairs, directly beside the family blanket. Everyone sprawled on the quadrangle's grassy floor, basking in the warm spring sun and the smoke-free air.

After Lewis's opening set, Steve struck up a conversation with the affable legend, asking if he could come for a visit. Furry responded with a loud, jovial, "Yeah. Come on down to Memphis. My house is easy to find. You can't miss it. It's the first little red house painted green."

The burst of laughter did not last long, as, from across the room, Hammond—who had just arrived from the airport—let out a blood-curdling scream. When he opened his guitar case, the sight of his National steel guitar, its neck cleanly snapped into two pieces from the flight, was a sight that made him, as well as everyone within eyeshot, sick.

Our set caused some commotion, as word had begun to leak out into the St. Louis musical community—just as it had in Kansas City. That afternoon, each song was greeted with eager attentiveness, waves of applause and fits of dancing. When we launched into "River to the Sun," just like our fans on the other side of the state, everyone rose and frolicked in the sun—a sea of tie dye and sandals.

When we finished, our dressing room scene was hectic. I had a great time, introducing my new friends from Springfield to my old friends from St. Louis.

The funniest part of the whole afternoon, though, took place after all of our guitars were put away. I knew my family had no interest in hanging around for the rest of the day. So, I emerged from the dressing room to bid them fond adieus. As I did, I could hear the good Captain already storming the stage. Heading toward the now-folded-up Granda camp, I was stopped dead in my tracks at the sight of my two little gray-haired grandmothers, still in their lawn chairs, attentively watching Captain Beefheart and trying to figure out what in the world he was doing.

As I walked them to the car, they both let me know how much they liked my band and how much they didn't like the Magic Band. I kissed everyone on the cheek and watched them drive off. Then, with a hearty chuckle, I raced back, not only wanting to catch the end of the Captain's set, but to also watch Jaco play bass.

We played afternoon sets at St. Louis University (where I would meet Karen Johnson, my future wife) and across the river at Southern Illinois University at Edwardsville (where we would garner an invite to play the River Festival). Because we were only doing afternoon shows, we set up and played a little longer than usual. Electric songs were toned down to "lunchroom" volume, to go along with the "lunchroom-ready" volume of our acoustic stuff.

When we finished at SIU, we were descended upon by the campus newspaper staff. As we packed up, they anxiously wanted to tell us all about this concert series they were having. When I informed them that

I was from the area and had already attended many of their shows, I became the Ducks' St. Louis conduit.

When they asked if we'd be interested in playing one of their shows, I went completely out of my ever-loving mind. I had been out of my mind at the Mississippi River Festival several times. But, this was going to be a different kind of "out of my mind." Rusty passed out Good Karma business cards, along with instructions to talk to Stanley.

We got our first gig outside the Midwest—a weeklong stand at Tulagi's in Boulder, Colorado with Jerry Jeff Walker. Chuck Morris, a friend of Stan's, not only managed the Nitty Gritty Dirt Band, but ran the club. At Stan's insistence, the gig was booked and we headed from the Ozark Mountains to the Rocky Mountains.

Every one of us was just as thrilled as we were surprised. Not only were we already big fans of Jerry Jeff, we looked forward to playing in Colorado—two shows a night for six nights. After driving across Kansas, when we checked into our Boulder hotel, we met up with Walker and his own band of nuts and loonies—the Lost Gonzo Band.

Introductions went around, and the hanging out between a bunch of hippies from the Ozarks and a bunch of hippies from Austin, Texas began at once. Breakfast and lunch were eaten in whatever combination of Gonzo Ducks happened to stumble into the coffee shop at the same time. When show time rolled around, the hanging out spilled over to the club.

After the first couple of nights, word began to spread around town about the cool evenings of music that were being provided by one of Texas's most gifted songwriters and this band of long-hairs from Missouri—who had some pretty good songs of their own.

As we played, Jerry Jeff and his boys hung at the bar. When they played, it was our turn to occupy the stools. By the end of the week, we got to know each other's material—as well as each other—very well. Both bands were smoking—on stage and off.

Bob Livingston, Walker's long-time bass player and I decided—so as to minimize delays between sets—we would share the same bass amp. I found this sense of cooperation rewarding and not as prevalent with some of the bigger artists we would soon meet.

He and I both played Fender basses and played them through my Fender Bassman amp. Plus he had an extra Precision Bass with him that had been disassembled into pieces. When I expressed interest in it, he offered to sell it to me for a good price—just to get it off his hands. I bought it, reassembled it and played the shit out of it.

By midweek, we began making friends around town. Nitty Gritty's, Jeff Hanna and Jimmy Ibbotsen, both Boulder residents, began coming by to hear some music and drink some beer. As they visited the dressing room, which housed both bands, cordial friendships were struck up all around.

Ibby invited everyone up to his house for a bunch of lunch and music. Here, we met Jimmy Fadden and John McEwen, as well as Morris. Food, wine and hospitality flowed freely, as did the afternoon. Then, we all headed back down into town for another night at Tulagi's.

By week's end, we felt so comfortable with Boulder (and vice versa), that Larry, Buddy and I took the opportunity to visit the local health food store (an idea that hadn't reached Springfield yet) to buy packets of Wood Rose seeds (an idea that also hadn't reached Springfield). After crushing the psychedelic seeds up and washing them down with hot tea, we headed to the mountains for a day trip, watching the clouds in the clear blue sky swirl above our heads and the mountains melt beneath our feet.

When we returned to town for Saturday's gig, the place was packed. Like everyone in the place, we were still stoned to the gills. It didn't matter. Jerry Jeff was drunk as a skunk.

As we stomped through our sets, the crowd hung and swung on every note and nuance. When the Gonzo's final set rolled around, Gary P. Nunn had to sadly inform the audience that Jerry Jeff was, unfortunately, not going to be able to make it. No one seemed to mind, as they called an audible in the huddle. Livingston shifted from bass to guitar and Nunn asked over the PA if there was a bass player in the house. That would be me.

To help finish out the last set of the night, I became Gonzoed. No one cared. Everyone danced.

Sunday morning, we headed back to Springfield, a trip that would inspire Larry to write "Kansas, You Fooler".

The week also found John writing "Colorado Song." Both tunes would soon appear on vinyl.

As we neared Kansas City, we drove right past "Go," did not collect $200 and returned directly to Springfield. This time, we were met with no fuss or fanfare. No one knew where we'd been—or that we were even gone. But, we knew where we'd been and what we'd done.

Later that spring, we would meet up with the Dirt Band again, as we were both slated to play the Ozark Mountain Folkfair in Eureka Springs, Arkansas, along with Lester Flatt, Earl Scruggs, John Lee Hooker, James Cotton, Big Mama Thornton, Clifton Chenier, Jimmy Driftwood, Mason Proffit, and fellow Missourian, John Hartford. The three-day festival was met with overwhelming attendance and an exuberance that not even rain could dampen.

All of the performers, ourselves included, were housed in Eureka's historic Crescent Hotel. Though we only lived ninety miles away, we took them up on their offer of hotel rooms in this grand old palace. Here, we were able to hang and mingle with some of America's greatest musical artists. With the bad weather outside, the pickings inside the Crescent were outstanding.

When we hit the stage that Saturday afternoon, we were the "local boys make good" portion of the show. A wonderful congregation of friends and neighbors gathered on the mountain. The sight of them, stretched out on the hill in front of us, put lumps in our throats and shot us into overdrive. The music elicited wild dancing. "Chicken Train" went into hyperspace, transforming into a tribal chant. We stomped the shit out of our set. The crowd stomped the shit out of the mountain.

The following year, when organizers began initial preparations for another go-round, when they visited the festival site to begin clearing it, they found massive amounts of watermelons and marijuana growing at the foot of the stage, the result of last year's seeds, washing down the hill. There was no second annual Ozark Mountain Folkfair.

Shortly after the Folkfair, we were invited to return to St. Louis to play the Mississippi River Festival with a young singer named Jimmy Buffett. Within the first half of 1973, I had played the Kiel Opera House and the River Festival. For years, I'd walked into these venues as a member of the audience. When I walked onto their stages with my guitar, I walked on Cloud 9,999.

It Shined

While we were burning up the highways between Springfield, Kansas City and St. Louis, Plesser was burning up the phone lines between Kansas City and Los Angeles. As he dealt with Buddha Records for Mike and Tom, he began making duck calls to A&M Records.

CHAPTER 9

"I remember bad weather and possible tornadoes, the night we played Cowtown for Glyn [Johns] and David [Anderle]," Randy recalls. "Michael Sunday, for some reason, was there, too. He said, 'Oh. This is a completely different band'—as he passed on us a second time. It was a big night.

"The onstage sound that night wasn't good. But, I thought we did great. I thought it was fine. It was. As far as what we'd been doing and the places we'd been playing, we were good ... and the crowd loved it. We had a good night, but, by Glyn's standards ... The crowd was going nuts, but he wasn't, which I always thought was a bit odd."

Possible tornadoes is not what you want to hear when flying over Kansas. With visions of Dorothy and Toto dancing in their heads, Glyn Johns and David Anderle white-knuckled their way from L.A. to KC. When the two finally landed, with no time to spare, they were whisked directly to Cowtown—where we were stalling for time.

Everyone in the place knew what was happening. Everyone knew the situation—and why we were waiting. Everyone knew that the man who'd worked with the Beatles—along with the man who'd worked with the Beach Boys—were coming to town to see if they wanted to work with the Ducks. Luckily, we didn't have to wait too long. We weren't about to start until they were there to hear us.

Afternoon weather reports of doom and gloom were replaced with sighs of relief when the two renowned producers walked in the door. After brief handshakes, we tuned up, hit the stage and hit the gas.

David Anderle headed the A&R department of A&M Records—the third company to hear our tape. "He liked what he heard," Stan recalls. "I went to a couple other companies with the tape. I went to Warners. I went to Capitol. Nobody was picking up on it—until Anderle. Generally, A&R guys don't want you in their office when they're listening to stuff, but David let me come in. He played two or three songs, stopped the tape and called up Glyn—on the spot.

"He says, 'Hey, Glyn. You know that group we've been looking to do? I just found it.' That was it. When David got that excited and called Glyn, that was a signal I didn't have to go any further."

Glyn Johns was already rock royalty, with a résumé that held, none other than the Beatles, the Stones, and the Who. Along with close friend, Anderle, the two just happened to be looking for a project to work together on—and have some fun with.

Having just produced the Eagles' first album, Glyn wanted something a little funkier than the slick L.A. cowboy box in which he'd been working. What he and David found was something a lot funkier.

Glyn didn't want to hear our demo tape, preferring to just hear us play. David didn't press the issue, booking two airline tickets to Kansas City. Neither of these men HAD to do this. Neither of these men HAD TO DO ANYTHING. Both were already successful producers—who could hand-pick who they wanted to work with. Both came to Missouri.

With no time to eat, they had empty stomachs as we took the stage. We had butterflies in ours. The buzz in the air had also reached the crowd, who, once again, embraced us. We ripped through an intense, animated set, reconvening in the dressing room to a rousing, hometown reception.

Glyn picks up the story: "When we went to Cowtown, I liked them all right—but not enough. I didn't think they were ready. When I first met them, they all knocked me out as people, although they didn't knock me out in concert. But that turned out to be a diabolical sound system which really screwed it up for them.

"When we first met them, David and I ... We were like the moguls from Hollywood and London, and 'I worked with the Beatles,' and it was a bit too much for them. They all expected me to be like someone who says, 'Shut up. I'm right and you're wrong because I've done all this before.'"

His first observation was that we weren't playing together as a band. David may have agreed with Glyn's assessment. But David had a record company on the line—who wanted us. David knew what he had. Glyn still wasn't sure. By the end of the evening, both would know what they had.

Then, they informed everyone that they were literally starving. At Stan's insistence, they went out for a quick bite and, at Stan's persistence, they came back to the Good Karma House for another listen—this time in a more relaxed atmosphere. Stan, knowing that Glyn was not knocked out by the gig, decided that this would be the time for the Englishman to hear what had knocked him out in the first place.

"That's what turned me on the most," he recalls. "It never got any better for me than when you guys would just be sitting around and say, 'Hey, listen to this,' and play me a song. I could almost touch the creativity. It never got any more exciting for me than that. To me, the closer I came to the creative source, the more it, obviously, energized me.

"So, that's what energized me to do the things I had to do with the record company. Record companies would rather there wouldn't be a manager. Then, they're in control—in control of how the deal is structured; in control of how much you work.

"The memory of that—and how stimulated I was by that—was the key in the end, when Glyn and David saw you at Cowtown. Glyn was not totally convinced at that point. I thought, 'Shit, I'm going to show him the energy that I first felt.' That's when I said, 'Let's go back to the Good Karma House.' When you guys played acoustically, that's when it all came together for Glyn. That's when he fell in love with it—just as I did.

"The tape was really good," he concludes, "but ..."

Glyn recalls, "I went back to their management's offices after the gig and they played one song ['Beauty in the River'] for me. I stood up and told them they didn't have to play any more. I was ready to work with them. I said, 'When can we start?'"

It Shined

We sang our hearts out, with vocal blends much better suited for the Duck Room than the Cowtown Ballroom. Plus, the two were listening on full stomachs. The ice was broken and crushed into small cubes. The cubes were placed into glasses. Beverages were poured over the ice. As we dove into song after song, another typical Good Karma House party kicked in.

Glyn and David heard our acoustic sound, enjoyed what they heard and, after hearing a dozen songs, knew that they had enough to work with. As the party broadened, conversations took place in other rooms. Glyn seemed to be just as intrigued with us as we were with him.

Naturally, talk about music had to turn to talk about the Beatles and the Stones. His stories of John, Paul, Mick, and Keith were spellbinding. That night, Glyn Johns was E.F. Hutton.

He liked the fact that we recognized that some of the most rocking Stones songs were made completely with acoustic guitars. He liked the fact that we knew that the key to the Stones was not Mick Jagger, but Charlie Watts. At that point, the Brit picked up his drink from the table, stood up and proclaimed, "That's exactly right. Here's to Charlie."

At this moment, the English gentleman and his Hollywood sidekick became just another couple of flailing ducks. After a while, when the

David Anderle and Glyn Johns at Ruedi-Valley, 1973 (photo by Billy Higgins)

party began to lose steam, the two, who had spent the entire day looking for funnel clouds, were ready to look for their hotel rooms. Plans for breakfast were made. Backs were slapped. The deal was done. Contracts would eventually be drawn up. But, that night, the deal was sealed with a handful of handshakes.

Breakfast didn't last long. Over biscuits and gravy, details were easily worked out. Glyn and David had two simple questions: where and when. Our answers were equally as simple: anywhere and anytime. As they caught much smoother flights back to California, we climbed into the Duck Truck and floated back to Springfield.

Happy with his discovery—as well as our eagerness—David reassured Stan that he would get the ball rolling as soon as he got back to the A&M offices on Monday. Glyn asked if we minded coming to the studio, where he felt the most comfortable. Because he would also be taking on engineering duties, he asked to work where he was familiar with the equipment. Nooooo problem.

That happened to be Olympic Studios—site of some of the greatest records ever made—many of which have Glyn's fingerprints all over them. He'd just finished recording *Let It Be*, *Beggar's Banquet* and *Who's Next* at Olympic. At this point, we knew American Artists was out of the question.

Further reasoning was sound. By removing ourselves from our familiar environs, distractions of everyday life would be eliminated. This would also help us concentrate solely on the music—free of "honey do" lists, car trouble, obligations, last-minute emergencies, and friends, who thought it would be a good idea to stop by with a bunch of beer, just to see what was going on.

It was an approach Glyn had just used, quite successfully, with the Eagles. It ought to work with the Ducks.

The decision was unanimous as passports were obtained and flights to London were booked.

Pre-production was scheduled for a cool, spring weekend at the Ranch. While we assembled, as we always had, Glyn and David flew in to pick and arrange songs. This time—after less-traumatic flights—when they arrived and saw the splendor, they knew they had entered fertile ground. Spring was springing. Ruedi-Valley was in full bloom.

It Shined

Small fires, just to take the chill off the place, were built in the fireplaces, as Rusty hustled to keep the place toasty. David lived in a big house in the Hollywood Hills. Glyn lived in a big house in the English countryside. Rusty spruced up his big house in the Ozarks, nicely.

As we set up in the front room and got the sound we liked, two extra chairs were pulled up. Work began, as we ran through song after song. Glyn and David sat intently—all ears, notepads and hand-held tape recorders. Some songs were immediately written in ink. How could we have made that first record without "Chicken Train" on it?

Randy's "Country Girl" and "Road to Glory" were placed on the list. We'd been playing both songs. Both were already well arranged. We'd been doing Larry's "Spaceship Orion" and "Within, Without" in our acoustic sets and in our living rooms. "Black Sky" was another gimme, as was "Standing on the Rock."

"Beauty in the River" was Glyn's pick. After all, it was the first song he'd heard us do and the one that convinced him that he wanted to work with us. It went to the top of the list—also written in ink, the indelible kind.

Songs were picked. Others were nixed. Some made a "maybe" list. Others just mercifully floated off, unhindered into thin air. Those that were picked received a facelift from Glyn and a rough recording from David.

They rearranged our meandering style, moving verses and choruses around, while paring away massive chunks of the musical drivel many of our songs contained. Sixteen-bar passages were trimmed to four bars. Others were eliminated altogether.

Instrumentation and harmonies were left alone. We had been singing a lot—and were blending well. By the end of the weekend, we had amassed a list of a dozen songs—ten of which would make it onto the actual record.

While we worked, Good Karma staff photographer, Billy Higgins was invited to drop in. Not only was he a photography major at the University of Kansas, he operated his Kansas Film Works from his rural, Lawrence farmhouse.

He had attended our very first gigs in the area, became an instant fan and was never without a camera around his neck. He was there the night we played Cowtown. He was there the night we played the Lawrence

Opry House. He was there the afternoon we played the Olathe High School Auditorium.

The meek Kansan hung out, joined in and became part of the creative atmosphere. Not only did he aim his cameras at us, he aimed them at the Ranch and the larger picture—the Ozark hills.

The atmosphere was so relaxed, no one minded when he snapped photos of the proceedings. Nor, did we mind when he asked if he could get a group shot on the front porch. We just put our guitars down, picked up our jackets, walked out onto the porch, and said "Cheese." The candid shot, which would appear on the back cover of the album we were about to make, took all of forty-five seconds.

Glyn and David were there. Stan and Paul were there. Rusty and Prince were there. No one even bothered to sit in the only chair on the porch. It remained unoccupied. The window on the far right side of the photo is the window to our music room.

At weekend's end, Glyn and David left with heads full of ideas, a tape full of songs and a hearty, "See ya in London."

Once again, we had to pinch ourselves.

While we were making the music in Missouri, Stan headed to the West Coast to begin hammering out the deal with Jerry Moss—the "M" of A&M. When both sides are eager to get things done, good things happen. The two got down to work.

Things happened very quickly, as a deal was struck for eight albums and twelve round-trip airline tickets from Kansas City to London. On May 1, 1973, after only a couple of months of courtship, i's were dotted, t's were crossed, papers were signed, sealed, delivered. We're theirs.

The eight-album deal was broken down into four groups of two—with A&M holding all the options. After the second album, if they didn't feel like working with us anymore, all they had to do was decline to pick up their option. This would void the remainder of the contract.

If they decided to pick up their option, albums number three and four would be made. After album number four, they would hold another option for albums five and six. After album six, they held one last option for albums seven and eight—and the end of the deal.

Things went smoothly, but for one minor/major/very major point— who would retain the publishing rights to the songs? This was the only thing we demanded. We wrote the songs. We own the songs. This is what Si and Wayne preached from the halls of Top Talent. We wanted to form our own publishing company and own our publishing royalties. On this point, there would be no room for negotiation. We made this clear to Stan. It was his job to make it clear to Jerry.

Stan summed up our approach: "When they [A&M] wanted to take the publishing, two things happened at that time. Glyn was saying, 'I want to do this project.' They were not about to piss Glyn off and say, 'We're not going to sign these guys because we can't have the publishing.'

"The other thing was—when I was first talking to Jerry, he had a little statue of Mahatma Gandhi on his desk. I said, 'How can you ask for the publishing with that statue on your desk?'

"He said, 'What's Mahatma Gandhi got to do with their publishing?' I answered, 'Well, he has a quote that I love—*There's enough in this world for all our needs—but not all our greeds.* Jerry, you're a collector. This is just another piece for your collection. You don't need this. They do. It's their annuity. When the music industry is done with them, they'll still have this. It's something for their future. I can't give it up.'

"The head of their publishing department got up and stormed out of the room. But we cut the deal. Jerry loved this band."

The "monkey business" part of the deal was also easy. Broken down into a party of twelve (the six of us, Rusty, Stan, Paul, Elizabeth, Larry's wife, Janet and Steve's wife, Sidney), we took to the friendly skies. It was only the second time I had ever been on an airplane. On May 1, 1973, we became A&M recording artists. That June, the Ducks got on the big plane and flew across the big pond.

We were eager. So was A&M. We flew from Springfield to New York a couple of days early, to take the opportunity to meet their staff and take a bite of the Big Apple. We were met at the airport by two limousines, that swept us right into the heart of Manhattan. Here, we were greeted by label honcho, Rich Totoian and promotions manager, Heavy Lenny Bronstein.

With hotel rooms on the thirty-seventh floor, Buddy and I had to laugh as we checked into our room. As *Towering Inferno* blared from our television, we looked out the window, looked back at the TV, looked at each other, chuckled, and headed back down to the lobby, where a waiting limousine swept us off to Mama Leone's and into the New York night. There were restaurants and nightclubs to get to, cocktails to drink, tickets to Broadway plays and parties to attend.

We learned about record company expense accounts for the first time.

We cut an impressive swath around Manhattan—a troupe of boots and beards. Wide-eyed, we visited A&M's offices, were introduced to the staff and given the grand tour of their fourteenth-floor complex. We were handed catalogues, containing all of A&M's releases, order forms and assurances that our orders would be waiting for us at home when we returned from England.

I became an actual kid in a candy store. As I took off, on my way to Olympic Studios in England, a large box of A&M records took off, on its way to the House of Nutz & Loonies in Springfield.

These New York folks hadn't heard our demo tape. They had no idea what we sounded like. They were just following Jerry's instructions to show us a good time—and we were more than happy to let them do just that.

The two days passed in a blur. Details are hazy, except for a lot of eating and drinking with Heavy Lenny—who hadn't earned his nickname for being a svelte man. Wonderful restaurants were visited, as we made our first foray into a Benihana's and an introduction to hot sake.

It's safe to say, we had a very nice stay. A couple of interviews may have taken place, but we were not pressured into anything. This suited us fine. We were just as interested in the monkey business, anyway.

On our last night in town, we were invited to Totoian's Greenwich Village apartment. Here, in a scene straight out of Dylan's "Don't Look Back," he assembled a group of friends for a bon voyage party, complete with incense, peppermints, berets, goatees, Charles Lloyd on the stereo, and soft light streaming in the windows from the streetlamps below. I couldn't believe my eyes, ears, nose, or throat.

I couldn't believe it earlier, when I looked out the thirty-seventh-floor window of the hotel at the ant-sized people below.

Then, I couldn't believe it when I looked out the fourteenth-floor window of the A&M offices.

Now, I couldn't believe it as I looked out Rich's second-story window onto the quiet Village street below.

Windows were thrown open. Cocktails flowed. People quietly talked, laughed and mingled. When asked, questions were politely answered. Though the party was for us, we didn't want to bogart it. We were just as interested in these people as they were in us. Joints passed around the room, along with bowls of hash. As the party floated along, one of the guests produced a small tin of cocaine—which was a new one for us.

As he came around to everyone's nose, when it came my turn, I stepped right up to the plate and let her snort—I mean, rip. This shifted the party into a higher gear, turning Rich's apartment into the Duck Room East. The drinking and dancing went through the night. I figured I'd sleep over the ocean tomorrow. Tonight, I had me a big slice of Big Apple pie.

I fell in love with the place, a feeling that remains with me to this day. Though, we would soon get lumped into the category of "Southern rock," I must confess: I'm a Yankee.

CHAPTER 10

It is common knowledge that, when you spend long periods of time flying from one part of the world to a distant other, one of the side effects you will invariably suffer will be jet lag. Jet lag is a real deal, folks. It is not a phony excuse, concocted by some rich folks in their silk-upholstered chair, making bets on Kentucky Derby Day.

Jet lag hits everyone—no matta the strata. Today, it hit us—and it hit us hard. A dozen new victims.

It is also common knowledge that, when you fly west to east, it will benefit you in the short run, as well as the long if, once you've landed, you stay awake as long as you possibly can. No matter how tired you are, the sooner you can adjust your body clock to local time, the better off you will be.

Thus, was the advice we were given as we landed at London's Gatwick Airport on the evening of June 22, 1973. Our late-morning departure from JFK, complete with seven hours of flight time and five hours of time zone difference, zoomed us right through the day.

It was a rainy night when we stepped onto British soil. Though our body clocks were telling us it was dinnertime, the clocks on the wall said it was close to midnight. All of this, on top of the fact that several of us had stayed up all night in the Village the night before, made for a ragged bunch.

It Shined

As we wove our way through baggage claim, Immigration, and Customs, we emerged from the terminal to a very loud and jolly greeting from Donald Bromage. Bromage, a large man with a thick English accent and even thicker biceps, would become our personal driver/tour guide for the duration of our stay. Having just worked as personal bodyguard for Phil Collins and Ron Wood, his stories were hilarious—his imposing presence, wild. His manner, though, was milder than mild.

He grabbed our suitcases—three and four at a time—placing them into the back of our vehicle, which resembled a small bus more than it did a limousine. We all jumped up front and were whisked into the dark, damp London night.

Though there wasn't much traffic on the streets at this time, the terror of driving on the wrong side of the road was overwhelming. Donald raced around town like it was nothing. Though it was late when we got to the Hyde Park Hotel, we were not tired. We were ready for dinner.

This grand old hotel, directly across the street from London's famed Hyde Park, would become our headquarters for the next couple of days. Here, we would try to acclimate and assimilate (some more successfully than others).

Headley Grange, our "home for the month," would not be available until Sunday. Studio time at Olympic didn't begin until Monday. We were afforded—just as we were in New York—a couple of unencumbered days to see the sights, visit the A&M offices and try not to step out in front of oncoming cars.

As we checked into the hotel, all we could think about was food. After just tossing our bags into our rooms, Donald whisked us right back into the night and off to the Speakeasy. They served food late. To us, it wasn't late.

The basement room—a notorious hangout for the British rock scene—was already in full swing by the time we walked in. The place was filled with smoke and flashing lights, as pub rockers, Ace were taking the stage for their final set. The dance floor filled with stoned people, including Pete Townshend, stoned to the gills and oblivious to everyone and everything around him.

John sets the tone, "There were all these really hip English, Carnaby Street folks all over the place. This was obviously the hippest place in town—and it was open after hours. After all the other pubs closed, if you had a membership, or knew somebody at the door, you could get into the Speakeasy."

We were seated at a long table in the corner, where carafe after carafe accompanied pint after pint. Just like the other night in New York, when we were introduced to sake, tonight in London, we were introduced to Guinness.

Donald told stories of the ale's vivid myths and colorful history. When it was delivered, we carved our initials into the foam. As the level of the liquid lowered, this identification remained in the head of that crazy little thing call Guinness. As mug after mug disappeared, I fell in love with the stuff—just like I did with sake.

Dinner took quite a while to arrive, its delay causing one round of drinks to turn into several rounds of drinks. Members of the A&M staff dropped by to introduce themselves. We found out that they liked to drink and dance as much as we did. With each pint, the laughter grew. With each quart, it turned to cackling.

As we waited on our food, everyone recognized the self-detonating Townshend—who had neared our table. Once again, John picks up the story: "I was on the end of this long table and a guy walked by. I knew it was Pete Townshend, because I'd seen him hovering around different parts of the restaurant all night. When he passed, I said, 'Excuse me. Are you the waiter?'

"He turned around and replied, 'Well, I AM waiting.'

"I said, 'Oh, good. What are you waiting for—the beginning or the end?'

"He sort of got sullen, and said, 'I'm waiting for the end ... So, what are you waiting for?'

"I said, 'I'm waiting for the beginning.' He turned around and yelled into the room, 'Hey. This bloke missed the beginning.' I remember that you and Cash were in shock. I mean, here's Pete Townshend and we're having this very strange conversation, after being in London for only a couple of hours. He mumbled a few more things. Then, he stumbled off. There was no confrontation. It was just a completely absurd exchange with one of the greatest guitar players in the world. Here we were, having this amazing conversation about existentialism, based on my interest in trying to get our food to come quicker."

Everybody laughed. Everybody drank. Pete really drank.

By the time we got our food and Ace was winding down, it was very late. By the time we got everyone rounded up and back to the hotel, it was very, very late. We were also very, very awake, running into each other in the hallways all night.

After a short, terrible night's sleep, the next thing I remember was the knocking on the door. All I wanted to do was roll back over. My body was telling me that it was still the middle of the night. Stanley, on the other hand, was telling me that we had places to go, things to do, people to see. The man's energy was (and still is) boundless. Don't get me wrong; I was excited about being there. I was also jet dog tired.

Donald drove us to the A&M offices, which were in a much smaller building than their Manhattan counterpart and in a much quainter section of London. Both these things were much more to our liking.

Here, we didn't have to take an elevator to the fourteenth floor.

Here, we met Coral, the lovely secretary with the lovely Australian accent, who was to become our Girl Friday.

Here, the hustle and bustle of New York was replaced with an atmosphere that took tea at three.

Effervescent label head, Derek Green burst from his office with shouts of glee and handshakes. Assembling his small staff, introductions went around. Pleasantries were exchanged. Tea was taken at three.

Sandy Denny, David Mattacks, Dave Pegg, and Richard Thompson of Fairport Convention (with whom we would share many stages over the next few years) just happened to be in the offices that afternoon—as were Benny Gallagher and Graham Lyle. Graham and Benny played freshly mixed tracks from *Willie and the Lap Dog*, their newly completed, Glyn Johns-produced album.

With biscuit in hand, Stanley, Paul and Rusty disappeared into Derek's office with the rest of Green's administrative staff in tow. When the doors closed behind them, members of the art department took the rest of us aside, slipping chunks of hashish into our pockets with an apologetic, "This is the best we can do. We don't get much weed over here."

Our collective reply was a hale and hearty, "No problem, mate. Cheers." After being shown how to smoke it off the head of a pin, under a glass, some of us filtered off, finding quieter quarters. Most of the afternoon was spent listening to music and hanging out with Mattacks and Pegg.

They had already released a couple of A&M albums, which I was well aware of. They made a wonderful sound—one that resembled ours.

We became A&M's distant American cousins to Fairport—two groups of long-haired hippies on opposite sides of the Atlantic, with complete artistic control and no disruption from the record company. We were both afforded the luxury of being able to play absolutely what we wanted, while paying absolutely no attention to the current musical trend of the day—DISCO.

This artistic control (which doesn't exist today) was given to all of A&M's artists—a characteristic that differentiated A&M from the rest of the labels. It also solidified their bohemian presence throughout the industry. It was a perfect fit. Their musical tastes were wide and varied. Our musical tastes were wide and varied. Their loyalty to their artists, second to none.

Glyn and David stopped by for a brief visit. Glyn felt fine. He lived right down the road. But I recognized the jet lag in David's eyes. Handshakes and hugs went all around. Everyone was glad to see each other, and VERY anxious to get started.

As the afternoon began to wane, the office emptied with toasts to A&M's newest band from America. Plans for happy hour were made, as well as another night of dining, drinking and dancing. That was just what I needed—another night of dining and drinking and dancing. This all sounded great, except for the fact that it was still the middle of the day and I could barely keep my eyes open. Like I said, jet lag is a real deal, folks.

Luckily, I have always been good at taking short "power naps." This afternoon, though, my much-needed power nap was reduced to a not-quite-long-enough power nap. Things were fine until I, once again heard the characteristic banging of Stanley's fist on the door. I pulled myself out of deep sleep, still in a serious fog. But it was nothing that a hot shower and a couple of pin hits couldn't fix. Then, it was into the lobby, into the limo, and into the London night. There was Guinness going to waste in those pubs.

I'd say Saturday morning came mercifully, but it was almost over by the time we started stirring. After several cups of strong coffee, it was a short hop across the street and into Hyde Park—which was jumping.

It was a brilliant, clear blue day, as the crowded sidewalks lined with artists, their work attached to the wrought iron fencing that surrounds the park. Here, we would join jugglers, musicians, street performers, ice-cream men, and assorted minglers from around the world—all just enjoying a nice day in this wonderful park.

The hotel clerk at the front desk exchanged a handful of dollars and cents for a handful of pounds and pence. I walked into the sunlight. As I neared Speaker's Corner, the din was deafening. Amid a sea of soapbox orators, the symphony of bullhorns was thrilling. A turbaned man shook his fists and screamed about injustice. His ranting crossfaded into another's view about something else. Viet Nam was still a popular subject—even here in England.

I drifted from discussion to discussion, soapbox to soapbox. I loved that corner, revisiting it every chance I could get. I also loved the ice cream.

A late lunch with Tom and Frances Bissell at the Tate Gallery was light and lengthy. Frances, who would become the food editor for the *London Times* and Tom, who picked out the wines to accompany her gourmet meals, became fast friends. Over our stay, the couple invited us on numerous occasions to their cold-water flat, where she would prepare wonderful meals in her small kitchen, while he prepared and served wine from their extensive wine list. Theirs may have been one of the only cold-water flats in London with a wine cellar.

Sunday finally came, which marked our evacuation of the Hyde Park (and its urban atmosphere), for our occupation of Headley Grange (and its rural isolation). The Grange, a three-story mansion located between the two small English boroughs of Headley and Alton, would become our actual home for the next month.

Located fifty kilometers southwest of London, eighty kilometers east of Stonehenge, and forty kilometers north of the English Channel, the Grange's ivy-covered walls, manicured lawns and ominous presence, regally stood atop 200 acres of pure English countryside.

The "Headley House of Industry" was built in 1795 for the parishes of Headley, Bramshott and Kingsley, to shelter their infirm, aged paupers and orphaned or illegitimate children. Having survived several riots and insurgencies through the following century, the building—which was still being utilized as a workhouse—sold in 1870 to builder, Thomas

Kemp Junior of Blackmoor, who converted the place into a private house, now known as Headley Grange.

In 1908, Colonel Francis Frederic Perry, professor of surgery at the Medical College of Calcutta, and honorary surgeon to the viceroy of India, bought the place, utilizing it for his practice and studies. In 1939, he died at the age of eighty-five.

After the Second World War, Lieutenant Colonel Michael Smith and his family moved in. Smith, belonging to the Indian Medical Service, continued his practice here until his untimely death in 1961. His widow decided to rent the house, which became a hostel for students from Farnham School of Art.

Arford Wi, in his essay, "Paupers to Pop," would observe, "Eventually, various recording companies such as Virgin Records and A&M, heard of the availability of Headley Grange. So it came about that for five or six years, it housed a variety of pop groups. Some of them came down to the quiet of the country, where they could practice undisturbed to try to 'get their act together.' Others, like Led Zeppelin, Fleetwood Mac and Genesis actually recorded in the large drawing room, which they had discovered possessed perfect acoustic conditions."

Groundskeepers, who occupied the servants' quarters in the back, kept the estate cloaked and tidied. Plus, as an added bonus, the place came complete with a dog—a big, old, scraggly dog named Sinbad.

Sinbad, complete with his severe gastrointestinal problems, presided over the place in the same manner Prince watched over Ruedi-Valley. John Paul Jones, on explaining how their song, "Black Dog" got its name, explains, "We never did really know his name, so we called him Black Dog. Had we known his name, the song would've had a different title."

With "Headley Grange" stoically scrawled onto the stone stele that marked the entrance, when we pulled up to the place, we were whisked back in time. Just as Glyn must have felt the Ghost of Americana Past when he entered Ruedi-Valley's gates, when we entered Headley Grange, we came face to face with a real-life storybook/history book setting.

With a large kitchen, equipped to feed a large amount of people, a larger dining room, and a larger-than-large formal parlor/living room/drawing room, the Grange had the capacity to easily accommodate many boarders at one time. So, to provide us with an undisturbed, rural environment, A&M rented the entire place for our entire stay. The Ducks roosted.

Previous tenants, the aforementioned, Jimmy Page, Robert Plant, John Paul Jones, and John Bonham had recently moved in along with a truckload of recording equipment. Here, they captured the mood, sound and aura of Headley Grange with *Led Zeppelin IV*, their critically acclaimed and commonly referred to "ZOSO" album.

The Grange feels just like that music.

That music sounds just like the Grange

Though the Zeps had moved out, their presence hadn't. Though the parlor was now devoid of their equipment and restored to its natural state, it retained the lingering vibe of "Stairway to Heaven" and "Black Dog"—in the same way thick curtains retain the lingering aroma of pipes and cigars.

Sporting a fourteen-foot-high ceiling, massive chandeliers, floor-to-ceiling bookcases, large thick rugs, and an enormous fireplace, the giant room was spectacular. This is where we would practice our vocals, the natural reverb of the room making them sparkle. As we stood next to each other, though, you couldn't help but imagine what it must've sounded like to have stood next to Bonzo's drums, as he thundered them off these walls.

There was enough room for everyone to have their own room—as well as share of space. John, Elizabeth, Larry, Janet, Steve, and Sidney took the larger rooms on the second floor. The rest of us occupied smaller quarters that were scattered throughout every nook and cranny of the place.

I scampered up two rickety flights of steps to a small room in a far corner of the third floor. Here, complete with low-slung rafters, a small fireplace, and a small window that faced the back of the estate, I could quietly sit and stare at the countryside that lay below.

Donald even had a room of his own, if we worked too late for him to make it back to his home. He was also an excellent cook. His specialty—hearty, hearty breakfasts. "Donald taught us all how to make omelets," Buddy recalls. "And to this day, I can make a fabulous omelet. That's directly because of Donald."

Unfortunately for Buddy, the thrill of cooking was replaced with the agony of the crab lice. He continues the story: "The bad thing about the whole deal was, I didn't have any fun catching them. Apparently, I got them from my bed at Headley. At the time, in England, pharmacists could dispense the medication without a doctor's prescription. So Donald had gone to get this ointment for me to put all over myself. I was so upset and eaten up. But he didn't tell me that the pharmacist had said you were only supposed to leave it on for a few minutes, then wash it off.

"So, not only did I have crab lice, I had blisters—an actual chemical burn—all over my skin from the medicine. It was really bad."

Mornings began slowly and quietly at the Grange, complete with the wonderful dairy products that were delivered daily to the doorstep. We ate like the royal family of Headley. Sinbad hung around the kitchen door, as did the horses and sheep. Everyone knew when it was mealtime.

After breakfast, we would load up in the bus, Donald would slide behind the wheel, and we would make the forty-minute trek into Barnes—and the site of Olympic Studios—our home away from home away from home.

Our itinerary for July, 1973 was simple: Headley to Barnes. Barnes to Headley. Rinse. Repeat.

CHAPTER 11

Olympic Studios sits in the pleasant suburb of Barnes, quietly located on London's southwest side. The large, brick building, built in 1906 as an Edwardian music hall, had remained a popular entertainment venue until the mid-sixties. In 1966, amid the fervor of the British Invasion, Cliff Adams bought the building, transforming the old minstrel hall into London's quintessential rock studio.

One look at the roster of artists who have used the place reveals the absolute pinnacle of British rock royalty—unless your idea of the pinnacle goes any higher than the Beatles, the Stones, Jimi Hendrix, and the Who. If this isn't enough to convince you, take another leaf though your record collection. There you'll find the proof in the Olympic pudding.

"All You Need is Love" and "Hey, Jude" were recorded here. In one of the rare Beatles/Stones collaborations, John and Paul visited to sing backing vocals on Mick and Keith's "We Love You" and "Dandelion."

When you walk up the steps leading to the big double doors, you cannot help but feel yourself walking in some mighty big footsteps.

When you walk through the front doors, like those before, the first thing you see is the directory hanging in the foyer. Olympic was active history in the actual making, and Glyn's favorite studio.

When you duck your head into the main studio room, every corner echoes with the memory and creation of some of the greatest and most colorful rock 'n' roll music ever made. You could feel John Lennon's voice still echoing through the room. The Stones had spent years camping here, even managing to set the place on fire.

When we walked into the place for the first time, the directory informed us that we would be working in studio A. It also informed us that Badfinger was in studio B, finishing their self-titled debut album for Warner Brothers.

We were not in Springfield anymore.

Stacked in the middle of the big room stood a pile of brand-new forest green Anvil road cases with the words "Ozark Mountain Daredevils" boldly spray-painted across every piece. One of the first things we told A&M we needed (which they gladly agreed to) was an upgrade of the sorry-ass gear we'd been dragging around the Midwest for the past couple of years.

When they recommended Anvil cases get thrown into the deal, that was fine with us. We weren't going to be carrying the stuff around anymore anyway. That's because, right before we left the States, we hired Cowtown stagehand/Kansas City resident Patrick Byrne (who had been working for Mike and Tom) to be our road crew.

The color of the cases was not a mistake. Patrick figured that with just another set of black road cases on another stage at another festival, one might mistakenly get loaded into another truck. Shit does happen, but not in our case. If it was green, it was ours.

Years later, Patrick's partner, Larry Tucker, instead of buying black guitar cables, bought spools of bulk green cable and soldered them up. All of our cables were bright green and easy to spot. Once again, if it was green, it was ours.

Glyn and David had not arrived. But Glyn's assistant knew what to do. He asked us to set up in the middle of the room, as if we were playing a gig. This was the same way he set up the Stones. This was the same way he set up the Who. This was the same way he'd just finished setting up the Eagles. This was how he wanted the Ducks to set up.

As we began unpacking, Larry placed his drums twenty feet from the front wall and smack dab in front of the thick pane of glass that looked up into the control room.

Directly to his left, I set up my new Ampeg STV amp—the "hernia model." For sound separation, a large baffle was set up between it and the drums. On the other side, another set of baffles buffered it from John's amp.

Randy's amp was placed just to Larry's right, and Buddy played the house grand piano—a twenty-foot Steinway that belonged to Nicky Hopkins. When it was rolled into place, tuned up, and miked up, Buddy bellied up.

Our more fragile instruments were carefully wrapped in blankets and packed into a smaller green case covered with HANDLE WITH CARE stickers. Our amps may have been shiny and new. Our green road cases may have been shiny and new. But our sound still depended on these old wooden instruments.

Randy brought his mandolin, his Gibson Hummingbird acoustic guitar, and his Gibson 335 electric guitar.

John brought his old Fender Telecaster, his fiddle, and a couple of Martin acoustic guitars—one which was to be "high strung." (A high-strung guitar consists only of the six higher-pitched strings of a twelve-string guitar. Not only does this make the guitar much easier to tune, it also gives it a light, jangling quality. When played alongside a regularly strung guitar, the sound is as light as Keith's chiffon).

Steve brought pockets full of harps and I played the old '64 Fender Precision bass I'd bought from Bob Livingston. All instruments received new strings. All sparkled.

As we were putting the final touches on our setup, Glyn and David arrived. When they walked in, Joey Molland and Pete Hamm emerged from studio B to greet them. Introductions went around—along with a neighborly "open-door policy" between the two bands and the two studios. For the next two weeks, sticking our heads into each other's control room for listens was commonplace. Once we started recording, the Badfinger guys were some of the first people to hear what we were doing.

After a brief chat, everyone headed back to work. As a myriad of microphones began getting plugged in, Glyn began to position some on Larry's drums. As he worked, he and Larry and I chatted about the Beatles, the Stones, restaurants, jet lag, and how a rhythm section should play.

It Shined

He talked about Paul and Ringo. He talked about Bill and Charley. When he began to talk about Supe and Larry, the only thing he stressed was that the two of us listen to each other and try to play as solidly as we could. (Insert "a house is only as sturdy as its foundation" adage here). When Glyn talked, Larry and I listened.

Then, when we noticed he was only placing three mikes on the entire drum set (one in the bass drum, one stuck between the snare drum and high hat, and one placed equidistant between the rack tom, floor tom, ride cymbal, and crash cymbal), we couldn't help but ask about the technique.

Glyn's eyes bugged out, as he emoted, "You want the drums to have some balls, don't you? You want them to sound BIG and lively ... not all squeezed up. Look at this room." Bingo. He said the magic word. The duck came down from the ceiling. Lights flashed on and off over my head. It's just what my "lively" St. Louis ears wanted to hear.

Two overhead mikes were placed a few feet above Larry's head to catch the ambient sound of the overall kit and the room—a sound that would then be mixed in with the three main mikes. When Glyn left the room, Larry and I could only look at each other, shrug our shoulders, and smile at what was happening.

This was the man who recorded Keith Moon. We were learning from the master. He walked back into the control room and took his seat at the recording console.

"The control room was just overwhelming because of the way the board looked." John recalls. "It surrounded Glyn, who had built it. If we saw it now, we'd probably say it looked like *Star Trek* from the '60s.

"And the lights were always up. This was just a workplace to them. This is where you came to do work. This is where you came to forge music. It was not a plush place. We had to fight occasionally on playbacks with, 'Can we turn the lights down a little lower?' The lights were up. These guys were working. They came to work every day."

As Larry began to play and test the drum sounds, slight adjustments were made to the microphone placements. Over the headphones, Glyn would instruct Larry to move this mic up a smidgen, or that mic down a bugger. After a while, the two had dialed in a nice, full drum sound.

When things started to take shape, I plugged in and jumped in on the groove Larry was hitting. Buddy sat down at the piano and the three of us got dialed in, quickly. As we played, we could look up through the glass and into the control room, where Glyn was twiddling knobs like a madman. It didn't take long to get the rhythm section in tune.

When focus shifted to the guitars, it was John and Randy's turn to provide Glyn with his "knob-twiddling" music. Electric guitars were plugged in and turned up. Acoustic guitars were placed in an isolation booth and tuned up.

While this was happening, Larry, Buddy, and I stepped out back, where we met Rusty, Paul, Steve, Donald and a couple of the Badfinger guys, all catching a smoke. On occasion, David would join in. But Glyn had no interest, as twiddling knobs and smoking hash don't go that well together. He let us know that he didn't mind if we did, just so we didn't smoke it in the control room. This was no big deal. We didn't mind stepping out back. Barnes is a very nice place of an evening.

Then he demanded that we not get too fucked up to play, citing Keith Richards as an example. We had no problem with this. We also had no problem when he would sit back and reminisce. His stories of Keith, falling asleep in the middle of an overdub, had us in stitches. A less funny story was when he showed us the spot in the back corner of the studio that had mysteriously caught fire during the recording of "Sympathy for the Devil."

As the evening wore on and the different sounds of the different instruments got dialed in, a collective sound began to emerge. While Glyn continued to prepare the control room, we began to run through the arrangements with David.

We hadn't played together in a few weeks, taking the evening as an opportunity to knock off some of the rust. We hit a few licks, knocked a few back, took a few tokes, and, in general, just loosened up.

When Glyn finally joined us in the main room, we blasted through each song one last time. Then he called it a night, instructing us to go home, get a good night's sleep, and get ready to come to work in the morning. We all agreed on a time—the crack of noon.

Donald pulled the bus up to the Olympic door; we climbed in and headed back to the Grange. We were feeling good, joking around and beginning to get the upper hand on the jet lag thing. Everyone slept well that night in Headley. The next day, work began in Barnes.

By the time we lumbered in, Glyn and David were already at it. While Glyn was making final knobulations, David formed a game plan. We put a real nice tuning on our instruments and gathered in the control room to look at the song list. Though there were a dozen songs on it, we knew we'd only be able to use ten. Still, we decided to record all twelve, just in case, somehow, shit didn't happen.

We had to start somewhere and David had the list. When he suggested "Country Girl," "Country Girl," it was. We'd been playing the song and playing it well for a while. It was a snappy, upbeat way to begin the session. Plus, we figured we could get a nice, solid track after only a few attempts. We were ready to rock. The tape rolled. The red button lit.

After a couple of rough passes and a couple of false starts, we laid down a very solid track. When Glyn suggested that we give it a listen, we all clamored into the control room. As the track boomed from the giant monitor speakers, goose bumps claimed every arm.

Randy's shoulders sagged, though, when Glyn and David declared that the track was a keeper and we should move on to the next song. When the floor was opened for discussion, Randy stated that he hadn't felt comfortable with the take. When Glyn asked why, he explained how he wouldn't feel comfortable until he'd played the song many more times.

Glyn raised an eyebrow, and with a bewildered, "You must be daft," turned to the rest of the room with, "Does anybody else NOT like this track?" We were all in total agreement. We loved it. Glyn and David put their foot down. We moved on. After all, they were the producers and, after all, the track does sparkle.

Here came the difference in opinion between Randy and the rest of us … again. It started on the very first song. We may not have played it as many times as he would've liked, but we played it well and we played it joyously. The Ducks moved on.

Then, with a "Supe, old boy? Could you come and play your bass part for me?" Glyn took me aside and back out into the big room. I strapped my bass on and began playing. After a brief listen, he held up his hand, stopping me with a sincere, "May I make a suggestion?" I was all ears and fingers.

When he advised that I lighten my touch and not play so hard, he reached over to the volume knob on my amp and nodded, "Let the amp do the work." As he turned it up a notch, he informed me that McCartney,

Wyman, and Entwhistle all played with light touches on their basses and slight nudges on their amps. That was good enough for me.

Then, when he asked if I had ever played with a pick, I answered, "No." When he asked if I would start, I answered, "Yes."

He suggested that I stay where I was and lay down another bass part onto the track we'd just cut. While the song was still fresh in my mind, I had no problem laying down another track in a single try—with a lighter touch. When we listened back, Glyn was all smiles and nods. The new, less-plodding bass track added even more lilt to the song.

Glyn's stories of Paul overdubbing his bass parts after everyone had gone home intrigued me. So, that's how he wove those wonderful bass lines through those songs? I figured, if it was good enough for Paul, it was good enough for me. Ever since that day, I've heeded Glyn's advice, playing with a lighter touch on my bass and an added pinch on my amp.

"Black Sky" was next. Steve stepped into the isolation booth, which allowed eye contact among all of us. After a few tries, a cool, swampy groove oozed from the studio monitors. He had no problems with the fact that we'd only played it a couple of times.

David changed the pace with Larry's "Spaceship Orion." Buddy moved to his Fender Rhodes electric piano, which smoothed things right out.

In this manner, song after song was focused upon. Each received individual treatment with the appropriate style, timbre, and instruments.

After taking a dinner break for a bite and a pint, we returned to the studio, spending the entire evening drinking, smoking, laughing, and cutting "If You Want to Get to Heaven." That night, we had a great time playing the shit out of it. By the end of the day, we had solid tracks to four songs.

The next day, we shifted gears and set up acoustically, to record John's "Standing on the Rock" and "Beauty in the River." Both have the same instrumentation and feel. Though they don't sit back-to-back on the record, they were recorded back-to-back in the studio.

Then we attempted "Colorado Song"—a song we hadn't played much, but were doing at Glyn's insistence. John remained in the isolation booth, with his acoustic guitar. Larry climbed back onto the drums. Buddy, Randy, and I assumed our positions and we ran the tune several

It Shined

times, getting two really nice versions with only one minor difference. We commenced to choosing.

When we listened to them back to back, it became readily apparent that we had played the first take with far more precision but far less abandon. Our second stab featured a long, rolling outro that swelled with confidence and built much nicer than the first take. We decided that if we could only have the body of the first take, combined with the ride out of the second take, we would have the best of both worlds. Glyn grabbed a razor blade. Open-tape surgery began.

After demanding silence, he inched the two reels of tape back and forth by hand, until the last note of the first half of the first take sat directly over the recording head. With a small grease-pencil mark and a swift swipe of the blade, our two-inch master tape was sliced in half. Everyone gasped.

Then, with the undesired "first outro" draped over his neck, he respooled the remaining tape and fast-forwarded to the corresponding spot of the second take. Another slice was made at the beginning of the outro we liked so much. At this exact point, the body of the song's first take was reattached. Surgery was a success. Calling Doctor Howard, Doctor Fine, Doctor Howard. Everyone exhaled.

The version of the song on the record is actually a hybrid of the two takes we did that night. The main body lopes along nicely to the splice. Then, it seamlessly blasts into its long, long outro.

Glyn assured us that this happened all the time, taking us down into the Olympic tape vaults, where he showed us the two-inch masters of *Are You Experienced?* Every twenty feet of tape had a splice. A lot of chopping went into Jimi's chops.

Glyn's open-tape surgery took us right up to happy hour. After happy hour, we were to spend the evening recording the only track left—"Chicken Train."

Work had been progressing smoothly, with each song getting checked off the list. When we got down to this, the last song, you could see Glyn and David scratching their heads, trying to figure out how in the world they were going to get this thing on tape.

There were no drums. There was no bass. There was just a bunch of stomping and banging and clanging. The entire song consists of nothing more than Steve's harp, John's mouthbow, and the rest of us just grabbing stuff from the percussion table.

Deciding to just mike everybody up and let 'er rip, David drew six chairs into a circle in the middle of the room. As John began to twang away, Glyn curiously walked around him in circles, trying to figure out where in the world he was going to put a microphone.

I found it funny that, in the middle of a studio full of state-of-the-art recording equipment, Glyn and David were trying to figure out how to record one string, stretched across a piece of wood.

We knew we weren't going to be doing multiple takes. Being well rehearsed is not essential for "Chicken Train." Spontaneity is. We knew we had to get on the train in time, on time, and right off the bat.

We sat down, and after all the final adjustments were made, David hit the talkback button with, "Okay. Let's try one." The twanging began. Then the stomping began. Then the harp began. Then the clucking began. Then it all faded away, leaving John to head for the finish line alone.

We'd ripped right into it, right through it, and right out the ass end of it. We'd done the song many times and were well familiar with its nuances. We knew, when we gathered in the control room to listen back, that we'd stomped the hell out of it.

Everyone took their seats. But there was only silence. That is, until a loud, groaning, "GOD DAMN IT" shattered the quiet from the back of the room. Glyn's assistant, with his head in his hands, had inadvertently hit the *record* button, resulting in a gaping two-second blank spot in the middle of the take.

While he was moaning, we were laughing. It was no big deal. It was spilt milk. We did our best to assure him that it would be nothing for us to do the stupid song again. Plus, we all knew we HAD to. Everything was still set up. The mikes were still plugged in. We just tromped back out and stomped through it again.

Though the second take was good, it just didn't seem to have the spark of the first take. It was also the only version we had—a recording that has been beloved by children, young and old, for years. Still ... you should've heard the one that got away.

With all the tracks cut, we shifted into overdub mode. All of the little mistakes we'd made along the way got punched in and fixed up. There weren't many. We were playing real well. We were also singing real well. Vocals were doubled—and sometimes tripled.

By this time, not everyone was needed in the studio at once. This afforded those of us who weren't needed the opportunity to catch up on sleep and sightseeing. Day trips were made to Stonehenge. The atmosphere that week was very relaxed.

Glyn's approach to background vocals was the same as ours—blend as a gang, instead of singing individual parts to be blended electronically. Stereo mikes were set up, we sang out, and Glyn recorded the blend—twice and, like I said, sometimes thrice.

The evening we were to lay the background vocals onto "Beauty in the River," we were joined by Elizabeth, Sidney, Janet and Donald, who could carry a tune quite well himself. Instead of having a chorus of six guys, we had a choir of ten people. We were all handed headphones, as we gathered in front of the microphones and began tabernacling as loud as we could.

When we finished, Glyn said, "That was really good. Now, I want everyone to stay close to the mikes. But just move around a bit." After shifting and shuffling through each other, we sang the song again. This placed individual voices into different locations of the stereo balance. After the second pass, David asked, "… And how about a third?" We just looked at each other and said, "Sure." We were just singing along, having a great time. When we finally finished, the song had acquired a mighty chorus—thirty voices strong.

When it was suggested that a nice percussion track might be the rhythmic sawing of a two-by-four, a trip to the hardware store was made. Saw horses were set up in the isolation booth. When Larry commenced to sawing, the sound was perfect. Plus, he had no trouble sawing "in time."

As the song rolled by, the sight of Larry sawing a board got funnier and funnier. As the song swelled with one final, "We can roll away the stoooo-ooooo-ooooone," Larry had sawed completely through the board. The end kerplunked onto the studio floor, exactly on cue.

The control room exploded with laughter, as we couldn't decipher whether the song was one two-by-four long, or the two-by-four was one song thick. Either way, the song was over, complete with a very cool, rasping percussion track. When the topic arose of whether to keep the "kerplunk" in the final mix, our jubilance was quickly overridden by a couple of adamant producers.

Our point? It just happened—and it was funny.

Their point? The "kerplunk" we found so amusing would not stay so for long—and the listening public would probably consider it to be a big, annoying, useless pop on the vinyl. The "kerplunk" hit the cutting-room floor, nixed from the mix.

Mixing mode was entered, our equipment was sent back to Kansas City, and we hit third gear. With all of the actual recording finished, our job consisted of sitting around, listening, and shaking our heads yes or no when we heard something we liked or disliked.

The mixing phase went as smoothly as the first two. We all pretty much agreed upon what sounded good. Every song got shined up with a real nice mix. To hear them finished and sounding so good was a real thrill.

The last phase of the ordeal was the selection and sequencing of the ten songs that would make it onto the record. Because a vinyl disc has two sides, two separate song lists had to be made—one for side A, the other for side B. As the listener finished hearing the last song on side A, if he flipped the record over, the next song he would hear would be the first song on side B. It's not rocket science, but it did take a little extra pondering, a pondering that has been lost with today's CD format.

During the recording, certain songs began emerging as 'a good way to start Side B,' or 'a cool way to end Side A.' David tore out twelve scraps of paper from his notebook—big enough to see from across the room. With a song title written on each one, he arranged them in two small columns on the mixing console.

Changes were simple. All you had to do was walk over and switch around a couple of scraps of paper. Everyone did their share of switching. Everyone threw their two cents' worth in. This also meant that we had almost as many opinions as we had guys in the room.

When Glyn instructed everyone to take a break, get some dinner, and leave him alone for an hour, we did just that. While we were gone, he would splice together the two running orders, as he thought they should be. We marched off to the pub. When we returned, everyone was excited about finally getting to hear the final version. Things went well. Side A began with "Country Girl," nicely ran through its five-song program, and seamlessly flowed into side B, ending with "Beauty in the River"—a rousing, kerplunkless finale.

When the last note faded, befuddled looks darted around the room. We knew a couple of songs were not going to make the final cut. No one thought one of those songs would be "If You Want to Get to Heaven." Glyn's logic was a simple, "You guys aren't a rock 'n' roll band. Your other material is much better. The album is stronger without it."

To which Steve pointed out, "I said, 'Glyn, this may not be rock 'n' roll, like the Who. But it's our rock 'n' roll.'"

When Stan heard Glyn's reasoning, he hit the roof. I vehemently agreed with him. I love that song and knew our friends did too. It had to be included. Its exclusion would give the record a completely different, more subdued feel.

Discussions continued, as opinions were strongly expressed from both viewpoints. As a compromise, a second running order was compiled with "Heaven" sitting in its slot. When we walked out of Olympic that night for the last time, we walked out with two different running orders under our arms.

Our last couple of nights in town were spent celebrating. With the album "in the can," we were treated by Derek Green to one last feast at the Elizabethan Room in Kensington, which stressed the quaffing of mead, and the total disregard of conventional table manners or eating utensils. We dug right in—with our hands.

As we assembled along the two sides of the long table, the wenches kept our chalices filled. As the meal began, the seat at the head of the table remained conspicuously vacant. That is, until Stan arrived, sliding onto the throne to hearty toasts of "All hail, King Stanley," as glasses were raised. The drinking began—and began—and began. Then the feasting began—and began.

Then, in a scene directly from the inside cover of *Beggars' Banquet*, the singing began. The festivities continued until the restaurant staff politely asked us to leave; then the merriment, led by Derek, spilled out into the quiet Kensington streets.

On our last night before flying out, Coral invited us to a smaller, less rambunctious party in her flat. Those of us who wanted to spend their last night in England at the hotel did just that. Those of us who didn't, didn't.

Coral laid out a modest spread of food, complete with a cake, baked full of hash. The massive amounts of alcohol from the night before were replaced with small wisps of smoke and cake. The boisterousness of the night before was replaced with the cool sounds of Bob Marley—who I was hearing for the first time. As the cake started to take effect, the dancing began. After being introduced to Johnny Nash, riding high on his hit, "I Can See Clearly Now," I transfixed into reggae hypnosis. She handed me a copy of *Natty Dread* to take home with me.

As the party progressed, smokes and jokes were shared with Mitch Mitchell and Humble Pie guitarist Clem Clemson. They asked how long I was staying and if I would be interested in playing a gig with them later in the week at a small pub. The lineup would be the three of us, along with whoever would stop by for jam or a bevy—or both.

I couldn't believe my ears. I also couldn't believe I had to decline their offer. We all had plane tickets out in the morning. We'd been gone a month and were ready to fly back to America. I was ready to fly to South America.

Stan assured me there wouldn't be any gigs until A&M released the record in the fall. Coral had arranged for my ticket to include a thirty-day visa and a side trip to Bogotá, Colombia.

The following morning, I waved to my mates—now, a party of eleven. As the "V" headed to Springfield, I headed across the terminal, waiting by myself for my much later flight to Bogotá.

CHAPTER 12

"Buenas noches damas y caballeros. Abrochen sus cinturones. Vamos a aterrizar en aeoporto internacional de Bogota El Dorado, donde la hora local es la media noche. Gracias por volar con nosotros y disfrute su estancia en Colombia."

The flight attendant's voice, blaring from the speaker right above my head, was a rude awakening. As I rubbed my eyes, trying to remember where I was, I looked around, quickly figuring out that I was sitting on an uncrowded airplane, en route to South America. When I looked out the window, it was the middle of the dark night.

This, only the third time I had ever flown anywhere, found me on a nine-hour flight from London to Bogotá. Here I would reconnect with Karen Johnson, who I'd recently met at one of our St. Louis University gigs, fallen for, and had remained in close contact with. She attended school in St. Louis. Her family resided in Bogotá.

When she invited me to dinner for the first time, I eagerly accepted, sharing a meal in her Central West End apartment with friends and her father, Tom, who just happened to be in the country on business. As wine flowed and laughter rang, my tales of the Mississippi River Festival paled miserably to his stories of international commerce and intrigue. By evening's end, I had dubbed him Don Tom.

It Shined

As my band mates where touching down onto the friendly runways of the Springfield Regional Airport, I was landing at Bogotá's El Dorado Airport. As they deplaned into a lazy Ozark summer evening, I walked into a scene straight out of a James Bond movie.

The flight attendant bid me a fond *adios*, as I stepped off the plane and into the late-night airport silence. I could not read the billboards. I could not understand the announcements over the terminal speakers. I couldn't even talk to the guy next to me, unless HE knew English. I knew "*sí*" and "*señor*."

I could, though, read the clock, which read midnight. I was tired, but I felt good, due to the fact that I had just been deposited back into the Central Time Zone. My body clock rejoiced, even if it happened to be 2,000 miles south of my house.

It was an eerie scene, as dozens of heels clopped up the empty concourse. I made sure I had my passport, my phone book, and a wad of cash close at hand. I also made sure there were no misplaced chunks of hash anywhere in any forgotten shirt pocket.

The first uniformed officer greeted me with a mustachioed nod and a sleepy eye. I shrugged my shoulders, showing him my passport. He pointed me to a second uniformed officer, who spoke a little English—but not much. I shrugged my shoulders and showed him my passport. He disappeared into an office.

I took a seat in the stark concrete waiting room that sat quiet, but for the tick-tocking clock on the wall. Upon his return, he brought a third uniformed officer, who spoke fluent English.

"Who are you here to meet?," he asked.

"Tom Johnson," came my simple reply.

"Okay. Wait here."

"*Sí, señor.*"

I already was waiting here, so I continued to wait here some more. I tried to pick up a magazine, but couldn't read it. The night janitor rolled up with a small, distorted transistor radio blaring the news. I could not understand a word they were saying, as he and his weird radio began to empty wastebaskets. When he strolled off down the hall and disappeared around a corner, the cement room regained its silence.

I'm not sure how he did it, but somehow, Tom made his way back through the Customs and Immigration stations and had found the office where I continued to wait. When I saw him, I knew the cavalry was on its way.

When he walked into the room, he reassured everyone that things would be fine. Then, after a brief exchange, the officers replied with a resounding, "Ohhhhh."

I was handed my passport, complete with smiles and visas. Tom had explained to them (in Spanish) that I was harmless and they should all just go back to sleep. As we walked off, he explained to me (in English) that I had just witnessed the Latin legal system at its finest.

When morning came, I couldn't wait to start seeing shit. I wanted to go everywhere and do everything. To this, Tom offered three simple pieces of advice:

1) "Even though you don't speak the language, try—no matter how poorly." The simple gesture would be a show of respect for the culture. This I was more than happy to do. My broken Spanish would be better than no Spanish at all.

2) "Don't carry all of your money in one pocket." Self-explanatory.

3) "Eat these." He produced a small bottle of ultra-hot Colombian peppers that blew the tops off of all thermometers. If I could learn to eat the hottest of hot, I would not have to worry about Montezuma—or his revenge.

All three tips were taken to heart/mind/intestine.

Buses were boarded—I hopped right on. Markets were visited—I walked right in. Train schedules were procured—I handed them right to Karen. I tried to talk the talk, expanding my vocabulary to *"baño"* and *"por favor."*

I also made a concerted effort not to cower in the shadows and create suspicion. I knew there was no way I could hide the fact that I was a big white guy with a long red beard in a land of small, brown faces.

I wanted to go to the beach, but Bogotá sits 10,000 feet in the mountains and 400 kilometers from the ocean. We jumped on a noisy, crowded train full of people, produce, and you guessed it - chickens—all bound for the northern coastal town of Santa Marta, a sleepy fishing village directly on the shores of the Caribbean Sea.

Sweaters were left in the mountains, as we detrained on the coast with sandals, a hammock, a few T-shirts, and a knapsack for food. We hit town, hit the market, filled the knapsack, and hit the beach, walking as

It Shined

far away from town as we could. Here we found a little niche to hang the hammock and fall asleep to the sounds of the sea in front of us and the jungle behind us.

This is where we spent the next couple of weeks—in and out of the ocean, in and out of the sun, and more importantly for my skinny, white skin, in and out of the shade. My most valued possession was a bottle of aloe vera gel. Fires were made. Rice, vegetables, and an occasional fish were cooked. Dessert consisted of mangoes, avocados, and bananas. The sun came up. The sun went down. Time was told not by the clock, but by the calendar.

As we based out of Santa Marta, jaunts to the Spaniard fortresses of Cartegena, the pirate-laden Barranquilla, and the salt mines of Cali were taken. After a month, though, my thoughts began drifting north to Springfield, Kansas City, Los Angeles, and the impending album.

On the beach, there was no way to find out anything about anything. I didn't even know what songs were going to be included. Was "Heaven" going to make the cut? I had two tapes, with two running orders, in my suitcase. But here I was in a hammock on the beach, without electricity. All I knew was, I didn't have to get back to Springfield for a gig until the sixteenth of the month. My ticket was arranged to leave Bogotá on the twelfth.

Until then, it was *"uno mas cerveza y tequila, por favor."* My Spanish was becoming less broken.

Eventually, the calendar struck 'one', the mouse ran down, and we hopped on a train to Bogotá—just in time for me to catch a flight to Springfield and meet in St. Louis.

Here, we packed up what few possessions she had and she moved to Springfield, transferring from St. Louis U. to SMS. Then we moved out of town, transferring from the House of Nutz & Loonies to the Nixa Trout Farm.

For the past month, I had been in an environment with absolutely no knowledge or interest in the Ozark Mountain Daredevils. When I landed in Springfield, the Ozark Mountain Daredevils were about to hit the shelves.

When I learned that after heated discussions between Glyn and Stanley, "Heaven" would be included on the album, I breathed a huge sigh of relief. For the past month, as I sat on the beach, decisions were being made about the song's inclusion. Both men were adamant about their stances. The final straw came with a late-night phone call between the two. Plesser recalls the brief conversation:

"You're going to do whatever it takes to get that song on the album, aren't you?"

"Yes, I will."

"You're going to go to Jerry [Moss]."

"Glyn, I'll do whatever it takes to get that song on that album, because I believe in the song that much. That song is an American hit record and I will do whatever it takes to make sure it gets on there."

The call to Jerry wasn't necessary. It wouldn't be the last time Glyn and Stan would tussle.

The next thing I did was catch my breath when I saw the cover art. It was gorgeous, tastefully done by Englishman Michael Doud. The front cover was simple—a modest logo, quietly placed onto a patchwork quilt. The back cover contained Higgins's black-and-white photograph of us on the front porch of Ruedi-Valley, complete with empty chair.

A six-panel insert, with an entire page devoted to each one of us, was not only icing on the cake, but whipped cream, nuts, and two tons of cherries. I could not believe my eyes. Each page contained candid photos of life at the Ranch, including a photo of Prince—the "King of Ruedi-Valley."

Lyrics were a must, as was the long "thank-you" list we had amassed on a notepad atop the Olympic console. Every one of us had many some-ones to thank.

I didn't mind any of the decisions that were made on my behalf while I was in Colombia. "Heaven" was on the record. That was important. It sounded great, and the artwork was marvelous. The ball was rolling. A&M was rushing the project through.

As we were about to hit the shelves, I was about to hit the Trout Farm.

The Nixa Trout Farm sits on a seven-acre strip of rich creek bottom, quietly nestled into a small dale, twenty miles south of Springfield. Located halfway between the small towns of Nixa and Clever, in its heyday, the place sported three large ponds of trout, a small house for the keeper, a large shed for supplies, and the happy fishing clientele of the entire area.

Built in the early '60s, business boomed. When a flash flood ravaged the entire valley in the spring of '68, the banks of the ponds were all but washed away. As hordes of trout swam downstream, the landlord walked away, not wanting to incur the expense of rebuilding the business or the ponds. Both lay fallow.

With three large, empty craters and a disappearing clientele, the entire place had been rented to Granny's, who, over the past few years, had proceeded to fix up the house as lodging and the shed as a rehearsal hall.

Upon my return from Bogotá, I learned they had just been hired, en masse, by Martha Reeves, as her band for her first solo tour. Because of this, they were forced to give up the place.

I moved into the house. The Ducks moved into the shed.

Granny's had fixed up both buildings, but had never quite completed either task. As I worked on the house with hammer and nails, the Ducks fixed up the rehearsal hall with foam rubber and burlap. Large rugs were brought in and laid on the floor, along with large, comfortable couches. All provided their share of soundproofing. It may not have been the parlor of Headley Grange. But it was the parlor of the Trout Farm—and where we hung our hat.

Patrick was able to pull our big green truck—which would not make it up the small lane into the Ranch—right up to the Trout Farm door. Even though we continued to assemble at the Ranch, most of the rehearsing shifted to Nixa.

Here, we could set up, play loud, and gear up for the larger stages we would be playing. Patrick hired fellow Kansas City native Larry Tucker to man his crew. We showed them how we wanted to be set up—close to each other, so we could easily hear each other.

As autumn began, I stayed out at the Trout Farm, played my guitar, made fifty bucks a week, and waded through the mountain of free A&M records that continued to come in the mail. While Springfield was abuzz, it was a quiet valley I settled into. Once settled, songs began to pop into my head—and I had the time to work 'em up and write 'em down.

As I just began writing about the things I saw around me, "It Probably Always Will" and "Roscoe's Rule" emerged at once. "I've got a mountain of dreams to climb, before I get to the top of the hill," and "He lives in a valley where the creek runs by him, every single day" were both written at the Nixa Trout Farm.

At this point, I must give credit and applaud the writers I was working with. As I played their songs, the care I saw taken with each lick and lyric, sparked licks and lyrics in my own skull. When these first two songs hit me, I caught them like fireflies in a jar.

This very high quality of material would continue to be our strongest asset, as we still considered ourselves a group of songwriters, as much as we considered ourselves a band. We knew we were not going to dazzle anyone with musical calisthenics or a twenty-one-guitar salute. We knew we were just a pretty good band. But we had some REALLY good songs.

That fall, I pulled these two pennies out of my pocket, ready to throw them into the hat. The valley floor was very fertile.

CHAPTER 13

As the autumn leaves of '73 began to fall, everyone in our camp began to hunker down. A&M announced "ASAP" as the release date—and that was just around the corner. So were the holidays.

"A&M was really pushing to get this thing out," Randy recalls. "They [David and Glyn] came in May. In July, we went to England. We turned the record in and the label put it out that fall. Labels don't do that anymore. Things could really happen quickly, then—and did."

We settled into the Trout Farm for the winter. I lived in the house. The Ducks rehearsed in the shed. Two large stacks of firewood got packed in. The valley was really, really fertile. When it wasn't really, really loud, it was really, really quiet.

I began to meet my neighbors, who all knew what went on at the place—not only when Granny's was there, but when it actually was a trout farm. I avoided suspicions by visiting their homes. When I began to tutor their high-school-aged kids in algebra, I became a valuable neighbor.

Algebra was a chore for these simple country kids, who already had enough chores. They came by once a week for dinner. Afterward, we hit the books. I laughed and tried to explain to them the sense of fun I always found with numbers—in ways their small-town teachers couldn't.

I was quite proud of the passing grades on their report cards. This was reward enough for me, though I did enjoy not having to buy eggs or milk for the entire time we lived at the Trout Farm.

The Ducks continued to practice, but there weren't many gigs. Instead of continuing to run over the same old songs from the album, we shifted focus toward new songs for a new album. We still had a slew of old songs, left over from the first record and there were new ones coming in daily. Plans to record at Ruedi-Valley next summer were initiated.

Everyone wrote and everyone sang, as "Fly Away Home," "Walking Down the Road," "Look Away," "Homemade Wine," and "You Made it Right" were placed on the front burner. It was a rainy afternoon at the Trout Farm, when Larry brought in a new song he'd written, entitled "Jackie Blue." As he sat at the piano, the song quickly acquired its very catchy Granny's groove. Then he began to sing:

> Ooh, ooh, ooh, ooh Jackie Blue.
> HE was da da, and da da doo.
> HE did this. HE did that.
> HE went here. HE went there.
> Blah, blah, blah
> Ooh, ooh Jackie

Yes. Jackie was a man. Though his sex change was still to come, we had a great time playing the song. It was immediately inserted into the "live" show.

We played a night at Cowtown with Danny Cox, along with a couple of small swings through Midwest theaters with Jesse Colin Young, Steely Dan, Shawn Phillips, Johnathan Edwards, and the Dirt Band. Things was gettin' cool.

December was a different story. We only had two gigs. But they put a swinging punctuation mark onto the end of a very interesting year. Patrick and Tucker loaded the big green cases into the big green truck, and with a "wish you a Merry Christmas," we hit the road.

The first run was made to the West Coast—and our first gig in Los Angeles—a six-night stand at Doug Weston's Troubadour with Commander Cody & His Lost Planet Airmen.

The second run was made downtown to the Landers Theater for "Perry Allen's Christmas Parade of Thrills."

Patrick had already made it to California with our equipment. With our fearless road crew in place on the coast, Rusty became our fearless road manager at the Springfield airport.

He handed out boarding passes and cups of coffee, as we jumped onto a Delta flight to Dallas, where we had a short—very short—layover, before connecting out to the coast.

When we landed in Texas, we knew we had to hustle to get from plane A to plane B. We didn't realize that in order to get there, we had to take a train from Terminal A to Terminal B.

Still, we were fine and things were running smoothly. That is, until we approached the line of twenty-five-cent turnstiles that separated us from our waiting train. We, frantically began rummaging through our pockets for quarters.

The train we needed was sitting right in front of us, with its doors wide open. We knew we had to be on it. We also knew that only a few of us had quarters. That train would not be sitting there long, and there was no time to go running off on a wild goose chase, looking for change.

Those who had quarters dropped them into the slot and walked right through. Those of us who didn't have quarters said "Fuck it" and jumped over the railings. When the train left Terminal A, we all breathed easier.

When we emerged into Terminal B and dashed down the concourse to our gate, we arrived just in time to hear last call being announced for our flight. We were greeted by a very friendly flight attendant with a sparkling eye. Then we were greeted by a very unfriendly Dallas policeman with a sparkling badge.

With an "Oh boy, a rock group" gleam in his eye, he placed all of us under arrest for not paying our tolls back at Terminal A. Security cameras had spotted us jumping over the railings, and this guy was here to do something about it.

Those who paid their quarter quickly began speaking up with an emphatic, "Hey, wait a minute. I paid my quarter." But this didn't cut no ice with this good ol' boy. Nor, did it carry any weight with his fellow officers, who began arriving on the scene.

It Shined

There were no handcuffs. There were also no boarding passes. As our plane headed to Los Angeles, we headed to the Dallas Airport police station—yes, even those who paid their quarter.

A phone call to Patrick alerted him about what was happening. We told him just to go ahead and set up the gear at the club and we would do our best to get there. There was still a chance we could make it in time. But if these uniformed Texans wanted to be real jerks, they could screw up the whole day, as well as our L.A. debut.

One by one, we were summoned to the judge's bench. Buddy was called first. He answered a long list of questions, took off his shoes, took off his belt, emptied his pockets into a manila envelope, and stepped into the holding cell. The heavy metal door slammed behind him.

Larry—who had paid his quarter, but realized how futile it was to try to plead any kind of case—went next. He and Buddy became cellmates. Randy (who'd also paid his quarter) and Rusty (who hadn't) followed.

The clock on the wall, as well as the afternoon, was ticking away very quickly. Each interrogation seemed to drag on and on, with most of the time being spent itemizing every little item being tossed into the manila envelopes.

I was next. By the time they got to me, it became embarrassingly apparent to everyone in the room that this was all just a complete waste of time. We were fucking up their quiet afternoon as much as they were fucking up ours. Plus, there were still several of us left to process.

Even the cops started to get bored. They weren't having any fun. They weren't finding any drugs. My stash was already in L.A. When I began to see that they were wanting us out of their hair as much as we wanted out of it, I decided to do something about it.

I walked right up to the bench and began a three-act play, set on a sandy beach, with lots of money, called "Going, Going, Gone." We had a gig to make, damn it, and there was no time to fool around with these macho Texas assholes about not paying a quarter. I handed the judge my wallet. I knew what was in it. As he opened it, a pile of sand sifted out onto his desk. The curtain rises:

Act 1: When he asked, I let him know that I'd brought the sand back from South America—Going.

Act 2: With a confused look, he discovered my wallet was full of Monopoly money—Going.

Act 3: When he started having to count it for the manila envelope, he snapped—Gone.

He waved his gavel, loudly declaring, "Okay, that's enough. Everybody put your shoes on and just get the hell out of here. ALL OF YOU!" The judge scowled at me, as he swept the sand off his desk and handed me back my wallet. I smiled as politely as I could. We gathered our things and headed back out into the terminal.

Rusty rushed to a payphone, where new flights were booked. We just wanted to get the hell out of Dodge. Ground transportation in L.A. was rearranged. If everything went right, we would get to the club right at show time.

We were a frazzled mess as we made a mad dash through the streets of Los Angeles. When we made a second mad dash in the door, Patrick was set up, with a case of beer iced down on stage. (Insert "skin of your teeth" adage here.)

The marquee of the Troubadour, not nearly big enough to fit the complete names of both bands, read "Comm. Cody & the Ozarks."

The epilogue to "Going, Going, Gone," reads as follows: 1) No, I don't know why I was carrying sand and Monopoly money in my wallet. 2) No, I did not put a quarter in the turnstile.

As we rushed in the Troubadour door for the first show, there was no time to get nervous. A day's worth of pent-up frustrations flushed to the surface and blasted through our amps. Not until we finished our set did we finally get the chance to sit down, relax, have something to eat, and listen to the Commander.

I'd been looking forward to this for some time, as the Airmen were already a staple on my turntable. Last week, they made me dance across the floor of the Trout Farm. This week, I was looking forward to dancing across the floor of the Troubadour.

They finished their set as we finished our dinner. As the audience cleared and the waitresses began wiping off tables, Patrick began to reset the stage for our second show. At this point, the two bands met, to tales of the "Texas Turnstile Massacre." Robust laughter burst from everyone, as our day had made their leisurely drive down from San Francisco pale miserably in comparison.

Like us, they were playing L.A. for the first time.

Like us, they were quite nervous about it.

Like us, they liked to drink and smoke pot.

They didn't know many people here either. So we got to know each other. The week began.

Reminiscent of our time with the Gonzos at Tulagi's, when we encountered the Airmen, our two entourages hit it off, right off the bat. Also, like the Gonzos, communal stage gear kept the changeover between sets to a minimum. Buffalo Bruce Barlow and I shared a bass amp. Larry and Lance Dickerson combined drum sets. Buddy and the Commander banged on the same piano.

Then, when faced with the logistics of how we were going to cram two large bands, with two dozen guys, into two small dressing rooms for one whole week, the answer was obvious: Take the doors off the hinges and just get rid of them.

Patrick did the handyman work, remodeling the two upstairs rooms into a smorgasbord of musicians from the Ozarks, topped with a healthy scoop of musicians from San Francisco. Cultures collided into one large, very smoky room at the top of the steps.

This set the scene for our weeklong residence on Santa Monica Boulevard—and entrance onto the Hollywood stage. Both bands played smoking second sets. This was going to be fun.

The next evening, after a much less traumatic day, when we arrived at the club, Roy Clark and the cast of *Hee Haw* were sitting there. Roy, with a new album, had scheduled a showcase with his new band. This was fine with us, as well as the Airmen.

Clark, who had just recently visited and fallen in love with Branson, Missouri was in the process of moving into his own theater—one of the first in town with a celebrity's name attached to it. The Baldknobbers were there. The Presleys were there. In 1971, Roy Clark was there.

Tonight, though, he was at the Troubadour. Both bands (especially the Airmen's Bill Kirchen) intently watched Clark's fingers. We were all fans of his guitar playing. We were also fans of *Hee Haw*.

Hoyt Axton climbed onstage to do a handful of songs. Then he climbed up into the smoky dressing room and stayed—all night. As the evening turned into a madhouse, the Troubadour's double bill turned into a triple bill and a third group of musicians tried to cram into the already-cramped dressing room.

With each passing night, word spread about these crazy, stoned-out hippybilly bands who were setting them up and knocking them down.

With each passing night, crowds grew.

With each passing night, friends from both bands began showing up with the season's harvest.

With each passing night, many of the A&M staff stopped by to hang out at the top of the stairs. Many became friends.

With each passing night, celebrities began dropping in. Label-mates Sneaky Pete Kleinow and Chris Etheridge of the Flying Burrito Brothers were regulars. David Anderle introduced us to Kris Kristofferson and Rita Coolidge (whom he was producing), along with songstress Kim Carnes. Glyn brought Joan Armatrading, Mimi Farina, Graham Nash, and Bernie Leadon in the door.

Glyn, who enjoyed our set much more than he had our Cowtown set, became quite bewildered with the Commander and his drunken antics, observing, "Why do they call him the Commander? He's obviously in command of nothing." The Ducks howled.

Robert Duvall, researching his role of Max Sledge in *Tender Mercies*, popped in throughout the week, just to hang around a bunch of good-old-boy musicians. Hoping that some of Billy C. Farlow would rub off on him, he did a lot of research that week.

Vic Morrow of the TV show *Combat* stopped in to hear Steve play harmonica. An aspiring harp player himself, Morrow hung around just to talk shop. As he did, the voice of Sgt. Chip Saunders filled the room, setting us all back in front of our black-and-white televisions.

With each passing night, all of the above crowded into those smoky little dressing rooms. The raw excitement of our two bands created a nice stir that quickly kicked into high gear. By Thursday, the club began to pack out for every show.

Fiddler, Andy Stein, who would go on to play an integral musical role in Garrison Keillor's *Prairie Home Companion*, would join in on "Standing on the Rock" and "Beauty in the River." Everybody sang.

With each passing night, we all felt more comfortable.

With each passing set, we all played better.

With each passing night, we all became really good friends.

On the last night, as a goodwill gesture, Patrick presented the Commander and his comrades a quart of Wild Turkey. The portly pianist immediately cracked open the bottle with a growling, "What are you guys trying to do, ruin our set?" The bottle made one lap around the room, disappearing in a matter of gulps.

Each night, we slept at the Tropicana Motel. It was late by the time we stumbled in every night. But the place was still wide awake, doors still open, lights still on, people still by the pool. Music, laughter, and aromas wafted through the arid night air. It did not matter what time it was. There was always something going on at the Tropicana. We walked right past all of the commotion and right to our rooms.

Ellen Vogt, David Anderle's longtime assistant, waved us past the guard at the front gate of the A&M offices, known as "The Lot." She would become our Girl Friday, the same way Coral looked after us in London.

David had alerted her with, "Don't worry. You can't miss them." From her vantage point, when she spotted us, there was no mistaking ten guys (our entire scruffy entourage) and Ganja (Patrick's scruffy dog). Not only did Ganja like to curl up and take naps next to my bass amp when we played, he provided an organic, effective security system for the big green truck.

As we drove through the gate for the first time, when we stepped out of the van, we cut an imposing figure of flannel in a sea of shiny sports cars. Everywhere we turned, it looked like a movie set. That's because it was.

In 1917, Charlie Chaplin bought this five-acre property at the corner of Hollywood's Sunset and LaBrea avenues. Here, he built and opened the Charlie Chaplin Movie Studios, utilizing every nook, cranny, balcony, stairwell, and rooftop of the place to set the scenes of the 131 films he would make at this location.

In the 1950s, the television series *Superman* was filmed on its soundstage. In 1958, Red Skelton purchased the property and used it for his weekly television series. In 1962, Skelton sold the facility to CBS and it became the home of the *Perry Mason* series.

In November, 1966, after years of shipping Tijuana Brass albums out of their garage by the thousands, trumpeter Herb Alpert and business partner Jerry Moss bought the place. Here they began shipping Tijuana Brass albums by the millions.

1416 N. LaBrea became "The House the Lonely Bull Built." Alpert (the A) and Moss (the M) became modern-day Rumplestiltskins, spinning brass into gold.

David emerged onto his balcony and trotted down the steps to greet everyone with hugs and photographs from the Olympic sessions. President Jerry Moss emerged from his/Chaplain's office, tucked off into a small, fountain-laden courtyard. Vice-President Gil Friesen, Promotions Director Bob Garcia, and Art Director Roland Young stepped out into the bright December sun. Introductions went around. We took up residence in David's—I mean, Ellen's—office.

One by one, folks from other departments began sticking their heads in the door to say hello. Art Coordinator Jeff Ayerhoff and Publicity Head Barry Korkin jumped in to meet the guys who were making that crazy music that had been floating through their offices for the past couple of months—the same music they were starting to sell.

We were given the grand tour of the compound, meeting Bernie Grundman in the recording studio with Joe Cocker and all of the Burrito boys, on one of the soundstages, rehearsing for their album, *The Last of the Red Hot Burritos*.

No one found the legal department to be very interesting. But we all found the art and shipping departments to be very cool. A stroll through Young's art department scheduled a photo shoot. A stroll through the shipping department garnered another box of records for the Trout Farm.

Everyone we met loved music. More importantly, they loved their job—a common trait of A&M employees. All were invited to the Troubadour. As the week progressed, many began to hang around the top of the stairs for the passing of the pipe.

Over the years, on a sporadic and very unannounced basis, one of our big green cases would fill with fresh green buds. A large part of the A&M staff enjoyed the fringe benefits of having a band from rural Missouri signed to their label.

For the next six years, this five-acre complex in Hollywood would become our California home away from home.

As we finished out our week at the Troubadour, we left L.A. and returned to Springfield for our last gig of the year—a Christmas parade of thrills at the Landers with none other than the one and only Perry Allen.

Granny's shared the bill.

Perry Allen stole the show.

Born from a rubber Halloween mask of a smiling, suburban, Ward Cleaveresque alpha male, Perry slipped out when Steve slipped the mask on. If the silly mask wasn't enough to make you laugh, Steve's hilarious impromptu skits were.

Perry had been bringing down the house for months. The decision was unanimous. The most horrible man in the world should make an appearance at our Christmas concert. Then, to show his total commitment to being a pillar of the community, raffle off a turkey. Then, to show his total lack of taste, sing a song.

The entire community dressed to its holiday nines and trod through the snow, drawn to the bright lights of Walnut Street. The theater once again sparkled. Even though we had appeared here several times, we were about to take the Landers stage for the first time as the Ozark Mountain Daredevils. We were no longer the Family Tree. The air was thick with electricity.

Friends and families came from miles around. Stanley brought his entire family down from Kansas City for the spectacle. Paul brought aspiring freelance writer and future brother-in-law David Rensin from Los Angeles.

Rensin, whom we'd just met the week before at the Troubadour, was hired by A&M and *Rolling Stone* magazine to begin finding out what the hell we were doing back here in Missouri. Becoming as enthralled with the band's DNA as he was with our music, when informed of our upcoming parade of thrills, he talked A&M into a plane ticket to Springfield and a ticket to the Landers.

Granny's started the night with their usual spirited set of tunes by Shuggie Otis, Amos Garrett, Harvey Mandel, the Meters, and the Sons. Larry sat in and did several of the songs he had written with Bill and

Bunge. The holiday stage was set. *Rolling Stone* was in the house. All awaited the arrival of Perry Allen.

By the time we took the stage, everyone was already warmed up from the inside out, as well as the outside in—chock full of eggnog and holiday cheer. We were really playing well, having just played twelve sets with the Commander last week (there's nothing like a weeklong gig to tighten up a band).

Bill left his horns on stage. Mike left his guitar plugged in. We all became Ducks. That is, until we all became Dogs. Coughing dogs.

At the appropriate moment, toward the end of our set (a.k.a. a song he doesn't play harp on), Steve sidled offstage for his personality transplant. As we finished the song on stage, it became "show time." Steve donned the mask and became Mr. Squeaky Clean. As he morphed into Perry Allen, we morphed into the Coughing Dogs.

On cue, we blasted into "Hold It," America's quintessential break song. I introduced the masked marauder with a hearty, "Here he is, ladies and gentlemen. It's the moment you've all been waiting for. Earth's only twenty-seven-year-old Perfect Master. The King of Horribleness. Mr. Perrrry Allllen."

With white shoes, a white belt, and a red golf sweater, Steve—I mean Perry—threw the curtains aside, emerged from the wings, and hit the spotlight, his pearly white rubber teeth beaming into the crowd like Liberace's jacket.

Sidney (as Trixie) and Janet (as Roxie) escorted the "ever horrible" Allen to center stage. Sporting beehive hairdos, tight bathing suits, high heels, and rhinestone shades, the theater of the absurd was about to become just that.

We had arranged for the evening's tickets to be numbered. Audience members were instructed to hold on to their stubs, as the other halves were placed into the large fishbowl Trixie carried on stage. Right next to her, Roxie held a twenty-pound frozen turkey on a silver platter. Both blew lipstick kisses to the crowd.

The place went nuts. That night, someone was going to get the bird, and "the most horrible man in the world" was going to give it to them.

The room was rolling with laughter as Steve stepped up to the microphone and bellowed through his mask, "Thank you. Thank you, boys and girls. I know you've been waiting for me. This is one of my gorgeous girls. Her name is Trixie. Would you welcome her, please?"

The hooting and hollering began.

"And this lovely woman here is named Roxie. My God, will you welcome her?"

Add whistling to the hooting and hollering.

"This is what you've all been waiting for. Isn't it great and horrible? Do you know that to one of you fucking gooses out there, we're going to give away a turkey?"

Add howls to the whistling.

"It's unbelievable, isn't it? Oh my God. It's beyond your most horrible expectations. Can I have a drumroll, please?"

Larry obliged.

"Now, I'm going to draw an unknown, selected—notice my eternal smile—number from this fishbowl. It's all completely fake. I already know the winner. A twenty-pound turkey, mind you!

"The winning number is number 4-4-7. Come on down, 4-4-7; come to the stage right now. Show me your ticket"

As the crowd began fumbling for their ticket stubs, we struck up the band with a rousing rendition of the "Billboard March." With guitars, drums, and kazoos ablaze, Perry continued to scream "4-4-7" into the microphone. His Coughing Dogs began to oompah.

After a while, the song died out and it became apparent that whoever had number 4-4-7 was not paying attention. Allen turned to the audience with, "What's wrong with you? Don't you want a turkey for Christmas? Since 4-4-7 is obviously a fictitious number, we're going to pick another. Roxie's going to read this one."

Roxie (in a slow, deep, sultry tone): "Fiiiive—Fooooour—One."

We blasted back into Kazooland. Perry again began to chide the crowd with, "Come on down. Don't be afraid. Who has number 5-4-1?"

5-4-1 also garnered no winner.

Allen disgustedly muttered, "Okay. What about five hundred and four? We've got to give away this fuckin' turkey."

With each failed number, the bit got funnier. Unfortunately, the air under Perry's rubber mask did not. When Steve moaned, "This is getting really old," a scream from the back of the room changed everything. We had a winner.

We were laughing so hard, we could barely play our kazoos. When old friend John Leonard walked onto the stage to claim his prize, Steve didn't even bother to check for a ticket stub. The "turkey giveaway" came to a merciful end.

Then, Allen turned his attention to the band, and with Trixie and Roxie at his side, launched into "Commercial Success," Steve's whimsical tune (my mother's personal favorite) about sniveling rock stardom. It had them dancing in the aisles.

Rensin turned to Peterson with an inquisitive "Do they do this every night?"

As we finished the song and blasted back into "Hold It," Steve left the stage to a standing ovation. He could not rip the mask off his face fast enough. After a few minutes to catch his breath, he took off his white belt, replaced it with his harp belt, and rejoined us for the rest of the show.

Perry Allen is a hard act to follow. But we finished the night with a handful of songs, and the curtain came down on another year. Everyone headed into the snowy night with light hearts and smiles on their faces. John Leonard headed into the night with a turkey. The Ducks headed into the night, as the Daredevils had a new record under their Christmas tree. Fa-la-la-la-la, la-la-la-la.

CHAPTER 14

If Springfield music fans listened to their music at Be-Bop's, Half-a-Hill, and Lindberg's, they definitely bought their music at Kaleidoscope.

"The original name was to be the Rock Shop," recall proprietors Tom and Pam Pierson. "We incorporated under that name. But as we were standing in the line at the bank to deposit this first money we'd borrowed, we saw a guy, two people in front of us, wearing a 'Rock Shop' T-shirt. That was John Gott, who'd just opened a music store named the Rock Shop. We had to change our name before we even opened."

On October 9, 1972, Tom and Pam did open the doors of Kaleidoscope, Springfield's first independent record store/rolling papers store/head shop. The sturdy two-story building on the corner of Fremont and Sunshine was in a prime location. The date, Tom adds, "just happened to be John Lennon's birthday. We didn't plan it. It just happened that way."

"We wanted a two-story house on a busy street, where we could live upstairs. We couldn't afford two rents. As we were driving through town, not fifteen minutes after C. Arch Bay put up the 'for rent' sign on the place, we passed by the corner and saw the building. The place was perfect. It was meant to be. We lived there for a couple years. Rent was $350. We were just a little family place that opened up. Nobody took us seriously, which let us get the camel's nose under the tent, so to speak. That's how we got our foot in the door. We were lucky, and made it stick."

Handyman friends built homemade shelves, and in the fall of '73, Tom and Pam filled them with Ozark Mountain Daredevils albums.

"In those days, albums came in boxes of twenty-five. We ordered them 100 at a time from St. Louis, who would get them to us overnight. We must've sold 500 to 600 of them over a few months. Remember, Springfield is not Chicago. You have a limited number of people. We did, though, sell more copies than any other one location in the country.

"The first record had set the pace for the second record [*It'll Shine When It Shines*]. Our initial order of that one was 1,200 copies. We had to actually go out and borrow money to even get that many. For us, that was a lot of money to shell out for one album. But we took a chance. We knew we were going to sell 1,200. But we didn't know how fast we were going to sell them. To commit that much money to one thing was scary."

Stanley had alerted A&M that they would be selling lots of records around here, and to stay on the ball. They supplied demand very well, making sure that everyone who wanted one found one.

Tom and Pam's shelves remained stocked, as our album became the official stocking stuffer for the '73 Christmas season.

"Country Girl" was released as a single. It made no waves.

We all began to move out of town, settle into new houses, and start new lives.

Randy and Rusty remained at Ruedi-Valley.

John and Elizabeth continued to live in their cabin, south of town.

Steve and Sidney moved into a small house at Turner's Station and welcomed the arrival of daughter Star Lisa.

I had moved into the Nixa Trout Farm.

Buddy and his bride, Jerri, moved right down the road into an old rock house near Dogtown.

Larry and Janet moved into an old, stately home overlooking the hills outside Clever.

Roscoe and Clarence Jones lived in an old, unstately house near Boaz. Clarence, in his '70s, and son Roscoe, in his '50s, were our neighbors. They worked their asses off, farming forty acres of rock and cedar trees, located midway between my house and Larry's. When I went to Larry's, I took the dirt road that passed right by the Jones boys. They never failed to wave. When Larry came to the Trout Farm, he passed them too. They never failed to wave.

When the Jones boys went to town, they passed right by the Trout Farm. We never failed to wave. Like a good neighbor, the Jones boys were there. (You will learn more about the Jones boys soon.)

As the outside world became interested in the Ozark Mountain Daredevils, the Ducks became more interested with their retreat into the hills. We did fly out to California for a string of gigs with the Burrito Brothers and the Steve Miller Band in Long Beach and Santa Barbara, followed by a couple of nights in San Francisco and Berkeley with old pals Fairport Convention and new pals the New Riders of the Purple Sage.

Between the two jaunts, a couple of days were set aside to do some interviews A&M had arranged. With six guys in the band, along with Rusty, we could break off into groups of twos and threes and accommodate several pundits at once. This was the best way to do it, too, due to the fact that group interviews were usually too cluttered and chaotic.

Each interviewer—depending on the interviewee—learned one of two things. They either learned about Ruedi-Valley Ranch, the Nixa Trout Farm, and how cool it was to be out here playing music, or they learned that the interviewee didn't really want to be here, didn't want to be on the road, just wanted to stay home and help their ladies plant the crops and blah, blah, blah.

This is the side the media chose to emphasize. Though it wasn't really true, it was intriguing. A&M scratched their heads, asking, "WHAT DO YOU MEAN, YOU DON'T WANT TO BE HERE?"

Some of us were excited about being here.

Some of us were ready to work hard.

None of us had crops in the field, back home.

Stanley summed it up nicely: "While you guys were playing, I was the one who took all your wives shopping. They kept telling me to keep you guys working. They didn't want you hanging around. They told me you guys didn't do anything while you were home anyway, except lay around and drink beer."

It Shined

When the articles began to get printed, comparisons to the Band peppered the pages. Noting our multi-lead-singered approach, our wide range of musical styles, and our laid-back attitude, the St. Louis Post-Dispatch called it, "Americana music made by bearded, flanneled men, who were just as content to stay home and lead normal lives."

We thought our interviews were boring. We were the opposite of glamorous. We didn't know anybody famous. We couldn't talk about hanging out with any rock stars. We'd just as soon, talk about things other than music. Our stories were about our lives, more than they were about the Ozark Mountain Daredevils.

We hit our first milestone when we made it not onto the cover, but into the pages of *Rolling Stone*. Still, I bought five copies for my mother. The headlines of the February 28 issue read, "The Cosmic Corncobs Go North."

Once again, there was our Phelps Grove Park photo, as David Rensin observed, "When the reviews of the album came out, the Daredevils were pegged as a cross between the Eagles and Black Oak Arkansas: the former since they were co-produced by Glyn Johns, the latter stemming from their geographical origins. Neither are close to the truth. Instead, the Daredevils' sound is peculiar to them in the tradition of the Band. Their music, a mixture of country, Appalachia, the South and rock & roll, always takes a fresh approach."

As witness to our recent Parade of Thrills, he continued, "When the band hit the stage, the hoots and hollers from the audience were the equal of, say, an LA boogie crowd. These 754 Missourians knew they were hearing a band they could call their own."

Plesser finishes the thought, observing, "[We] represented a lot of guys around there that never got a chance—that were as good as you guys, or maybe even better. They just never got a chance. You've got to take this opportunity and run with it."

We flew to Toronto to participate in an experimental multimedia presentation called "Cin-A-Rock." When we left Springfield, we had no idea where we were going. All we knew was, someone in Toronto was going to pay us a lot of money to go up there and play. We shoved off for Canada-AY. It turned out to be a complete flop.

Scheduled to play two shows a night for a week in one of Toronto's numerous grand old theaters, we shared the bill with local rockers Barefoot, which featured Levon Helm's nephew Eli on drums. Both bands set up their gear directly behind the giant movie screen that could be raised and lowered with the flip of a switch. A bald-headed man controlled the switch.

The bald-headed man, who turned out to be the promoter, maniacally rushed around the stage, dramatically barking orders and making ridiculous demands of everyone. The fact that no one seemed to be listening to him didn't seem to matter. His rantings continued. Though none of us can remember his name, we do remember the name we gave him—Mondo Preminger. For one week—and one week only—Mondo Preminger presented "Cin-A-Rock."

Barefoot opened the show with a short set. Then Mondo lowered the silver screen, the stage darkened, and an hour-long movie ran. As the film began on the screen, we quietly rearranged the stage directly behind it. As the movie ended, Mondo Preminger barked instructions for us to take our positions.

We could only look at each other and chuckle, as we stood in the dark, the movie screen two feet in front of our faces. When the final credits rolled, Mondo threw the switch, the screen raised, the lights came up, and we blasted into "Chicken Train."

The concept was nice. The theater was very nice. The fact that there were only a couple of dozen people, slouched down in their plush theater seats from the movie ... wasn't. Though we blasted through our set, Mondo Preminger's balloon was bursting—and it was only opening night.

The crowd grew to almost three dozen for the late show. The second night brought in crowds of fifty and fifty-one, respectively.

The third night turned out to be our last night, as Mondo pulled the plug on the Great "Cin-A-Rock" Experiment. When he asked if we would mind just going home, Rusty got paid and the Ducks flew south. We didn't mind. That empty theater wasn't a lot of fun for us either.

Though I didn't become a fan of Cin-A-Rock, I did become a fan of Toronto, Younge Street, hockey, and Canadian beer. It is a marvelous city. Though our first of many, many, many, many gigs on Canadian soil was less than memorable, Canada will become an important and valued part of our equation.

We were met at the airport by Stanley and our wives, all excitedly waving copies of *Billboard* magazine. On February 16, 1974, on the heels of a dismally failed "Cin-A-Rock," we found that our record had cracked the *Billboard* Top 200 album chart.

Directly attributed to the good people of the Midwest and their hippity-hop to the record shop, initial sales neared 30,000 copies. This was great and, in those days, good enough to get you onto the charts. To the good people of Kansas, Iowa, Oklahoma, Nebraska, Colorado, Illinois, Arkansas, and especially Missouri, each one of you deserves a heartfelt *thank you*.

Weighing in at a whopping #198, we were in good company. The Commander's *Live from Deep in the Heart of Texas* sat at #192. Neither of us posed any imminent threat to Bob Dylan, whose *Planet Waves* was perched at #1. But we were ON THE CHARTS.

We excitedly grabbed the next week's issue (Feb. 23) to find out that we'd jumped all the way up to #191. The next week, we slipped back down to #197. The week after that, though we quietly shuffled off into the two hundreds, we were thrilled. So was A&M. We'd sold 30,000 copies and things were looking up. A&M was already looking ahead.

"After the album came and went," Stan recalls, "I walked into Jerry's office, with all of the head guys there. They were ready to start the next album. I said, "No way, gentlemen, in my wildest imagination, did I not see there be a hit on this album. I know your loyalty and it's much appreciated, but there's a hit on this album—and that's 'If You Want to Get to Heaven.'

"They said, 'He's doing something negative.' Of course. Otherwise, they would've done it their way and their way would've been ... You would've never had a hit with 'Heaven.' They were ready to go on to the next album.

"To their credit, A&M would always say this. I knew they would stick with a group. They were very loyal to their artists. If it took three albums to break through, they would do it. They'd sold 30,000 records and said, 'Hey, that's a nice start.'

"I said, 'No way. Time out. This isn't going to happen. There's a hit on this record. I would like for you guys to release this [Heaven] as a single.' They did."

Plesser concludes with, "Those are the kind of things that sometimes don't endear you to the record company. But I had to do it. I didn't have ten other groups I was managing. I didn't have fifteen other releases coming out next week. I only had this."

When the song was released as a single, every station got one. Better than that, they all began to play it—and play it a lot. What was once underground was now in the air.

On April 20, "If You Want to Get to Heaven" cracked the Top 100, weighing in at #99 with a bullet. The next week, it went to #87 with a bullet. Each week, it made jumps of ten to fifteen slots.

As the song began climbing the charts, we began climbing onto small chartered airplanes, following Patrick around the country. A week in Cambridge, Massachusetts with Roger McGuinn was followed by a week in Denver at Ebbet's Field with Mike and Tom.

From Denver, we flew directly to Texas, playing two nights in Dallas, three nights in Houston, one night in San Antonio, and a night at Austin's Armadillo World Headquarters. Dallas and Houston were as unimpressed with us as we were with them.

We had a great time, though, drinking margaritas in San Antonio and an even better time drinking them at the Armadillo.

Thus would become our relationship with America's second-largest state—one that would linger through the years. We continued to visit Austin and San Antonio, but we would drive right through Dallas to get there.

We knew that "Dallas is an important market, blah, blah, blah." But we didn't care. The way we looked at it, there were two schools of thought on the subject:

SCHOOL A: "We've got to continue going there until we break the market."

SCHOOL B: "Fuck this place—and the horse it rode in on."

There were a lot of other places to play—places that enjoyed it when we came to town. We weren't nearly macho enough for these Texans. Nor were we interested in trying to be. We had a fiddle in the band, but the guy who was playing it wasn't wearing a big black hat and a big, obnoxious belt buckle.

Last year, we didn't enjoy the Dallas airport police.

This year, we didn't enjoy the Dallas musical palette.

Then it was on to Alex Cooley's Electric Underground in Atlanta, where we hooked up with the Doobie Brothers for a long swing of one-nighters through Florida. I was having the rock 'n' roll time of my life. Unfortunately, I was also having flashbacks to the severe motion sickness I suffered as a boy.

Each night of music was pure ecstasy. Each day of jumping into our little eight-seat Cessna was pure agony. Each morning, I sought the refuge of the back seat and the solace of not one but two barf bags. The first thing I did was fill the first one on takeoff. The next thing I did was fill the second on landing.

I sat right by the door, learning how to work the latch. This way, as soon as we landed, I could open it and climb out of the plane quickly. When my feet hit solid ground, all I wanted to do was sit directly on the pavement until all of the bobbing and weaving stopped.

Needless to say, I felt like hell for the rest of the day. That night, though, when it came time to play, the aching went away. This became my routine for the summer—sing out every night, throw up every day.

I hated jumping into that little airplane—absolutely HATED it. I began to ride with Patrick and Larry in the equipment truck, simply because I couldn't physically tolerate the airplane. Anything was better than the motion sickness and the chilling childhood memories along the Missouri roadsides.

Plus, I had never been to Florida and thought it a better idea to enjoy it while driving through it than to puke while flying over it. I prefer my Capricorn feet planted firmly on the ground.

I could not wait to get home. Did I mention that I HATED that little airplane? This eighteen-day trip was our first actual extended tour. Some fared better than others. Others complained more than others. None felt any worse than I did.

With the infusion of Heaven's success, on April 27, the album re-entered the charts at #160. After a determined climb, by the end of June, it had cracked the Top 40 at #39. "Heaven" was stretching its neck to #25 with a bullet. The song needed one last booster shot to catapult it into the Top 10, where it could really raise a little hell.

The boost it needed was to be added to playlists in Chicago, Detroit, and New York. Everywhere else the song was being played, it was a hit. Not only did it hit the top of the charts in Kansas City, St. Louis, and Springfield, it hit the top of the charts in Denver, Tampa, Cincinnati, and Seattle. Even Dallas radio played it.

If the song could only get picked up and played in the Big Windy Motor City Apple, the record would keep its momentum.

But the Fourth of July came and went without any rockets' red glare. The final boost never came. Both the album and the single had bullets. Both acquired anchors and started parachuting back to earth.

As summer faded, gigs became fewer and further between. We took this opportunity to make our way back to L.A. and our maiden voyage onto the tube—videotaping a segment for *Don Kirschner's Rock Concert*.

Wally Heider's mobile recording truck was pulled up alongside the Concert Hall of the Long Beach Auditorium, as an entire season's worth of performances could be captured on tape in a matter of weeks.

This was sound strategy for us, as a fall appearance on network television would not only be a shot in the arm, but could do nothing but provide further exposure and longevity for our record.

At the time, Les Garland still hadn't started MTV. There was no "round-the-clock" cable access to anything. There were only two syndicated rock 'n' roll shows being broadcast. On Friday night, America gathered around their televisions to watch the *Midnight Special with Wolfman Jack*. On Saturday, everyone watched Don Kirschner. If you missed either of these two shows, you were shit out of luck until next week.

When we walked into the Long Beach Auditorium that night—with all its lights, cameras, and action—we were overwhelmed. It didn't help, either, when the stage crew seemed to take forever to get ready, though they were sporting enough clipboards, headsets, and walkie-talkies.

Microphones were endlessly tested. Multiple camera and lighting angles were endlessly adjusted. We waited endlessly in the back. Rusty tirelessly tried to ease the tension with his best, "C'mon, guys. You gotta be loose. You gotta be loose, before you can be tight" banter. This was television and we were wound as tight as a drum.

I had to chuckle, though, as I sat in the make-up chair, getting make-up applied to my ever-oily, ever-bulbous nose by a make-up girl, trying not spill any powder onto the red Izod shirt I'd chosen to wear for my big television debut. Patched jeans and work boots completed my ensemble.

I also had to chuckle when, right before we started, the hyper stage manager was giving the audience specific instructions on how to act like they were having a good time. There's NO business like SHOW business.

When he finally clapped his clap board and hollered "action," John walked up to his microphone, said, "This is for the folks back home," and we launched into "You Made it Right," "Spaceship Orion," "Chicken Train," "Road to Glory," "Standing on the Rock" and "Heaven."

It was a nice cross section of our material, but we were all so tense and afraid to make a mistake that we made lots of them. I was so scared, I couldn't even look up from my bass. When we ended "Heaven" with my traditional, "Come on, everybody, stand up and clap your hands" routine, I felt very awkward, not being able to tell if the standing ovation we were receiving was sincere, or just per the stage manager's directions.

Though we hadn't played very well, we knew we were a good band. We also knew that our stage show—a half dozen guys, just standing around, playing their instruments—was less than spectacular. A&M knew this too. We couldn't refute it. That's just how we were.

When we suggested that it might be interesting if we could replace our ugly mugs on screen with a montage of sights and scenery from around the Ozarks, A&M agreed to the added expense. Billy Higgins and his Kansas Film Works were brought on board.

Higgins, along with his extensive files of photographs and videos, was flown out to L.A. for the post-production of our segment. As our songs played, his images of the Ozarks replaced our boring stage show. The effect was impressive and very cool, as once again, the affable Kansan did a nice job of portraying life in Missouri.

Co-starring with Roy Buchanan and Return to Forever with Chick Corea, our segment aired—one of the first to incorporate video images over the soundtrack. That Saturday, the entire populace of Springfield gathered around our TVs.

As we began "You Made it Right," long, panoramic sweeps of the gentle hills and dales around our homes appeared on the screen, followed by additional shots of dogs, cats, horses, cows, creeks, wildflowers, spider webs, and the Trout Farm.

Kirschner, who we never even saw during the whole ordeal, brought everyone back from commercial break with his adenoidal, "When two talented pros like Herb Alpert and Jerry Moss of A&M Records find a group worthy of recording, and *Rolling Stone* magazine describes this group as a mixture of country, the South, Appalachia, and rock 'n' roll that always takes a fresh approach, and the Daredevils' sound is peculiar in the tradition of the Band, then we became anxious to put them on our rock concert show. Here they are, the Ozark Mountain Daredevils."

When John's solitary fiddle started Randy's "Road to Glory," a blazing sunrise filled the television screen. Additional footage of a fog-filled valley enhanced the story.

When "Chicken Train" began, the sight of strutting chickens perfectly interpreted the sound of the mouthbow. Additional footage of busy sidewalk scenes, traffic jams, and garbage trucks were humorously spliced in between the chickens.

When we ended our segment with "Standing on the Rock," Larry stepped to the front and grabbed an acoustic guitar. Randy joined Steve in a double harmonica assault. When "Heaven" was reprised for the show's outro, the credits rolled. We might not have played well, but we were on television—and that lump in my throat was real.

It had been an interesting and active year. We'd been gone a lot. Now it was time to not be gone. It was also time to start thinking about making another record. Glyn and David came back to town to work on songs. The sun was about to shine.

CHAPTER 15

Rusty didn't have to take out too many trees, as he and his father Dale prepared the Ruedi-Valley driveway for the arrival of the Record Plant's mobile recording truck. The twenty-five-foot-long, twenty-four-track truck was driven from Los Angeles, California to Aldrich, Missouri. Here, we set up camp.

A&M did not put up much of a fight when we asked if we could make our second record here at the Ranch. Glyn and David also loved the idea, reassuring Jerry Moss that everything would be just fine.

After all, we were on a roll. We'd just had our album AND our single in the Top 40. While "Heaven" was blasting from everyone's radios, we shifted our focus out to the Ranch and another record. A two-week stretch in June was booked to cut the tracks at Ruedi-Valley. Two weeks in July were booked to mix the tapes at Sunset Sound in L.A.

Though the driveway was widened a bit, branches scraped against the side of the truck, as it inched its way up the lane, squeezed its way through the front gate, and found its way up the hill, to the far side of the house. For the next two weeks, it would sit directly outside the window to our music room.

Once in position, the truck was leveled and the parking brake was set. We had to make sure the electricity was sufficient. This was a very old house with very shaky wiring, and the recording truck had very strict power requirements. Rusty contacted Bolivar Electric, who sent out a crew. The crew ran a separate, much sturdier electrical line back in to the place.

When they yelled "CONTACT!" the switch was thrown. Everyone held their breath. Though the truck powered up just fine, we continued to keep our fingers crossed that we would not encounter one of the giant summer storms that could sweep through at any moment (like they are known to do), and knock out power to the entire area (which they are also known to do).

While the studio gear was turned on and adjusted, an umbilical cord of microphone cables was fed through the open window into our room. It was June. The weather was great. All the windows were already open.

Directly behind the recording truck, Dale and Rusty pulled in several smaller trailers and Winnebagos, to be used as housing. After all, the big house was only so big. Not only did the delicate recording equipment need a steady current of electricity, the array of trailers needed a steady current of air conditioning. Glyn and David each had their own. Several others were scattered about for visitors who wouldn't be able to handle un-air-conditioned air.

We stayed, as we always did, throughout the house. I strolled off to the barn at the far end of the glade, hanging a hammock from its support beams. Not only had I become comfortable sleeping in a hammock, at the end of the day, I could step away from the fray. It was quiet down by the barn. Visitors were few. The early June air hadn't hit the sweltering point yet. The evenings were cool (in more ways than one) and spent sleeping in a hammock in the barn.

The Winnebagos were followed in by a portable kitchen, which was manned by Polk County neighbor Lydia Bonham. The spunky seventy-one-year-old grandmother of eleven was hired to prepare a couple of meals a day, for a couple of dozen people for the next couple of weeks. All meals were eaten family style at the long picnic tables that were gathered in "Lydia's World."

She was described by Rusty as, "a phenomenal lady. I've never met anyone her age who was so self-sufficient. She built her own bathroom onto her house. Then she dug the ditches and installed the water and sewer systems herself."

On a recent trip into Aldrich (population thirty-three), Rusty struck a deal with her to come out to Camp Ruedi-Valley and feed the troops. A second deal was struck with Bob and Vetta Rae Blauvelt of the Aldrich Mercantile, who agreed to place larger-than-usual grocery orders and deliver them out to Lydia on a daily basis.

Staged directly outside the kitchen door of the big house (used for storage) and directly beside the well house (used for water), Lydia filled the crisp morning air with the aroma of a crackling campfire, crackling bacon, eggs, coffee, pancakes, orange juice, biscuits and gravy.

The birds filled the morning air with song. The wildflowers filled the yard with color. Lilacs, wisteria, and honeysuckle were in full bloom and very aromatic. Rusty made sure everything was in working order, the lawns meticulously mowed. The Ranch spruced up well.

Prince, like the twelve-year-old puppy he was, hung around, lumbered about, laid by the fire, scratched his fleas, and waited for people to spill things. This was the most excitement his big brown eyes had ever seen around the place. He and Lydia became good friends, as she only had to bang him on the head with her spoon a couple of times. They quickly learned to co-exist. After all, Lydia's World WAS in Prince's World.

Everyone woke to the smell of smoke and began gathering. As the breakfast crowd grew, preparations for the day's recording were mapped out. Once again, this duty was placed into David's hands. After the first, few gallons of coffee, we filtered into the house to begin working.

When our focus shifted inside for the music, Lydia's focus shifted to lunch and dinner. Breakfast dishes were washed. Potatoes were peeled. Grills were fired up. It was her job to uphold our motto—"Groceries take precedence." This, she did magnificently.

Close friend Jim Mayfield was invited to come out with his cameras. Mayfield, a staff photographer for the *Springfield News-Leader*, not only turned his lens onto the band, but—like Higgins—also turned it onto the Ranch, in all its glory.

While we were capturing a feeling on tape, Jim was hired to capture that same feeling on film. His laid-back demeanor put everyone at ease, as he was given free rein to roam the place. Because he knew how to blend into the mix, as well as the woodwork, no one minded that he was there. Because he knew when NOT to make his presence felt, no one minded when he turned his lens toward them.

One person he could not turn his lens onto, though, was Lydia. No matter how much we all begged and pleaded with her, she would not allow Jim (or anyone else) to photograph her. When approached, she would quickly turn away with a stern "NO."

It wasn't until one of the last days that she allowed Jim to finally snap her likeness—primarily because she was just too tired to get up from her chair. It had been another long breakfast, as she decided to take a

Lydia sitting in the sun (photo by Jim Mayfield)

break and sit in the afternoon sun. As she relaxed, she half-heartedly consented with, "Okay. Just one."

As she smiled and threw her arms into the air, Jim snapped the shutter. At the time, no one knew that the only shot we would ever get of her would end up on the album cover. Her smile perfectly sums up what was going on at the Ranch. The sun was shining on us all.

We set our gear up in the music room like we'd been setting it up for years. Larry's drums were placed in the corner by the fireplace. Once he got them muffled just right and thumping real good, Glyn miked them with the same three-mike approach he used at Olympic. I set up my amp in the next corner.

Buddy's piano occupied a third corner across the room, and Randy's amp sat in the fourth. John took a chair by the front door, as Steve and Rusty sat near the window with all of the cords running through it. Glyn and David sat in the truck.

Though most of our rehearsals had shifted to the Trout Farm, there was just a special atmosphere about Ruedi-Valley. It not only held the heart of our music, but was where we felt most comfortable making it. We knew how to make this little room sound nice—by "playing well with others."

We knew this music HAD to be recorded here. The time had come.

David started us out with "Look Away" and "Walking Down the Road"—a couple of songs we'd been playing for years. Both had been considered for the first record. Both were well rehearsed. Both went onto tape, quickly. This started things off with a bang. At this point, we went on a two-week roll, like no other two-week roll we'd ever been on.

Songs started coming from every imaginable direction—under shady trees, on the front porch, on the back porch, in Lydia's kitchen, around Glyn and David's trailers. Some were written in the morning, worked up at lunch, and recorded that afternoon.

Every idea was explored, as microphone cables were run all over the place—under shady trees, on the front porch … well, you get the picture. When the weather was nice, songs could get recorded outdoors in perfect silence. If it rained, all we had to do was step inside.

It was stormy night as we set out to record the track to "Jackie Blue." Thunder rolled softly across the hills in the distance. The sensitive microphones picked it all up. As we worked through the evening, we laid down several tracks to the song. The loping version we liked the most, though, held a string of subtle thunderclaps that bled onto the song's long ride-out.

Unlike the "kerplunk" at the end of "Beauty in the River," neither Glyn nor David seemed to mind this extemporaneous noise. We didn't mind either. The thunder clapped along to the funky Granny's groove.

We all really enjoyed playing the song, even though it sounded quite a bit different from the rest of our material. This disparity, which we enjoyed and kind of prided ourselves in, would soon begin to confuse people. The song really doesn't sound like it's being played by a country rock 'n' roll band.

When we finished the track, Glyn turned to everyone in the truck and loudly proclaimed, "Gentlemen, that's a number-one record." Then he set up microphones on the front porch and began to record wave after wave of thunder for future use.

The next day, after the storm had passed, we utilized a slow morning to record a series of songs, each done individually. Informally dubbed "Morning Sickness," one by one, we pulled out one of our more obscure tunes and recorded it while the rest of us ate breakfast. One take—no second chance—no overdubs.

I sang "Plainity," which I'd just written and worked on in the barn. Steve sang "Lazy." Buddy sang "Dreams." Randy sang "Rock 'n' roll Dream." John sang "Lowlands," which would receive eventual inclusion on the record. Larry, who had gone to town for the morning, missed out.

When he returned, we decided to use the afternoon to fortify the "Jackie" track we had recorded the night before. As Randy added lead guitar, his notes sailed out the open window of the house like the Frisbees that sailed across the lawn. Our sails were full.

A gorgeous afternoon turned into a gorgeous evening, as we set up on the front porch to record "It Couldn't Be Better"; Glyn asked that we sit silently for a minute, after we finished playing the tune. This would allow him to record the wave after wave of crickets that accompanied us.

When the final mixing took place, the decision was made to keep the crickets on the end of "It Couldn't Be Better" and cross-fade them into "E.E. Lawson." Crickets—the official summer soundtrack of Missouri.

While some of us were working on songs with Glyn in the house, others were playing songs for David out in the kitchen. It was at Lydia's where I first played, "It Probably Always Will." David's reaction was, "That's cool. Let's go play it for Glyn." Glyn's reaction was, "That's real cool. Let's cut it," finishing with a wink and a, "Leave this one to me, mate."

He miked the guitar in my lap, began positioning people, and showed us all, one by one, exactly when to come in. Then he stepped out to the truck to hit the red button. After starting the song by myself, with each verse and chorus, Glyn introduced a new instrument. By the time we got to the end of the song, we were all gently rolling down the hill together.

When I joined him and David in the truck to hear my song for the first time, my skin crawled off my shaking bones. With each new instrument, the song swelled. When we got to the end, I could not catch my breath.

When the two turned to me with a quizzical, "That's okay, isn't it?" I was absolutely speechless. When Glyn explained how he tried to record the song as if it were a Fairport tune, I knew exactly what he meant. Years later, Sandy Denny would approach me to express her fondness for the song, though she mistakenly called it "It Probably Never Will." We both laughed.

When David ended the conversation ended with, "Now go back in and put on a bass part," I flew out the door of the truck. These guys didn't have to ask me twice. In a matter of a few hours, my song went from a thought in my head at the breakfast table that morning to that very same thought on tape that afternoon. Songs continued to materialize out of thin air.

Another picnic-table session found John and Steve putting the final touches onto "It'll Shine When It Shines." After playing it for David, Dale, Rusty, Prince, Patrick, and whoever else happened to be in Lydia's World at the time, it was also recorded in short order.

As we got close to having enough material for the album, new songs continued to emerge. I suggested one morning that we take a little time to go back and pick up a couple of our older songs. Our fans loved

It Shined

them. They wouldn't take long to record. This idea went over like a lead balloon.

I was really getting off on what we were doing. But I also thought we were leaving out an essential part of our deal—the humor. "All of these new songs aren't better," I contended. "They're just newer—like a new girlfriend. We all know about tears and fears and mystical dreams. But we're not making a Leonard Cohen record. This is the Ozark Mountain Daredevils. What about 'Time Warp'? What about 'Homemade Wine'? What about 'Leatherwood'? What about 'Sonora'? People have been getting off on those songs for years."

My suggestions fell on deaf ears as, this time around, Glyn made it known that he was in charge and he wasn't interested in our sillier stuff. Wanting to concentrate on the mellower, more serious material, John was feeding him a long line of ballads. When the album finally came out, six of his songs were included. Only one of Randy's hit vinyl.

As the session neared its end, two silly songs became points of serious discussion. One was Steve and Randy's "Time Warp," which we'd been playing and laughing at for years. The other, Steve and John's "Journey to the Center of Your Heart" had just been written and had been making us laugh for days. We all knew both of these songs needed to be recorded.

That is, everyone except Glyn, whose response was a defiant, "I'm not going to waste my time." Both songs lay neglected. That is, until the day Glyn got called into town to tend to some business.

That afternoon, while the Brit was away, the Ducks did play. We pleaded with David—though we didn't have to for long—to let us cut these two songs. He knew how essential they were to the mix. He immediately took the helm, grabbing the duck by the horns and instructing everyone to assume their positions.

We spent a very light-hearted afternoon laying down these very light-hearted songs. No one minded when Larry burst out laughing in the middle of "Time Warp," his guffaw bleeding right into the drum mikes and onto the tape. The spur of the moment was being caught. Everyone laughed.

Complete with stumbling banjos, bumbling recitations, silly guitar solos, sillier kazoo solos, whistling, and a healthy dose of mayhem, they represented the comedic side of the band I felt most comfortable

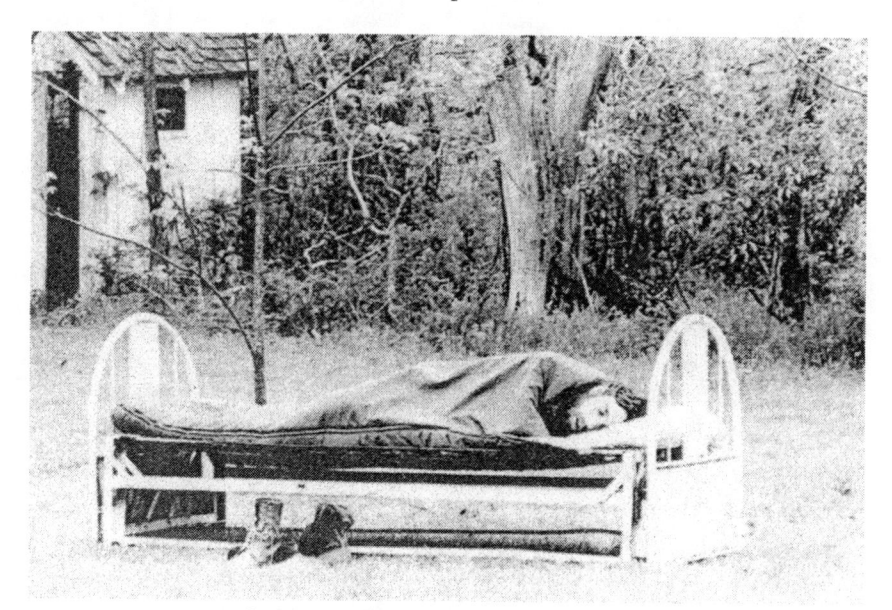

Hard at work, Ruedi-Valley (photo by Jim Mayfield)

with—and responsible for. After all, I was the one who used to play the blues on a toy xylophone.

I felt this sillier side of the band was being ignored. I also felt that this wasn't a very good idea. With all of these serious songs, Perry Allen found himself on the sidelines, his hands in his pockets.

This sentiment is best described by Stan, when he recalls, "The best part of your music was left in the locker room. Glyn didn't want to do those kind of songs. But to me, that was the essence of the band. Those songs are what separated you from everyone else out there. No one was doing that kind of shit."

When Glyn returned to the Ranch, "Time Warp" and "Journey" were greeted with a polite clearing of the throat. That evening, we got back to work.

With the inclusion of these last two songs, our grand total came to fifteen. We knew we could only squeeze twelve onto the vinyl. Three had to go.

Once again, Glyn laid out his vision of the song sequences. Needless to say, neither "Time Warp" nor "Journey" made the final vinyl.

Also hitting the cutting room floor was Randy's "Better Days," which would be relegated to the B side of future singles. I was disappointed

It Shined

"Time Warp" didn't make it. I was disappointed "Journey" didn't make it. I wasn't disappointed Glyn liked "It Probably Always Will."

As the end of the fortnight neared and all the tracks got cut, friends started to catch wind of what we were doing—and knew where to find us. Mike and Tom came down with Stan and Paul from Kansas City. A slew of friends came up from Springfield.

The moon was very full, as the natives converged on the Ranch for one last night of imbibing, hanging out around the campfire, and listening to rough mixes. For the past couple of weeks, we would listen to the same song over and over while working on it. This evening, we were ready to hear them back to back to back to back.

Plus, we were ready to blow off some steam and share the music with friends. The campfires were stoked. All cautions were thrown out the window—I mean, into the fire. No one had to be quiet. No one was.

Rusty set up a small table and chairs on his candle-laden balcony, dubbed Cafe Royale. He and his visitors sat directly above the front porch, with a bird's-eye view of the proceedings below.

David opened his trailer, which we named Dave's Ribs.

After a visit to Cafe Royale, where you were treated to a fine wine and a fine puff of pot, at Dave's Ribs, you were treated to a fine line of cocaine. Both men were running fine, upstanding establishments. Both stayed open all night. After imbibing at the two locales, silhouetted Ducks began howling and jumping through the fire.

Steve Canaday, Curt Hargus, Bill Ware and Ken Knauer brought sacks full of beer and pockets full of posies. We drank all the beer and smoked all the posies. As the fire raged into the night, the Coughing Dogs emerged.

As the Coughing Dogs became the Snorting Dogs, the party got louder, instruments got broken out, and even more songs started blurting out. As a jam started with not one, not two, but three harps (Cash, Kurt, and B. Ware), we all sang chorus after chorus of "There's an H-Bomb Crawling in the Back of the Bus." Everyone wailed. Everyone laughed until we cried. Everyone danced in the fire.

Throttles, as well as the door to the recording truck, were thrown wide open. As Glyn sat and blasted extremely loud rough mixes across the fields and into the clear night air, every song sounded magnificent.

Eventually, he wandered off to bed. But not before assuring us that we wouldn't be disturbing him with our revelry. Then he reminded us that, after all, he used to hang out with Keith. He said, "Carry on." So, we did. The next morning, Lydia nursed severe hangovers, as Glyn acutely observed, "I was intrigued by the primitiveness of it all."

Our work was done. The Record Plant truck was packed up, ambled back down the driveway, and headed west. We all bid each other a fond adieu and an excited, "See ya next month."

Glyn flew home to London to record with the Eagles. David flew home to Los Angeles to record with Kris and Rita. I drove home to the Nixa Trout Farm. Randy and Rusty were already home.

Camp Ruedi-Valley was disassembled and we all re-entered the real world. My real world involved another sojourn to Latin America, and fatherhood. That's right. Fatherhood. Ta-da.

CHAPTER 16

It was the middle of June when everyone left Ruedi-Valley. I tended to the Trout Farm, which seemed tiny in comparison. Though my unborn child was still seven months away, I began at once preparing the nest. When I was informed that there wouldn't be anything going on until the middle of July (when it'd be time to mix the record in L.A.), I headed south.

By this time, Don Tom had moved his entire family from Bogotá to Guatemala City. Planes to South America could be replaced by trains to Central America. Amtrak was boarded in St. Louis. The border was crossed at Laredo. Mexico flashed by our window.

When I stepped onto Guatemalan soil for the first time, I knew I was going to enjoy it more than I did Colombia. The tropical sun is nice. But this small, volcanic country is not labeled "Land of Eternal Spring" for nothing. Once again, we hopped on buses and vanished into the countryside, hammock in hand.

This time, instead of sleeping on the beaches of the Caribbean Sea, we slept at the foot of the volcanoes that surround Lake Atitlan. Taking up residence in Panajachel, we could easily get wherever we wanted. Guatemala is not a large country. Trips were short, wherever we went. We went everywhere.

I immediately felt more comfortable among the Guatemalan indians than I did among the Colombian caballeros. I also fell in love with the marimba, unable to pass a marimba band without becoming totally enchanted by the sound.

A jaunt to Tikal was my introduction to the Mayan culture, which I fell in awe of. As we strolled among the ruins, I became convinced the Mayans were not of this world. Now, Spanish fortresses dating back to the 1600s are one thing. Entire civilizations built of stone in the middle of the jungle THOUSANDS of years ago is another.

Where did all these people go? There had to be multitudes of them. While I'm on my soapbox, where are the people who built Machu Picchu? Where are the people who built the pyramids? How did those stone heads on Easter Island get there?

I can't accept that primitive cultures built these massive structures by rolling eighty-ton rocks on tree trunks across the jungle and desert floor. I don't think so.

I came back to this country a changed man, heading straight to L.A. with the rest of the boys, who'd been hanging around Springfield. After listening to rough tapes for a month, we were more than ready to get them mixed up and smoothed out. We took up residence at Sunset Sound and checked back into the Tropicana.

Each morning began with breakfast at Duke's. The rest of the day and night was spent at Sunset. We brought no instruments, due to the fact that all of the recording was done. The piano was replaced on "Jackie Blue," at Glyn's insistence. Knowing he had a hit on his hands, he demanded the giant grand piano at Sunset be played, instead of the funky upright piano at Ruedi-Valley.

All we had to do was sit around the studio and mix. Plus, we didn't all have to be there at the same time. Afternoons were spent poolside at the Tropicana, sunning to the sounds of James Cotton. In town, for a gig at the Troubadour, he was using his motel room on the second floor to rehearse his band. As they played, his harp blew cool breezes through the hot afternoon air. It sounded great. As we sprawled out at the pool, they crammed into a hotel room. They were wound up and laying it down. We were loving it and lying around.

Tutti Camarata was Walt Disney's director of recording in the late 1950s. At one point, Camarata asked Disney why he didn't have an in-house recording studio. The Missouri native's simple reply was, "I'd rather be a client."

Camarata took the hint and went shopping for a studio. After sussing out several locations, he settled on the perfect spot—a former auto-repair garage on Sunset Boulevard.

The floors were slightly tilted, so motor oil could drain away from the cars. Tutti intuited that this would bode well for the studio's acoustics, stating, "No studio worth it's salt has parallel surfaces, since the sound waves tend to bounce back into themselves, resulting in a mire of 'standing waves.'"

Tutti took the plunge and bought the place, opening Sunset Sound Recorders in 1962. Soon, the Mouse That Roared came to his new studio, recording scores and soundtracks to *101 Dalmatians*, *Mary Poppins*, *Bambi*, *The Jungle Book*, and many more. Sunset became known as a great sounding studio, featuring state-of-the-art equipment.

After many fits of frustration at not being able to record the singer as he wished, Camarata is best known as the creator of the isolation booth, claiming, "Why are we always having the singer in the same room with the band, and we can never get the band sounding the way we want it to sound?"

As the singer stood alone in his own isolated room, the engineer would acquire more control over the sound of the singer's voice. Many singers, ranging from Bing Crosby to Neil Young to Frank Zappa, stepped into Tutti's iso booth.

But for all the success Camarata was having with jingles and Disney soundtracks, it was the burgeoning rock 'n' roll scene a few blocks down Sunset Strip at the Whiskey a Go-Go that set Sunset Sound in stone (as well as the Stones in Sunset). What started out as the place where Uncle Walt made his merry Mouseketeer music turned into the house of the doors of perception. Not only did the place play host to the Doors, the Stones, Buffalo Springfield, the Turtles, and Zappa, it was where Brian Wilson built "Good Vibrations" and "Pet Sounds." Sunset became the epicenter of the vibrant L.A. rock 'n' roll scene.

Just as Olympic was Glyn's favorite place to work in London, Sunset was David's. Numerous other A&M acts also worked here, including

It Shined

Herb Alpert himself. We checked into the smaller mixing room and got to work.

One by one, each song got nice, warm mixes—crickets and thunder intact. It was exciting to hear the older songs done correctly, just as it was to hear the new ones come to life.

Layers of Brian Wilsonesque vocals were stacked onto John's "Morning Sickness" version of "Lowlands." David brought in old friend, Nick De Caro, to put the finishing touches on "It'll Shine When It Shines" with his accordion.

One of the last tracks to get mixed was "Jackie Blue." The only problem was, it still had no vocal. When it came time to sing the song, Larry stepped up to the mike.

He picks up the story: "I hadn't even thought about changing the lyrics until we got to L.A. I remember singing them through one time. Then I could see Glyn in the control room talking to David and whoever else was in there. It was one of those instances where you're just sitting there. You know something's going on in the control room. But you don't know what it is. I was sitting there, with my headphones on ... and nobody was talking to me.

"After a bit, Glyn got on the intercom and said, 'Larry, come in here, please.' When I walked in and sat down, he just looked at me and asked, 'What the hell is this song about?' I told him the story about how it was influenced by a friend of mine back home who was just a drugged-out, fucked-up guy.

"Glyn just said, 'No. No. No, mate. Jackie Blue has to be a girl. Now, you and Cash go back there and change it.' So Steve and I went into one of the other studios with a piano in it, where we just knocked some new lyrics out in about thirty minutes. Instead of some drugged-out guy, we changed Jackie to a reclusive girl."

When the rest of us heard the new lyrics for the first time, our collective jaw hit the floor. Not only had Steve and Larry written new words, the song had gone through an entire sex change. Jackie, the guy who used to swing at every nightclub in town, turned into Jackie, a girl who lived her life from inside of her room. The new lyrics were great, and Larry sang them wonderfully. But for a few days, the gender switch threw us all for a loop.

Not Glyn. He was going nuts. So was the rest of the A&M staff, who began stopping by to hear the new band, the new album, and the new single. None of them had any idea that just last week, Jackie Blue had been a man.

Randy's guitar solo on the song posed another puzzle. "There's also a strange timing on his guitar solo," Larry points out. "If you listen to it, it's not quite as he played it. In those days, you had to manually change the heads back and forth on those old twenty-four-track machines. If you didn't, the recording and playback heads would be slightly out of alignment. Glyn had forgotten to sync them back up before Randy started overdubbing his solo.

"When he recorded the solo and played it back, everything was lazy on the backside and slightly behind time. It's all..... kind of, in time. But, it's a strange way to descend down to places. His notes fell in such odd places. It was so cool, Glyn just said, 'Let's keep it that way.' So we did."

It was at this point that the album acquired its identity, its title, and its cover. We had all been leafing through Mayfield's photos from the Ranch, when his only shot of Lydia sitting in the sun stood up and yelled, "Here I am, boys. It'll Shine When it Shines." We handed the idea off to art director Roland Young, who compiled another tasteful package, complete with another six-panel insert of lyrics and photos of us in our individual homes. This was just more icing on more cake.

All sixteen songs got finished, though we mixed "Time Warp" and "Journey" without Glyn. Though neither of these two songs made it onto any album, I will always be thankful to David for helping to preserve them. If the humorous element of our deal was not going to be represented on record, I'm glad there's proof that it was there. The day the two got mixed, I sat at David's side, throwing in two bits, four bits, six bits, a dollar.

Other members of A&M's artistic departments began dropping by—some just for the pot. All stayed for the music, which they enjoyed, and more importantly, was selling. This was still only the third time we'd even been to California, and they wanted to see, firsthand, what all the stomping was about.

We were given clearance to walk right past the guard at the front gate of the Lot. We'd hit the big time.

It Shined

Because Sunset was right around the corner from A&M, it was easy to shuttle between the two locales. After each mix, Glyn would tell us to get lost for a few hours, while he began to dial in a new song. This meant hours of free time. As we scattered, some of us listened to James Cotton. Others preferred to hang out on the Lot.

This is where we concocted a very funny publicity stunt for the album. We thought it'd be a hoot to bring a little bit of the Ozarks to Hollywood.

Glyn and David weren't the only ones who hated ticks. Everyone who flew in to see us was also deathly afraid of them. No one seemed to mind the coyotes howling at night or the occasional snake. But when the mighty little mites were spotted, everyone coiled in fits of terror.

The stunt was simple. When "It'll Shine" was released, with our entire crew, we would visit the Lot—a virtual guerilla party. With pockets full of time-released capsules—each one filled with ticks—we would spread out through the entire complex, stroll around, and inconspicuously drop them behind cabinets, under desks, and in closets. The following week, a telegram would arrive, reading, "Greetings from the Ozarks."

The plot was funny but, at Stanley's insistence, never implemented.

Label-mate Hoyt Axton was aware of us (he got free A&M albums too). Through his mother, Mae, he was also aware of the Ozark Jubilee. We were fans of his. He became a fan of ours. He and Rusty quickly became smoke-'em-if-you-got-'em buddies and buddy, they smoked 'em. Hoyt loved to smoke our pot. His husky laugh and healthy sense of humor garnered him honorary Duck status.

It was a quiet evening at Sunset, when Hoyt invited those of us who weren't busy to sing background vocals on "Idol of the Band," his tribute to small-town, teenage rock 'n' roll lust. The song, as well as his 1975, A&M release, "Fearless," was being produced by David Kerschenbaum.

Many Springfieldians remember Kerschenbaum from his rock-star days at the Half-a-Hill, as leader of David Kerr & the Playboys—which featured Steve Canaday on drums. In search of broader horizons, he had recently left Southern Missouri for the warmer climes of Southern California.

In the '50s, he was childhood friend and neighbor of Steve and Larry, all growing up in the shadows of the KWTO studios.

In the '60s, he became a teenage heartthrob around Springfield.

In the '70s, he moved to Los Angeles to continue working in the music business.

You will learn more about him and his hand at producing the Ducks later. Tonight, he was producing Hoyt. The two were gracious hosts.

That night, when we walked into the studio, we stepped directly into a full-blown Hollywood blow party. Introductions went all around, as Cash and Kerschenbaum started talking about the old neighborhood. Hoyt and Rusty started their smoke fest. There was plenty of everything to go around.

We gathered around the microphone with Hoyt's band, which included Kansas City native Nicolette Larson (on loan from Neil Young's band) and L.A. singer/ songwriter Rosemary Butler (on loan from Linda Ronstadt's Stone Ponies).

Everybody had a great time. Everybody sang their hearts out. Everybody talked—a mile a minute. We were in Hollywood, baby.

On quieter evenings, promotions director and A&M stalwart Bob Garcia set up a large movie screen in his modest home, which he then proceeded to fill with interesting, artistic people. As we watched private screenings of old classic movies, more members of the A&M community stopped by.

Though their aim was true and their gesture appreciated, we had to chuckle on the afternoon they invited us to a small company picnic. Because they thought us country boys would probably like to get out of the city for a day, we headed for the hills—the Hollywood Hills.

It was only a thirty-minute drive up the canyon from the hustle and bustle of the A&M Lot to the quiet roadside campground, shrouded with scenery, directly out of a Hopalong Cassidy movie. A leisurely Tuesday afternoon was planned, an extended lunch catered in.

It wasn't until we reached the campground that we discovered we would be sharing the facility and the adjoining canyon with a bunch of cavemen. No, literally, a bunch of cavemen.

Lunch was filled with beer, stories, and laughter. After lunch, as several of the staff wandered off with us to burn one, we heard the commotion coming from up the canyon. Curiosity killed the duck. As we hiked onward and upward, we came upon a large cave, its entrance completely covered with a large black tarp. No light was allowed to see the dark of cave, as inside, MGM was filming "Korg: 70,000 B.C.," their less-than-classic 1975 Saturday morning children's show.

Outside the shuttered orifice sat video trucks, film crews, trailers, and catering tents full of cavemen extras, all waiting for their scenes to be shot. Some sat cross-legged in the shade, wearing glasses and reading the newspaper. Others drank coffee, smoked cigarettes, played cards, milled about, and watched TV. All were getting their caveman make-up applied.

When we realized what we'd stumbled upon, Rusty, Buddy, John, and I were beside ourselves with laughter. When our A&M liaison informed the show's director who we were, we were told we could stay, but we could not go into the cave. We could, though, hang out with all the cavemen.

We called back down to our picnic for a photographer to come and get a shot of this. Our friends back in Springfield were not going to believe it. Because we were laughing so hard, we could barely talk to any of the cavemen. We did finally convince one to pose for a picture.

We walked a few yards away, where Rusty quietly offered the caveman a hit from the joint he held. The caveman quickly took a long drag. I would tell you the actor's name, but I don't remember. I also don't remember much else, other than he was dressed up like a caveman and, as you know, if you've seen one caveman, you've seen 'em all.

As we became better acquainted with the A&M staff, we learned that we all shared an affinity for sports. When we learned that they had a company basketball team, which included producer Lou Adler and comedian Cheech Marin, in our finest bullshit bravado, we challenged them to a game.

After all, Steve and Rusty had been very good players in high school, each going to the state tournament with his team. Larry, Paul, and I were all pretty athletic. Danny Cox was in town. We figured it would be fun to get together and play a light-hearted game of hoops with Cheech. We were already huge fans—Cheech & Chong were on A&M. We already had their records.

A nearby community center was procured and an afternoon game time was set. It would be a nice break to get away from the studio for a while, play a friendly game, and be able to make it back for dinner and an evening of work. We were equipped for music. We were not equipped for basketball. Some of us had to cut off our Levi's to make shorts. Others just went ahead and played in their jeans. Several of us had to stop by the store to buy sneakers.

Due to the time spent shoe shopping, that part of our team fell behind schedule. Stanley slid behind the wheel of the rental car, as we raced from the shoe store and began racing to the gym—new shoes in hand.

Then, we hit the traffic.

Then, we came to a grinding halt in the traffic.

Then, in a total lack of judgment and driving prowess, Stan decided to take a shortcut, steering the car directly into a section of freshly poured concrete and sinking the right front tire up to its axle. We were stuck, as the hard-hatted construction workers (who had just smoothed the concrete) walked up with a disgusted, "What the fu …?" and a push.

Once our car was extracted from the bog, we squealed off down the street, flinging wet cement every which way. We were still laughing as we entered the gym. We were looking forward to laughing with Cheech.

Cheech, though, was not laughing. When we walked into the gym, we found him, Adler, and the rest of the A&M team running organized lay-up drills, led by Philadelphia Eagles tight end Tim Reed, who was currently starring in NBC's *Doctor World*. It became quite clear, quite

Stan calls time out as Steve hits the floor. Cheech says, "What the................?"
(photo by Jim McCrary)

quickly that our vision of a light-hearted game was not to be. They became "shirts." We became "skins."

From the opening tip, it took almost two minutes for the coughing and hacking to begin. It took Cheech and his boys another two minutes to dash out to a 27-4 lead. They ran the fast break. We were still trying to break in our shoes. In a matter of mere seconds, they led 36-4; then 44-6; then 52-8.

Then they started giving us some of their guys, just to even out the game. At this point, some of them joined back into the spirit of fun. Others didn't. Cheech was not amused.

Work at Sunset continued. As we neared completion, Glyn used a lull in the action to play some of the fresh mixes he'd recently made for the Eagles' *On the Border*. As he bounced back and forth between the two bands, each of us got to hear the other's work, long before it even hit the pressing plant.

As the Eagles began soaring into the platinum stratosphere, the Ducks continued to flutter at the treetops. Glyn would point out, "You guys laugh a lot more than they do. They never laugh. When they're in the studio, they are all business. There's never any laughter. You guys laugh all the time."

You bet I was laughing. I just played basketball against Cheech Marin, got stoned with Hoyt Axton, and met a bunch of cavemen. I was having the time of my life.

When we got home, we only had a couple of weeks to snap out of "studio" mode and switch back into "gig" mode. We hadn't played in more than three months. But with the addition of some of the newer songs, we had no trouble whipping together a sixty-minute show.

As we got the music together, Patrick and Larry Tucker got the gear together and we hit the road. We may have had our new material in our minds, but the crowds still had "If You Want to Get to Heaven" on theirs.

August and September were spent on the East Coast, playing long runs of outdoor sheds and theaters with Loggins and Messina. October and November were spent on similar runs through the South with Chicago and the Doobie Brothers.

Once again, I fell in hate with the little airplanes we continued to charter. I continued to ride in the truck on a regular basis.

I was at the airport, though, the morning we saw the Doobie Liner. Actually, we saw the Doobie Liner every morning, as, for weeks, all three bands adhered to the same daily travel schedule. We all had chartered airplanes, which would get parked side by side by side every night. Every morning, it was a funny sight, as we drove past Chicago's huge, sleek jet and the hulking Doobie Liner to get to our tiny, eight-seat Cessna.

Our little brown-and-tan plane blended in well with all of the other little brown-and-tan planes scattered about. There was no mistaking the Doobie Liner. Complete with oil leaks running down its side and it's moniker roughly painted above the door, it was the only plane on the entire tarmac that appeared as if Dwight Eisenhower could emerge at any moment and start waving to the crowd.

The poor old gal had millions of miles on her—and looked like it. Every morning began with a chuckle, as we marveled that she'd made it another day. That is, until the morning we arrived to see her completely scorched in a charred heap.

Overnight, she had sprung a mysterious electrical fire. Though it wasn't really funny, we laughed until we cried. I laughed until we took off and I started throwing up. I'm not sure how the Doobie Brothers got to their next gig, but it wasn't on the Doobie Liner. The Doobie Liner was toast.

We finished out the year with a small run through the Midwest with the Marshall Tucker Band, and another string of gigs with the New Riders from Seattle to San Diego. Here we met Ted Giannoulas.

Giannoulas picks up the story: "In 1974, KGB was the main radio station in the San Diego area. That Easter, as a promotion, they rented a chicken suit for an Easter egg giveaway at the zoo. With gold eggs to promote the AM station and psychedelic eggs for the FM side, their angle was 'We've Got Music for Everyone.' The only problem was, no one at the station wanted to wear the suit.

"So they came onto the campus of San Diego State University to find the first college kid they could find to wear this suit and go to the zoo. When they walked into the college radio station where I was working, several of us were just sitting around, bullshitting about what we were going to do for Easter break. With an offer of $2.00 an hour, they pointed at me and said, 'You're the shortest guy in here. You'll fit into the suit.' I was game. There was no interview, no audition, no application. I just told them I'd do it, and spent Easter at the zoo.

"The promotion was such a hit that I started wearing the suit to lots of other functions, becoming a walking billboard for the station. I went to a lot of Padres games, Chargers games, and KGB-sponsored concerts. I was making a dozen appearances a day. Though I became the San Diego Chicken to the rest of the world, people in San Diego knew me as the KGB Chicken.

"When A&M sent a box of promotional albums down to the station, I saw this song called 'Chicken Train' by this group of crazy-looking, long-haired hippies called the Ozark Mountain Daredevils. When I heard the song, I went nuts. It was perfect.

"When they came to play Montezuma Hall on the San Diego State campus, not only did I have to go for work, I wanted to go to hear the band. As I did my usual deal of just wandering through the crowd, acting silly, I felt a tap on my shoulder. It was one of your road crew members, asking if I'd like to join the band onstage for Chicken Train. We headed directly backstage.

"When the song started, I waited in the wings. When they got to the middle section and all the chicken squawking started, I walked out on stage and started acting like more of an idiot than I usually do. The crowd, as well as the band, went absolutely apeshit. I wasn't sure you guys were even going to be able to finish the song, you were laughing so hard. I used it as my theme song for years."

With chickens dancing, we were having a good year. That fall, when A&M released 'It'll Shine When It Shines," our good year turned into a great year. Under our Christmas trees, for the first time, we began finding these crazy little things called publishing checks. Si had told us about them. Here they were. Lost Cabin was on its feet.

Lost Cabin Music was our most important item of business, when negotiations with A&M began. We insisted on keeping our publishing money. Here it was.

We set up the company so that we would all share in the spoils. Each individual writer was awarded the writer's half of the check, with the publishing half evenly split seven ways—Rusty as the seventh share. As soon as a publishing check came in, numbers were crunched and it was divided up. This would be in addition to the fifty bucks we continued to receive on a weekly basis.

At this point, unlike our neighbor, Jim Dandy and his Black Oak Arkansas boys, what each of us decided to do with our share of the money was our own business. They communally bought massive chunks of Arkansas real estate. Unfortunately, when they started leaving the band one by one, they ended up giving most of it to the lawyers and accountants they had to hire to figure out how to divide everything up.

We like Jim Dandy. He's a great guy. But we paid no attention to him when it came to this topic. We did listen intently to Si Siman. We may have been hillbillies, but we weren't stupid hillbillies. The money began coming in just in time for us to provide very nice lives for our new families. It was a very merry Christmas.

CHAPTER 17

Over the years, we always tried to take the first couple of months of the year off — winter. This is something we adhered to, even before we began traveling more extensively and further from home. We felt that people were less likely to spend a bunch of money on a concert ticket after having just spent a bunch of money on Christmas.

The entertainment industry, on the whole, uses this same approach—take some time to regroup from the holiday push to formulate strategies for the upcoming summer season. The winter of 1975 was no different.

On top of all this, I heated my home with wood and felt it important that I be there to keep everything from freezing up. In years to come, our lame "We don't want to go on the road because it's summer and we have to stay home to help our ladies" routine was just that—lame. On the other hand, our "We don't want to go on the road because it's winter and we'd like to stay home in order to keep everything from freezing up" routine was legitimate.

Plus, my first child was on the way and I was not about to leave. This is one topic we all felt the same about—the importance of being present for the births of our children.

Steve and Sidney had recently welcomed their daughter Star into the world. It was only after they settled back into their home as a family that we began to schedule gigs.

It Shined

In the winter of 1975, it was my turn to be the reason why. We continued to gather and rehearse at the Trout Farm. But we would only play a gig if it was close enough to make it home that night.

This drove Good Karma and A&M berserk, as they repeatedly tried to point out that this was part of the job description, something entertainers did on an everyday basis. But we were just not going to do it. So we didn't.

In the middle of the night of March 14, I drove through a snowstorm to reach Dr. Harold George's small clinic in Mt. Vernon. In the early-morning hours of March 15, I witnessed the birth of my daughter, Sya Leena. There was no gig worth missing this for.

After baby was swaddled and nestled to her mother's breast, I turned to Doc George, the large, jovial country doctor and pointed out, "You know what, Doc? You didn't do much, did you?"

"Nope," he replied with a wink. "The mother does all the work."

"Well, I could've done that."

Placing his hat on his head and heading into the cool morning, he quipped, "Yes, you could've." These were words I would take to heart when my second child came knocking.

Later that morning, as mother and baby rested in their small clinic bed, I returned home alone to prepare Sya's cradle. The snowy night had melted away into a brilliant blue spring day. As I strolled through the sunlight to the top of the hill overlooking the Trout Farm, I fell onto my knees, vowing to work even harder to provide a nice life for my daughter.

On the evening of March 15, we were allowed to come home as a family. A few close friends were invited to stop by. All shed tears of joy at the sight of Sya's sweet little smile. A toast went something like, "Here's to you, Sya Leena. Welcome to the planet. One year from now, we'll all meet again to celebrate your first birthday, which must make tonight your … zeroeth birthday." That night, we celebrated Sya's zeroeth birthday party with wine, bread, and friends.

On March 16, I called Stanley and gave him the green light. I was ready to get back to work.

As 1975 started to unfold, what a pleasant surprise it was to walk out to the mailbox on Friday afternoons to collect my fifty bucks, only to find an additional check with the word "publishing" written in the lower left-hand corner.

The first album was well on its way to selling a half million copies, and "It'll Shine When It Shines" was entering the charts. We all prayed that this record would not fall prey to the sophomore jinx. "If You Want to Get to Heaven" had made a nice impression. A&M was getting ready to hit everyone with "Jackie Blue."

The first three months of the year were spent at home, keeping our homes from freezing, paying off IOUs and living snugly.

The first thing I did was head up to the Nixa Bank, where I opened something I'd never had before—a savings account. When the bank president caught wind of my frequent visits, he emerged from his office like Mr. Drysdale—all smiles and handshakes.

Then I walked across the street to the Nixa Hardware, plunking down a handful of cash for a brand-new chainsaw. Though I was still tutoring algebra to my neighbors' kids and knew they would gladly continue to lend me their saw (to go along with the eggs and milk), I just felt better about having my own. In no time, the Trout Farm was well stocked with firewood.

The next thing I did was drive my 1960 forest green Volkswagen Beetle (which we had named Phil Forest), with its cracked windshield, rusted floorboard, and sporadic heater onto the Montgomery GMC Truck lot in Springfield.

Here I met with Tom Montgomery, the middle of three Montgomery brothers. He was my age, a fan of the band, and possessed the ability to bypass a lot of the bullshit you have to go through to buy a vehicle. In thirty minutes, I drove off the lot with a brand spanking new, 1975 Hawaii blue GMC pickup truck (which we named Bill Hawaii).

Then, it was back to Nixa Hardware, where I bought a garden tiller, and back down to the Trout Farm, where the fertile pond bottoms were tilled up. Lots of vegetables were planted. The three of us ate very well. The creek still ran right by the place. Water was not a problem.

Several late-night excursions were made up the creek without a paddle—but with a tiller. Here I reopened the pot beds Granny's had been using for the past few years. With a handful of seeds that I'd procured from botanical friends, I sowed and tended to a dozen marijuana plants.

Once again, the creek ran right by the patches—water was not an issue. The valley floor was fertile. I had a new baby in my house and a dozen new babies up the creek. All began to grow tall, strong, and healthy. I made sure all were nourished, loved, and tended to.

By summer, the Ducks were back in business. As the "V" headed back into the sky, back onto the road, and back onto the charts, things were about to change drastically.

A&M contractually had ninety days after the completion of "It'll Shine" (record number two) to notify us whether they intended to exercise their option for records number three and number four. It didn't take them ninety seconds to do so.

All systems were go. Glyn was not so sure. On our first trip out to the West Coast, he called, asking to set up a "band members only" meeting. A&M had just extended our contract for two more records, and he wanted to talk to us about it.

As he and David came by the Tropicana, we all crammed into one room—James Cotton style. As we sat about on the beds and dressers, Glyn explained that he was still interested in working with us as artists, but he could no longer work with Stan.

With a simple "me or him" proposition, we were confronted with a decision. There was no yelling. There was no screaming. Voices were not raised. Glyn calmly and succinctly explained his situation. Then we all went out for dinner and drinks. He treated. The choice was ours. I chose steak and shrimp.

Our choice was simple. Our lives were still simple. Out of a genuine sense of loyalty to Stanley and his efforts, our decision was simple. John explains, "We pretty much felt like we oughta stay with the one who brung us to the dance." Glyn's torch was passed on to David.

We figured, with everything we'd learned over the first two records, we could work well with David. He is one of the dearest people you will ever meet. We'd had a great time working with him before. There was no reason why we wouldn't have a great time working with him now.

After all, he WAS the one who "brung us" to the A&M dance. The lanky, affable man signed on to produce our next two records by himself.

As we headed home, "Jackie Blue" started making headway up the charts. By the middle of April, as Sya was kicking the sides of her cradle, Jackie was kicking down the doors of the Top 10.

We teamed up with the talented and gorgeous Emmylou Harris and the talented and ungorgeous Elvin Bishop for a swing through the South, playing smaller theaters in the cities we'd visited the year before with Loggins and Messina and the Doobies.

It was a very nice ticket, attended well everywhere we went. Emmylou had just released "Elite Hotel" and "Pieces of the Sky," fronting her Hot Band, which contained luminaries James Burton, Glen D. Hardin, and Emory Gordy, Jr.

Elvin, in support of "Let It Flow" and "Struttin' My Stuff," had an equally hot band of good old boys in cowboy hats from Georgia, which featured Mickey Thomas's voice on "Fooled Around and Fell in Love."

Every night was a game of skee ball at the county fair. The music was delightful from the first song to the last. Everyone—performers, as well as audience members—had a great time. All three bands were firing on all cylinders. All three bands had exciting new records out. All three bands became fast friends. Every evening was a great night of music, followed by a great night of partying into the wee wee wee wee hours.

As our logistics became more and more complex, it became clearer and clearer that Rusty was not going to be able to maintain his road-managing duties for much longer. Keeping gas and hotel receipts was not one of his long suits. Keeping the party afloat was.

We knew something had to be done about the situation: hiring Patrick's older brother Maple, fresh from a five-year stint at San Francisco's Boarding House.

"First, I worked at Don Weston's Troubadour," he recalls. "At the time, Doug had two Troubadours—one in L.A. and one in San Francisco. When he closed the San Francisco Troubadour, David Allen took over the building, kept most of the staff, and started the Boarding House.

"I did sound and lights, did some booking, did the posters, lived in the building—you name it. It was a complete co-op thing. Back then, one person did sound AND lights, because not many people at that level had road crews. We just had one big pile of levers and knobs. That's where I met Mike and Tom.

"When I came back to Kansas City to take this gig, I hadn't really ever been on the road. I knew a lot of people who had come through the Boarding House, and for the brief time I worked at the Egress in Vancouver. But I had never been 'on the road.' I had a lot to learn."

The slender five-foot-four-inch Byrne, with long tresses of frizzy brown hair, recalls his first gig. "Patrick, Tucker, and I had driven the truck all the way to New York for some record company gig at the Palladium and a 'live' radio broadcast from Electric Ladyland. We checked into the City Squire Hotel real late on the Wednesday night before Thanksgiving. We were really blitzed and had no sense of what time it actually was.

"The following morning, we opened the curtains just in time to see a thirty-foot Bullwinkle floating by the window, followed by Underdog. The Thanksgiving Day Parade was going down the street, right outside our window. We'd been driving for three days and didn't even think of it as being Thanksgiving. That was the last thing on our minds."

As '75 progressed, duties slowly switched over from Rusty to Maple. This was a good thing—a very good thing. Actual itineraries were produced. Our wives actually knew where we were and where we were going. Actual hotel keys were waiting for us, when we walked into the hotel lobby. Of course, we were still in those STUPID LITTLE FUCKING AIRPLANES. But things ran much, much smoother with Maple on board.

For the first few months, in order to make the transition easier, both Rusty AND Maple were part of our entourage. Maple kept the receipts. Rusty kept the "love mics" on.

Things were awkward at times, due to the fact that Rusty had never NOT been to one of our gigs and had never NOT been part of the entourage. The only problem was, he didn't sing, or play anything. After a while, when it became apparent that he had nothing to do, he bailed. But not until he bailed me out of a New Orleans jail.

The long southern swing with Emmylou and Elvin ended with a couple of days in New Orleans, a gig at the Warehouse, and a *Billboard* magazine informing us that "Jackie" was receiving that one last push "Heaven" hadn't. The transsexual Blue had cracked the Top 10 at #6 with a bullet.

As our traveling caravan of vagabonds, minstrels, and dogs hit the French Quarter, we all checked into the Marie Antoinette Hotel for a day off and an evening of rest. Emmylou and her band decided to do just that. Elvin and his band decided not to. Neither did we. The date—Cinco de Mayo, Steve Cash's birthday.

Both bands had hit singles.

Both bands had a night off in New Orleans.

Both bands hit the town that night as one large posse—a recipe for disaster.

I fell in love with the place immediately, realizing why my uncle Don had fallen in love with it years ago. When I also realized that this is where a lot of that music he had turned me on to as a boy came from, I fell in love with it even more.

I enjoyed the slow pace and crazy nuances, along with the sights, sounds, and smells that reminded me of St. Louis. These two lovely, lively cities have always been just a short journey up- or downstream from each other. Throw Memphis into the middle, and you have a rich musical palette along the banks of the Mississippi River.

We ate many oysters at Felix's on the evening of May 5. We also had many cocktails. As the dining, drinking, and dancing in the street carried into the night, one by one, members of our party began to fade and filter back to the hotel.

When the last couple of Ducks decided to throw in the towel, Steve bellowed at the top of his lungs, "It's my birthday, damn it, and I'm not ready to go down yet! Garcia Lorca, you jazz people. Here I come." Then, there he went.

Though I was also quite smashed, I was also not tired. As the two of us headed deeper into the Quarter and deeper into the night, not only did I want to continue to soak up more of this wonderful city, I wanted to keep an eye on my drunken friend. Neither of us needed to find the wrong end of an alley.

Many jokes, smokes, and birthday toasts later, we found ourselves having a nightcap on the corner of Bourbon and St. Charles. Casually watching a platoon of police cars round up a platoon of hookers, Steve stood inside the bar, leaning out an open window. I stood on the sidewalk, directly outside that window, leaning against the wall. It was great theater for a couple of drunken yay-hoos from Missouri.

Then, from out of nowhere, the policeman appeared, demanding identification and ordering me into one of the police cars. As he rhythmically poked me in the chest to accentuate each syllable, "You're-under-arrest. Let-me-see-some-ID. Take-a-seat-in-the-back-of-that-car," all I could babble was, "What? Who? Me? I—I—I wasn't—I'm not—What?"

"Hey, wait a minute," Steve chimed in. "He wasn't doing anything."

"Get in the car," the officer forcefully reiterated.

When I was advised by our waitress that "You'd better do what he says," I did.

"Now wait a God damn minute!" Steve yelled, his dander definitely up.

Turning to Steve, the cop's final words were, "And you'd better pipe down, Buster."

Before I knew it, I found myself in the back of a New Orleans police car with a couple of other unsuspecting Joes. The cop jumped behind the wheel and we sped off to the precinct. I turned around, just in time to see Steve screaming, shaking his fists into the air, and jumping up and down on the corner. It all happened in the blink of an eye, as things are wont to do in the middle of the night in the middle of the Quarter.

The clock on the wall read 3:00 as we checked in at the night court desk. The hookers had already been booked and were yelling and screaming at each other down the hall. By the time I was processed and charged with "loitering with intent," it was four.

When the dust started to settle, we were told we could use the payphone attached to the wall directly outside the cell—within arm's reach. When it came my turn, I dialed the operator and asked her to put me through to the Marie Antoinette.

I woke up Rusty with, "Rusty, you're not going to believe where I am."

"Mumble, mumble," he replied.

"I'm in jail."

"Mumble, mumble, mumble?"

"No. I don't know which one. But I'll find out."
"Mumble, mumble, mumble, mumble?"
"Yeah. $150.00."
"Mumble, mumble?"
"Let me see. Twenty-two bucks."
"Mumble."
"Okay. Hurry."

I knew things would be all right. What were these guys going to do—kill me? The only thing I was guilty of was getting toasted with my friend on his birthday. I hadn't robbed anybody. I hadn't shot anybody. I was arrested for loitering, for God's sake. Isn't loitering standard behavior in the Quarter?

As the sun rose on Seis de Mayo, Rusty, Maple, and an even more irate Steve came busting through the police station doors. Once again, Steve was advised to settle down—which he did. Rusty began talking with the jailer. Maple, wondering what kind of gig he was getting himself into, pulled out a wad of cash. Dotted lines were signed. Papers were shuffled. I was released and given a court time of 10:00 that evening.

We pleaded our case that this would be impossible, due to the fact that we would be on the Warehouse stage at 10 PM. The judge shrugged his shoulders and handed us a list of attorneys in the area.

It was a bright New Orleans morning when we emerged from the police station, merged into morning rush-hour traffic, and headed back to the Marie Antoinette. Tensions slowly eased, giving way to waves of laughter at the absurdity of it all. Once we were at the hotel, I started calling the list of lawyers.

After contacting the Law Offices of Somebody, Somebody, & Somebody, Maple, Rusty, and I hopped back into another cab and headed across town. Steve headed to his room, to sleep his birthday off.

Once in Mr. Somebody's office, we were informed that mine wasn't an uncommon occurrence. He explained that it was no big deal for the cops to make random late-night sweeps of unsuspecting out-of-towners, haul them off to jail, collect their bail money, and send them on their merry way.

Then, Somebody informed us, "If you really want, I'll appear in court for you at 10 o'clock tonight and get your $150.00 back. But I'll have to charge you $250.00 to do it."

His advice was to not even show up and not even worry about it. Then he stressed not getting arrested again. If I did, my name would be on the books. "Then, you're fucked," he finished. I fell in love with the city even more.

By the time we headed back to the hotel, everyone in all three bands—except Steve—was awake and eating breakfast. Word about my Cinco de Mayo escapades had already spread among the troops. I pulled up a chair and began the story.

Laughter shattered the quiet morning in the fountained courtyard, as a dozen musicians can make a lot of ha-ha racket. That night, this same festiveness transferred to the Warehouse, as we all sang and played our butts off. At 10:00, I saluted the New Orleans Police Department. The crowd went nuts. The party roared.

Elvin laughed harder than anyone, all night long saying to me, "Man, you're a goofy son of a bitch."

All I could say in return was, "Man, look who's talking."

After the gig, a loud, late-night knock on my hotel room door sent jolts of terror through my entire body. As I slowly opened the door, there stood Elvin in his overalls, with no shirt on, guitar in hand. When he asked if I had any blow, and I told him I didn't, he barged right past me with, "Good. Then, we'll do mine."

I hadn't slept the night before. I didn't sleep tonight, as the two of us sat there all night long, playing guitar, singing, laughing, and calling each other "goofy sons of bitches."

It was Mardi Gras the next time we visited New Orleans, but I still hadn't forgotten Somebody's advice, staying in my room with the shades pulled. This didn't last long, though, as I figured, "Hey, wait a minute. Fuck this. This is New Orleans. I'm not going to just sit around this hotel room anymore. Let's go."

We played Mardi Gras many times in the years to come. I never got arrested again.

"Jackie Blue" had some stiff competition when it finally cracked the *Billboard* Top 10. As I sat in the New Orleans jail, it sat at #6. Tony Orlando & Dawn had a stranglehold on #1 with "He Don't Love You (Like I Love You)" and was showing no sign of relinquishing the spot. Orlando stayed there for three weeks, as we jockeyed for position behind him with Freddie Fender's "Before the Next Teardrop Falls," Elton John's "Philadelphia Freedom," and B.J. Thomas's "(Hey, Won't You Play) Another Somebody Done Somebody Wrong Song."

On May 10, Jackie climbed to #4 with a bullet.

Though at the time, *Billboard* was still the big dog, there were two other publications that ran concurring Top 10 charts—*Cash Box* and *Record World*. On May 10, *Cash Box* placed Jackie at the #1 spot. On May 17, *Record World* did the same.

Still, *Billboard* was the bible. On May 17, it charted Jackie at #3 with a bullet behind Freddie and Tony. On May 24, it stayed at #3 but lost its bullet, as Earth, Wind & Fire streaked past everyone to the top spot with "Shining Star." The next week, we fell from the Top 10, relinquishing our spot to John Denver's "Thank God, I'm a Country Boy."

Jackie returned to her room. Her run was over. But it was a good run—twenty-one weeks on the charts. In addition to the album, A&M agreed to put out a music book. We thought this was a great idea.

When we asked if we could expand the book a little, to represent some of the other artists among us, A&M thumbs went up. When paying customers opened to the first page, we didn't want them to see a picture of us standing around, mugging for a camera. Instead, they were treated to a funny photograph of a handful of ducks, waddling and mingling alongside an old, rusted-out pickup truck. It was a fitting opening for those who STILL referred to us as the Ducks.

Several pages of photos, taken by Higgins and Mayfield, featured the Ozark landscape around our homes. The twelve songs (which we made sure were musically correct) were followed by six pages of poetry, including Steve's "Dharma Berries"—a poem he'd already had published in *Rolling Stone*, but had not been paid for. This was followed by a trio of small vignettes written by Karen in Spanish. All were accompanied by Elizabeth's wonderful Sumi-e paintings.

Having lived in Kyoto, Japan from 1966 to 1969, Elizabeth had studied Sumi-e under the tutelage of Toriumi Nirakushi. When she relocated back to the Ozarks, she brought her love of the medium's sparse style with her. Though she wasn't performing with us anymore, when we first began gathering, she was one of the artists in the creative stew. We always contended that one of her paintings would make a beautiful album cover. Her contribution to the book is splendid.

A&M scratched their heads, trying to figure out what Japanese Sumi-e paintings and poetry in Spanish had to do with our music. They also scratched their heads when they listened to the album for a follow-up single. What they found was nothing that even remotely sounded like Jackie.

No other single was released—well, not really.

When we suggested that the follow-up single be "You Made It Right" and that it should be released to country radio, they looked at us like we were crazy. Our rationale was simple: "Why not? We play country music. We like country music. When we play gigs, we play more country music than we do stuff that sounds like 'Jackie Blue.'"

"You Made It Right" was released, reaching #84 on the *Billboard* country charts, staying there for four weeks. We thought this was a natural move and a great idea. But it only seemed to confuse people, many of whom didn't even realize that these two songs were by the same band. We often heard, "You're the guys who do 'Jackie Blue'? You're kidding. We thought you were a country band or something."

This also seemed to confuse A&M, who asked, "What bin do we put your records in? The country bins? The rock 'n' roll bins? The pop bins? How do we market this stuff? How are we supposed to explain this shit to people?"

To us, it was easy. There was nothing to explain, as we asked why copies of the same record couldn't be placed into more than one bin. But this just didn't seem to comply with the compartmentalizing world of selling records.

We must give A&M credit. They knew how to market "Jackie Blue"— and did a fabulous job. But when they wanted "Jackie Red" or "Jackie Green," they got "You Made It Right." We were even confusing people in our own camp.

As *It'll Shine* continued up the charts, we continued up the East Coast with Emmylou, having a great time through the Carolinas and Virginia. Here we hooked up again with the Airmen for a couple of bashes at Washington D.C.'s Constitution Hall and the Capitol Theater in Passaic, New Jersey. Then we headed into the Big Apple for a three-night stand at the Bottom Line with Mike and Tom.

The lines at the Line went down the block, as the storied place was packed for all three nights—two shows a night. As we played, we looked out at the widest and weirdest assortment of people imaginable. Hippies, executives, bikers, lawyers, and street people all rubbed elbows, sharing tables, ashtrays, bar stools, and space.

Once again, Heavy Lenny and Rich Totoian made sure their chart-topping artists were well taken care of. As we became better acquainted with the better restaurants of Manhattan, the company credit card got a good workout. Jerry Moss flew in from L.A. for the occasion. Derek Green flew in from London. Stan and Paul flew in from Kansas City.

Rob Mackie of the *Village Voice* called *It'll Shine* "effortless, clean Thanksgiving music, vaguely religious, and entirely natural sounding. Back porch music for a hot summer night, but far from rough—Glyn Johns, co-producer and engineer has kept the sound finely honed as a lumberjack's axe. They're versatile as an egg and, definitely, sunny side up. If this music had a colour, it would be golden brown, like a ripe cornfield."

With each night, the crowds grew. The *New York Times*'s Penny Valentine reviewed the show with, "They're so damn at ease with each other and with you—out there in the dark—that they make you feel like you're being wrapped up and looked after. It's an un-histrionic, but equally a non-lazy performance.

"The last time I can remember feeling like this—not being able to take my eyes off a band and wanting to say thank you (for making me feel so good when I could feel so bad) was when I saw the Band at the Albert Hall five years ago."

When we left the Big Apple, we returned to Missouri. But only for a cup of coffee. Wheels for the follow-up to *It'll Shine* were already in motion. A&M was anxious to have another record ready to release on the heels of Jackie's success. We were anxious to spend time with our families. They were gung ho. We wanted to go home.

We all went to Nashville.

CHAPTER 18

After a brief stop at home, we found ourselves heading to Nashville and into Norbert Putnam's Quadraphonic Studios. Quad was chosen for two reasons:

1) We'd be closer to home than we would if we went to L.A. This would allow us to get back and forth to Springfield easier.

2) A&M, having just learned something about country singles, wanted to establish more of a presence in town.

We'd been traveling around the country quite a bit. Each city we visited, we were met by the local A&M field rep, who wined us, dined us, and took us to the radio stations that were playing our records. Oddly enough, Nashville was not one of those cities.

They had the Flying Burrito Brothers on their label. But the Burritos preferred their California style to Nashville's slick approach. We'd just had a song on the country charts with "You Made it Right," which couldn't be labeled "country rock," or "country this," or "country that." It was flat-out country music, and we meant it to be that way.

We made "Jackie Blue" sound the way it did on purpose, too. Neither song was compromised to the homogenization the industry's "formula thinking" is based on. Our rock 'n' roll songs sounded like rock 'n' roll songs. Our country songs sounded like country songs. Period.

This lit a little light bulb over A&M's head. Other than Hoyt and the Burritos, they didn't really have many artists on their roster doing anything that even remotely resembled country music—except us. And our last hit was "Jackie Blue." I know, I know, confusing! You're surprised?

When we stepped into Quad, we knew this record was going to be different—for two reasons: 1) It'd be the first time Glyn would not be producing, and 2) It'd be the first time he wouldn't be engineering.

Still, we were confident with David at the helm, though he was not an engineer. When initial talks took place between him and Norbert, Norbert recommended Marty Lewis, a young, brash staff engineer who had recently moved from Detroit to help Putnam record albums with Jimmy Buffett and Dan Folgelberg.

The short, stout Lewis, who dubbed himself "the Sculptor of Sound," looked like a square peg in Nashville. In a sea of cowboy hats and Western shirts, his barrel chest and Andy Capp cap stuck out like a sore chin. When he opened his mouth, his thick Detroit accent informed everyone within earshot that he wasn't from around "theeese heeere parrrts."

His Yankee engineering sensibilities resembled Bob Seger more than they did Pete Seeger. There was no doubt about it. We were going to have a different sound—a bigger sound. The team was in place; a producer from L.A., an engineer from Detroit, and a band from Springfield.

Quad Studios sits at 319 Woodland St., smack dab in the middle of Nashville's famed Music Row. As was the case with many of Nashville's studios, Quad was housed in an actual house. The large two-story dwelling had been converted into a studio, which utilized every square inch of it. Norbert's offices occupied the bedrooms on the second floor. The studio occupied the entire downstairs. The mixing console occupied the front porch, which had been boarded up, rocked up, and finished off.

As Larry set up his drums in the spacious living room, Buddy played the grand piano in the dining room. Randy put his amp in one of the empty fireplaces. I plugged into the board—and sat on the porch.

When we assembled, not only was our production team different, so was the band. Bill Jones, who always had a welcome mat into the mix, but was not included on the first two albums, was asked to come along.

Bill, a childhood friend of Larry's, always raised our level of musicianship every time he joined in. Now, with the added influx of royalties and the flexibility a hit record allows, we were able to have him join us in Nashville. When we asked if we could incur the added expense, David didn't mind. Amenities come easily to those who are having success.

As the recording started, we hit the studio as a seven-piece band. As the recording started, David came to town with a subtle agenda from the record company. Though he didn't constantly bang us over the head with it, it was a factor that would soon prominently figure in. Let's just call it a strong suggestion—a suggestion that would shape the sound of our next two records.

We'd just had a hit single with a pop song—and Larry sang it. A&M had looked through the rest of the album for more of him, but did not find it. This new record was to have more of Larry's voice on it. David was to make this happen.

This was only natural. They were in the business of selling records. We couldn't blame them for wanting to make their job easier. They did a great job with "Jackie Blue." But "Jackie Green" we did not have. They got the Quacky Ducks.

In keeping with tradition, David started the sessions with a couple of tunes we knew well—"Leatherwood" and "Keep on Churnin.'" Then, after a couple of days, for the first time, we were faced with the dilemma of what to record next. Once again, my suggestion of looking into the song cupboard went unheeded.

Our recent touring schedule had become quite restrictive for a rehearsal schedule. We were confident we could come up with enough songs for a record. We just hadn't worked them out as a band. The last thing in the world we wanted to do when we came home from road trips was get together and rehearse. So we didn't.

When we went in to make our first two records, before we even stepped foot into the studio, we knew what songs we were going to do. This time, we went in with rough ideas. Glyn had the luxury of having pick of the prime material in our virgin catalogue. He chose wisely. Now *we* had to choose wisely from what remained.

With monetary constraints no longer an issue, when royalties from Jackie started to become available, studio time was not an issue. Instead of working up a definite number of songs, we decided to just start going to Nashville and recording things.

We set up camp—in two-week blocks—at Quad. We also set up camp three blocks away at the Holiday Inn on West End Avenue. It was a well-beaten path between the two doors—one we didn't veer far from. We remained holed up in the studio, not really socializing around Nashville. Nashville, in turn, didn't come knocking on our door.

As the recording progressed, instead of sitting down with a band, David found himself sitting down with a group of songwriters—each with individual ideas. Tracks were worked up on the spot. Others were pieced together. Unfortunately, because of this, some of our cool older songs remained property of Mother Hubbard.

Randy describes the scene: "We went into our Buffalo Springfield phase. We started breaking down and printing tracks with nothing on them because people didn't have parts worked up. Close to half of it, I'd say, we hadn't rehearsed. We didn't really know the stuff, and it wasn't a full band deal. There were a lot of times when not everyone was playing.

"I think it happens to a lot of people. They work up so many songs. Then, if they have some success and go on tour, they're tired and burnt out. They don't want to go home and rehearse. Their second, third, and fourth albums are material that they haven't worked up together. This makes things take on a different character.

"Sometimes, that's a good thing. In most cases, it's not. That record [this record] is very disjointed. None of it made sense—not even the cover. Everything was up in the air."

"There were some cool songs and I loved playing them," Larry adds. "There was some interesting music being made. But I don't remember it being as creative. I remember a lot of experimentation and 'How weird can we make this?' going on. I loved a lot of the stuff we were trying to do. Whether we accomplished it or not ... at least we were trying."

When Marty began hitting the red button, song after song after song got laid down in one form or another. Though we had enough material, we still continued to cut tracks—just because it was fun. We gladly would've been content to continue down this road. But when David got what he wanted, he steered us into overdubs.

Once again, we had recorded a few extra songs—quite a few extra songs. Buddy and I both utilized his honky-tonk piano style, recording his "Dreams" and my "Plainity."

Once again, we recorded a couple of Steve's funny songs, "Dollar's Worth of Regular" and "Hannibal's Crossing the Alps." Though none of these tunes would make it onto the album, we were afforded ample time to finish them properly.

Then it was Bill time. His presence could immediately be felt. When the album opened with "Keep on Churnin,'" the listener heard a chugging baritone sax instead of a chugging harmonica.

The next song, Larry's "If I Only Knew," was being groomed as the follow-up single to Jackie. It contained a horn arrangement, complete with orchestra bells and a flute solo.

If you'd played these first two songs for a blindfolded veteran Springfield music fan, they would swear they were the first two cuts off a Granny's Bathwater album. Our sound sure was different.

All of this took time, as Bill meticulously made sure every note was right where he wanted. This was not a problem. We had time. We were also having fun listening to him build these tracks. His intricate string arrangement helped Randy's "Whippoorwill" crescendo. His classical harpsichord etude was spliced onto the beginning of Larry's "Mr. Powell"—a song that also sported a VERY intricate vocal arrangement.

This was a new approach for us. This was the first time we had sung harmonies, one voice at a time. Bill had been given permission to write out the parts, which he scribbled onto score paper. This seemed funny, due to the fact that none of the rest of us could even read music. Taking us into the studio, one guy at a time, he utilized the timbre of each of our voices, taught us our part, and directed us through it. Marty hit the red button for each one of us.

The final result was an astounding sound that complimented each song quite well. You can literally hear "Mr. Powell" rowing down the mighty Colorado. We marveled at these cool Beach Boys ensembles.

Bill heard all of that stuff in his head. The public scratched theirs.

Also, for the first time, instead of figuring out our own parts, outside musicians were brought in. Several of Norbert's Nashville Cat friends were hired to sweeten up some of the tracks. Weldon Myrick placed a weeping pedal steel guitar track on John's "Out on the Sea." Nancy Blake played cello on Steve's "Cobblestone Mountain." I was enthralled with these musicians, their approach, and their professionalism.

We became quite comfortable at Quad. We also became quite comfortable at the Holiday Inn. Our schedule was pretty consistent. Breakfast at the Loveless Cafe was followed by a morning of music. Lunch at the Elliston St. Soda Shoppe was followed by an afternoon's worth of music. Spirited dinner breaks broke into spirited evening sessions.

As the royalties began to come in, round-trip plane tickets between Springfield and Nashville were purchased by the dozens. If we ever needed—or just wanted—to go home for a day, we jumped on a plane. Many of these tickets were used by our wives, who didn't want to stay at home alone. There were no crops depending on them. They wanted in on some of this big-city action too. The money was coming in and they were happy to help us spend it.

During the day, while we worked, they shopped. When we broke for dinner, we all met at Viscaya or Julian's on West End Avenue. The staffs from both of these fine restaurants got to know us quite well. They also got to know our reputation, the amount of our tabs, and the company credit card we flashed.

When they saw us coming, wine lists were produced as soon as we walked in the door. Nice bottles were ordered up, and downed, followed by another round. All were accompanied by long meals, capped off with coffee and cognac.

At times, our consumption at dinner turned the evening session into a sloppy, unproductive mess. Some were blown off altogether. When the girls were in town, the party raged. When the girls left town, the party continued.

Stanley had bought us a nice portable Sony tape recorder, to be used by anyone who needed to lay down a rough song idea. We used it a lot, as it bounced from hotel room to hotel room. Many ideas were hummed into it. One night, the Soldier of Talent sang into it.

The Night of the Soldier began with a very, very, VERY spirited dinner. Afterward, when John and Larry headed back to the studio with David and Marty, Steve, Randy, Rusty, and I, not wanting to hang around and have to concentrate on things, headed to the Holiday Inn.

Here we continued to drink beer and write songs that made us laugh so hard, we fumbled and stumbled for the tape recorder. As we congregated in Rusty's room, we assembled around the microphone to record the "Soldier of Talent"—our cynical observances of Music City.

I played Randy's acoustic guitar. Randy played harp. Steve operated the "record" knob on the recorder. Rusty, who had just come to town to hang around, kept the libations flowing. When we started to play, we started to laugh. When we started to record, we laughed even harder. Completely unable to stifle any kind of laughter, we didn't even try. The Soldier sang:

> We are living in Nashville, writing all those groovy tunes
> It is a guerrilla party. It won't be over 'til June
> I am the Soldier of Talent. Meet me on the avenue.
> I will sing you some songs and tell you what is wrong with you.
> Soldier. Soldier. Soldier. Do it again.

The Soldier was followed by "Hello, Rustler":

> Hello, Rustler in my brain.
> Ego hustler with no name.
> You stole the cattle of my mind.
> Now, my Herefords I cannot find.
> Oooooooooooh.

The long night ended when "Invisible Ortega" claimed:

> Why, oh why, am I so invisible?
> Any day I could be miserable.
> Invisible Ortega is my name.
> I take my chances with the cance.
> I'm so happy, it's bumming me out.

We could barely get through any of these songs without the clang of toppling beer bottles. But get through them we did—cackles and all. The tape kept a-rollin' all night long. Crickets and thunder were replaced with farts and belches.

Usually, drunken, late-night tapes are not nearly as funny the next morning. This one was. When we got up and listened back to what we had recorded, the hilarity picked right back up where it had left off. When we played the tape in the studio, those who weren't at the guerilla party laughed as hard as those who were.

One of those laughing was John Sebastian, who was utilizing a quiet morning to stop by, pay Norbert a visit, and check out the place. Those of us who weren't working in the studio sat on the sunny deck, drinking coffee and strumming guitars. The actual author of "Nashville Cats" took his place at the table. When he stuck his head into the control room, he heard our slick material. When he sat down on the deck, he heard the Soldier of Talent.

The only other celebrity sighting came as we worked late into the night one night. Norbert had installed a security system, with a camera that looked directly down on the front door. A television monitor above the recording console allowed those in the control room to be able to see who was knocking at the door, without having to stop working.

That evening, when the doorbell rang, the studio monitor revealed nothing but the top of three gigantic cowboy hats—faces completely hidden. Knowing there were other Ducks in the foyer, we stayed at the board. When the door opened on the monitor, we saw the three hats walk in. They were followed by two more hats, which were followed by a whole slew of them. We had no idea who was under the hats. We saw not one face.

If the sight of a hat parade marching in the door wasn't funny enough, the sight of it parading right back out two minutes later was. We were informed that it was Charlie Daniels and his band, looking for a "kick-ass" Southern rock party. When all they found was a couple of guys sitting around, watching television (and not kicking any ass), they bored quickly and left. Those of us in the control room still never saw one face. They had nice hats, though.

After a couple of months in Nashville, the recording was done, and we headed back out to Sunset Sound to mix everything. Instead of checking into the Tropicana, we were able to afford residence at the Chateau Marmont. The quiet of the Chateau was much more to our liking.

It took us quite a while to mix all of the songs, but we decided to stay until everything was finished—even the extra songs. While Marty mixed away, we visited Roland Young to discuss the artwork. We'd brought a poster with us from a gig we'd just done at the Red Dog Saloon in Lawrence, Kansas. It had caught our eye as we strolled back from a quiet dinner in a quiet restaurant. When we walked past the window of the local record store, we were stopped in our tracks.

The hilarious picture of three people, cut out and hastily pasted into the seats of a '57 Oldsmobile as it inexplicably flew through the sky over a quiet lake, was just that—hilarious. The people hadn't been pasted in with any finesse—or attempt at any. The guy in the back seat had his head sticking completely out of the window at a goofy angle.

Lawrence artist Murv Jacob was not trying to fool anybody. It was meant to be funny—and it was. Before we left Lawrence, we made sure we took one of those posters. When we flew to Los Angeles, we made sure we took it with us.

When Roland saw the picture, he chuckled with his best, "I guess you had to be there." When he asked if we had a title, our response was, "Well ... it is a picture of a car going over a lake. How about *Car Over the Lake Album?*" At this point, we were calling the shots. The *Car Over the Lake Album* was released to cool reviews.

Though we thought the cover was funny, the music inside did not reflect its humor. At the record company's suggestion, Larry's voice was to be more prevalent. At the record company's suggestion, the overall sound was to be steered in the direction of the smoother Jackie, instead of that "country stuff."

Though each song was done well, none of them really related to each other. Nor was there a cohesive thread woven through them. The album was a long string of individual songs.

The thing that bothered me the most, once again, was the fact that there wasn't one laugh on the entire record. This didn't bother those of us content with making melodramatic masterpiece after melodramatic masterpiece. The Soldier of Talent joined Perry Allen on the sidelines. Both remained AWOL. This bothered me—A LOT.

A picture of us on the inner sleeve, making Junior Airmen goggles with our hands, was another attempt at humor. The most important element—the music—had none. The crunchy outside had a marshmallow filling.

It Shined

Because of this, when talk arose of inserting a thin, flimsy disc into the album jacket that would include "Time Warp" and "Journey to the Center of Your Heart," I was the biggest cheerleader. The Little Red Record was born. At last—a hint at some kind of humor. The idea came from the least likely source.

Stan recalls, "The Little Red Record. That was [son] Joey's idea. He said, 'Dad, they ought to make a little red record.' He was really into comic books and had been writing to this company he'd seen in the back pages for samples of these thin, flimsy records. He kept typing them letters, until one day they called and said, 'Joey Plesser. Is he an adult?' My mom—Joey's grandmother—answered the phone and said, 'Um, I don't know. I'm just a guest here,' because she didn't want to give him away. He knew about this company that made these little floppy records you could get in any color. He loved this kind of shit. I thought, 'Joey. This is great. You just solved the problem.'"

David, trying to convince the powers that be at A&M that this little red record was not such a stupid idea, wrote them the following memo. It made it into his bosses' hands. Then it made it onto the back side of the record itself.

It reads:

September 12, 1975
TO: Jerry Moss, Gil Friessen, Kip Cohen, Jeff Ayerhoff
FROM: David Anderle
RE: "Ozark Mountain Daredevil" E.P. Insert—"Establish Yourself," "Journey to the Center of Your Heart," "Time Warp."

"I am going to try to explain, as fully as possible, why the inclusion of the three song EP in the forthcoming OMD album is absolutely imperative. The Daredevils, to a man, voiced the desire to include the above mentioned songs as part of their new album. To do this meant excluding two or three songs presently on the album. I fought this idea primarily because the flow and feel of the new material did not, in my estimation, meld evenly with the older tunes. The band stated quite frankly that to exclude the humor inherent in these songs was to avoid the essence of who they are, i.e. the Ozark Mountain Daredevils. Now, they know as well as anyone that not everybody is going to respond positively to this type of rural humor. They also know that a great many people will.

They know this because they have seen it work. I, myself have seen it work. First, in Kansas City when I first saw them and again in St. Louis. I personally responded greatly to this type of humor. It is no different really from the humor of Brian Wilson, Frank Zappa, Kris Kristofferson, or Leon Russell. I mention these people because I have worked with them closely over the years. All have one thing in common—a sense of humor. If you negate this humor and look merely to the music, as you want it to be, then you are missing the point of who these people are. You cannot judge 'Time Warp' and 'Journey to the Center of Your Heart' on purely musical terms. It is rural satire. People looking at themselves and laughing. Looking at their parents, their peers, their leaders and teachers. You may want these people to be the Beach Boys, the Allman Brothers, or whomever else. They are not. They are the Ozark Mountain Daredevils. Their people are from there. They have as much trouble understanding you as you apparently do them. But here is the difference; they are willing to listen to reason and adjust. They understand that this humor may be lost in L.A., New York, Detroit, Chicago. Therefore, why not make it easy. Deal with the humor separately. If you don't dig it, throw the EP away, roll it up and smoke it, send it to someone you hate. If, on the other hand, you dig it, then play it. Believe it or not, I have met people who love 'Journey' and hate 'Jackie Blue.' Kids from Kansas, Missouri, Arkansas and Tennessee have gotten me backstage and on the farm in Missouri and asked me why we won't let the band do their real music instead of all the 'stuff everybody else does.' The type of humor found in these songs is directly related to the life styles of the people who wrote them. You cannot take only what you want from these people while rejecting what they must give. I can control the flow, but only as long as everyone is willing to be sensitive to one another's needs and desires. It is never just black and white when you deal with people and their music. We have to respond to one another, creatively. That is, unless you are willing to look at someone and tell them that you know better than they do what all the people want and need, and not only that, but that you think that that person's sense of humor also stinks. If you can do that, then you can also come up with all the cliché reasons why the EP idea won't work, instead of trying to figure out how to make it work. Anything we do at this point is an investment in the future with these people.

"If I am being naive, then let me know. It there is some reason why the EP idea is totally out of the question, other that a reason based on musical judgment, let me know. I am willing to learn. All I know for sure in this situation is that this group is named the Ozark Mountain Daredevils. It is no accident that these six people call themselves that.

D."

In the end, David's efforts did produce, though begrudgingly, the insertion of "The Little Red Record" into the *Car Over the Lake Album*. Plesser observes, "But Gil would only allow the Little Red Record in the first pressing that went out to the promotional people and the radio stations. It never really made it out to the public. The public never got the Little Red Record. There was only a couple thousand of them."

A&M relented, but only to a certain point. Some of the people at the label were enjoying our little art projects. Others weren't. To them, we became a case of chiggers. They hated chiggers almost as much as they hated ticks. The chasm formed.

For every hoop we asked them to jump through, they asked us to jump through one in return. When we asked them to do this or that, they agreed. When they asked us to work more, we balked. The chasm widened.

Then, when offered the hoop of a lifetime, we decided not to jump through it.

Jerry, knowing he had the quintessential American band (and two hit records) under his arm, asked us to relocate to Los Angeles. This way, we would be more readily available to Johnny, Merv, Cher, the Smothers Brothers, David Frost, Dick Cavett, and their TV shows.

We didn't think about it hard—or long. Our answer was a collective "Thanks, but no thanks." I didn't want to uproot my family. I liked it where I was. Missouri was where I wanted my kids to grow up—not Los Angeles.

Life was good where we were. The checks were rolling in. The creek was rolling by. Jerry's hoop was taken off the table. He was in the business of building careers in the entertainment industry. We wanted to build log cabins in the woods.

At this point, his time, his attention, and his money was diverted to another band who was willing to jump through the hoops—the Police. They were everywhere. You saw them.

Though showing the first signs of strain, our relationship with Jerry was still a nice one. He understood why we weren't moving. He respected our decision. He also realized that if this was what it was going to take, we weren't willing to do it. The *Car Over the Lake Album* would not get the same attention the first two records got. The chasm widened.

The album was released to mixed reviews.

The *New Musical Express* had praised *It'll Shine* with "The Daredevils sing real songs with lyrics stripped to the bone, always with a point and an atmosphere. These Feds have got the edge over all their Southern counterparts when it comes to melody, arrangements and downright taste."

They panned *Car* with "The trouble with *The Car Over the Lake Album* is complacency—and it's right there in the title. All the Ozarks can provide is a handful of nice songs. There are only a couple of tracks that are worth a third listen. I put off reviewing this as long as possible, as I couldn't think of anything to say about it. It's not that *The Car Over the Lake Album* is a bad LP, it's just not a very good one."

High Times loved it, calling us "the world's first heavy metal jug band."

Car would eventually climb onto the charts, but only stay for a couple of months, reaching #57. "If I Only Knew" was released as a single, but only hit #65.

As *Car* was released, we packed our bags and headed to Great Britain, where *It'll Shine* was still jumping. Here, we stepped off the plane and onto the train. All aboard!

CHAPTER 19

It was late August when we left the sweltering Ozarks for the British Isles. After spending most of the spring and summer in Nashville, it was time to hit the road and begin playing "live" again. The fall of 1975 began with a ten-day trek through England and Scotland, beginning with a slot on the Fifteenth Annual Reading Rock Festival.

Upon landing at Gatwick Airport, we moved into Emerson, Lake, and Palmer's Manticore Theater for a couple of days of rehearsal. Here, we not only acclimated ourselves to the British time zone, Patrick, Larry, and Maple acclimated themselves to our British sound crew.

ELP, which had bought the old, ornate theater to prepare their elaborate stage shows, agreed to vacate the premises for a few days. We came in and set up. Though the stage was empty, their massive amount of equipment was piled everywhere—in every aisle, in every hallway, on every balcony. It was impressive to see Keith Emerson's flying piano, stuck off into the corner. We had to laugh when we noticed that his organ rig was as large as our entire stage plot.

Amid the Reading Festival's weekend bill of Yes, Supertramp, Lou Reed, Richard and Linda Thompson, Robin Trower, Wishbone Ash, and the Mahavishnu Orchestra, not only were we one of the newer acts, we were definitely the smallest.

This became quickly evident when we were informed that we were to set our stuff up directly in front of Yes—who were in the process of constructing an entire fantasy world onstage. Complete with cloudlike fiberglass structures filled with interior pastel lighting, massive backdrops, and elaborate risers, it was impressive.

As we played, Supertramp was setting up their own little world on the far half of the stage. This was the first time I'd seen this half-and-half approach to staging. When one band finished, all the crowd had to do was shift their attention fifty feet to the right (or left), where the next band was set up and ready to go. It was a great idea. The music was nonstop. Unfortunately, so was the rain.

As we walked onstage, the drizzle continued. As we played, Yes's crew continued to work behind us. Standing in front of Yes City, we opened with "Absolute Zero." The English sound man, more accustomed to bombastic openings, was startled and confused by the little sound we were making with our kazoos.

It took him most of our first song to figure out what was going on, and where that farting oboe sound was coming from.

It took the muddied audience most of our first song to figure out that we had even started playing. The song received no reaction, but for a smattering of applause from a few people up front.

On a crummy, rainy day, our first show on the British Isles was literally a wash. Once again, we experienced our inability to bloat our little sound onto a giant stage—a trait that will also take its toll at the Canada Jam in Toronto in front of 300,000 people and the Southern Jam in Charlotte, North Carolina in front of 400,000.

We hit our stride and played well, but never reached the level of intensity—or decibels—it took to cut through the pouring rain.

We did reach one guy, though, who waited until we went into "E.E. Lawson" to stand up in the middle of the crowd and do a manic little dance. Wearing a leather aviator's helmet, goggles, and a cape, with "E.E. Lawson" scribbled across his shirt, his devilish grin and funny routines amused us greatly.

When we finished to a less-than-rousing reception, we huddled off the stage to a dry dressing room. Here we were briefly introduced to the Supertramp guys, who were on their way out to the stage. With A&M's

staff fawning all over their hottest new group of English rockers, they had just released their *Crisis? What Crisis?* album.

Though we were label mates, there wasn't much time for chitchat. They were British rockers with spiffy clothes and entourages. We were the scruffy Americans in flannel shirts and work boots. They squired secretaries on their arms. We held our kids in ours.

When they hit the stage, they sucked all of the air, as well as all the people, out of the dressing room. We strolled out to see their show, but only stayed for a couple of songs. We saw the flashy opening, but were not really interested in hanging around in the rain to hear them.

As we left the site, the cold drizzle that had been coming down all day intensified. So did the hammering on Yes City. We had dinner in a warm, dry restaurant on our minds.

The next morning, we met our train at the station. Here we also met Andy Fairweather Low, who was promoting his latest A&M album, *La Booga Rooga*. Not only had Glyn produced his record, Low brought along an all-star band that included Fairport drummer Dave Mattacks, bassist John David, pedal steel wizard B.J. Cole, and Who keyboardist Rabbit. When the train left the station, we all swung on behind.

A&M had leased a private coach that would easily accommodate both of their acts. Each morning, the car would be hooked onto the appropriate train, headed to the appropriate town. Each morning, instead of herding us through airport concourses, Maple guided our scraggly circus through the busy streets, into the bustling train station, and onto our quiet coach.

Our reliable A&M staff member hooked up both bands with large chunks of hash, which started getting consumed immediately. Along with a well-stocked bar, every day was a party that rolled through the English countryside. Merrily, merrily, merrily, merrily, life is but a dream.

The sight of stone walls covered with green moss, flocks of sheep, fields of clover, and ancient castles floated by our windows. Because train tracks do not have to adhere to road maps, we really enjoyed veering off the beaten path—no traffic, no billboards, no stop signs, no litter. It is a great way to see the British Isles. It helped that the daily treks were filled with card games, adult and children sing-a-longs, smoking, joking, and trucking.

From London, we headed north to Liverpool, Leeds, Newcastle, Birmingham, Edinburgh, and Glasgow, before finishing with a gig at the Hammersmith Odeon and a few days of sightseeing and souvenir shopping. Every night was a blast, as we played small theaters that were much more to our liking than the giant festivals. Not only did every theater sound great, large amounts of very knowledgeable fans showed up.

Maple would recall, "The thing that got me was all these people were coming to the gigs—and we were a long, long way from home."

Everywhere we went, the reviews were glowing, many commenting about how much fun we seemed to be having and how "at home" we appeared on stage. How could we not be having fun? How could we not feel at home? We were playing a long string of Landers Theaters.

The party was nonstop—in the theater by night, on the train by day. Old theaters and train stations are a wonderful way to see the soul of a city. We've already discussed how much I hate airplanes. I LOVED that train.

As the fortnight passed and we returned to London, it was time to souvenir shop. I took the last hundred-dollar bill from my wallet and hit the streets. As I approached the sidewalk exchange kiosk, the glassed-in Pakistani teller was on the phone. With the receiver nestled into the crook of his neck, he was yelling and screaming at someone in his native tongue.

Strewn all about his disheveled counter were piles of papers, receipts, empty fish-and-chip boxes, half-empty bottles of soda pop, overflowing ashtrays, open money drawers, and complete disorganization.

He waved me up to the window and took my C-note. Continuing to smoke, wave his hands, and scream into the phone, he began to count out my exchange. I could tell something was wrong. I relate well to numbers. The day's exchange rate would have garnered maybe forty or fifty pounds. But as he began to count, he laid down "20—40—60—80—100—120—125—126."

I could tell he had mistaken my bill for some other kind of currency. As he handed me close to 250 dollars worth of cash, my mind quickly debated whether or not to bring it to his attention. My mind was made up for me, when I couldn't even get his attention—due to his incessant screaming. I didn't try a second time, calmly taking the money, folding it, putting it into my pocket, turning away, turning the corner, and blending into the London landscape.

After buying some very nice souvenirs, I found a department store, where I procured two large greeting cards. Then it was a beeline to the A&M offices, where I procured an ounce of hash. After flattening it into thin sheets, sticking it into the greeting cards, sealing the cards tightly, and smothering them in cologne, I headed to the post office. Postmark—the Nixa Trout Farm.

After several more days in London, we headed home. When I walked through the screen door and into my house, the first thing I asked was if the cards had made it. Karen's reply of, "Yeah, it came today," puzzled me. *It* was supposed to be *they*.

The next morning, I, anxiously watched for the mailman. When I rushed out to open the mailbox, it smelled like a Turkish factory. The cologne had worn off. But both cards made it fine. We had a nice, lovely stash—an exotic treat—which we liberally shared with our friends.

The rest of the autumn was spent flying around the heartland, headlining every Sioux Falls, Cedar Falls, Cedar Rapids, and Rapid City big enough to have a civic center, college gym, or rodeo arena. Of course, these venues didn't sound nearly as good as the theaters we had just played in Britain. But they were larger and we were a hot ticket—which we sold lots of.

We hired Carlo Sound out of Nashville to provide the sound system, which they did, magnificently. Rich Carpenter and John Logan joined the entourage, driving their big truck alongside our big truck. Dipping back into the Kansas City gene pool, we hired Danny Mayo and his Cowtown Lights. When he climbed into the cab with Patrick and Larry, we had a road crew of three. When he hired Rick Redford as his assistant, they grew to four—all in one big, happy, green truck.

Though we headlined most shows, we did continue to hook up with other national acts, sharing numerous bills with the Allman Brothers, Marshall Tucker, Charlie Daniels, and Lynyrd Skynyrd. This, consequently, lumped us into the Southern rock genre—one we felt awkward with.

We were never comfortable with that label, as we never considered what we played to be Southern rock in the first place. We played rock 'n' roll songs. But only a couple of them remotely resembled Southern rock. Plus, we were never quite macho enough to fit in and hang out with these guys. We didn't wear big belt buckles, big hats, or big fu manchus. When these guys played, they all invited each other on stage for long, drawn-out jams. Invitations never came our way. We didn't mind. We didn't find many of their whiskeyed meanderings to be very interesting anyway.

While we played our sets, they threw their arms around each other and stomped off, past their bikes, to their dressing rooms. When they played, we would leave.

We also began to play shows with country artists, which we enjoyed very much. We found the backstage atmospheres to be much friendlier, much less macho, and much more to our liking. When we asked Skynyrd or the Doobies if we could move one of their amps a few feet, so we could set up one of ours, we were chided with, "Don't touch anything." When we asked the country guys if we could move a piece of their gear, they said, "Sure. Let me help you with that."

After all, we'd just had a song on the country charts. Some of these country music fans seemed to know who we were. They may not have been familiar with "Jackie Blue," but they knew "You Made It Right." When we played "You Made It Right," they danced. When we played "Jackie," they scratched their heads.

We played basically the same set list for both country and rock audiences, only having to substitute a song or two, to put an entirely different slant onto the show. The crowds loved it.

We hooked up for gigs with Waylon Jennings, Willie Nelson, Johnny Paycheck, Merle Haggard, John Prine, Johnathan Edwards, Rusty Weir, and Asleep at the Wheel. We also continued to get invited to bluegrass festivals. Here, we tailored our set even more. This was no problem. We enjoyed the flexibility this crazy music was giving us.

I was—and still am—proud of the fact that, one night, we could blast away with the Allman Brothers on a huge outdoor festival stage, and the next night play with Earl Scruggs on a flatbed trailer in the middle of a field. This approach may have been confusing to some. We found it to be interesting.

We found some of the odder bookings to be even more entertaining. Maple recalls one of the more bizarre: "I remember the outdoor gig we were on the bill with Chubby Checker and Tiny Tim. That was the gig where we knew we weren't going to get paid. It was a big festival and we said, 'We're here. Our fans are here.' It was raining and we decided to go ahead and play for our fans, who were sitting in the rain. Tiny Tim left. But if Chubby Checker was going to play, that would really make us look bad."

We twisted the night away.

As the venues got bigger, so did the band. Bill started playing on an everyday basis and Steve Canaday became the opening act. Canway, who had just quietly returned to Springfield, had begun coming out to the Trout Farm to join back in musically.

Before the burning of the Bijou, we had worked up several of his songs. When he returned, he had several more in his briefcase. We all liked his songs, including Stan, who helped him procure a publishing deal with Warner Brothers. When he pitched "Fair Play" to Mike and Tom, they included it on *ST-11261*, their inaugural album for Capitol.

When Canway went into American Artists to make his demos, we were his backing band. Bunge engineered the sessions. It was old home week—a perfect fit—like a favorite, well-worn sweater.

When we would head for a string of gigs, Stan would convince promoters that, for a few hundred extra bucks, they could book this hot new songwriter by the name of Steve Canaday. Canaday, with his recent cut on the new Brewer & Shipley album, would open the show. His band, unbeknownst to the promoter, was us.

This was fine with everyone in our camp. Plus, he was already a licensed pilot, easily jumping into the plane—sometimes taking the wheel. All Patrick had to do was set up another amp. When the evening began, Steve was introduced and we unceremoniously became our own opening act.

When he finished his set, we would take a little break and come blazing back out with "Chicken Train." Some noticed. But no one minded. His amp remained plugged in, and he was also given the green light to be a Duck.

He also played drums, which gave Larry the mobility to move out front to the piano—where the audience could see him. A&M loved this idea. Buddy would slide over to the Fender Rhodes, which gave Larry's songs the extra fullness they had on record. Canway became a valuable utility player.

Still having some "nightclub guy" in his blood, he began booking small gigs around Springfield as Steve Canaday & the South Side Boys. Larry, Buddy, Randy, and I became the South Side Boys. We all lived on the south side of town, which made it easy to get together and rehearse Steve's stuff at the Trout Farm.

We knew we would have to play under this alias, as any mention of the words *Ozark*, *Mountain*, or *Daredevil* would've created enough chaos to ruin everything. Our close friends knew who the South Side Boys were. They knew what was going on. They knew they weren't going to hear "Chicken Train." Everyone wanted to remain under the radar. Everyone did.

Steve's unique brand of funky, filled the club with funky people, happy to be hearing music that reminded them of the sorely missed Bijou. We worked up a couple of sets of his songs, including "Fair Play," "Lost Cabin," "Back Roads" and "Horsetrader"—all of which would find their way into Ozark song lists.

The year ended with a new album on the shelves and a string of gigs down the West Coast. Starting in Vancouver, we made our way south through Victoria, Seattle, Portland, and Eugene before a night at San Francisco's Great American Music Hall and three nights at the Roxy in Hollywood.

The entire Pacific Northwest embraced us warmly. We embraced them right back. Our stay in Vancouver was wonderful and a much nicer encounter than the last time we stepped foot onto Canadian soil. Remember Cin-A-Rock? We had the same herbal good time in Seattle, Portland, and Eugene that we were used to having at home.

The *San Francisco Examiner* called us "Mad, Mod Country Music," noting that we "play a very tight ensemble style, but seem to retain their sense of humor. They understand, collectively, the value of occasional solos, but still have as powerful a group sound as any around. They are as complete a musical ensemble (a sextet, plus one) and certainly as entertaining a band as you're likely to encounter anywhere around. They swap instruments around so much that, sometimes bassist Supe Granda plays both bass and drums."

Bass AND drums? Let me explain. This was a little trick I'd begun several years before—when Canway wasn't around. When Larry stood up and walked out front to pick up an acoustic guitar to play "Homemade Wine," "Standing on the Rock" or "Beauty in the River," I walked two feet over to his drums and sat down—with my bass in my lap.

As I played my bass with my hands, I had no trouble keeping time on the bass drum and high hat with my feet. It was simple. I didn't even pick up a stick. I had no trouble playing, singing, and boom-chuck, boom-chuck, boom-chucking at the same time.

Things were boom-chucking along nicely. We were playing really well and being treated like kings in these great northwestern cities. The morning after playing the Great American Music Hall, Maple and I went shopping.

We got up early, hopped into a cab, and visited the Alembic musical instrument factory. Here, Maple introduced me to his friend and longtime designer of the Dead's Alembic gear, Rick Turner. We ordered a couple

Left to right: Bill Jones, Randy, Steve, Buddy, Larry, John, and me on bass and drums (photo by Jim Mayfield)

of large "B-15" bass bins with heavy-duty, JBL speakers in them—Phil Lesh models.

I had always been a big fan of Lesh's playing—especially his deep, full tone. The speaker cabinets were thrown into the truck, along with two large—green, of course—Anvil cases. Once again, Patrick and Larry didn't mind hauling them around. When they stacked them on top of each other, it made for a verrrrry solid bottom.

Then, it was on to L.A. and into the Roxy—Hollywood's newest, now-est club on Sunset Strip. The Whiskey's heyday may have been in the '60s. The Roxy's heyday was RIGHT NOW—and we were booked for three nights.

All three nights were sell outs, as the backstage area became an absolute zoo of Hollywood schmoozers, boozers, and scene-makers. Mike and Tom opened the show each night, while courting people from their new record company (Capitol). We were hosting our A&M friends. There were cameras filming and radio stations broadcasting live. Did I mention that the place was a zoo?

Friends began coming out of the woodwork, loaded for skunk, causing the Roxy crew to liken our stay to that of Bob Marley & the Wailers—who had played just a few nights before and whose aroma still lingered in the furniture. "You guys smoke a lot of pot," the backstage manager laughed. "But they had an entire room with a bonfire in the middle."

The last show of our last night was wacked out, for obvious reasons. It was also to be broadcast live on WHATEVER-FM radio. The Roxy was busting its buttons, like five pounds of bologna crammed into a four-pound skin. Jerry and the A&M brass sat at a prime table in the back of the room with Stan. As the place danced in the aisles, the brass sat with a watchful eye. By the time we got to the encore, everyone in the place was bonkers.

When we came back onstage for the encore, Steve decided to lead everyone in a Coughing Dogs' version of his poem, "Fifteen Chihuahuas." We had been laughing at the silly little four-line verse for days. Tonight, the Coughing Chihuahuas blasted out, over the late-night L.A. airwaves. Unfortunately, inside the Roxy, it went over like a lead balloon.

Steve sang, "I saw fifteen Chihuahuas in my kitchen," as we echoed, "Divine. Divine. Divine." When he finished with a final chorus, "But that don't matter. Meet me in Bangkok with a sandwich," a confused audience didn't quite know what to do. Jerry turned to Stan with a bewildered, "What the hell was that?"

Then, when we finished the evening with "Time Warp," Gil turned to Stan and asked, "Isn't this one of those songs off that stupid Little Red Record? How come they're not playing something off their new album? They're live on the radio, for Christ's sake."

And so it went. Some of our A&M brethren were amused with our antics. Others were not. Though three sold-out crowds went nuts, the brass didn't. Things were still cordial, though "Car Over the Lake" and "If I Only Knew" were not setting the woods on fire.

The Police released, *Outlandos d'Amour*.

Peter Frampton released, *Frampton Comes Alive*.

We found the back burner.

The new year brought more abundance to the Ozarks. Once again—much to A&M's chagrin—we stayed home for the winter. In Europe, though, folks were still latched onto *It'll Shine*. Though "Jackie Blue" was never a hit single over there, the album was still being listened to.

In the spring of 1976, we headed back over the big pond. This time, we took a larger entourage of roadies, engineers, managers, spare drummers, saxophonists, wives, and babies.

Bill played his horns. Canaday played guitar and drums. Marty Lewis was hired to mix our bigger sound—the same sound he was already familiar with from recording *Car Over the Lake Album*. We figured that, even though he had to deal with a different mixing console in a different country every night, it would be much better than us having to deal with a different sound man in a different language every night. Marty made us sound good and big. Europe, here we came.

When we landed in England, a couple of days of rehearsal at London's Pinewood Studios preceded appearances on Mervyn Cohn's International Festival of Country Music at Empire Pool Wembley and the BBC's *Old Grey Whistle Test* at Shepherd's Bush Green.

As we gathered on one of Pinewood's smaller soundstages, we were allowed to wander freely through the grounds. Everywhere we looked, we could see the fancy gardens and movie sets from James Bond, Pink Panther, and Monty Python films. We were also able to see the Stones' unfolding lotus stage, being built in one of the larger hangars.

It Shined

When we headed back into London for Mervyn's bash, the clamor arose. We took residence in the Hyde Park Hotel, which just happened to be headquarters for the festival's formal lunches, formal dinners, and formal press conferences.

The pomp and circumstance was wonderfully entertaining and wonderfully British. When the forty-piece marching band—in complete Beefeater parade regalia—strutted into the ballroom, the hair on the back of my neck stood up. Marching bands are loud.

We were slated to headline the third day of the festival—an experimental third day—which was being added for the first time to the traditional two-day format. Billed as "Progressive Country Night," we shared the evening with Buffy St. Marie, John Hartford, Ricky Nelson & his Stone Canyon Band, the Dillards, and Carl Perkins.

This gave a more modern slant to the strict country lineup of the previous two nights, which included Jack Greene, Connie Smith, Wanda Jackson, Jim & Jesse, Tammy Wynette, Johnny Gimble, Dolly Parton, Red Sovine, and Marty Robbins.

When the crowd started filing in, we could not believe our eyes. It looked like Halloween. Everyone was decked out in big cowboy hats, fancy cowboy shirts, gaudy cowboy boots, scarves, fringed vests, chaps, lassos, guns, and holsters. That's right—phony guns in holsters.

Throughout the venue, vendors set up country-western stores to outfit the country-western fans, going to the country-western festival. It was country-western funny.

The spacious Wembley Pool had housed wonderful crowds, but by the time we ended the festivities on Monday evening, we were the thirty-seventh of thirty-seven acts to play. By the time we were up, the country fans were countried out.

When I heard we were to immediately follow Carl Perkins, I cringed. I had attended his showcase at the hotel the day before. I saw how apeshit the people went for him. I was one of those apeshitting people. All of this, along with the fact that we would be on another large stage, in a cavernous room, did not paint a rosy picture.

When Perkins hit the spotlight that night, the dwindling crowd went crazy—just like they did the afternoon before. After their manic rockabilly dancing, the dwindling picked up. Our set was met with a subdued reaction. We played well. But Carl had just plain tuckered everyone out. The moral of the story? Never try to follow Carl Perkins.

The next day, we peered into the BBC television cameras, recording a ten-song segment for *The Old Grey Whistle Test*—Britain's answer to *Don Kirschner's Rock Concert*.

Hours of tediousness were spent, to make sure every cord was plugged in, every knob adjusted, every light focused, and every camera positioned just right. Having worked with Glyn, we were used to this meticulous approach. This was an important show—well worth our time.

When everything was placed just right, the cameras rolled. This time, instead of a large crowd in a concert setting, a smaller crowd enjoyed plush studio seating. Though we were still nervous, it was nothing like our Kirschner appearance. We felt comfortable playing over here.

So comfortable that in the middle of a segment that included, "Walkin' Down the Road," "Homemade Wine," "Road to Glory," "You Made It Right," "Chicken Train," "Keep on Churnin'," "Standing on the Rock," "Shine," "Jackie," and "Heaven," Steve gave an oration of his poem, "The Servant's Quarters."

Then it was on to the continent, for trips into France, Germany, and Amsterdam, before a second week in the UK and a final trek through Scandinavia. With each new country, we were met at the airport by the A&M man. Our luggage was handled for us, as we were whisked to extensive press conferences, brunches, and dinners. The Europeans were intrigued.

With each new country, we were also provided with plenty of hashpitality. If our prescription ran out, it was easily refilled. If we had leftovers at the end of our stay, we figured they couldn't find it *on* us if it was *in* us. What we didn't smoke the night before, we ate on our way to the airport the next morning.

By touchdown in the next country, we were quite mellow. Once through Immigration and Customs, we were met by another A&M man with another fistful of fun. My number-one rule of international travel has always been do not … let me repeat, DO NOT EVER carry anything, at any time, through any border. That is, unless it's safely in your stomach.

France was a wash. Our sparsely attended evening gig broke out into a raging Paris discothèque as soon as we finished. When we played, we played to a hundred people. By the time we packed up our gear and left, the crowd had swelled to a thousand. As Paree went gay into the night, we went to eat a quiet meal.

Multiple days in Amsterdam found us walking along the canals, admiring the houseboats, visiting the coffee shops, and playing at the Roundchurch. Everything Paris wasn't, Amsterdam was. The slower, friendlier pace struck a chord with the Dutch in my blood, as my thoughts rang back to my dear great-grandparents—Big Mom and Pop, a stubborn old Dutchman who had come from here on the boat.

Not everyone was as enthralled with the place as I was. Unfortunately, Larry Tucker saw the other side of the Guilder. "I was traveling with the English crew in a rented van and we were leaving right after the Roundchurch gig to drive to Hamburg," he recounts. "We had all of our personal stuff in the van, which got broken into outside the church. My briefcase got stolen, which had the equipment manifest and my passport in it. We didn't notice this until we were packed up and ready to start the all-night drive to Germany. All of a sudden, I figured out that I didn't have a passport and I would have to stay in Amsterdam. I went to the police station to make a report of the robbery that night.

"Early the next morning, I went to the American Consulate. They told me it would take four or five days to get out of town, because they didn't want to issue another passport, in case my original passport showed up. Then I'd have two passports out there.

"I started in with the biggest lies I could tell. I wasn't only the equipment manager, I was the producer, I had to sign all the contracts, and they couldn't play if I didn't sign the contracts. I went back to the police station, where the officer who filed my original report the night before signed a handwritten note I'd drawn up, stating that, in his opinion, the thieves were after my money and not after my passport—which was probably already thrown in a canal somewhere.

"I stopped at a photographer, took some quick passport pictures, and headed back to the American Consulate, where I continued to talk to agent after agent. Finally, thirty minutes after the consulate had closed, I ran into the head guy, who was still in the office. I was still there too, begging him to give me a temporary passport. He finally conceded that he would issue me one the next day.

"As I walked out, I turned and said, 'Wait a minute. If you can issue me a passport tomorrow, you can issue me one right now.' His jaw dropped. He sat back down, reached in his drawer, pulled out a passport, glued my pictures in it, stamped it, and assigned me a ninety-day temporary passport. I thanked him profusely and walked out of the place. There was a cab about a half block away. I jumped in and said, 'Let's go. Get me to the airport. Here's some money.' I walked into the Fabrik, just in time for the last song of sound check. But I made it."

Hamburg found us playing near the Rapierbahn section of town. Though our jaunt into Germany was short and we didn't have much time to explore, I did take what little time there was to wander the streets of the Rapierbahn, wondering what it must have been like when the Silver Beatles hovered.

We routed our way back through Amsterdam and back into Great Britain for a short string of gigs, which included two nights in Glasgow and Edinburgh and a pilgrimage to Liverpool's Cavern Club—which had been converted into a clothing store.

We had made it completely through Customs at the airport and were about to step into our cabs, when I felt the tap on my shoulder. Then I heard the Customs agent politely say, "Come with me, please." Our entourage had been traveling for a couple of weeks, which made us even more ragged and shaggy than we normally were.

Coming in from Amsterdam raised red flags. I wasn't worried. We were clean. We were stoned. But we were clean. They wanted to see Sya. We were escorted back inside the terminal and searched. I was completely incensed. The bastards didn't even check me, but they checked to see if we smuggling drugs in my baby's diaper.

Once in the county, we hooked up with A&M's new acoustic duo, Splinter, and headed for a Friday night at Edinburgh's Usher Hall and a Saturday night at Glasgow's Apollo Theater.

Both gigs were cool, but quite different. The crowd that filled Usher Hall sat stoically, intently listening to every note and lyric before bursting into thunderous applause. The crowd at the Apollo went nuts from the very first note. They knew every lyric to every song, becoming a chorus of thousands on every chorus. It sounded heavenly. Jerry Moss had flown up for the weekend to see three encores, complete with a stage full of splinters, roadies, wives, and babies.

It Shined

Then we were off to Scandinavia, landing in Bergen, Norway. Here we would spend a couple of days eating, drinking, and being merry, before visiting the capital cities of Oslo, Stockholm, and Copenhagen.

While experiencing the beauty of Bergen's fjord-filled shoreline, we were treated like royalty by the jovial Norwegians. The fish was fresh, as the open-air markets bustled straight out of a *National Geographic* magazine. The beer flowed like wine, and let me tell you, it flowed. Because Bergen—known as the San Francisco of Norway—is not a large city, we became men about town in no time.

Here we met local country band the Flying Norwegians. We had a night off. They had a gig in town. Accepting their invitations, we walked into the small, smoky club to hear their band which, like ours, was a cool blend of acoustic and electric guitars. Plus, they did several of our songs. It was very entertaining to hear them sung with Norwegian accents.

Though everyone in the band was a fan of American music, the definite ringleader was their tall, blonde guitar player. At six feet four with long, unruly locks of hair, Rune Walle is a virtual encyclopedia of American country music. Not only did he know every song on every album, he knew every lick on every song—licks he had taught himself to play, using only his long fingers and his record player.

He was able to reproduce a myriad of pedal steel licks on his Stratocaster. Oftentimes, the fingerings he contorted into were astounding. But when the Flying Norwegians played, you could not tell that Buddy Cage or Sneaky Pete were not on stage.

The evening turned into a modern-day Viking fest, complete with food, drink, smoke, song, and healthy doses of laughter. They sounded great. Everyone had a great time. Afterward, they joined us at our table, where the drinking and smoking went deep into the night. The Vikings and the hillbillies hit it off famously.

Our concert the next evening was more of the same festiveness. The Koncertpaleet Cinema was filled to capacity with friends, old and new, hugging each other, raising their glasses in toast, and swinging each other around like children. When Rune and his boys took the stage, the place went nuts. When we took the stage, the place erupted.

I learned two phrases, which I liberally used throughout the night—"*Tousan Tak*," and "*Hey, Skol.*"

As we stepped onto the plane the next morning, bound for Oslo, Rune sent us on our way with, "I hope to see you guys again soon." Little did we know, we would be seeing him sooner than soon.

After Bergen, Oslo and Stockholm were anti-climactic. Both cities were flown into. Both gigs rushed to. All meals rushed through. Both cities hastily departed. By the time we landed in Copenhagen for a day off and one last gig at Daddy's Dance Hall, there were some frazzled tempers in our camp. Fuses were short.

Not only had we spent the entire month dashing around Europe, we had spent the entire month traveling in close proximity to each other—more than enough time to get on each other's nerves (another reason for our self-imposed, seventeen-day limit). A couple of days in Copenhagen didn't do much to settle anything. When we got to Daddy's, things flared.

Our set was marred from the start. Our 10:00 show time got pushed back, then it got pushed back some more. It was almost midnight by the time we took the stage. The Danish crowd, which wasn't overwhelming in the first place, was less than happy about the long wait.

When we started to play, bad sound didn't help matters. The air was thick with tension—and nobody had the energy to defuse any of it. This was the last gig of the tour—and it showed. Everybody just wanted to go home. As the set progressed, Randy snapped, beginning to play much louder than usual—*obnoxiously* louder.

Tucker, with a bird's-eye view from the wings, recalls, "I remember the incident at Daddy's Dance Hall. It was the last show, and I remember the band saying, halfway through the set, 'Randy, you're playing too loud. We can't hear ourselves.' He replied, 'Oh. I'm too loud, am I?' and walked over to his amp, and just rolled his hand across the top of his knobs—rolled every one of them all the way up. He finished the set that way. That was the last day of the tour."

His stunt put everyone at odds, only adding fuel to an already tense atmosphere. As we finished the set with "River to the Sun," his guitar outro became quite unpleasant. Instead of feeding everyone the guitar lick as the cue we used to end the song, all we heard was the squealing feedback. The cue never came.

When the rest of us turned to each other, we took it upon ourselves to end the song—cue or no cue. The gig, the tour, and the band as we knew it came to a screeching halt that night. A brief shouting match broke out in the dressing room, but everyone was just too damned tired to even give a shit.

Tempers tempered the next day for the flight home. Everyone was drained. No one wanted to talk to anyone about anything—including the night before. We just wanted to go home. When we landed at the Springfield airport, everyone went their separate ways. Let me rephrase that: We went ours. Randy went his.

After several days of peace and quiet, Stan began calling with information about our next tour (which was to begin in a few weeks) and our next album (which was to begin in a few months). Then he finished the conversation with, "And by the way, has anyone seen or heard from Randy?" Our collective answer was, "Nope."

He hadn't called me. I didn't know where he was. No one else knew either. The last time we saw him, he was ruining "River to the Sun" in Copenhagen. Calls to Ruedi-Valley went unanswered. Rusty offered no information. Contact was absolute zero.

After a week, everyone started to become concerned—not only about him, but about the band. Stan flew in from Kansas City, as we called a meeting to figure out what the hell was going on and what the hell we were going to do if Randy didn't resurface. The *Car Over the Lake Album* had stalled, and "If I Only Knew" had already fallen from the charts.

With an entire summer of work ahead of us, we couldn't locate our guitar player. Plus, we had another album to make—a very inopportune time to throw monkey wrenches.

We began to discuss Plan B in earnest. It would be stupid to cancel all of the work coming up. If he was going to continue to hide, our decision was simple. He did; he hid. We did what we had to do.

The search for a new guitar player started immediately. We came up with a handful of suggestions, which was basically a list of guitar players in Springfield. When someone mentioned, "Hey, what about that guy we just met in Norway?" light bulbs went off. "He already knows our songs."

The phone call was made to Bergen. The Viking would soon come to the Ozarks.

CHAPTER 20

As you drive south from Springfield on Highway 160 (more commonly known as Campbell Street), the last thing you encounter before crossing the Christian County line is the James River Valley. Over the years, the lazy James has cut a wide, friendly swath through the hills.

When heading south, you notice nothing but Mother Nature's splendor. When heading back north across the valley floor, you will see, embedded into the far face of the river bluff, the Rock.

The Rock, a stately three-story home, sits halfway up the bluff. Having received its moniker from the appearance that it took every rock and field stone for miles around to build, the estate, complete with high-ceilinged parlors, tall arched windows, fireplaces, gardens, courtyards, and verandas was owned by Paul and Ruth Canaday.

Son Steve occupied one of the smaller buildings (also made of rock) that populated the grounds. Father Paul, an avid proponent of the band, was always willing to offer the Rock as our in-town meeting place when we were unable to make the trek out to Ruedi-Valley.

It was a rainy spring day when one, such occasion arose. No one wanted to go out to the Ranch, due to the fact that the main reason we were gathering in the first place was to discuss Randy's replacement. We didn't think this would be a very good thing to do out at his house.

The call was placed to Paul and Ruth, who handed us the keys to the place, with instructions to make ourselves at home, help ourselves to the pool table, the well-stocked refrigerator, and to relax on the verandas, with their magnificent views. The valley below was springing to life and coming into bloom. But it was a serious flock of Ducks who gathered at the Rock.

The first item on the agenda, naturally, was Randy. Our general consensus was the logical, "If he doesn't want to be here, we don't want him here." No one was overly anxious to try to talk him out of his decision either.

After unanimously deciding to contact Rune, Stan informed us that Patrick and Maple would also be leaving. Patrick had agreed to become a member of Fleetwood Mac's road crew. Maple had accepted a gig to road manage Vassar Clements, which would lead directly to a four-year stint as Steve Martin's personal banjo roadie.

Both cited the fact that we weren't working enough for them to make a living.

Both were correct.

We bid the Byrne brothers fond adieus.

When it was suggested that Larry Tucker stay on and take over as equipment manager, everyone gave an enthusiastic thumbs up.

When it was suggested that Canway take Maple's place as road manager, all thumbs remained up. Both selections were natural choices. Both were easily and quickly made.

After listening to Rune's splendid guitar work on *Wounded Bird*—the Flying Norwegians' latest album—the call was placed to Norway. Our invitation was accepted in a matter of seconds. Plans were made for him to arrive in a matter of days.

In a matter of an hour, business at the Rock was taken care of. The new team was in place, and the serious tone of the proceedings gave way to the pool table, the refrigerator, and the majesty of the James River Valley, which lay at our feet.

Life was good in all our valleys. We had a few weeks off to just relax and do nothing but attend a Paul McCartney concert before starting back to work.

When we learned Paul was bringing Wings through Kansas City, we all wanted to go. When we learned Cowtown was promoting the gig, we knew we'd able to get good seats. When we learned Stan might be able to arrange a backstage visit with the ex-Beatle, we jumped at the chance.

Kansas City's cavernous Kemper Arena is not acoustically gifted—built more for basketball games and monster-truck shows. But that night, Paul made it his living room. I packed my shirt pocket with a handful of my hefty homegrown joints. I knew Paul also liked to smoke pot and, if this meeting were to come about, it would be the thrill of a lifetime to burn one with a Beatle.

After a wonderful evening of music, when the lights came up and people began to file out, we lagged behind. When we were summoned backstage, it was requested that only band members come in. Grumbling rippled through the wives section. But there was nothing we could do. As we walked into the dressing room area, Stan stayed behind to unruffle spousal feathers.

When John, Larry, Steve, Buddy, and I walked past Wings's dressing room, the place was aroar with boisterous laughter. Denny Laine and Jimmy McCullough emerged from the fray to greet us with invitations in.

When we were shown into Paul's dressing room, it was a much different atmosphere. At the far end of the long room sat the McCartneys, quietly smoking a joint, towels draped over their drenched shoulders.

"Ah, it's the Ozark lads. Come in. Come in," he cheerfully called, standing to greet us. Linda became the most gracious of hosts, making sure we all had cocktails from the massive catering table in the middle of the room.

As introductions and handshakes went around, the first thing Paul did was make sure we knew that he was aware of our band—as well as our relation with Glyn. The second thing he did was ask if any of us would like a hit off his joint. I couldn't believe my lungs. I reached into my pocket and handed him one of mine, accompanied with a fatherly, "Try one of these. I grew it." His eyes lit up as he lit up.

Conversation steered toward our shared fondness of Scotland. When we told him of our recent gigs in Glasgow and Edinburgh, he let us know that he'd heard the buzz. Then he conveyed the mutual fondness he, as well as his countrymen, had for our music.

When we asked about recent photographs of him wearing a *Car Over the Lake* T-shirt, he candidly answered, "I can't really remember where I got it. I just like the way it feels. I wear it when I'm knocking about the house."

Linda chimed in with, "He wears it all the bloody time."

After a brief, cordial visit, it was time to leave. When I shook his hand, he thanked me for bringing the joint by. I handed him the remaining contents of my pocket with a sincere, "Thanks for all the bass lessons."

With smiles and "Cheers," we left the room, reunited with our families, walked into the quiet Kansas City night, and headed home. It was time to get to work.

When Rune stepped off the plane at the Springfield airport, it had only been a month since we'd seen him in Bergen. The Trout Farm was readied and we quickly headed into rehearsals. With only a short period of time to familiarize himself with the material, he dug in his heels with a stubborn, Viking determination—one that resembles that of a stubborn hillbilly.

He already knew many of the songs from the records and was a quick study on the others. His willingness to listen and cooperate fit in quite well, as did his friendly demeanor.

Though we would eventually work up new material for a new album, these first rehearsals concentrated on the live show. As we were breaking in a new guitarist, Tucker hired Kansas City native John Aikin to move to Springfield as his aide. While the two of them learned about the equipment in the big green cases, Rune learned the songs.

Rune's addition could be felt right off the bat. His chicken pickin' gave many of the songs bounce, as well as ballast. His searing pedal steel licks sent others into outer space. His banjo lent our bluegrass material the appropriate spice it needed. He was three-for-three right off the bat—and that's batting a thousand.

Though he had been one of the main singers for the Flying Norwegians, he shyly stayed back from the microphone. He had a nice command of the English language, but he spoke as well as sang with a thick Norwegian twang.

Even though he's a much better guitarist than Randy, Rune isn't nearly the vocalist Randy is. I am not the vocalist Randy is either. But overnight,

I acquired his harmony parts, and though I knew what they were, the vocal blend changed. Emphasis was no longer being placed on vocals.

In lieu of casually sitting around, singing as we did in the early days—on the porch, in the living room, at the Trilogy, at the Bijou, in the Duck Truck—vocal rehearsals were shrugged off with a simple, "Eh. We'll run over them in the hotel room." We never did. The only time we really sang was on stage. No one was worried.

As we began running through the songs, it became apparent that Rune had listened to our records very closely. It was also apparent that he had listened to Randy's guitar parts even closer. After only a few songs, we suggested, "Don't try to play like Randy. Play like Rune."

With a freshly rolled cigarette from his ever-present pouch of Drum tobacco, he softly replied, "Yaaahh. I caan doo thaahhht."

Giant clouds of smoke engulfed his head at all times, as his large fingers rolled perfect cigarette after perfect cigarette. (We all received rolling lessons.) Bill Jones, whose horns were set up directly next to him on stage, could only shake his head and mutter, "Man, that guy can smoke."

When we took breaks and everyone left the rehearsal room, the shy Norwegian would pull his chair alongside mine. Not wanting to take a break, he wanted to continue to play. He and I did just that. I broke out the mandolin I had just acquired, as he picked up his banjo. After a few songs, I would hand him the mandolin and pick up an acoustic guitar.

I taught him several of the bluegrass tunes I had been writing, as he taught me traditional tunes he had adapted from his homeland's Harding fiddle. The two of us would sit and play until everyone else decided to come back inside. He liked to play music as much as I did. In no time, we had a nice little repertoire of songs.

I began carrying my mandolin on the road, as the sound of these little songs began to fill our dressing rooms. Occasionally, John would join in, playing fiddle on "Hubcap Souffle." Most of the time, though, it was the Viking and the Polack.

We all took turns housing Rune for the first few months he was in the country. Still self-conscious, he remained relatively silent in a crowd. In quieter circumstances, though, the man was well spoken, well read, intelligent, jolly, animated, and just a hell of a lot of fun to hang around.

It Shined

He went absolutely berserk when Steve Martin and Dan Aykroyd portrayed Jortuk and Jorge Festrunk on *Saturday Night Live*. We all laughed, but he laughed hardest of all. Not only did his normal speaking voice resemble the "wild and crazy guys," he memorized and re-enacted their skits, word for word, inflection for inflection. He kept us in stitches with "Now, are the foxes."

His sense of humor fit right in. One day, after hearing "I Only Have Eyes for You" on the radio, he turned to us, asking what the background singers were singing. As we listened intently, he inquired further, "Are they saying, 'Did you wash your butt?'"

"Didja washya butt?" doubled over the entire room. The phrase became his mantra for the festive times that were soon to come. The next time you hear the Impressions sing the song, try not to laugh. The man was a fountain of pure humor.

Though he would eventually become more comfortable and get a place of his own, we were all happy to invite him into our houses. He was a very gracious and courteous guest. But though he was having the rock 'n' roll time of his life, he was a long, long way from home.

Our first gig was a bright Saturday afternoon at Kansas City's Arrowhead Stadium. For the rest of us, our forty-five minute warm-up slot before the Beach Boys was just another gig. Rune was a nervous wreck. This was the first time he had ever played in this country, and the most people he had ever played for—EVER.

As we stood on the side of the stage, minutes before we were to go on, I tried to ease tensions with, "Don't worry, Rune. Leave it to us. You just relax, play your guitar, and have fun."

He replied, "I haave to pee real bahd."

I understood his predicament. I also realized that the bathrooms were a long way away. I suggested he do what I sometimes did—as quickly and inconspicuously as possible, wander off among the stacks of empty amplifier cases strewn about behind the stage and pee into a bottle. Off he went.

He was terrified when he returned, explaining in his deep voice, "I was so scared they were going to show me up on that big screen." When I reassured him that the Arrowhead Stadium Jumbotron had not shown him taking a leak, we threw our heads back with a howl. Then he slapped me on the back and said, "Now let's have some fun."

When we began, our faithful Kansas City crowd went nuts, paying no attention to the fact that we had a new guitar player. As the set progressed, you could literally see the nervousness leave Rune's body. We shouldered the burden of the show. He played very nice guitar. Everyone danced.

As the set ended and the Beach Boys prepared to take the stage, we retired to the luxury suite of Kansas City Chiefs' owner Lamar Hunt. Here we picked up where we left off last month in Bergen. Beer flowed like wine. Laughter followed suit. His first gig was behind him, and it was time to celebrate. It was gravy from here. Then it was on to Tulsa's Cain's Ballroom, which he was familiar with from listening to Bob Wills records.

A summer's worth of gigs ensued, including Denver's Red Rocks with the Dirt Band and the Dixie Dregs, our first of many trips to Montana, and another visit to the Mississippi River Festival, where we headlined for the first time to an enthusiastic crowd of more than 5,000 people.

Cain's was an un-air-conditioned, but satisfying, sweat bath. Red Rocks provided the best sound and most magnificent views we've ever experienced on stage. Montana introduced us to some of the silliest fun people we had ever encountered. The River Festival hosted the first "Bob Granda Show."

My dad—who had gained a bit of notoriety about his boy's band—had shed his suspicion of my hippie friends and that crazy weed we smoked. When we played the St. Louis area, he became Canway's unofficial assistant road manager/bouncer/backstage host/beer go-getter. He became quite good at discerning between drunken party crashers and actual friends of the band.

His natty attire and thinning white hair made him look like Johnny Carson in a sea of Jerry Garcias. The quintessential St. Louis host made sure everyone was comfortable, everyone knew everyone, everyone was introduced to everyone, and everyone had a cold beer in their hand. Of course, when an unsuspecting reveler handed him a joint, he would politely pass it on, taking every precaution not to get it anywhere near his face.

While my mother, as well as my siblings, found the quieter corners more to their liking, Bob felt comfortable right in the thick of things.

We began referring to the backstage scenes at our St. Louis gigs as "Bob Granda Shows." He and Rune took an immediate liking to each other, though each had a hard time with the other's name.

Bob just could not understand the non-silent "e" on the end of Rune's name, often saying, "Well, it *looks* like June."

Rune's pronunciation was "Baaawwb."

The shy Norwegian fit in nicely, and slowly began to emerge from his shell. When he did, boy did he, feeling more and more comfortable off stage, as well as on. After all, he had a whole slew of big brothers watching out for him.

The gigs got better, the music got tighter, and THANK GOD, we no longer chartered those stupid little airplanes. When that large, shiny, sixty-foot-long customized Silver Eagle bus drove in from Nashville to pick us up, I embraced that cold mass of steel like a teddy bear.

The summer came and went. We didn't miss a lick. We didn't miss a beat. We didn't miss a gig. Though he couldn't totally shed his accent, Rune began to venture up to the microphone and sing. The most important element he re-introduced to the band, though, was the enthusiasm Randy was no longer able to maintain—and the sense of fun Randy never had.

When it came time to record, rehearsals stepped up. By this time, I had moved from the Trout Farm, which we still maintained as a rehearsal hall. David came to town, met Rune, we got down to work, and for some cockamamie notion, we thought it'd be a good idea to try to make the album at American Artists.

As the griping about being on the road intensified, when we asked A&M if we could stay in Springfield to record, our wish was granted. We should've watched what we wished for. Once again, Marty Lewis was called in to engineer. He walked in the front door, took one look at the place, and laughed.

Though it was the same studio in the same building on the same corner, the whole atmosphere had changed. Now, instead of a clientele of artists recording songs, the place catered to a clientele of advertising executives recording jingles.

Tucker set up our gear in the studio. Marty reluctantly slid behind the board. David started the proceedings with "Homemade Wine"—a song that had been a crowd favorite for years. This is the theory I had been suggesting for the past couple of albums. I was thrilled to death. Plus, I was able to lend a hand on mandolin, which helped give the tune a lilt. This also thrilled me to death.

When it came time to play the closing lick, I was ready. I had been practicing it for days. When Marty hit the red button, though it took me several attempts, I hit the lick. David and Larry said, "That sounds good." We moved on.

With the addition of Rune's banjo, "Fly Away Home" acquired proper feel and texture. Unfortunately, American Artists' gear was also acquiring something—a chronic state of disrepair. The sessions only lasted a couple of days. "Homemade Wine" and "Fly Away Home" were the only two songs we cut before the plug was pulled. This turned out to be a blessing in disguise.

Marty didn't want to have to put up with the outdated and broken gear. David didn't want to have to put up with the toupeed and turtlenecked Higgins. This, along with the onslaught of friends just wanting to drop by the studio to see what was going on, was not conducive to productivity. We HAD to move. So we headed for the mountains.

Caribou Ranch sits at an elevation of 6,000 feet, directly outside the small town of Nederland, Colorado—a mere thirty minutes up the canyon from Boulder. Owned and operated by famed producer James Guercio, this state-of-the-art studio sat in the middle of an actual 4,000-acre working ranch, complete with stables of horses and staffs of hands.

The Chicago native— not only responsible for the brassy sound of the Buckinghams in the '60s ("Kind of a Drag"), had taken that same approach to shape the sound of the Chicago Transit Authority (who would later shorten their name to Chicago) in the '70s. In much the same way Herb Alpert parlayed the sound of a trumpet into a flourishing A&M Records, Guercio parlayed that same sound into a flourishing Caribou Ranch.

Nestled a half mile off the road, Caribou features breathtaking vistas in any direction you look. The studio, housed in the large barn, sported tall ceilings, fireplaces, and the warm sound of a wooden structure. A short walk up the hill from the barn/studio sat a dozen smaller log cabins. At one time, the cabins housed dudes at the ranch. Now they housed musi-

Caribou Ranch with Rune Walle, 1976 (photo by Jim Mayfield)

cians in the studio. All came complete with large, comfortable beds, piled high with quilts and blankets to fend off the Colorado nights.

A large dining room/kitchen was centrally located smack dab in the middle of everything. Manned by a full staff of cooks and waitresses, anytime we stumbled in, they were there to cheerfully make breakfast, lunch, or whatever our little old pea-pickin' hearts desired.

After a day in the studio, dinner was served family style around the long, oaken dining room table. The menu was superb, oftentimes consisting of fresh trout caught that afternoon from one of the many streams that ran through the place. Other times, large grills were fired up on the huge wooden decks that surrounded the kitchen, sending billows of smoke into the air. Combined with the scent of pine trees and fresh air, the entire place filled with wonderful aromas.

Once again, Jim Mayfield was hailed, to visit with his cameras. One of his main objectives was to photograph the cover for the album, which we had tentatively titled *Nuclear Fishin'*—after the hilarious cartoon Canway had drawn in the pages of Caribou's large guest book. The tome was a virtual roster of the Rock 'n' roll Hall of Fame, containing page after page of magnificent penmanship, witty sayings, drunken musings, and a whole section of monsters and dinosaurs, drawn by seven-year-old Dweezil and three-year-old Ahmet Zappa.

The cover for *Nuclear Fishin'* was simple—a candid snapshot of a man, sitting on the end of a dock, quietly fishing into a small pond. With a cane pole in one hand, while waving at the camera with the other, he would be wearing a full-body asbestos radiation suit.

Nuclear Fishin' at Caribou (photo by Jim Mayfield)

It Shined

Jim agreed to take the shot. I agreed to go fishing. We rented the silver suit from a Boulder costume shop, waited for the sun to come out, and walked down to one of the many ponds on the place. I put the suit and helmet on, grabbed a fishing pole, walked out to the end of the dock, and sat down. Then, all I had to do was sit there, while Jim snapped away from various angles with various lenses.

The small crowd of bystanders who had gathered laughed themselves silly. Several times, shooting was delayed while the photographer stopped to wipe tears from his eyes.

We thought the photos were hilarious. A&M did not.

After *Car Over the Lake Album*, they wanted something a little less obtuse, and a little more connected to the music inside. *Nuclear Fishin'* was scrapped. Years later, the photo would see the light of day, when A&M Canada used it for the cover of our greatest hits package. There I can be found, happily waving to the Canadians.

If we didn't want to, we never had to leave the place. Most of the time, we didn't. Why would we? Everything we needed was right here. Room, board, work, play. All went neatly onto the A&M tab.

When we settled into our cabins, everyone was happy. When we settled into the studio, David and Marty were extremely happy. Caribou was one of the hottest studios around. American Artists was, once again, relegated to jingles about banks and lumber yards.

Over the past few years, we had continued to return to Colorado on a regular basis, playing colleges, ski resorts, a slot on the Telluride Rock 'n' roll Festival, a snowy week in Crested Butte that almost killed us trying to learn how to ski, and a handful of gigs at the Boulder Theater. Now we were living just up the road from the Boulder Theater.

On occasion, we would wander down into Nederland's Pioneer Inn, to spend the evening playing informal, unannounced sets of acoustic music. There was no publicity. There was no pressure. There was no pay. There was no stage. None of that mattered, as we sat around in the middle of the room, having a great time playing music for—and getting buzzed with—the locals.

One of those locals was Jerry Mills, who lived in nearby Evergreen. Fresh from a stint playing mandolin with the Nitty Gritty Dirt Band, when Stan invited him to stop by the Pioneer, he did. His high level of musicianship kicked "Homemade Wine," "Fly Away Home," "Standing on the Rock" and "Hub Cap Souffle" up several notches.

The Nederlanders filled the place for these low-key evenings. They usually knew who was working up at Caribou. They also knew that a lot of the time, those artists never came out to play. Our love affair with Colorado deepened.

As work geared up, things quickly fell into a cool groove. If we had to be away from Springfield, this was a great place to be. We felt right at home in the idyllic setting, one that was very conducive to wives and kids. Over the course of the month, all were able to fly out for a few days of being pampered, Rocky Mountain High style. The A&M tab grew.

The atmosphere was wonderful, the fishing was great. The food and wine were magnificent. The evening softball games are legendary. If one of us wasn't needed in the studio, there were hikes to be taken, fish to be caught, horses to be ridden, waterfalls, swimming holes, mountaintops, and secluded valleys to be visited.

This relaxed atmosphere carried right into the studio. Though the end of summer was still hanging on in Missouri, small fires were built in the fireplaces to take the chill off the crisp Colorado air. All of this provided a wonderful place to work.

Rune, in an American studio for the first time, would often look around, shake his head, and say, "I am in heaven."

We started the sessions by listening to "Homemade Wine" and "Fly Away Home." Both sounded fine. Marty breathed a huge sigh of relief. Then David began with a couple more of the older songs, which already had proven track records. "Noah" benefited from Rune's slide guitar, and the aptly named "Mountain Range" benefited from Buddy's scenic oboe solo.

Canway and I laid down a solid track, as Larry played "You Know Like I Know" on piano. A&M, still clinging to the theory that it was going to be Larry's voice that would get us back onto the charts, groomed, "You Know" as our single.

Cash-o had picked up my mandolin early in the sessions, taught himself a couple of chords, and wrote "The Red Plum," a tale of black-smiths, cobblers, fletchers, and ivory queens in full-length, white lace gowns. After teaching me the song, Jerry Mills was summoned to the studio.

As we set up to record the song, Rune droned a detuned guitar. John droned on the fiddle. Larry clanged a triangle, as Jerry and I strummed mandolins. Then I overdubbed a big bass fiddle, filling the bottom with deep, comfortable notes. It was a very cool sound—one that nicely matched the timbre of the tale.

When we finished cutting the track, Jerry hung around for the rest of the evening. After numerous rounds of beers and cheers, Rune and I began to dive into the material we had been playing. Jerry dove right in with us.

One of the songs was "Roscoe's Rule," which I had just finished with Steve's lyrical help. When I played it, it caught David's ear, and he wanted to record it the very next day. It's a tight little up-tempo tune that reflected the atmosphere of the sessions, as well as the album's eventual cover art. Though the song never mentions Roscoe by name, the simple man was woven throughout the lyrics of the song, written in the Trout Farm valley.

When we finished the track, David turned and asked if I'd mind if Larry took a crack at singing it. I didn't mind. If A&M wanted more of his voice on the album, so be it. It could only be a selling point for my song's inclusion on the record. I was disappointed when it got passed over for Larry's "It's How You Think."

I argued that I thought the fans would prefer a song with a harmonica and a funky guitar on it, to a song with a flute and a synthesizer. Both songs featured Larry's voice. That was not an issue. Plus, the title of my song was the name of one of the characters on the cover. I was VERY disappointed when David took me aside to inform me that "Roscoe" was not going to be included.

Though I felt horrible, I swallowed hard and participated in the "name the album" party. Because Mayfield's whimsical shot of my fishing expedition was discarded, we decided to use his stunning photograph of Roscoe and Clarence. The photo was set atop the recording console. We began imbibing and shouting titles at it.

Some titles were serious—*Men from Mars*.

Some were not—*Ralph, the Rubber Tornado*.

When *Ralph, the Rubber Tornado* was suggested, we all laughed. When *Men from Mars* was suggested, we all "oohed." We knew we were close. With the next suggestion, *Men from Earth*, we all "aahed." We knew we'd hit the nail on the head. Roscoe and Clarence. Men from Earth. Our business was done. We had spent a month in the spectacular Rocky Mountains. We couldn't wait to get back to the subtler Ozarks.

Clarence and Roscoe Jones, Men from Earth (photo by Jim Mayfield)

The bad news was, when David took the tapes to L.A. to be mastered, we found that the big sound Marty had sculpted at 6,000 feet had dwindled. The tapes that sounded so huge in the rarified air of the mountains did not move nearly as much of the denser air at sea level. This is a dilemma every artist who records at Caribou faces. But the place is just so damn cool, this minor detail is easily and often overlooked.

When *Men from Earth* hit the streets, like *Car Over the Lake*, it was greeted with a cool response. This, along with the last-minute dealings with "Roscoe's Rule," caused my enthusiasm to wane. We'd also recorded another of Steve's hilarious songs, "Dollar's Worth of Regular." This tale of fulfilled sexual fantasy for a young, small-town gas station attendant was wonderful. It also didn't make the record.

Men from Earth had a somber tone. You could see it in the unsmiling faces of the two men on the front cover. You could see it in the unsmiling faces of the six of us on the back. I had an odd feeling our fans weren't going to go for—or buy—a record devoid of humor and the harmonica. But the money was rolling in, and I was still part of the team.

When we turned the album in, this fulfilled the second stage of our contract, marking its halfway point. Once again, A&M had ninety days to notify us, in writing, whether or not they intended to pick up their option for albums number five and six. Jerry Moss flew to Missouri.

Deciding that he ought to just come and see for himself what the hell was going on back here, he paid us all a visit. When he stepped off the plane, he came to each of our homes for brief chats and long conversations about not only music, but other varied and passionate interests we all had. The man has many—one of which is music.

I had moved from the Trout Farm (which had become too crazy and too noisy for an infant) and into a small, quiet house in the middle of 160 secluded acres near Highlandville (a mile up the road from Buff Lamb). I felt honored when Jerry came to my house.

As the president of A&M Records sat in my kitchen, drinking coffee and whiling away the morning, conversation was light. We discovered that we shared an affinity for travel in Latin America. Of course, our modes of transportation were different. I traveled on chicken trains, filled with screaming children. He traveled in Herb Alpert's private jet.

The hills around my house were ablaze in their fall glory. As a pleasant morning was spent in the shade of the sycamore trees that sheltered the valley, the worldly man was a gracious guest, possessing the wonderful ability to put everyone at ease.

When the conversation turned to the state of the band (as it was bound to do), this ease turned to candor. I felt comfortable talking to him. He shot straight with me and expected the same in return. He got it. After expressing his continued fondness of our music, he expressed his concern about our lack of motivation and work ethic.

When he stated that he wished the band would work harder, I could not have agreed with him more. As I began to echo this, he waved his hand and cut me off with an assured, "I know. Stan's told me. You're one of the ones who want to work."

Soon afterward, the conversation ended with, "Why didn't you guys just get an American guitar player?"

After lunch, I invited him for a short stroll up an overgrown path to one of the outbuildings behind my house. He asked about ticks. When I assured him that the chickens had alleviated the problem, he breathed a sigh of relief. Then he let out a gasp, when he stepped into the small shed to see a dozen pot plants hanging upside down, curing.

After catching his breath, he slowly turned and asked, "Do you sell this stuff?"

"No, I don't," I answered. "But I'll give you some."

He laughed. He didn't really want any. He was just taken aback at the sight of it—a sight he would also see when visiting the other guys. After all, it was fall.

Over the course of the next few days, he made the rounds, visiting each of our homes and seeing the sights. The morning he left to return to Los Angeles, he gathered us for a brief meeting in the airport coffee shop. Here he notified everyone that he intended to pick up his option for two more records. His notification may not have been in writing. It didn't have to be. His eye contact sealed the deal.

We were all men from Earth, living good lives. When he boarded his plane, we were all smiles in the terminal. Handshakes went around. Stan and Paul went to Kansas City. We went to our homes. It was a beautiful, fall day in the Ozarks.

CHAPTER 21

By now, the money was starting to roll in at a very healthy and steady clip. We scattered even further, buying farms throughout the area. John and Larry bought 500 acres near Yellville, Arkansas. John moved into the house. Larry began designing one. Steve bought thirty acres and a marvelous cabin on the Niangua River near Buffalo, Missouri. Buddy bought 180 acres and built a house near Crane, Missouri. I bought 279 acres of wilderness on the Buffalo River near Ponca, Arkansas—and a house in downtown Springfield.

When I first entertained thoughts of investing in real estate, Don Tom wanted in. Wishing to filter some of his money out of Guatemala and back into this country, he offered to match me dollar for dollar. This was great. It meant I could look for a REALLY big place. Where his money came from was never discussed. I had no problem with this. I didn't care where it came from. I just knew that healthy checks were coming from Central America—and they were never late.

We found paradise. We also found the middle of nowhere—two heavily timbered valleys, forming the headwaters of Possum Trot Creek, merging into a larger valley that stretched, untouched, as far downstream as you could see. Smack dab in the middle stood a seven-acre glen, a dozen springs, and the old homestead.

It Shined

The ramshackle house, which had been occupied by nothing but critters and Mother Nature for decades, had severely collapsed, resembling the imploding face of a Jack-o-lantern in November. Any attempt at restoration was completely out of the question.

I bought a large army tent and pitched it directly beside one of the babbling brooks. Days were spent watching the sun go up and down, while watching Sya run around the fields. When we packed up, it was a short, ninety-mile trek back up to downtown Springfield.

The unassuming, two-story white house at 422 South Main appears deceptively plain from the outside. But after walking up the front steps and through the big front door, the interior exploded with elegance and craftsmanship.

A dazzling, crystal chandelier occupied the foyer, which opened into three giant rooms, all containing high ceilings, sliding Dutch doors, bay windows, and fireplaces, shrouded with tile and mirrored mantels. An ornate wooden staircase frolicked its way from the foyer up to four large bedrooms, all with giant windows and sunny views of the city. Recalling days when Springfield was a young, ambitious community, it was easy to see large, healthy families living along this tree-lined street.

It had been almost ten years since I had moved to Springfield. But I could see the city shifting. When I first came to town, I fell in love with the sense of community that thrived on its vibrant square. Now, a shopping mall on the outskirts of town lured merchants, as well as shoppers, from the heart of the city.

Springfield is not alone. This is an affliction that is prevalent throughout America—Mom and Pop get stomped into oblivion by jackbooted supercenters, with acres of free parking. It is a trend I am not fond of.

As concerned friends began gathering to form an association to preserve the heart and soul of their community, I decided to put my money back into the downtown area. I did not want to live close to a mall. I did not want to see my adopted home wither to dust and blow away to the suburbs—which, over the years, it has done.

As the world rushed by, all it saw was the plain exterior of my big, white house. Inside, the crannies and nooks of the old place made our transition from the middle of nowhere to the middle of town much easier. I had the best of both worlds—a big piece of rural America AND a small piece of Main Street, U.S.A.

In the fall of 1976, when *Men from Earth* was released, it seemed that my personal assessment of the record agreed with many of the critics.

Some were kind, pointing out that, "They are trying to entertain through musical variation and not rest on a successful formula, unlike many of their more illustrious, country-rock competitors."

Others observed, "I enjoyed this band best when they were a lot rougher on their first album. 'Jackie Blue' was a fine piece of Top 40 music off of album two. But it has seen the band's focus change to a slicker and more bland Los Angeles sound—and made them just a little too anonymous as a result."

Car over the Lake hadn't made much of a splash. Neither would *Men from Earth*. *Car* had spent fifteen weeks on the charts, clawing its way to number fifty-seven. *Men* would spend ten weeks, only making it to number seventy-four. "You Know Like I Know" also peaked at number seventy-four.

Our fans didn't buy it in droves.

One of our first appearances after leaving Caribou was another taping of *Don Kirschner's Rock Concert*. This time, after Kirschner deadpanned into the camera with one of his robotic intros, we hit the stage. When we did, boy, did we. As John played the opening fiddle lick and we launched into "Homemade Wine," the cameraman went into a long, panoramic sweep across the stage. It took him quite a while to make it. There were eight guys on screen. From left to right: Buddy, Canway, Rune, Cash-O, Larry, me, John, and Jerry Mills.

Then, as we began, it became apparent that most of the guys had found their way to the barbershop before they found their way on camera. In addition to the expanded roster and trimmed-up appearance, the same sense of somber that permeated the album permeated our seven-song segment.

The first time we appeared on the show, we were wide-eyed and scared shitless. This time, there was a lot of staring off into space. Though we were doing songs off our new album, they were old songs we'd been playing for years. Tonight we played them like we'd been playing them for years.

We also played them as if we hadn't been playing much. That's because we hadn't. We'd been at Caribou for the past month in "studio" mode.

Instead of just ripping into the songs, like we usually did, we played them like we were still in the studio—timidly and afraid to make a mistake. We played this one close to the vest—nice and safe.

The only new song, sandwiched between "Homemade Wine," "Noah," "You Know Like I Know," "Jackie," "Heaven," and "Beauty in the River," was "The Red Plum." I dug this a lot, as I was able to hand my bass to Canway, pick up my mandolin, and join Jerry Mills up front. John played the fiddle. Buddy squeezed his accordion. It was a very cool sound.

As the taping wound down, one of the few humorous moments came at the beginning of Heaven's outro. As Steve began his harp lick and I once again began chiding the home viewing audience to get up on their couches and dance, you could actually hear the reed pop in his harmonica. This is not uncommon. Reeds blow out all the time. It's no big deal. There's nothing you can do. When they blow, they blow. When this would happen, Tucker would simply reach into a big box of spares and Steve would be back in the saddle by the next chorus.

This time, when the reed blew, Steve, in mid-lick, looked up at John and me with a wide-eyed look of humor, horror, and dilemma. Should we stop or should we just keep on trucking? We decided to truck. Though the harp is an essential part of the song, it was successfully buried in the mix. With seven other guys blasting away, getting buried in the mix is not hard to do. With seven other guys blasting away, it was easy to just barge our way through the song. This did put a light-hearted stamp onto the end of an underwhelming set.

This time, when the episode aired, all the home audience saw was the eight of us, standing there, playing our instruments. We had never relied on any kind of rock 'n' roll flash or showbiz sizzle—an approach that doesn't necessarily translate well to television.

This time, there was no additional footage of home spliced into the show, as A&M had not agreed to the added expense of any extra artwork. This was not surprising. They were not agreeing to the added expense of much of anything—even to the extent of sending a memo to all of their field reps, informing them NOT to take us to dinner and NOT to show us a wine list.

Our reputation for running up expensive tabs was catching up with us. Though the reps still came around to drink beer and chase girls, their Green Warriors remained in their pockets.

The Kirschner slot, as it would turn out, would be another major fork in the path—one of Buddy's last gigs. I was saddened when he broke the news, but completely understood his reasoning. He had been contemplating leaving the band, to return to medical school. The day had come.

"All of the crazy stuff that was starting to happen was fun and everything," he explains. "But it seemed that more attention was being paid to eating and drinking than was being paid to the music. I just didn't think this was a very wise approach—and wasn't really going to get us anywhere or produce any more hits. A&M was souring on us, so I decided that it might be a smart time to make the jump."

He and his family moved to Kirksville, Missouri, where he enrolled in the Kirksville College of Osteopathic Medicine.

Local barrelhouser Ruell Chapell was hired as his replacement. The short, rotund man with the loud—I mean *loud*—and shrill—I mean *shrill*—laugh, had been a fixture on the local music scene for years. Fronting his band, Spillwater Junction, he had been a frequent visitor to the parties and jam sessions at the House of Nutz & Loonies. He and I had been friends for some time.

When asked to join the Ducks, he jumped at the chance. His powerful piano style gave our onstage sound the gregarious quality we were acquiring off stage. His stage presence followed suit, with his long brown hair cascading from beneath his ever-present straw cowboy hat. Though his short, stubby fingers had difficulty shuffling a deck of cards, when he turned them loose on a piano, man, the keys flew!

Jerry Mills also jumped on the bus, hired by Stan to, not only play mandolin but be an advance publicist. Along with utilizing his mandolin on stage, most of his time was spent on the phone, lining up newspaper interviews and radio-station appearances in the cities we were visiting. I thought this was a good idea, hoping that *Men* could garner the attention *Car* did not.

His efforts were met with barrages of "No," "I don't want to talk to those people," and "That'll fuck up dinner." Consequently, many of the interviews were conducted with the bass player and the mandolin player of the Ozark Mountain Daredevils. When the others did join in, interviews once again focused on how much we hated to be on the road.

A&M, which had just committed to two more albums, was not thrilled.

Ruell would've participated, but he didn't know anything about the record, except how to play the songs. Rune did a few interviews, but they were from Scandinavia and conducted in Norwegian.

Though I still had an unenthusiastic taste in my mouth for the record, I agreed every time Jerry called with an interview to promote it. Radio stations were visited. Newspapers were talked to. Television cameras were talked into. He and I became a two-man gang in our assault of local media.

Oftentimes, we took our mandolins with us. While we waited in lobbies, we got them out and scrubbed off a few tunes. I started getting pretty good, just by hanging around the guy—another reason I was glad he was on board.

I didn't mind going to radio stations. I still don't. I like the role they play in the community. I understand the rhythm of radio. It is not fast paced—thirty-second bursts of talking, followed by three minutes of silence while the record plays. One of the most important qualities a radio man can have is to be full of hot air. I'm one of the fullest.

AM stations, which were only hip to "Jackie" and "Heaven"—and not playing "You Know Like I Know"—were visited. But I preferred the FM stations, with formats that were more flexible, allowing you get away with playing the seventeen-minute version of "In-A-Gadda-Da-Vida" while you stepped outside for a smoke.

One of our biggest supporters was K-SHE in St. Louis. The small cinderblock building sat on Route 66 (near my childhood home), directly under the screen of the Route 66 Drive-in Theater (the same drive-in I sneaked into as a teenager—in the trunks of cars).

Evening disc jockey Gary Kollander and I became good friends and running buddies. He played our records frequently. I'd visit him at the station during his seven-to-midnight shift, oftentimes not even letting his listeners know I was there.

When he informed station manager Shelly Graffman of my late-night visits, we were given the royal "okay." The atmosphere of the place was very relaxed, as Gary allowed me to browse through the station's record library and pick out tunes to play. Then we'd just hang out through the night. When we stepped outside for a smoke, we could look up and watch the movie playing on 66's giant screen.

K-SHE continued to play our records, even though many other stations around the country didn't. More importantly, they didn't stick exclusively to "Jackie" and "Heaven." Kollander, along with fellow DJs John Ulett, Ron Stevens, Gail Hrudnk, "Radio Rich" Dalton, Ted Habeck, Mark Close, and Randy Raley, prided themselves in playing many album cuts.

Because of this, our St. Louis fans became well acquainted with all of our music, not just our two hits. When we played in the area, K-SHE sponsored the show. They were there at Kiel. They were there at the River Festival. They would soon be there when we recorded our live album at the Fox. We were there for a couple of their legendary birthday parties. I felt honored to be involved with the very station I listened to as a youngster.

I knew the importance of these radio and newspaper folks. I saw, with my own eyes, what happened when they wrote about us and played our songs. I knew it was a mistake to blow them off. But blow them off we did. Despite Jerry Mills's efforts, coverage dwindled and records didn't get played. This reflected in sagging sales. Our new records may have gotten played in Missouri. But the rest of the country didn't hear them.

Sound checks also started getting blown off, due to the fact that they interfered with dinner. This frustrated Tucker, making his job harder. He took great pride and paid meticulous attention to our stage plot. We paid meticulous attention to wine lists. The sound of our shows took a back seat.

At times, when we went straight from the restaurant to the stage, it directly affected the show. As we tried to sing between belches, singing was less than precise. When we arrived full of wine, the singing was even more imprecise. The party, though, traveled well. In lieu of finesse, we began to rely more on ranting and raving.

Old friend Charlie McCall was hired to keep it all together and road manage the expanded roster. Canway, no longer interested in those duties, became a full-time member of the band. We began to insert a couple of his old Southside Boys songs into the show, as he preferred the trappings that came along with being a guitar player. Receipts and responsibilities were passed on to Charlie.

It Shined

Charlie McCall as Stinghead (photos by Jim Mayfield)

The gruff, mustachioed McCall, who had just left his position as road manager/lead singer for Zachary Beau (the band that lost ALL of their equipment in the Bijou fire), was hired to make sure the party made it from town to town and gig to gig. He was well suited for the job.

His persuasive manner rounded up folks well. When good manners didn't work, he would bellow like a stern Lou Rawls, "FIVE MINUTES, GUYS." If that didn't work, the large man could—and would—literally pick you up and carry you where you were supposed to be.

We hit the road that fall as an octet—nine when Bill joined in. It was a handful for Charlie to handle. But the man had boundless energy, as well as a voracious appetite for caffeine, nicotine, beer, whiskey, and cocaine. He jumped right into the middle of the fray, which was about to become an absolute circus.

Though it was not the Duck Truck, we used the same principle with the bus. In the Duck Truck, we would all pile in, head to the liquor store, and hit the road. We did the same thing with the Viking Bus. The only difference was, more guys meant more beer, more snacks, and more drugs.

More items were added to our catering rider, especially in the alcohol department. After the first gig, what we hadn't consumed in the dressing room was loaded onto the bus. After a few nights, we carried quite a booty. At any given time, there were cases of beer, gallons of whiskey and tequila, mountains of cheese, bags of chips, tubs of dip, piles of fresh fruit, and one large rolling rathskellar for the Vikings—I mean, the Ducks—to operate.

This also added another character to the cast—a bus driver. Bus drivers started showing up in all shapes and sizes. We never knew who it was going to be. Not only did you have to live with his driving abilities—or lack thereof—you had to live with him at breakfast. He became part of the entourage.

Sometimes older drivers with long résumés and a grasp of the atlas would pull up.

Sometimes young, eager beavers, solely intent on getting from Point A to Point B as fast as they could, would arrive.

Some had been everywhere, knew everybody, and knew where they were going. Others had no idea where they were, no background and no social skills.

It Shined

Some knew the roadmap of America like the back of their hand. Others, had never been out of Alabama.

Some were smooth. Others weren't.

Some had manners. Others didn't.

We took an immediate liking to the old pros, preferring the less-jostling style of the old guy who drove George Jones to the lunging of the knucklehead who drove Ozzy Osbourne. None of us liked being rolled out of our bunks in the middle of the night.

Most drivers were just good old boys, having a good time and enjoying life on the road. Because most of them were from Nashville, some were pretty good guitar pickers. It wasn't unusual to walk into the hotel bar on a night off to find our bus driver on the stage, with his guitar in his lap and an audience at his feet.

All of them liked to have a good time. The good ones knew when not to. When faced with overnight drives, some would prepare by napping at the hotel in the evening while we played. Others took bennies. I had no trouble with this. I felt more comfortable with a bennied-up driver of a big bus than I did with a coffeed-up pilot of a little airplane. I had no problem when, right before an all-nighter, I saw Sam break open a black capsule, containing a White Cross amphetamine and shove the two powder-filled halves into each nostril. I knew we would be in Amarillo by morning.

(Sam may not have been the man's name. In this, as well as the following stories, names will be changed—not necessarily to protect the innocent. I just can't remember.)

Don't get me wrong. All overnighters weren't chemically induced mad dashes. All drivers weren't crazed speed freaks. Some were full of guile and resourcefulness.

Ernie had a unique and effective way to deter the authorities when he got pulled over for speeding. On occasion, he was forced to implement "Operation Teens for Christ."

THE SCENE: Middle of the night. Middle of nowhere. Flashing lights. Side of the road. Ninety-two in a seventy. The Vikings slept in their bunks.

STEP ONE: Make sure Charlie keeps everyone in their bunks.

STEP TWO: Reach up and change the destination marquee on the front of the bus from "Private Coach" to "Teens for Christ."

STEP THREE: When the highway patrolman walks up, make sure to step out in front of the bus, where said patrolman can see said marquee.

STEP FOUR: When asked, "Do you know how fast you were going?", apologize profusely with your best, "I'm sorry, Officer. I know I may have been going a bit fast. But I've got Teens for Christ asleep back there, and they're just a bunch of young kids and they're really tired and they just had a late show in Indianapolis and I've got to get them to Milwaukee as quick as I can."

STEP FIVE: Once ticketless in Milwaukee, return marquee to "Private Coach" position.

Many all-nighters resulted in sunrise truck-stop breakfasts. On one of these mornings, I stumbled off the bus and into the Butte, Montana greasy spoon. As Howie (the driver) fueled up, everyone else remained racked out from the late party. The early morning after found me dining alone, anxious to get something in my stomach besides beer and potato chips.

I didn't feel so good, as I sat down at the counter and ordered a cup of coffee. With the bus idling at the gas pump right outside the door, biscuits and gravy, bacon and eggs, and a couple of Alka-Seltzers were my ticket back to health. As I ate, I didn't think anything of it when the bus pulled away. Oftentimes, after gassing up, drivers will pull them off to the side and out of the way.

I ordered another cup of coffee and turned back to the newspaper. When I paid my bill and strolled outside, the parking lot was completely devoid of anything resembling a bus. Big buses are hard to miss. The place was empty, filled with tumbleweeds, overflowing trash bins, flea-riddled dogs, and silence.

The curtain rises. "Operation Stranded Polack" begins.

SCENE ONE: Sunrise on an empty, rural truck stop in the middle of Montana. The gas pump—which, twenty minutes earlier, housed a big bus—now stood unoccupied.

Walking back inside, I approached the bespectacled waitress behind the cash register, politely asking, "Did you see that bus that was out there?"

"Yep", came her terse answer, not even looking up from the crossword puzzle in her lap.

"Do you know where it is?"

"Yep." Focus remained on the puzzle.

"It didn't leave, did it?"

With a lipstick drag of her cigarette, she looked up, answering, "Yep."

"Well, I'm part of the band that's on that bus, and I'm supposed to be on that bus, and …"

"Don't worry," she interrupted.

"What?"

"Don't worry. They'll be back. They didn't pay their fuel bill. I just called the Highway Patrol. They oughta be here in about ten or fifteen minutes."

Relieved, but more amused, I reclaimed my spot at the counter. I wasn't worried. I ordered a piece of pie and did my best not to laugh. No one else in the diner was amused with unpaid gas bills. I'd become collateral as I quietly sat and waited for the bus.

SCENE TWO: Flashing lights, a bus of sleeping Vikings pulled over to the shoulder of the highway. This time, "Teens for Christ" would not be of any help.

"How fast was I going, Officer?" Howie pleaded. "I didn't think I was going that fast."

"You weren't," informed the patrolman.

"What?"

"You weren't. You weren't speeding. But you've got to go back to that truck stop and pay for your gas. Plus, you forgot one of your guys."

SCENE THREE: As I continued to wait, I watched the police escort the bus off the highway, down onto the parking lot, and up to the station. Howie jumped from the bus with an apologetic, "I'm sorry. I thought Charlie had paid for the gas." Charlie, wiping his bloodshot eyes, explained, "And I'm sorry too. I thought Howie'd taken care of it."

The attendant was not amused. It was an honest mistake. No charges were pressed. Charlie smoothed everyone's feathers—a trait he was very good at. By now, the bus was awake. I jumped back on. Charlie paid the bill. Five minutes later, we were back on the road.

Now, getting back to me getting stranded. Howie didn't think anyone had gotten off the bus when we pulled in, and Charlie hadn't counted noses when we left. It was a funny Montana morning.

Navigating those buses over open roads and through large, empty Holiday Inn parking lots is easy. It got interesting—and very entertaining—when we took them into the narrow streets of the big city.

Joe Bob was a young, strapping, high-strung chain smoker who had never been north of the "Makes a Difference Line." With a short redneck temper and a loud redneck voice, he actually thought the South was going to rise again, wore a hat like his idol, Richard Petty, and hated anything remotely Northern.

It was ironic when he became our driver for a two-week jaunt through the Northeast that included stops in "bus-friendly" places like New York, Boston, Philadelphia, Providence, Baltimore, Hartford, and Washington, D.C. For the entire tour, he starred in a one-man show entitled, "Operation Yankee Cocksucker."

Daily drives were dashes. If someone cut in front of him, his switch would get tripped, the veins would bulge in his neck, and smoke would come out of his ears. With barrage after barrage of "Fuck you, you God damn Yankee cocksucker! Move over, you fucking asshole or I'll kick your God damn Yankee ass!" these tirades were a constant source of amusement for the poker game in the lounge area right behind him. He was not a happy camper.

He wasn't much happier as he sat parked behind New York's Lone Star Cafe—one of the most prestigious venues to play, as well as one the most inconvenient places to load in and out of. Silver Eagle buses are no picnic on these streets. Tonight, Joe Bob was not in a picnicking mood.

It was late. The streets were quiet. We'd just played a couple ferocious sets, as everyone was slowly meandering out to the bus for an overnight drive up the coast. With this many guys, it was always an ordeal just to go anywhere. While we waited, a fire engine pulled around the corner at the far end of the block. With lights and sirens ablaze, it raced directly at us.

There was only one problem: Our bus completely blocked the street. Still, the commotion came streaming our way. When the two behemoths stood nose to nose, it was apparent that somebody was going to have to back down—and back up. As the big bus and the big fire truck had the big stare-down, it became apparent that we were the ones who were going to have to move. They had stinking badges. Joe Bob put it in reverse.

Driving a big bus through narrow city streets is one thing. Backing one up is another—a much slower go. I jumped into the shotgun seat,

It Shined

amused with it all—a loud commotion outside, a continuous chorus of "Yankee cocksuckers" inside.

He got even, though, a few days later, when one such Yankee cocksucker pulled out in front of him. With Charlie's assistance, "Operation Golden Shower" was implemented.

THE SCENE: Middle of the day. Middle of the tour. Middle of some highway, somewhere between Boston and Providence. "God damn Yankee cocksucker!" he bellowed, as the car pulled out in front of the bus.

STEP ONE: Speed up and pass said Yankee cocksucker.

STEP TWO: Be a road hog, turn into a Southern asshole, and not give the Yankee cocksucker any chance of pulling back around.

STEP THREE: Draw a bead.

STEP FOUR: With the unsuspecting New Englander squarely in his rear-view mirror, yell, "Charlie, assume the position."

STEP FIVE: Charlie steps into the bathroom.

STEP SIX: "Ready. Ready. Ready. NOW."

STEP SEVEN: When Charlie pulled on the toilet's release valve, the entire contents—blue stuff AND yellow stuff—sprayed all over the startled Yankee cocksucker's windshield.

It was a horrible thing to do. It was also very funny. The poker players howled. So did the Family Feud players. So did the Dictionary Game players. With ten guys on the bus and Charlie—an avid games and numbers freak—at the helm, there was always some kind of action going on in the front lounge. Always.

On a daily basis, he would break out his briefcase, issue per-diem advances to players, light up a Marlboro, crack open a cold beer, do a big bump, and commence to dealing the cards. What would a good poker game be without a bunch of guys drinking, smoking, and snorting, anyway?

One trip into Kmart for toiletries found him returning to the bus with the home version of *Family Feud* under his arm. Daytime TV on a rock 'n' roll bus is a given. We all loved watching Richard Dawson, laughing mightily at the hurried answers of his harried contestants. When Charlie opened the box and set up the little board, we played "the Feud."

Families were chosen, which basically consisted of whoever was sitting next to one another. Charlie assumed the role of Richard Dawson.

The Fun Bunch, 1979. (back row) Ruell Chappell, Canway, Dillway, Larry (front row) me, Rune and Cash-o (photo by Jim Mayfield)

Everyone yelled, "Good answer! Good answer!" when one was given. Charlie issued a loud, obnoxious "EHHNN," complete with rib gouges, when an answer was wrong.

When outsiders joined in, cheering sections formed. The rooting and shouting was infectious. Many of the drunken answers were side-splitting. Many of the games, ear-splitting. When women joined in, they naturally had to be kissed by Richard Dawson.

When we pulled into fairground and festival sites, while our rock 'n' roll brethren stomped around in motorcycle boots and leather jackets, we sat on our bus, getting stoned and playing Family Feud.

Women loved it—especially the classier ones, who preferred sitting on a nice bus, sipping cocktails to admiring some guy's new tailpipes. Drivers, on more than one occasion, would comment, "You guys are nuts. I drive around a lot of bands and I've NEVER seen anybody just sit around and play Family Feud. Why aren't you guys out there chasing pussy?"

While the Family Feud was an exercise in boisterousness, the Dictionary Game was much more subdued—but, no less funny. The rules were simple—sit there with a pencil and a piece of paper in your lap, while the dealer leafs through a dictionary. When he stumbles upon a word he was unfamiliar with, the game began.

As the word was pronounced—along with its correct spelling—everyone began making up their own definitions. While, secretly, writing them down, the dealer writes the correct definition on his sheet. All are read, back to back to back to back. The object of the game? See how many people you can fool. More importantly, how many you can make laugh.

The game was easy to play. You didn't have to do anything, but sit around with a dictionary. One episode in Eugene, Oregon produced a definition so astoundingly absurd, it found its way onto one of our records.

As we relaxed around the hotel after the gig, the word game broke out with old friend David "Bean" Walter. Bean, a gifted songwriter and member of the Sound Farm (Columbia, Missouri's legendary hippie band of the '60s), had relocated to the Pacific Northwest in the early '70s—and never left.

Years before, nights were spent playing wild music and howling at the Missouri moon. Tonight, we spent the evening howling at the Oregon moon with a dictionary. As the tome passed into Cash-o's hands, he thumbed through the "P" section.

Finding "pachuco," the game got underway.

When all entries were collected, Steve began to read. Along with the real definition and a couple other feeble attempts (i.e. the ankle of a duck), Bean brought the game to a thrilling conclusion. His was obviously not the correct answer—just the cleverest and clearest.

As Steve began reading, "City street. Hang out. Thumbs in pocket. Black jacket. Blackjack. Dago red. Manhattanized Bohemia of Southern California. Tough punk of cool, futuristic Montana," the last few syllables were delivered from the floor. The game came to a screaming, screeching halt.

It was the definition of all definitions—a poem Steve began to recite on stage, as we tumbled into "Arroyo." When we recorded his funky song at Caribou, which also features a long, informal start, Bean's definition became an integral part of the canvas.

Even if it was only for an evening in Eugene or dinner in Denver, I enjoyed seeing, catching up, and staying in touch with old friends. I consider this to be a fringe benefit of the job—a privilege many people back in Springfield did not have.

Plus, with as many guys as we had on the bus, somebody always had a friend, somewhere—and these friends knew that all they had to do was show up and they'd be ushered in. They were well rested, loaded for skunk and coke. Even though we may have just had an evening in Eugene or dinner in Denver, with the correct medication, the party remained afloat.

To finish up about the bus, there was only one rule: "No Number 2." A no-smoking rule was out of the question. Smoke was a given, blending in with the smell of sweaty men, spilled beer, and Christmas tree air fresheners. What didn't blend in was the smell of a turd, sloshing around in the toilet, directly behind the poker game.

Out of respect for each other, we learned to utilize truck-stop bathrooms. The "No Number 2" rule was strictly enforced.

Smoking? That didn't bother anybody.

Smelling like a basketball team? Not a problem.

Diesel fumes? Horrible, but tolerable.

Taking a shit on the bus? Completely out of the question.

There were those among us who still preferred those small planes. I was not one of them. I liked the drives. I liked the bunks. I had no trouble sleeping in them. I liked being able to lounge around and watch *Monty Python and the Holy Grail* over and over, laughing hysterically with each viewing. I liked the horsing around. I liked the poker games. I liked substituting for Charlie when he was unable to fulfill his Richard Dawson duties.

If the gig was a shit hole, the bus was a great place to get away from the stench, the noise, and the people. Plus, it made quite an impression when it pulled into town. No matter what the marquee on the front said, all a driver had to do was cruise around campus with his door open. The things are babe magnets. Babes started to jump on.

The Viking Bus rolled. Even though our last two records hadn't sold very well, A&M had picked up the option for two more. When they did this, we drove the Viking Bus back out to Colorado.

CHAPTER 22

After a couple of albums that garnered little attention and disappointing results, we headed back up to Caribou Ranch. With a renewed commitment from A&M and a bolstered lineup, we began another month-long stay in the Rockies.

"It was like a vacation," John recalls. "A real expensive vacation. We were up there, probably longer than we should've been, spending a lot of money—our money—that A&M was fronting us. But it was great."

When we drove through the Caribou gate, it was a comforting sight—one as spectacular as we remembered. We were greeted as old friends by the tech staff in the studio, who helped Charlie, Tucker, and newly hired David Trask set up the gear. The girls on the kitchen staff were still smiling and accommodating, a staff which had grown to include Lydia Cornell, who would soon move to Hollywood and into the role of Sara Rush on *Too Close for Comfort*.

Guercio still presided over the whole place on horseback, his pistol at his side.

When all of the above had been alerted that we were coming, the tape vault, as well as the wine cellar, was well-stocked. Our daily routine was the same as it was on our last visit. We all passed through the kitchen on our way down to the studio for the day's work. Dinners were still served family style—though the family had grown—in the evening.

More guys in the band meant more wives, kids, and girlfriends. Friends from back home, having heard how cool the place was, started to find their way out. We did get our work done, though the parties, as well as the consumption, grew—considerably.

As the July concert circuit brought artists through the Denver/Boulder area, those who knew about the ranch made side trips—just to pay visits.

Dennis Wilson and Al Jardine of the Beach Boys stopped by for a couple of days of beer and barbecue.

Ann and Nancy Wilson of Heart stopped by to check out the studio and spend a quiet afternoon.

Gerry Beckley and Dewey Bunnell of America dropped in for a glass of wine, some peace and quiet and a visit to the site of their *Hideaway* and *Harbor* albums.

Bill Champlain, Terry Haggerty, and Geoffrey Palmer of the Sons, who had just recorded their *Loving Is Why* album here, stopped by for a smoke and a joke.

All were welcomed in. All were extended invitations into the studio. Though several stuck their heads into the control room, none were even remotely interested in concentrating on anything—except the Ranch itself.

The Sons, in Boulder for a two-night stand, returned our hospitality with invitations down to their gig. This was great. We were all huge fans. While some of us spent these evenings in the studio, others spent them hanging around Boulder. Though we already knew quite a few people in the area, more contacts were made with more local characters.

We gained wonderful access to whatever kind of adult libation we wanted. All the Rocky Mountain High delivery man had to do was tell them at the front gate who he was. He was waved right in.

We knew the sonic shortcomings of the place. But we decided to once again overlook this minor detail and have some fun. Plus, with the personalities in our new lineup, fun was rapidly rising to the top of our priorities list.

This time, when we headed for the hills, we rode in on a horse of a different color—I mean a David of a different last name. David Anderle had begun taking more of an active role in A&M's burgeoning film department. When his schedule disallowed him from producing our record, David Kerschenbaum was called in.

With a renewed commitment from the label, everyone involved thought this might be a good time for a fresh start. We hadn't had a hit on either of the last two records.

Not only was the energetic Kerschenbaum still riding high from producing Joan Baez's 1975 A&M comeback, *Diamonds and Rust*, the Springfield native had cut his boyhood musical teeth across the backyard fence from Steve Cash.

Steve recalls, "[Kerschenbaum] was just another kid in the neighborhood, all going to fourth grade together. It was maybe fifth or sixth grade when he said, 'Come on over to my house today. My mother just got a tape recorder.' That was exotic. I thought, 'Tape recorder?' Then he said, 'And they got me an electric guitar and an amp.' He didn't really even know how to play the guitar. But I went over there and he taped his first sounds."

The bespectacled Kerschenbaum, who would be responsible for bringing Joe Jackson and Bryan Adams into the A&M fold, was also the man responsible for fronting David Kerr & the Playboys, his wildly successful Springfield '60s rock 'n' roll band. "They played at Rockaway Beach all the time," Steve continues. "My brother-in-law, Jimmy Baird, played bass and Canaday played drums."

Though I would've loved to have heard the Playboys, I never did. By the time I moved to Springfield, David had already uprooted to California and changed his name back to Kerschenbaum. I heard all of the stories, though. That June, he greeted us like long-lost friends.

David, who would go on to produce Tracy Chapman's Grammy-winning "Fast Car," was now the man hired to produce us. It was a natural selection. He was a hit-maker. We needed a hit.

I enjoyed the short, energetic man right off the bat, immediately identifying with his unbridled passion and animated enthusiasm for what he did. Though sometimes he would get a little too animated and a little too enthusiastic, his track record was irrefutable.

In another fine example of the coincidence-laden Springfield music scene, I dug the irony of this old Springfield guy, who, after making a name for himself in Hollywood, was going to make a record with some more old Springfield guys. I looked forward to working with him—a bunch of Springfield guys with Springfield ears. I was glad to be a Springfield guy, even though I maintained my St. Louis ears.

When he came to town to pick songs for the album, logistics were easy. He just stayed with his folks, who still lived on the south side of town.

Conversation around the Caribou dinner table oftentimes took on a very "Days of Springfield Yore" atmosphere. I enjoyed hearing tales of the music scene before I arrived. I was well acquainted with the entire cast of characters, laughing heartily when I heard about their teenage rock stardoms.

David's negotiations with the label were simple. The only thing he demanded was that his producer credit be displayed on the outside cover. When record buyers picked up the album in the store, he wanted them to read his name. He was hot. He made it clear to everyone, right off the bat, that he was the producer, it was his name on the line, and he was in charge.

I had no problem with this Napoleonic approach either. His ideas about the direction of the music completely coincided with mine. When he observed that he didn't think *Men from Earth*—though aesthetically pleasing—was what the fans wanted to hear, I let him know I was in his corner.

Instead of downplaying the word *daredevil*, which we had been doing since its inception, he wanted to liven things up, putting the emphasis back on the name of the band. That fall, when the album was released, the artwork was not a subdued photo of a couple of guys and their mules, awash in a rainbow of browns and grays. It was a whole bunch of guys, horsing around under a loud banner that blared DAREDEVILS in bright red and yellow letters.

With his inexhaustible energy and a couple of old drinking buddies in the band, we commenced to drinking and recording. I thought these were two grand ideas. The Viking Ducks were taking roost at Caribou again. I was ready to roll.

Young Englishman Pete Henderson was flown in to engineer the sessions. Henderson, who had started his career at George Martin's AIR Studios, trained exclusively with Beatles' recording engineer Geoff Emerick (*Sgt. Pepper, Abbey Road*). Along with this, he worked on numerous sessions as an in-house engineer with the legendary Sir George.

As a freelance producer himself, he had worked in top studios all over the world, co-producing *Breakfast in America*, Supertramp's 20 million-selling platinum A&M album (for which he won a Grammy for Best Engineered Album). Having also worked with Paul McCartney, Ringo Starr, Rush, Frank Zappa, Jeff Beck, and Tina Turner, the affable knob-twiddler had agreed to come to Caribou to record the Ducks.

But only if he could return to London to mix the songs at AIR.

Though we were satisfied with the sound Marty had gotten on our last two records, we looked forward to having a pair of British ears listen to our music again. We knew the drawbacks of tapes made at Caribou. But Pete reassured us that he could make them sound as good as ever—if he could mix them on gear he was familiar with.

This was only natural. When Glyn asked to work at Olympic, we didn't have a problem. When Pete asked to work at AIR, no one objected to flying back over to England to mix the record.

Dates were decided upon.

Studios were booked.

Cocktails were served.

In place of Anderle's laid-back approach of just letting us figure out for ourselves what to do, Kerschenbaum lit into our songs like David Scissorhands. He ripped into the first song of the session, "River to the Sun," paring our eight-minute rant down into a three-minute pop song. We'd been playing it for years. He was hearing it for the first time.

With this new band, we had become accustomed to playing in a raucous, inebriated state on stage. We wanted that same approach in the studio. We lit into "River" and ripped up the new arrangement real good. Though it was odd to hear the condensed version, I was glad the song finally got recorded. It had always been one of my favorites and a blast to play. It would open the album with a bang. I thought it was a great idea that the first sound you heard was Steve's harmonica.

Right behind that, we did "Snowbound," one of John & Steve's new songs about the joys of being stranded at home in the middle of the winter. The tune nicely showcased Rune's funky Lowell George-style guitar.

It Shined

Don't Look Down (left to right) Steve, Larry, Ruell, Jerry Mills, me, John, Rune and Steve (photo by Mark Hanauer)

Larry chimed in next with "Moon on the Rise," which also played right into Rune's chicken-pickin' hands.

When we followed these with "Backroads"—Canway's ode to the Ozark pastime of aimlessly driving along dirt roads with a cold bottle of beer between your legs—Kerschenbaum danced around the control room. The song, which had become a staple of our live set, featured Ruell's barrelhousing. Larry and I had been playing the song since the "Days of Southside Boys Past." It went onto tape, smoothly and quickly.

Another song we'd been playing nightly—and went onto tape in a flash—was an instrumental bluegrass tune I had written on mandolin. After teaching the tune to Jerry, I strummed the acoustic guitar, Rune chimed in on banjo, John played his fiddle, and we became a string band. For the past six months, we had used the simple tune—which I referred to as "Baked Potatoes"—to warm up in dressing rooms.

When we took the song to the stage, I walked out front with a guitar, Canway picked up my bass, and Larry played a lightning-fast tick-tack beat behind us. We began kicking off our encores with it. The lively tune goosed audience members out of their seats on a nightly basis.

One spirited evening found Charlie leaping onto the stage in the middle of the song, scaring the shit out of everybody. With no shirt on, a red bandanna around his neck, and a small pair of white sunglasses that made his large head appear even larger than it already was, he ran to the front of the stage and did a silly little jig that made everyone in the audience, as well as everyone in the band, laugh. His nightly cameos never failed to bring the house down or get the dancers up.

Those same sunglasses, worn on the bus in the middle of the day, garnered the same reaction, inciting Cash-o to observe, "Those things make you look like you just got stung all over your head by a million bees." Thus, Charlie acquired the nickname Stinghead, which got shortened to Sting. Now A&M had two acts with a guy named Sting on their payrolls.

Kerschenbaum loved the song, its contribution to the up-tempo style he was after, and its reinforcement of the band's name. The song had become an important part of our show. I made it my main focus to see that it became an important part of the album.

Unlike last time, I was going to make sure one of my songs made it onto vinyl. I wanted in on a larger slice of the publishing pie. I had a farm, a house, and a family to support. I made this clear to David. He agreed.

We recorded the tune the same way we recorded "The Red Plum"—with Jerry, Rune, John, and me all sitting in a circle, facing each other in the middle of the studio. Though we weren't really a bluegrass band, we did have a good time playing the song. After several passes, we laid down a very snappy track. Charlie didn't burst into the room and do his little dance. He did, however, make sure libations kept coming.

When David asked if the tune had a name, I shrugged my shoulders. I'd just been referring to it as "Baked Potatoes"—after mishearing one of Jerry Mills's first lessons in mandolinology. The length of a bluegrass tune's intro is often measured in potatoes. You can have "two potatoes" (two beats), "four potatoes" (four beats), "six potatoes" (six beats), or "eight potatoes" (eight beats). When Jerry asked how long I wanted the intro to be, my misguided answer was, "I'll take baked potatoes."

When it got down to it, though, I thought it was appropriate to pay homage to Charlie, his little dance, his little sunglasses, his large forehead, and his extremely large sense of humor. I dubbed the tune "Stinghead."

Over the past year, Rune had taught us the meaning and mythology of the Norwegian phrase, "Hey Skol." The ancient Viking battle cry, which literally means "Death to the enemy," became our mantra. Though we never meant death to anyone, "Hey Skol" became our "Hip-hip-hooray" on a nightly basis.

When we decided "Stinghead" deserved a "Hey Skol," we all (Charley included) gathered around the microphone. As the song swung into the last stanza, Pete hit the "record" button and we shouted in Norwegian. The toast-filled overdub took less than thirty seconds.

As work continued, Henderson—who enjoyed a libation or two—became quite fond of our convivial intake. One afternoon, he good-naturedly expressed the fact that he thought that he, an Englishmen, could outdrink us Americans.

The hair on Ruell's neck bristled as he yelled, "BULLSHIT! I bet you twenty bucks you can't."

"Oh, yeah? You're on," replied a defiant Pete.

"Hey, I want in on that," I chimed.

"Yeah, me too," yelled the Steves—Cash and Canaday.

When Rune caught word of what was going on, he rushed in from the other room, piping in with, "Hey. Vait a minute. Vhat are you guys tawking about? Wikings can drink all you pussies under the table." In a matter of minutes, an international beer-drinking competition was in the works. The Olympic Games were to begin on the evening we finished tracking all the songs.

THE SCENE: the dining room table at Caribou Ranch.

THE CAST: one dozen contestants (consisting of representatives from the United States, Great Britain, and Norway), surrounded by two dozen not-so-innocent bystanders (consisting of friends, family, staff members, various Boulderites and Nederlanders).

THE RULES: one shot of beer every sixty seconds. Last man standing, wins.

As the party began, the crowd gathered in the dining room. The principals took their places around the table. On one corner sat Pete, a strapping young English lad who liked to drink beer, but whose youth didn't provide him much experience.

On another corner sat Rune, a tall, stout Norwegian who was never without a beer in his hand.

The rest of the contestants were all Americans—Ruell, me, Cash, Canaday, Charlie, Larry Tucker, and Springfield engineer Pat Shikany, who had just recorded the demos for this record in his Dungeon Studios. He'd come to check out Caribou. Everyone threw twenty bucks into the pot. The Olympic torch was lit.

David Trask became the official timekeeper, equipped with a watch (with a second hand) and five cases of Heineken at his side. The (ahem) athletes from the three participating nations filled their shot glasses. When Trask counted, "Five, four, three, two, one, drink," all shots were downed. Glasses were set back on the table and refilled. The party resumed for fifty-five seconds—until the next countdown started.

With each minute, the party grew in hilarity. Mock national pride and cheering sections emerged. With each shot, word got out. Phone calls were made down the canyon. Additional locals made it up to the Ranch. Beer was not the only libation consumed in large quantities that evening. The party chugged into the night.

The first hour (sixty shots or five twelve-ounce beers) went without a hitch. Everyone excitedly talked about the record and laughed at the absurdity of the contest we were staging. If you had to take a leak, you had exactly fifty-nine seconds to make it to the bathroom and back to the table. If you could not find your way back in time for the next shot, you were disqualified.

Amid shouts of "Hey Skol," things turned into complete chaos.

When I could not lift my head off the table to answer the bell for the ninety-seventh shot, it was all I could do to crawl off into the kitchen and pass out. When I came to, an hour later, the contest was still going strong. The two remaining contestants—Canway and Shikany—were getting ready to down their one hundred eighty-first shots.

When I walked back into the room, I walked into the Twilight Zone. I have been around some stoned people in my life. That night, there were some stooooned people around that table—onlookers as well as contestants. The music on the stereo was turned up real loud, as Trask continued his countdowns.

The Englishman had fallen by the wayside after a mere 127 shots. The Norwegian had walked outside and fallen off the deck after 170. As the contest entered its fourth hour, the two remaining Americans were having a hard time keeping their tongues from falling out of their mouths.

After 200 shots, both tried to go to the bathroom, but neither could stand on their own. Both had to be carried outside by their arms, where they just peed wherever they could. Both made it back in time for Trask to announce, "Three, two, one, drink." There was still more than $200 in the pot.

I had made it for an hour and a half. These guys were entering their fourth hour. When the evening mercifully ended (Shikany threw in the towel after 213 shots), Canway was pronounced the winner. His prize? Having to be carried to and poured into his bed.

Because the contest had lasted so long, I had time to get drunk, pass out, wake up, rejoin the party, get drunk again, and somehow make it back to my cabin. The next day, when I lifted my head from the pillow, I was still stone-cold stoned. When I read 6:30 on the clock, I panicked.

My first thought—"Oh, no. It's 6:30 and I've slept through the entire day."

My second thought—"Everybody's probably getting ready to eat dinner. I'd better get a move on."

After throwing on whatever I could find to wear, I rushed down to the kitchen. Here I was met by a startled kitchen staff—some of whom had been at the party. It wasn't until they asked, "What are you doing here?" that I realized it was 6:30 in the morning and I had only been asleep for a few hours.

After a couple of Alka-Seltzers, they sent me back up to my cabin. When I woke again, all the Olympians had begun stirring. Breakfast was eaten with sunglasses on. Bloody Marys were administered. As a bonus for winning the gold medal, Canway was excused from the day's recording. Work continued.

Though A&M no longer felt Larry's voice was our ticket back onto the charts, we all agreed that a hit single was essential. We had grown accustomed to the kind of money hit singles provide. "Crazy Lovin'" became that song.

Kerschenbaum became obsessed with it. He was the hit-maker, and he was going to make it a hit—even if it didn't sound like us. With its Billy Joel piano intro and fist-pumping, Styx-like power chords on the guitar, John became equally obsessed.

The rest of us cringed at the amount of time being devoted to this one song and the blatant pursuit of a radio single. If it had been treated like all of the other songs, no one would have minded. When session after session was dedicated to recording, re-recording, and re-re-recording things on the tune, the grumblings in the back room began.

We all wanted a hit single. There was no question about that. But I didn't think pounding all of the life out of the song was the way to go about it. While John and David fretted in the studio, the rest of us played pool and rode horses. Whenever he could escape, Pete would leave the control room and join us, clenching his teeth and shaking his head.

Stanley, as well as David, was already touting it back to A&M as the next big, chart-topping thing. Once again, the adage of "putting all of your eggs in one basket" would be put to the test.

The rest of the songs on the album were recorded smoothly, quickly, and had a funky cohesiveness that well represented the band in its present state. Our single was taking forever, filled with long, melodramatic, Dennis DeYoung-like vocals.

Work on it continued. With each new vocal and each new overdub, the song sounded less and less like us and more and more like a "not-so-weird" radio. We got good at playing pool and riding horses.

Each day, when we finished recording, David would pore over rough mixes of the song in his cabin—all night long. After a while, the rest of us just began to roll our eyes. Flogging the song until all spontaneity was squeezed out of it was the approach Randy had wanted to take in the past. We didn't like it much then. We weren't liking it much now.

Still, David and John pounded away. Our fans wanted us to sound like us, not Billy Joel—or Styx. Still, David assured us, "It's a hit. It's a hit. Don't worry. It's a hit." He was the producer. We left it up to him.

We pressed on and got the work done. Studio time was no object. Neither were the gourmet food and wine tabs we were running up in the dining room. Neither was anything else we wanted to add to the expense account—like blow from Boulder, or a plane ticket for Connie Hamsey.

When Little Rock's own Sweet Connie was called and asked if she would enjoy a three-day all-expenses-paid trip to the Rocky Mountains, she jumped on the plane. When our families flew home, Connie blew in. Without going into too many details, the next three days were filled with the things legends are made of. You've read about her in *Rolling Stone*. You've read about her in *Newsweek*. You've read about her in *Hustler*. Charlie entered it as "entertainment" onto the A&M tab.

By the end of June, we had finished recording. When Pete headed to London with the master tapes under his arm, we headed back to Springfield. Because we weren't scheduled to mix the tapes until August, this gave us the month of July to re-acclimate from the Rockies back to the Ozarks and make a short trip out to L.A. to shoot some kind of album cover.

This way, it would give A&M time to ready the artwork while we were mixing the songs. Slated to come out in October, the album would be on shelves just in time for the holiday shopping season.

The only problem was, we hadn't decided on a title. When we landed at A&M, we had no idea what we were going to do. After meeting with Roland Young and Jeff Ayerhoff, we decided to pursue several ideas. Three separate photo shoots were set up.

The first idea was—you guessed it—"Crazy Lovin.'" All eight of us donned straitjackets and acted—you guessed it—crazy, as we jumped around the racquetball court A&M had reserved to simulate a mental hospital. It unfortunately didn't look like anything but a racquetball court. The idea was funny, but not that funny. The pictures were funny, but not that funny. The pictures were crazy, but not that crazy. The idea was scrapped.

As we were in search of a second crazy idea, a chauffeured van pulled up to our hotel the next morning. We all piled in with coolers full of beer, pockets full of drugs, two voluptuous models dressed as nurses, and some wheelchairs. Our withered, sixty-three-year-old driver, sporting slicked-back hair, a white shirt, and a tie, drove us to Santa Monica.

It was almost noon by the time we entered the large stucco warehouse, which housed the practice facilities of the Los Angeles Thunderbirds' roller derby team. Arrangements had been made to rent the track while the team wasn't using it.

Here we met the T-Birds' general manager, who, in his day, happened to be a roller derby star. We also met his midget assistant. Both were happy to help us. Both were expert skaters. Both donned referee shirts to become part of the photo.

There was no real threat of injury, as they were not about to let a bunch of drunken yay-hoos skate around the track and break their necks. We were issued skates, uniforms, and roller derby helmets.

Because some of us couldn't even skate, we were forced to re-enact phony scenes. The nurses became nurses with wheelchairs, placed on the infield of the track. The bus driver leaned over the railing, waving his hands like a rabid fan.

When everyone laced up their skates and found their way onto the track, there was much off-balanced clinging. A roller derby track is not level. The tilt is steep, to prevent skaters from flying into the stands. The tilt also prevented some of us from being able to even stand up.

It was decided that those who couldn't skate should hold on to those who could, while the two referees held the entire mass of humanity upright and in place. Broken bones may not mean much to a roller derby skater. They mean everything to a musician.

When the photographer yelled "Action," he got action.

John and Larry were positioned directly on the track, five feet in front of the rest of us. They began pretending to elbow each other in the throat.

The bus driver started cheering, waving his arms, and leaning over the railing.

The nurses manned their wheelchairs.

The rest of us, who had been huddled into an interlocking mass, just let go of each other and slowly rolled four feet forward—a thrilling four feet filled with flailing arms and terrified faces.

When the photographer yelled "Cut," the two T-Birds grabbed and stabilized everyone. Cocktails were served to a soundtrack of "Hey Skol." We rolled back to our original positions for another four-foot, four-second stretch of imbalance.

After a couple of hours, everyone was ready to get off wheels. Those of us who were good skaters were allowed to take a few laps around the empty track. Rune, Canway, Larry, Paul, and I took off. It's quite an experience to accelerate around those curves and feel physics and inertia whip you through the corners.

After a half dozen laps, all five of us were panting and thirsty. We knew where there were refreshments—in the van that was going to take us to yet another photo shoot. We all hopped in. The driver sped off toward Hollywood. We waved good-bye, as the nurses and their wheelchairs were dropped off at the modeling agency.

Though the roller derby idea was funny, I questioned what it had to with "Crazy Lovin.'" By this time, things were so confusing, we were just grabbing at straws.

When we arrived at one of the A&M's smaller soundstages, the setting was simple, consisting of a long two-by-four placed across some cinder blocks. We were instructed to climb on, line up, and try to keep ourselves balanced. Afterward, the board would be eliminated from the photo and replaced with a tightrope.

Canway on one end and Cash on the other were instructed to hold their outer hands in the air, as if holding up the two ends of the rope. Those of us in the middle threw our arms over each other's shoulders for shaky balance. The doctored photo would then be superimposed onto a sky blue background, giving the appearance that we were mysteriously suspended in midair.

Charlie, Stan, and Paul became spotters, holding all of us in place atop the two-by-four. When the photographer yelled "Action," they let go and vacated the frame. This turned us into the Flying Wallendas, weaving back and forth, trying to keep eight guys balanced on one board. The length of each attempt was no more than five seconds—before someone would lose it and fall.

This didn't matter, as we were only a foot off the floor. That wasn't the point. The facial contortions were. When one of us caused all of us to jump off, all we had to do was have a good laugh and hop back up on the board.

This idea, just like the roller derby idea, didn't have much to do with the "Crazy Lovin'" theme. This was fine. Most of us were glad to see this crazy loving thing fading away.

We dubbed the record, *Don't Look Down*.

From here, John, Larry, Steve, Canway, and I flew over to AIR Studios, where we rendezvoused with David and Pete. The flight was uncharacteristically quiet and unburdened, due to the fact that every other time we had flown over, we hauled equipment and entourages. This time, all we needed was our ears.

It was a steamy August day when we landed in London. In lieu of staying in hotel rooms for the month, A&M leased a large, furnished five-bedroom flat in a quiet, unassuming neighborhood. This was fine with us. We weren't interested in making the daily forty-minute drive in from Headley Grange anyway. We much preferred the ten-minute subway ride from our flat to the studio.

Complete with high ceilings, tall windows, wood floors, and plush furniture, the most important furnishing in the entire place was, without a doubt, the giant stereo that had been installed in the formal parlor. The unit got quite a workout, as we sat, drank coffee, and listened to daily mixes.

When we first walked in, copies of *Sticky Fingers* and Elvis Costello's *My Aim Is True* lay next to the turntable—left behind by the technician who set up the gear. Both records received immediate and frequent spins. Both got played over and over, day and night, for two good reasons: 1) They're fantastic records, and 2) They were the only two we had.

By the first few listens, we learned that Mick and Keith had done it again, and this little funny-looking guy named Elvis was really, really good. A&M dropped off a selection of their latest releases, but we weren't really interested in Rick Wakeman's latest rock opera. When we came home, it was a bowl of hash, Elvis, and the Stones.

On the corner, a half block away, steps led down to the subway that would lead directly to Oxford Circus—site of AIR Studios. AIR, located on the third floor of one of the tall office buildings, could not have been more inconspicuous.

When you walk through the Circus, you rub elbows with a wide variety of British street characters. When you enter the building, you walk alongside a wide variety of British businessmen. When the elevator opens onto the third floor, you walk directly across the hall and in AIR's front door. Here, the hustle and bustle of Oxford Circus is replaced by the peace and quiet of a recording studio.

It was great to see Pete and David again. Kerschenbaum, as high-strung as ever, immediately began filling us in on what he'd heard on the tapes, what we needed to do, and what we needed to change. After a month of pondering, his to-do list was extensive.

The mellower Henderson quietly led us into the control room, introducing us to his assistant, Nigel Walker. Nicknamed "Wombat," the slender man had spent the past several years as Pink Floyd's live mixing engineer. When Pink wasn't touring, Nigel worked with Pete in the studio. He was accustomed to making things sound good. That August, the two Brits got our tapes sounding real good.

For the past month, Pete had been filling him in with stories of Caribou and the drinking contest. Nigel, no stranger to a pint himself, was anointed Minister of Silly Walks, and we all became regulars at the pub around the corner.

Things got off to a great start. Pete was happy to be working on gear he was familiar with. We were happy to be in England again. One by one, songs started getting transferred from David's to-do list to his been-done list. Plus, they all sounded great.

"River to the Sun" was filled with Steve's blasting harmonica over Larry's pounding tom-tom beat. "Backroads" and "Snowbound" got funky, fast. "Stinghead" took almost as much time to mix as it took to record. Days started to fly by, each ending the same way—with Elvis and the Stones.

Tom and Frances Bissell became welcome visitors again, inviting us to gourmet meals (prepared by her), complete with wonderful wine (selected by him). We got our cheeseburger and milkshake fix at the Hard Rock Cafe, which had recently opened its London doors.

Unlike any other studio we'd ever worked in, if you wanted to step outside for some fresh air, you couldn't. Well, you could—if you wanted to walk out into the hallway, wait for the elevator, take it down to the ground floor, and navigate Oxford Circus. "Stepping out" at AIR meant hanging around the lobby, with its large, overstuffed chairs, or down the hall in the break room, with its coffeemaker and pinball machine.

Sir George's kingdom consisted of three separate studios—the big room up front (where we were), a smaller room in the back, (where Gino Vanelli was—and where the Sex Pistols soon would be), and Martin's own personal mixing room, halfway down the hall between the two.

The occupants of all three studios had to use the same lobby, the same break room, and the same bathroom. Sometimes this made for a crowded hallway. It also made for some diverse combinations of people. After a couple of weeks, everyone got to know each other quite well.

It became commonplace to pass Sir George in the hall. No one blinked an eye when Pete's mentor, Geoff Emerick, walked in one day with a portable tape recorder under his arm. The red-haired Emerick, having just returned from Scotland, where he had been making field recordings of the bagpipes that would appear on Paul McCartney's *Mull of Kintyre*, asked if we'd like to hear them. Our answer was a simple "Suuure." He assured us it wouldn't take long. It didn't. Martin was called in. The tapes were cued. Every seat in the control room was taken.

How could we say no? These were the two men responsible for the Beatles' sound. We knew we were just a group of guys, in the right place at the right time. The moment was seized.

When played in their raw form, the pipes sounded like a million bucks. By the time they were inserted into the mull, they sounded like two million bucks and three million copies. Geoff and George apologized for taking our time, but we assured them that it was not a problem—thirty minutes well spent. Both became fixtures. Both stuck their heads in on a daily basis.

Sticking your head into other studios became commonplace. When label-mate Gino Vanelli invited everyone in for a listen, a crowd gathered. As he played one dramatic Mediterranean sex anthem after another, Wombat listened quietly—until he just couldn't take it anymore, observing, "Yeah, Gino. That sounds great. But who's going to buy that shit?" One by one, we slithered from the room. A&M had delivered copies of his records to our flat the week before. They didn't get played—just as Rick Wakeman's records didn't get played.

It was a quiet, slowly developing morning when I stumbled into Sir George in the hallway. Both of us had coffee cups in our hands. Mine was empty, as I headed for the coffee machine. His was full, as he headed into his studio. He smiled and asked if I had a minute. Of course I had a minute.

When he asked if I'd stick my head into his studio and give him an opinion about something, I couldn't believe my ears. When we stepped inside, he sat down at the console, took a couple of sips from his cup, made a couple of adjustments on the board, turned around, and asked, "Tell me if you think these guitars are too loud?"

I couldn't believe it—him, asking me if Paul McCartney's guitars were too loud. When they floated out of the speakers, they were perfect. When I expressed this, he responded with, "Thanks. Just wanted another opinion." I bid him a fond adieu and he sent me on my way with "Have a good day, mate."

When I pushed the door open and continued my trek to the coffee machine—after having just heard music from heaven—I walked smack dab into the devil. Sid Vicious's complete lack of civil behavior was the exact opposite of Sir George's manners.

The punk rock scene was busting wide open in the summer of '77—and I loved every minute of it. I liked the rawness of the music as much as I liked watching the escapades of its characters. I dug watching record companies clamor over each other, offering contracts to anyone with a safety pin through his ear. The epitome of the scene was the Sex Pistols—its epicenter, Vicious.

After having swindled several record companies (A&M included) out of a lot of money, they had booked the back studio at AIR for the week. As they recorded *Never Mind the Bollocks. Here Come the Sex Pistols*, they brought the entire London punk scene upstairs with them.

All we had to do, to get a bird's eye view of the parade was look out our door. If we wanted to hear the music, all we had to do was walk down the hall. Even though their door remained closed, we could hear them in there, bashing and crashing away. It was pure rock 'n' roll, with a hell of lot more passion than Rick Wakeman or Gino Vanelli. I dug the hell out of it.

Along with bumping into George Martin and Geoff Emerick, we were now able to bump into Sid Vicious and Johnny Rotten. Everyone had to walk through the same lobby. Everyone had to use the same bathroom. Everyone had to play the same pinball machine. We laughed our earlobes off.

The punks' antics splashed across the front pages of the paper on an everyday basis. We enjoyed reading about Costello, playing his songs on the street with a Pignose amp strapped to his side. It was an eerie feeling, though, to listen to Elvis Costello on the evening of August 15—then pick up the *London Times* the next morning to read about Elvis Presley's demise.

Though it was a terrible way to start the day, it didn't keep us from working. The scene around AIR held a subdued, "work as usual" climate. We came in to work in our studio. Martin came in to work in his studio. Rotten came in to work in his. When we went back to the flat that night, it was the old Stones and the NEW Elvis.

As we began to get close to finishing, only a couple of overdubs remained. Geoff Richardson came in to play viola on Larry's haunting "Giving It All to the Wind."

When Pete mentioned the water gong, we asked, "What's a water gong?" John and David, still searching for the magic elixir for "Crazy Lovin,'" eagerly agreed, "Yeah, yeah. Let's try a water gong."

Wombat began filling a very large tub of water in the middle of the studio. As we pulled a couple of chairs alongside, Pete pulled a huge gong out of the closet. Oh yeah, we get it. The gong goes in the water. Duh. We gathered around.

When the tub was filled and microphones positioned, Dillon and Canway climbed up on the chairs, holding the gong directly over the tub.

When Pete ran back into the control room and hit the "record" button, Larry hauled off and banged the shit out of the gong, sending spikes of overtones throughout the room.

When John and Steve slowly lowered the vibrating cymbal into the water, the ringing descended in pitch. Then it disappeared into thin air … I mean, thin water.

It was a technique Pete and Nigel had used on Supertramp's last album. But it just didn't work on "Crazy Lovin.'" Still, we had a good time listening to Larry bang the gong and watching John and Steve dip it into the water. After a while, the idea was scrapped. The water gong may have been essential to Supertamp's art. For us, it was a complete waste of time. We went to Happy Hour gongless.

Still we pressed on, finishing and finding our way home with stories of George Martin and Johnny Rotten, freshly mixed tapes of our record in our pockets, and a case of *My Aim Is True* under our arms. Right before we left, we arranged for A&M to exchange a case of our records for a case of Elvis's. We knew a lot of friends back home who were going to flip for this guy. When we got home, E's records got passed all over town. Three-year old, Sya went nuts for it, grabbing a copy and heading right for her room.

For the next month in Springfield, just like the past month in London, Costello's songs played constantly—not only on my big stereo, but on Sya's little record player. The following March, *My Aim Is True* was released in the States. We had been listening to it in the Ozarks since August.

Our album sounded good too, as we were anxious to get back on the charts. Kerschenbaum, as well as everyone at A&M, was excitedly convinced that "Crazy Lovin'" was our ticket back into the limelight. I wasn't so sure.

Neither was Larry, recalling, "Everyone was screaming, 'RADIO HIT. RADIO HIT.' I didn't really care that much if it was a hit. 'Crazy Lovin'' just didn't sound like us, and there were other songs that were much better on that record that did sound like us."

Still, Stan suggested that it would be a good idea if we showed signs of cooperation with the label. When they asked us to go on radio/press junkets, we went. With test pressings in hand, we scattered. Because there were so many of us, we could cover a lot of territory—sending a couple of guys to each part of the country. John and Larry hit the East Coast, flying to New York, Boston, and Detroit. Cash and Canway hit the West Coast, flying to L.A., San Francisco, and Seattle. I hit Tulsa, Minneapolis, and Kansas City, before ending up in St. Louis and Shelley Graffman's K-SHE offices.

When the disc jockeys asked about our new single, "Crazy Lovin'" was cued up. When the song began, there was something different—jaw-droppingly different. John and David had made one last-minute adjustment. The day before the record was to be sent to the mastering lab, the two decided John's vocal wasn't good enough.

Without consulting anyone, Ruell was flown out to L.A., where he re-sang the song. After a quick remix, the tapes were sent to the mastering lab. Once an album is mastered and sent into production, it's too late to turn back. Ruell became the voice of the song.

Steve recalls, "I remember being in Seattle when I heard the new vocal for the first time. I couldn't believe they did that. We just tried to write a nice, little pop song and it ended up turning into this mutated thing."

Ruell's vibrato-filled vocal made the song sound even more like Styx than it already did. When I heard it, I was shocked. Now we sounded nothing like us. If one of the radio guys mentioned this, I quickly steered him toward "River to the Sun" or "Moon on the Rise."

When the album came out, it created such a non-stir, it stayed on the charts for a mere ten weeks. Not only was this the shortest stint for any of our records, it didn't even crack the Top 100—topping out at #132. "Crazy Lovin'" never made it onto any chart, anywhere.

So much for all of your eggs in one basket. A second single was never released.

CHAPTER 23

Though *Don't Look Down* was floundering, that fall, we rounded the troops back onto the bus and hit the road in support of it.

That October, we got some good news and some bad news. Which do you want first?

The good news was that our first album had just gone gold, and Missouri governor Walkin' Joe Teasdale was declaring November 28 Ozark Mountain Daredevils Day. To commemorate the occasion, he extended invitations to visit his office in Jefferson City.

The bad news was, because Ozark Mountain Daredevils Day fell right in the middle of a swing of gigs, in order to get there, I would have to ride in a little chartered airplane again.

More bad news came on October 20, when we learned that Lynyrd Skynyrd went down in theirs. Though we'd played some gigs with the Skynyrd boys, we never were that close. Still, I had a horrible, empty feeling in my heart for their families. I never thanked the Lord harder for the bus than I did on October 20, 1977.

The good news was, Walkin' Joe, a Democrat from Sedalia—who earned his nickname by walking across the state during his 1976 run for governor—was throwing us a little party at the capitol. We had a new record, a gold record, and a day named after us.

The bad news was, reports on *Don't Look Down* were not good. Nor were they promising. "Crazy Lovin'" was nowhere to be found.

The good news was, we were selling out gigs wherever we went. We began to obtain the reputation for throwing very festive parties—a reputation that provided full arenas. Concert promoters lined up to book us. Every night, Charlie walked out of their smoky offices with bags of money. Album sales may have been down, but ticket sales were up—way up.

The bad news was, we were forced to be away from home more than we wanted to be. We had been gone all of June, recording, and all of August, mixing. We just wanted to chill out at home and play with our kids. When A&M asked us to pick up our touring schedule, to help flagging sales of *Don't Look Down*, we balked.

Refusing to budge from our stance of not staying gone longer than the allotted seventeen-day period, we didn't. A&M was not thrilled. Though we kept up what we thought was a good workload, it was not up to industry standards.

Nor was it up to Jerry Moss's expectations of what he thought we were going to do to help promote the records he had just opted for. He also didn't like our practice of ignoring radio stations and newspapers.

Jerry Mills, still on the bus doing daily promotions for the album, continued to ask us to talk to these media people. General consensus— "Nahhh." General consensus—"We already talked to them, and they still aren't playing our records." General consensus—"They're not interested in our new material."

The good news was, we were having a great time playing gigs. The parties were large.

The bad news was, royalties from "Heaven" and "Jackie" began to show signs of tapering off. More and more, we began to rely on the revenue from our shows to keep up with our farm and truck payments, as well as the standard of living we'd grown accustomed to.

In the chilly early-morning air of November 28, 1977, I gritted my teeth and climbed into the back seat of the small, single-engine plane on the tarmac of the Peoria, Illinois airport. As the rest of the guys jumped on the bus to Omaha, John, Ruell, Canway, and I headed to Jefferson City and our 10:00 meeting with the governor.

It'd be a piece of cake. When the ceremony was over, all we had to do was jump back into the plane and rendezvous in Nebraska—arriving about the same time as the bus.

No problem, except for the fact that this meant not one but two sets of takeoffs and landings. Overcoming an overwhelming sense of dread with a large dose of Show-Me stubborn, the only thing I was concerned with was my barf bag.

The small Jefferson City Regional Airport quietly sits in the wide Missouri River Valley. Along the opposite side of the river, massive bluffs form curtains of stone. Regally perched atop the bluffs stands the domed capitol building, sentinel to this purple valley's majesty, where quiet mornings with Lewis & Clark are easily invoked.

The flight was not too turbulent. But that didn't matter. I still felt like shit when we landed. Though I didn't have to use my regurgitation receptacle, my stomach was still queasy as hell—on top of the butterflies that were already there. I jumped from the plane, to sit on the solid Missouri soil.

Here, we were met by a limo that whisked us off into the brisk morning. We had to hustle to get to the capitol by ten. There was no time to fool around. I checked all of my pockets for forgotten joints. I was clean. My stash was safely on the bus to Omaha.

When the limo driver sped from the airport, reached the top of the bluffs, and pulled into the archways of the capitol building, even though my stomach was in a dither, a warm sense of pride ran through the rest of me.

The clock was striking ten as we clamored up the empty marbled stairwells and into the lobby of Teasdale's offices. When we opened the door, the quiet echo of the stairwell was replaced with the buzzing of a very noisy lobby. The place was jam packed with people.

This is when we found out that not only was it Ozark Mountain Daredevils Day, it was Girl Scout Troop #214 Day, Registered Nurses of Hannibal Day, and Amalgamated Plumbers of Local #6 Day. Behind them stood Other Organizations from All Over the State Day—all with ten o'clock appointments.

Knowing that we were on a tight schedule, we were summoned from the noisy room by a page, led down a series of quiet corridors, and shown into the back entrance of the governor's chambers. The affable Teasdale, a large, jovial man with large, jovial hands, greeted us with hearty handshakes and cups of coffee. Introductions went around, as members of his staff were there, just as much to meet the band as they were for the ceremony.

With a hearty, "Come in. Come in. I'm glad you guys are here. Have a seat," he just wanted to sit and bullshit with the guys, before opening his door to the masses.

He knew he wasn't the only one on a tight schedule. That's why he pulled us to the front of the line. The entire visit lasted fifteen minutes. We presented him with copies of all our records. He presented us with plaques, proclaiming:

WHEREAS, the popular band, Ozark Mountain Daredevils, is a band formed in Missouri, based in Missouri, managed in Missouri, and drawing from the music and culture of the State of Missouri; and

WHEREAS, the Governor and the people of Missouri are most pleased that audiences throughout the world have taken the Ozark Mountain Daredevils to their hearts, and have responded to this music of Missouri with exuberance and enthusiasm; and

WHEREAS, the Ozark Mountain Daredevils have, individually and collectively, helped make people throughout the world aware of the natural beauty of Missouri and the advantages of living in our beautiful state, as well as exposing the world to our music, art, crafts, and culture; and

WHEREAS, the Governor, on behalf of the people of the State of Missouri, takes great pleasure in congratulating the Ozark Mountain Daredevils for receding a Gold Record Award for their first album and on release of their fifth album for worldwide distribution by A&M Records:

NOW, THEREFORE, I, JOSEPH TEASDALE, GOVERNOR OF THE STATE OF MISSOURI, do hereby proclaim November 28, 1977 as OZARK MOUNTAIN DAREDEVILS DAY in Missouri and urge Missourians to join in honoring them on the release of their new album, and for enjoying its unique musical offerings.

Hands were shaken. Photos were taken. Smiles were two miles wide. Backs were slapped. The small crowd clapped. Autographs went all around. With this, Teasdale started his day. As he opened his front door to a long line of girl scouts, nurses, and plumbers, we were out the back.

I felt great, though still nauseated from the flight—a nausea that knew that, in a few minutes, it was going to have to climb back aboard that little plane and try not to erupt on its way to Nebraska.

This second leg of the trip wasn't too bad either. But I still felt like hell when we landed on that cloudy, windy November afternoon.

I was glad to see the bus, knowing that I had just the thing for a queasy stomach. A couple of hits that afternoon helped knock the edge off the nausea. A nice dinner that evening threw a blanket over it. That night, a sea of tequila wiped the sucker right out.

When we got to the gig, the place was packed. We tore into a set, filled with high jinks, highballs, and "Hey Skol" after "Hey Skol." The crowd went crazy when Charlie came out and did his Stinghead dance.

Even though we were in Nebraska, it was still Ozark Mountain Daredevils Day in Missouri. A good time was had by all. I don't know if "Girl Scout Troop #214 Day" was as big a success. But I'll guarantee they didn't drink as much. I'm not sure about the plumbers.

As the year came to a close, we decided to take the holidays off. I decided to spend them in Guatemala. I loaded back onto the train in St. Louis and headed south. Sya, almost three years old by now, had become quite travel savvy. This made the trip a lot easier. Once again, the train took a few days to meander across Mexico. Once again, I had a few weeks with nothing to do but meander. A-meandering we went.

Most of my three-week stay was spent in and around Panajacel, where I became king of the market. New Year's Eve was spent dancing on volcanic soil. It snowed in Missouri.

Thursday is market day in Panajacel. The small, makeshift agora, directly at the foot of the village church, was filled to capacity. Vendors noisily hawked their wares. Children with melting ice-cream cones in their hands laughed and ran through the narrow, undefined aisles.

It Shined

Women with baskets of produce balanced on their heads dodged the livestock and poultry that roamed freely. Others set up shop right where their baskets fell.

As we strolled into the market fray, I once again heeded Tom's advice by staying in the light and out of the shadows. Here I became king of the market. I didn't *try* to become king of the market. I became king of the market by being court jester of the market.

My eye had been caught by a game of three-card monte, taking place on a small cardboard box in an entranceway. Having always loved the mythology, mystery, and "base thirteen" mathematics of a deck of cards, I became an enthralled observer. I loved the game, as well as the beehive of activity that surrounded the box.

I watched intently as hand after hand, someone laid down a Quetzal on what they thought to be the odd card. I found myself correctly identifying the winning card at a surprising rate. After a handful of hands, I had him. Then I let everyone within earshot know I had him.

With a loud, involuntary, "OOOOHHH," I pointed to the card in the middle and reached into my pocket for a Quetzal. It was then, that I realized that I wasn't carrying any money. My money was in Karen's purse—and she was halfway across the market. All the small, brown faces turned my way.

As the murmuring turned to chuckling, I screamed, "HEY, COME HERE! I GOT HIM. COME HERE. I NEED A DOLLAR. COME HERE. HURRRRRY!"

The chuckling faded into curious whispers, as the dealer stood cross-armed, with a wily smile. I nervously smiled back. Then I smiled at the sea of faces all around me. I kept my finger, as well as my eye, on that card in the middle.

When word finally reached her, she worked her way back through the gathering crowd. After grabbing a Quetzal, I quickly turned to the dealer. With a confident "Gotcha," I triumphantly threw my money on top of the card in the middle.

He hadn't cheated. He hadn't switch cards on me. He had just flat out fooled me. The suspense was over. The silence was shattered with peals of laughter. My jaw hit the floor with a mighty guffaw.

When everyone around the box realized that I wasn't mad, and had actually enjoyed the drama, the guffawing escalated. We may not have spoken the same language, but we all understood the laughter.

I became king of the market, as word spread quickly about the big, goofy-looking white guy who lost his money and laughed about it. Extra avocados were tossed into our knapsack. Cold beers were shoved into our hands. It's good to be king.

On January 2, I headed home with my batteries recharged. It had been a very festive holiday season. But I was ready to get back to work.

CHAPTER 24

As the new year got underway, *Don't Look Down* and "Crazy Lovin'" disappeared altogether. By the middle of February, both were out of sight—literally. Knowing we were still contractually obligated for another album, this became a popular topic of discussion on the bus. When the logical—as well as fashionable—idea of a live album arose, nods—though reluctant—rang through our ranks.

None of us were big fans of live albums. But this rang A&M's bell—BIG TIME. After all, they had just sold twelve bazillion copies of *Frampton Comes Alive*. Though we hadn't listened to that record, we could not refute its impact or its success. A&M thought a live album was a GREAT idea.

We also knew it was the right thing to do—for several reasons.

1) After having spent a lot of money on the last few records, a live album could be inexpensively made.

2) After having spent large chunks of time away from home making those records, we would be able to stay in our own backyard.

3) This incarnation of the band had been playing together for a while and getting quite tight—as bands that play together are wont to do.

In the middle of all this tightness, though, we never lost sight of Rusty's "You gotta get loose before you can get tight" mantra. Getting tight is a lot of fun. So is getting loose. We got very good at both. A live album was scheduled to capture our traveling cocktail party onto tape.

Wheels were put into motion, as Brian Ahern's Enactron Truck was booked for the middle two weeks of April. With a list of clients as diverse as Black Sabbath and Barbara Streisand, that spring, the Ducks were added to its résumé.

Until then, we would continue to play, continue to get tight, and continue to get loose. Because Randy Erwin's booking agency was located in Missoula, Montana, numerous trips were routed through the part of the country with the big sky.

It was in picturesque Missoula where we met a five-piece band of mischievous, dope-smoking, coke-snorting hippie musicians, driving around in a bus, playing music and leading wonderful, bohemian lives tucked away up in Montana—the same kind of lives we were living, tucked away down in Missouri.

If the Mission Mountain Wood Band (who would shorten their name to the Montana Band) was the official band of the state, we became their close cousins. They had loyal followings, as well as a big sound and light system. Because Erwin also booked them, co-bills were easy, as well as often. Venue marquees may not have liked the weight of all the letters in our names. But the crowds loved it.

Their circle of friends shared the same zest for life as ours did—a voracious appetite for good music, good food, good wine, a good time, and as many recreational drugs as we could get our hands on. Crowds in Montana weren't that much different than crowds in Missouri.

When they pulled their bus alongside ours, it was a vision of the Doobie Liner. While we were driving a big, shiny Silver Eagle, they had an old, converted, blue '67 Greyhound Scenicruiser. And what a cruiser it was—the back half covered in sprayed oil and exhaust suet, the interior covered with tie-dyed sheets, American flags, piles of cowboy boots, and racks of fancy Western shirts. The place looked like a clubhouse for boys. We nicknamed it "the Goob Bus."

These boys spent a lot of time on their bus, as a Scenicruiser is a wonderful way to see this magnificent part of the country. The only problem was, you can drive 600 miles and still be in Montana.

These boys also spent a lot of money on their bus, as blown engines—whether from the altitude, the sheer amount of miles, or their crazy driving habits—were not uncommon. Maintenance on the thing was a never-ending comedy of errors.

We rented our bus. They lived in theirs.

Still, when we showed up, they never failed to make sure we had plenty of Montana hospitality—whatever variety we wanted. Not only did they show us a stupidly good time by night, they were articulate guys, who offered interesting history and geography lessons by day. We already knew about Custer's Last Stand at Little Big Horn. They showed us Evel Knievel's house in Butte. We already knew Montana was where the head waters of the Missouri River were. They showed us Glacier National Park.

They pointed out the difference between the two Montanas. One Montana is the beautiful, mountainous western half of the state (where they lived). The other is the prairie-filled eastern half of the state (which they referred to as West Dakota).

We weren't interested in West Dakota either. We were, however, interested in the mountains—and we had some of the hippest tour guides around. Whenever we were within range, we found ourselves soaking in the Chico Hot Springs, with plenty of poolside libations. They were just as proud of their state as we were of ours.

They were much better showmen than we were. When they hit the stage, their set was filled with scripted segues and synchronized leaps into choreographed lighting. Their nightly version of the "Orange Blossom Special" never failed to bring the crowd to its feet.

They only lacked one thing—songs. Their songs weren't bad, but they relied on a steady stream of regional themes and "I was in a honky-tonk, when ..." They had a couple of really nice records that sold like hotcakes in Montana, Wyoming, and Idaho. The rest of the world knew nothing about them.

They were wonderful musicians.

They were wonderful men.

They lived in a wonderful state.

We all became great friends.

A big, blue sky filled the clear autumn day, as we made our way into their home town of Missoula. Not only was it homecoming weekend for the University of Montana football team, it was a homecoming for the boys in the band. That afternoon, an invitation was graciously accepted for a home-cooked meal at the home of guitarist Terry Robinson.

The food was wonderful, a welcome break from Denny's. The atmosphere was nice, a welcome break from Holiday Inn.

After lunch, when their wives and girlfriends emerged from the back bedroom, mirror in hand, the party took off. They didn't have a little mirror. They had taken down the full-length mirror from the bedroom wall and spelled out Ozark Mountain Daredevils in cocaine across the glass. As their "key to the city," they had calculated the twenty-three letters on the mirror to coincide with the twenty-three people at the party.

When Terry handed me the straw, the games began. Heading straight for the giant "M," I helped myself to its four long legs. Rune attacked the large "O." As, letter by letter, our name vanished from the mirror, music began to appear in the room.

This feeling of fellowship danced right through the rest of the day, spilling over into the gym that night. By the time we all made it to the gig, both bands were well oiled and in high spirits. So was the audience.

As we finished our set with "It'll Shine," Terry Robinson, Mark Wittman, Kurt Bergeron, Rob Quist, and Jerry Zalnoski joined us on stage to sing. The place went nuts. Then we all headed into a crisp, fall Missoula night.

Over the years, this happened on a regular basis. We looked forward to going to the "non-West Dakota" part of Montana. Summer jaunts were filled with outdoor festivals along clear mountain streams. Winters were powder-filled at ski resorts. The party, no matter the season, carried on for days.

It also carried onto the stage. Occasionally, it carried onto the stage a little too much. No one was immune. Everyone took a spin on the Wheel of Inebriation.

Ruell took a spin in Milwaukee when, by the middle of the set, he was having Commander Codyesque trouble remaining upright on his piano bench. As he was bending over, mid-song, we could all hear him mumble, "Canway, get me out of here."

As the rest of us blasted away, Steve unhooked his guitar and helped the stumbling pianist offstage and across the darkened backstage area. As Charley packed his forehead with cold towels, Canway returned to the stage, picked up his guitar, and joined right back in where he left off. We didn't miss a beat.

The occasion was commemorated by the Coughing Dogs, who, on the spot, began to compose "The Ballad of Old Stolichnaya"—Ruell's vodka of choice and subsequent nickname. Sung to the tune of Gordon Lightfoot's "The Wreck of the Edmund Fitzgerald," we howled, singing chorus after chorus of:

> "He started to go when he switched to Pernod.
> The Ballad of Old Stolichnaya.
> At a quarter to ten, his main hatchway caved in.
> The Ballad of Old Stolichnaya."

I took a spin on the wheel in Memphis when, halfway through the set, I *knew* I wasn't going to make it to the end. I've finished many sets with a full bladder, but was always able to hold on. This muggy Memphis night, I knew this would be impossible.

I frantically began looking around, searching for my getaway. When I turned to Steve and Larry, explaining the situation, we called an audible. As I ripped my bass from around my neck, I grabbed one of the empty sixteen-ounce paper cups (the culprit) from the top of my amp. In the same motion, I jumped into the shadows and headed for the first dark nook I could find.

On stage, the rest of the guys started snaking into the extended intro to "Bo Diddley." As they started to fill the hall with that hypnotic beat, I started to fill the cup with golden fluid. Things started well, until it became apparent that I had more than sixteen ounces in me. As the cup filled, I was far from finished.

In a panic, I looked around to weigh my options—one of which was not having a whole lot of time to think about it. Making sure no one was around, I flung the contents into a far corner.

The last few ounces were deposited into the cup. I deposited myself back on stage. Having only missed about forty seconds of "Diddley" time, when I put my bass back on, Larry kicked in with the drums and we barged into the song. Charley immediately delivered another cup of cold, fizzy golden fluid to the top of my amp. We were a well-oiled machine.

Another incident found me making it through "Heaven"—well, kinda—before having to flee the scene. Now, don't get me wrong. Ruell and I weren't the only ones out there spinning the wheel. Everyone had their turn. Believe me. There are many tales in the naked city. This is one of them.

The smoky club in Toronto held 700 people. But that night, a crowd of over a thousand crammed into the place. Not only did this make it hard for the audience to move around, it made it hard for us to even get to the stage from the dressing room—which was behind the bar, in the back of the club. With absolutely no backstage area, the only way to get on stage was from the front. It was also the only way out.

With a thousand and one "Excuse me's," we made our way on. As we ran the set, golden fluid once again began to disappear from the top of our amps. As the set neared its end, I felt things getting critical. I thought I could make it. But it was going to be close—very close. With a couple of songs left, I stopped stomping my feet and jumping around.

As we began the outro to "Heaven," I turned to the rest of the guys with the international "throat slashing/let's get this shit over with" sign. That night, Heaven's outro was a short one. As I threw my bass off and turned around, there was nowhere to go. As the humanity pressed against the front of the stage, I realized there was no way I was going to make it all the way back to the restroom.

Then I noticed the front door. With a frantic, "LOOK OUT," I made a run for it. As I leapt from the two-foot-high stage, I thought I had it made. That is, until the impact of my foot hitting the floor caused my bladder to just burst. I made it out the door. But not before—well, you know what not before.

As I found the nearest tree and let loose, wave after wave of relief flooded over me. All I could hear, though, was wave after wave of "One more song. One more song," clamoring from the club. I knew I had to go back in and do an encore. All I wanted to do was crawl off into a hole somewhere.

As I looked down the front of my pants, it was all I could do to just hang my head and groan at the sight of a gigantic "pee-pee stain"—the phrase Rune had coined to describe those last few drops that always seem to find their way onto your pants. Tonight, I had the mother of all pee-pee stains.

When I climbed back on stage, the rest of my lovely band mates fell all over themselves laughing. Rune, Canway, and Larry laughed the hardest. After all, they were the ones I had been drinking with all day.

I adjusted my guitar strap to its very, very, very lowest Sid Vicious setting, playing most of the encore with my back to the audience. When I turned around to sing, I made sure my bass was crotch-high.

No one in the crowd noticed or even cared. They were just as smashed as I was. My fellow musicians on stage were very amused. When we finished, I made a beeline for the bus.

The good news was, the Coughing Dogs did not choose to commemorate the occasion with song.

In this manner, we played as much as we could, sang as much as we could, laughed as much as we could, drank as much as we could, worked up as many songs as we could, got tight, got loose, and got ready to record. On April 6, the Enactron truck pulled into Missouri.

We decided that, instead of just recording one show, we would set up a small tour through friendly territory. We knew that on any given night, we could play—and play really well. We also knew that on any given night, we could suck—and suck really bad. Recording a dozen shows would greatly increase our odds of getting an album's worth of acceptable material.

Beginning in Carbondale, gigs were scheduled for St. Louis's Fox Theater, Kansas City's Memorial Auditorium, Wichita's Century II Theater, and the Lawrence Opera House, before the grand finale—two nights at MacDonald Arena, on the SMS campus in Springfield.

Marty Lewis was called in from Nashville to do the engineering. Having done a couple of records and a tour of Europe with us, he had a good idea of what we sounded like on stage, as well as a good idea of what we needed to do to capture that on tape.

We also insisted that Carlo Sound be hired. John Logan, fresh from a stint playing banjo with Poco, was called in to mix our house sound. The man has a wonderful touch for making acoustic instruments sound nice on stage. Not only did we want our tapes to sound good for the record, we wanted our shows to sound good for the audience.

We knew that playing in our own backyard would feel good. John and Marty were hired to make it sound good. We felt no need for a producer. We knew what we sounded like. We would produce the record ourselves.

Old friends the Pure Prairie League were contacted to open the shows. Having played together on many occasions, we always had a grand time when we met up. They liked to smoke and drink and stay up late—just like we did. The soundtrack for the cocktail party grew.

As soon as the news hit the airwaves, gigs sold out in a matter of days. Each local radio station, eager about the idea of recording a live album in their market, promoted the hell out of it.

Each day, Tucker, Trask, Mayo, and Redford made sure our gear was set up just right. Each day, Marty and assistant Donovan Cowart made sure all of the microphones were plugged into the correct jacks. Sound checks—which had become a thing of the past—took place every day. After all, we WERE making a record. Knobs were adjusted. Instruments received new strings.

Each night, the Pure Prairie League boys played to enthusiastic crowds. Each night when we played, the place went bonkers. Each night, Donovan, with two twenty-four-track machines at his disposal, made sure a reel of tape was rolling at all times. Every moment of every show was to be recorded.

Each night, when we finished, as Tucker and Trask packed up our gear, and Logan and Dennis Fite packed up Carlo's gear, Marty threw the Enactron doors open to the April night. Among the swirl of post-gig activity, small crowds gathered. Tapes were loaded back onto the machines. One last listen was given to ensure everything got recorded properly. Rough mixes were dubbed onto cassettes.

The first night in Carbondale was a blast, a reputation this small college town proudly wears. Afterward, we excitedly crammed into the truck to listen to the tapes. What we heard was a lot of people having a really good time—and it sounded really, really good.

The second night, we headed to the Fox Theater in St. Louis. When I walked into the K-SHE studios that afternoon for an interview, I was walking on air. When I stepped onto the stage of the Fox that night, I stood stunned for several minutes before I could even put my bass on.

Having sat in that audience so many times not so long ago, to see the Dead, the New Riders, and Traffic, the largest lump I've ever had formed in my throat. The place was packed with thousands of friends, dancing in the aisles. Backstage, the Bob Granda Show was in full swing.

Lifted by the crowd, we played and played and played. Then we played some more. Solid versions of everything were laid down. By the end of the night, we were doing cover tunes and songs that had just been jams in the past. Rowdy versions of "Bo Diddley" and Bobby Womack's "It's All Over Now" were sandwiched around "Commercial Success"—which had NEVER been cut.

As I've said before, "Commercial Success" was always one of my mother's favorite songs. While we acted like idiots on stage, singing about groupies, smoking dope, and growing our hair 'til it touched our knees, she giggled in the shadows. When I asked her why she liked that particular song so much, she would meekly reply, "Oh, Michael, it just makes me laugh."

Over the years, she always asked why we had never recorded it. All I could do was shrug my shoulders and shake my head. Then, when she asked why we never recorded any of the funny songs we used to do, all I could do was shake my head and shrug my shoulders.

That night, every song shined.

That night, everyone in the place shined.

None, though, shined as much as the Fox herself.

As one of three Fox theaters built across the country in the '30s to house traveling vaudeville shows, the Egyptian decor of the ornate 4,500-seat venue is second to none. So are the acoustics. The place sounded as magnificent as it looked.

When we finished, Marty and Donovan were brimming with delight at the quality of the tapes. They sounded so good, Marty asked if there was any way we could record another night.

On the spot, Stan, Charley, and Contemporary Productions' Irv Zuckerman disappeared into Zuckerman's office, emerging ten minutes later with the good news. The following Thursday had been a "dark day" for the theater—but not anymore. It had been an "off day" for us—but not anymore.

We figured that while the recording truck was here, we might as well utilize it every chance we could get. The following Thursday was booked.

Tickets went on sale through K-SHE the next morning. Just as the first show sold out in a matter of a few days, so did the second.

Unlike the cavernous Kemper Arena, Kansas City's Memorial Auditorium was well suited to our style. Though a much smaller room, it had much better acoustics. We'd played there before. We knew how good it sounded. Instead of booking one big show in one big arena, two nights were booked in the friendlier auditorium. We had no desire to go anywhere near Kemper Arena.

A sellout crowd of 2,500 crammed into the place each night. Though the comfortable Kansas City crowd did not unleash the frenzy of the Fox, the tapes sounded just as good. Here we got more reserved but equally strong versions of our sets. After these first few nights, we were confident we already had enough material for the album. We had been playing well. It was time to let loose.

Lawrence, Kansas is the perfect place to let loose. The thousand people who crammed into every possible square inch of the Opry House became an absolute circus of students, teachers, crazies, doctors, dignitaries, and mayhem—all rubbing shoulders, all stoned to the gills.

When we listened back to the evening's tapes, the "theater of the absurd" had found its way onto them. The songs weren't real tight. But man, they were sure fun to listen to.

By the time we got to Wichita, we were hitting on all cylinders. All three crews were working well together. Sound check was a snap. This, along with the fact that the auditorium sat directly across the street from our hotel, made sure we all made it back in plenty of time for Happy Hour.

Happy Hour was a hit, becoming Happy Hours. The Pure Prairie League boys jumped in with both feet. Shenanigans began early and went late. One cocktail turned into two. Two turned into three. Charlie banked an eight-ball. I don't remember the rest. But we got it on tape.

Another enthusiastic crowd filled the theater, as we poured ourselves across the street. When we started to play, a guerilla party broke out on stage. When we finished, Marty stumbled into the dressing room, laughing so hard, he had to use the doorframe to hold himself up. When he said, "You guys gotta hear this," Charlie laid out some lines and we headed for the truck.

After four hours of Happy Hour and two hours of guerilla party, the tapes were a drunken mess. Donovan cued up "Commercial Success." Marty shook his head, mumbling, "You're not going to believe this."

The first thing we heard was Cash, screaming into his microphone, "This song is dedicated to every one of you wild cards out there who think you want to be an ace like me." Then, the song—a lazy, sloppy, blues shuffle—became lazier, sloppier, bluesier, and shufflier than ever. The beat was there. But neither Larry nor I was. Neither was Rune, whose sour slide guitar notes raised the hair on the backs of our necks. When Marty soloed his track, it sent ripples of laughter throughout the truck.

When Ruell's piano was soloed, it sounded as if he was playing it with boxing gloves on. When the song swung into its last verse, Steve replaced its lyrics by pleading, "And I want to sleep with Stevie Nicks every niiiiiiiiight." With this plea, we all tumbled into the last chorus and mumbled toward the finish line.

Marty muted everything but our vocal tracks, which resembled the Wichita Elks Lodge. The only difference between the two was you could have found better enunciation and pitch at the Elks. Still, we were having a great time. Needless to say, none of the songs from the Wichita show would make it onto the record.

We knew we already had solid versions of everything in the can. No one was too concerned with the fact that we had just completely blown off an entire evening of recording, as well as a dozen reels of tape. We just headed back across the street to the hotel and up to the bar on the eleventh floor, anxious to get to the party started again.

Overlooking the bright lights of Wichita, this eleventh floor would soon become the birthplace of the Condor.

If any of us at any time had ever been the life of any party, Rune was, without a doubt, the master. To find him smoking two cigarettes and drinking three beers at the same time, while pirouetting around the room with anyone who would dance with him, was commonplace.

So was Mr. Pillow Head.

In the '70s, smoking was still permitted on commercial airlines. Smokers were just seated in the back—an approach about as effective as the "no peeing" section of a swimming pool.

From the back of the plane, the laughter came. Those of us in the no smoking section turned to see Rune with the small airline pillow pulled over his head. Poking his head above the seats like a prairie dog, he'd torn a big hole in the pillowcase, roughly where his mouth was. When he lit up, all you could see was billows of smoke pouring from the pillowcase.

When the flight attendant came on the speakers to inform everyone that we were cruising at an altitude of 21,000 feet, she could not stifle herself either.

His antics, practical jokes, and sight gags were a constant source of amusement. That's why no one thought anything of it when he started crawling around on the floor of that Wichita bar, stalking the woman seated at a window table. The rest of us remained silent at the bar. We just wanted to see what was going to happen. Whatever it was, we knew it was going to be a riot.

Unbeknownst to Rune, the woman was not alone. When her date, who had merely stepped out for a moment, returned to the table, Rune was rolling around underneath it. Not amused, the guy coyly leaned over and sternly advised, "Cool it, condor."

Rune stood up in an uproar, offering the guy a cigarette, shaking his hand, slapping him on the back, buying them both drinks, doing a little dance, while defusing the situation with a hearty, "Hey, Skol," and a twirl away.

Rejoining the rest of us at the bar, he quietly sat for a few moments, pondering the situation. Things were fine until he turned and asked, "What did he mean by 'cool it, condor'?" We laughed so hard, we could barely explain that not only was the guy politely telling him to get lost, Rune—with his wild hair and long, gangly arms—kind of resembled one. From that evening on, he became The Condor.

A shy man by day. The Condor by night.

If we thought our previous gigs had attracted crazy crowds, nothing would compare to the friends and family who would cram into McDonald Arena for these last two nights. With a handful of shows under our belt, by the time we hit the stage, we were flying high. All Ducks had become condors.

As discussions about the album progressed, the only thing to decide was whether to make a single or double album. A&M wanted us to condense everything into a single album—one that would be cheaper to manufacture. We contended that this would not leave room for any new songs—and a record compiled of nothing but remakes of "Jackie," "Heaven," and "Chicken" would be boring.

A double album would give us room to include versions of "Commercial Success," Canway's "Horse Trader," my "Ooh Boys (It's Hot)" and Bobby Womack's "It's All Over Now." All were going over very well in concert. We thought they should be included on the record.

When we pointed out that *Frampton Comes Alive* was a double album, a double album ours became.

Plus, this would also allow us to include a song that had been a staple of our sets from the early days of the Bijou.

In 1964, fellow Missourian Porter Wagoner had recorded Jack Rhodes's "A Satisfied Mind" in Springfield's KWTO studios.

In 1976, we decided to record it in the men's locker room of McDonald Arena.

Everyone knows how good they sound when they sing in the shower. Our version of the song would sound great in one. After Friday night's show, we assembled the next afternoon to record it.

The entire building, which, the evening before, had held a noisy crowd, now held an empty locker-room silence—along with its wonderful, natural reverb. We also knew we only had a window of a couple hours to record the song before Saturday night set back in.

Donovan placed two microphones in the middle of the room. Outside in the truck, Marty balanced their levels. John, Larry, Ruell, and I gathered around to sing. Because it was a live album, Steve decided to play his harp solo at the same time. The five of us stood in a group, amid a sea of concrete, porcelain, glass, and mirrors. We sang the song several times. Each time, Marty moved one of us closer—or farther—from the microphones, until we had just the right blend.

We may not have been playing the song much in our shows lately. But at one point, it was a staple. The shower seemed like the perfect place to record it.

After an afternoon of singing in the quiet bathroom, that night, the entire arena filled back up with people, noise, and craziness. After another knock-down drag-out affair, Donovan began loading the truck to head for California. Marty labeled and stored boxes and boxes of recorded tapes.

We all agreed to reconvene in L.A. in May. Two weeks of mixing time was booked at Sunset. Between now and then, it was our job as producers to wade through this massive pile of tapes to pick out which version of which song from which night would make it onto vinyl.

None of us was really thrilled with this phase of it. But it had to be done.

The conference room of the North Glenstone Holiday Inn was booked for the week, outfitted with a nice stereo. Each morning, we would meet, drink coffee, eat doughnuts, and start listening to tapes.

Instead of listening to show after show, we decided that a better approach would be to listen to version after version of the same song. This is how we approached the task at hand. It took quite a while.

After eleven versions of "Black Sky" were cussed and discussed, eleven versions of "Walking Down the Road" were waded through. This was followed by—well, you get the picture. You do the math.

"It was not a whole lot of fun," John adds.

Some choices were easy. Others were not. Some versions were really good. Others were sour beyond repair. We all jotted notes, compared them at the end, and decided upon the best cuts. The tapes from the Fox were magnificent, as were the tapes from Kansas City. Most of the songs on the album were culled from these two venues. The tapes from Lawrence were good. The tapes from Wichita were worthless—except for "Commercial Success."

While we bumbled through the song and Steve pleaded with Stevie Nicks, what the version lacked in execution, it more than made up for in hilarity. We also had a solid version of the song from the Fox—with the correct lyrics. But nothing compared to the "Night of the Condor."

In the end, we chose the solid Fox version for two reasons:

1) The Wichita version was funny. But would it remain funny?
2) We didn't want to get sued by Stevie Nicks.

A week of listening and culling at the Holiday Inn in Springfield was followed by two weeks of listening and mixing at Sunset Sound in L.A. By the time we began mixing, thank God we no longer had to listen to any of those sour renderings. Some of them were downright painful. As John, Larry, both Steves, and I met Marty and Donovan at Sunset, the first thing we did was splice together the chosen versions of each song onto a master reel.

The second thing we did was divide them into the four groups of four songs that would make up the four sides of a double album. Once again, we used Glyn and David's technique of laying scraps of paper across the mixing console.

The third thing we did was amass an audience track. Thirty seconds of applause from the Fox was spliced into an endless loop, which was then fed into the board and assigned its own channel. This way, if we felt we needed an extra shot of mayhem, it was a simple push of a fader away. As each song ended, we could augment the audience's actual response with whoops and hollers from the Fox.

Trips to the Lot became less frequent, as our relationship with A&M became more strained. We were just as unhappy with the lack of promotion our last three records had received as they were with how much we didn't tour. Stan and Jerry had butted heads many times over the years, continuing to do so on an everyday basis.

We did connect with Assistant Art Director Jeff Ayerhoff on the cover art. As tensions mounted in the administrative offices, joints were still being smoked in the art department. As we mulled over album cover ideas, we broke out the roller derby pictures. Once again, they grabbed no one.

Then, the movie poster over Ayerhoff's desk jumped off the wall, onto the table, and did a little dance. We all recognized it from the '60s movie thriller, *War of the Worlds*. When Jeff turned around and hollered, "IT'S ALIVE!" we all knew, in one fell swoop, we'd found the cover art, as well as the title.

Overdubbing vocals became an issue. If a song had a solid track but a sour singing part, the sourness could be easily smoothed out with a trip into Sunset's vocal booth. Discussions centered around "Is this cheating?"

It Shined

I didn't think it was. But I chose a version of "Ooh Boys" from one of the Kansas City shows, due to the fact that it was the closest thing to an acceptable vocal I was going to get—and I didn't feel like replacing one of my average vocals with another one of my average vocals.

Larry thought differently, replacing most of his parts on "Jackie" and "You Know Like I Know." Steve disagreed, but gave in to Larry's insistence. Though disagreements like this occurred, they didn't last long. Nor did they ever become heated. We knew better. We were producing ourselves. We knew issues like this were bound to pop up. Out of artistic respect for each other, all attitudes were tolerated.

Though there wasn't an unusually large amount of fixing time, it did take away from mixing time. As we neared the end of the second week, not only were we rushed, we were getting sick of hearing these songs. Interest seriously waned. "Good enough" became good enough. A number of the songs could've gotten much better mixes. But we were just so ready to get done and get gone, we got gone.

With flights home already booked, work carried through that last night and into the morning light. When we walked out of the studio, the sun was already up and the day was well underway. We had just enough time to run by the Chateau, grab our bags, and get to the airport.

When Stan informed everyone that if we wanted, we could spend the evening at Kansas City's Uptown Theater with Elvis Costello and the Attractions, I jumped at the chance. No one else was interested. As they left the KC airport, headed for Springfield, I headed for the rental car desk. Then I headed for the Good Karma House. Then I headed for the Uptown.

When I walked into the ornate theater, I was introduced to the music of Rockpile. I was already a fan of Dave Edmunds, as well as Nick Lowe's Brinsley Schwartz. I could not take my ears off of this band. They played real hard and real fast—the way I like it. When they finished, I headed to the dressing rooms. I knew right where they were. We'd played this fine theater several times.

Here I met road manager Jack Rivera, who told me to hold tight while he let Elvis know I was here. It took Costello almost two seconds to burst from his dressing room with an outstretched hand and a hearty "Come on in, mate." This took me by surprise. The press had been portraying him as a snooty asshole. I expected a cold shoulder. I got a warm reception.

As the sounds of Mink DeVille began wafting up from the stage, we walked into the dressing room, where Rockpile was still catching their breath. Introductions went around, as Elvis—with the same courteousness Linda McCartney exhibited—asked if I wanted a drink. I told him to make it a stiff one. I fit right in, as stiff ones flowed freely throughout the Stiff Records' roster.

He had caught wind of us toting a case of *My Aim Is True* back from AIR last year. Tonight, he was a long string of questions about why we liked his record and why we went through all the trouble of lugging it home with us. My answers were easy: We loved the songs, we loved how simple the record was, and we knew a lot of our friends in Missouri would love it too.

He seemed most amused when I described Sya belting out "The Angels Want to Wear My Red Shoes," her little record player blaring from her room.

As DeVille finished his set, Elvis excused himself to get ready for his. When he stood up, Nick Lowe slid into his spot on the couch and introduced himself. This was great. I was too tired to stand up anyway.

When Jake rounded up the Attractions and headed them to the stage, Nick and I, with beers in hand, headed for the wings. After a ferocious evening of music and drunken camaraderie, we all bade each other fond adieus and headed for our respective vehicles.

Elvis pushed through a rabid crowd of fans and autograph-seekers on the way to his bus. I quietly walked to my rental car. No one even recognized me. He was the new kid on the block. I began to wonder if we were over the hill. Though I hadn't been to sleep in two days, I pointed my steering wheel toward Springfield.

There was plenty to think about. That night, Highway 13 was navigated to the music I'd just heard at the Uptown, along with the music we just mixed in L.A. All were sandwiched between musings of my second foray into fatherhood.

It would be a monumental summer.

CHAPTER 25

As the summer sun of '78 scorched, we scattered. We were all happy with "It's Alive." We were even happier that it was over with. After having heard those songs every day for the past couple of months, the last thing in the world we wanted to do was go out and play them some more.

All I wanted to do was focus on having a second child and, because we had decided to deliver the baby at home, I was not about to leave my house.

Larry, on the other hand, took the summer to head back to Nashville, hooking up with Norbert and Marty at Quad. Jerry Moss, after five Ozark albums, realized that it might be a good idea to let Larry do a record of his own and take a shot with the voice of "Jackie Blue."

There were fans who wanted to hear more of him—and they didn't want to have to wade through one of our records to get to his songs. On the other side of this coin, there were those who preferred not to hear him at all—only wanting to hear our rowdier country stuff.

Jerry realized that the diversity of our material—the flag we had rallied around for years—may not have been the best angle to take from a marketing aspect. He agreed to let Norbert and Larry produce an album.

Larry picks up the story: "After a couple weeks of tracking in Nashville, Norbert called me in Springfield from Miami, where he was working with [Jimmy] Buffett. He said, 'Buffett can't sing all day, and we've got the studio [Bay Shores] booked. Why don't you come down here for four or five days and we'll work at night when Jimmy's not?' So I did.

"That's how I ended up singing on Buffett's record [*Son of a Son of a Sailor*]. He knew I was there to do my vocals. When he asked if I'd like to sing some backgrounds on his stuff, I said, 'Shit, yeah. Put me in, coach.' Then, Norbert and I went to AIR, where we hired a thirty-piece orchestra to do all of these elaborate charts Bill [Jones] had written.

"There were some cool songs on that record, but the reason it sucked was because I was WAY into overproducing stuff—and I had a producer who was WAY into overproducing stuff. Anything either one of us thought about trying, we did. It was just an overproduced bunch of stuff.

"It didn't even have a title. At that time, I didn't even know if it was any good or not. I got to do it, and that was great. I thank Jerry. But he was just puzzled by it—and I don't blame him, because it was a puzzling thing. He heard it and said, 'I'm not putting this out.'

"We spent $180,000 on it. Me and Norbert ate big food every night with expensive wine. He was just signing the checks, taking them to the secretary, and putting them on the studio bill. We spent a lot of money on food."

At the same time, John and Steve had caught the ear of English songwriter Paul Kennerly. In the middle of recording *White Mansions* (A&M, 1978), his musical exposé of the Civil War, the tall, lanky Brit was working with Glyn Johns at Olympic. In search of American voices to interpret his songs, at Glyn's advice, he agreed to give a couple of guys from Missouri (a neutral state in the war) a shot.

John and Steve's voices fit the bill perfectly. With Waylon Jennings and Jessi Colter already on board, a phone call from London filled out the cast of four.

Though Waylon received the bulk of the work, it reunited John and Steve with Glyn and his cast of cronies, which included Bernie Leadon and Eric Clapton.

"I wasn't completely knocked out with the songs at first, because it's … It's just hard to tell history in a song," recalls Steve. "But once we got rolling, everyone really got into their characters."

This included the session for "White Trash," a song that not only featured Steve's voice but Clapton's slide guitar. Steve continues, "We were trying to cut the song and he [Clapton] was just average all day long. Here I was, sitting with the great Eric Clapton—and it just wasn't happening. We finally got a track, went to dinner, and had some drinks. Then we came back to do another song that evening. When we finished, he turned to Glyn and asked, 'Can we have another go at that first thing, mate?'

"Glyn said, 'I'll stay if you'll stay,' and we were off. We set back up and it happened. Boy, did it happen. Every time we turned the rideout around … Man, it took my breath away. The whole thing only took twenty minutes. But there was the great Eric Clapton."

Waylon (in the throes of his cocaine addiction) and Cash (always good for a jump or a joke) became bumping and grinding buddies. On occasion, Waylon would guffaw, "Hoss, you remind me of me."

When John and Steve returned to Springfield, Larry was filtering back into town from his sojourns with Norbert. I was still learning how to become a midwife. Yes, a midwife.

Gigs were scarce, as everyone just wanted to unwind from their summer ordeals. I wasn't going to go anywhere. When a short run of gigs with Fleetwood Mac came in, Jerry Moss called.

After conversation about our families, he asked about the progress of the baby. When I assured him things were fine, he asked if I would object to the idea of getting another bass player to play these gigs. They were only thirty-minute sets. They just happened to be warming up for one of the highest-profile bands in the world. He thanked me when I let him know I was not opposed to the idea.

When Stan called, asking if I had a recommendation, I was stymied. I had never thought of it before. This was the first gig any of us had ever missed.

When I suggested local bassist Larry Van Fleet, a session was set up for me to teach him the songs. This wasn't going to be hard. I play very simple parts. It'd be a snap to run through the seven songs. Along with being a good bass player, he was a quick study. When he came by the house, I taught him the entire show in a matter of an hour.

As they flew off, I stayed behind. When they returned, I heard the tales of Mr. Pillow Head, lost trousers, lost wallets, and the all-night shenanigans, interspersed with daily thirty-minute bursts of music. Details are hazy. They will remain that way. This time, I have an excuse. I wasn't there.

That summer, while John, Larry, and Steve were away, I had been reading every book I could get my hands on about natural childbirth. I began preparing packages of sterilized linens and obtaining belly button clamps. Instead of going to Lamaze classes, I bought the instructor's manual and ingested it completely. I knew I was about to undertake a very primitive task. But I could not get Doc George's "Yep. You could've done that," out of my head.

Close friend Dr. Colleen Kivlahan was placed on hold to help with the birthing. The only glitch—her practice was in Columbia, one hundred and sixty miles away. She assured us that when the time came, she would drop whatever she was doing and be on the first flight to Springfield; I sent her an open-ended plane ticket, along with a flight schedule.

On the morning of September 11, 1978, 422 South Main was transformed into a delivery room. The house was as quiet inside as the autumn morning was outside. As Sya ran around, playing with the neighbor kids, I jotted down a list of errands to run.

When I was informed, "You're not going anywhere," I laid the small stack of envelopes to the side. At this point, animal instincts kicked in. Things became very calm and very clear.

The first item of business was to call Colleen. As we synchronized watches, I assured her that someone would be at the airport, awaiting her 2:00 flight. The only problem was, the baby wasn't going to wait.

With one eye on the clock, we headed to the upstairs room we had converted into the birthing room, set up with soft bedding, clean sheets, sterilized instruments, and fresh baby clothes; the large windows filled the room with morning light.

At the most intense part of the process, an innate sense of just knowing what to do flushed through me. The entire birthing only took a couple of hours and went without a hitch. By one o'clock, my second daughter, Yari Autumn, had entered the world as calmly, easily, and pink as can be.

When the cord was cut, the sheets changed, and the baby swaddled, I acquired a fourth member to my family. By the time Colleen was landing, the dust had already begun to settle.

I took the opportunity to make a quick dash around the corner for a bottle of champagne. When Colleen made her final dash up the steps, I was waiting at the top of the staircase with two glasses in my hand. "Its a girl," I beamed.

By the time her doctor made it to her side, Yari was already a couple of hours old. While I recounted, step by step, what had taken place, Colleen made a few checks on the baby, to make sure she had ten fingers and toes, and a few checks on the mother, to make sure she was coming back together.

The entire post-natal exam took twenty minutes, culminating with a "Good job." Yari smiled.

By 5:30, Dr. Kivlahan was on her way back to Columbia. As the quiet afternoon faded into a quiet evening, the quiet evening faded into anything but a quiet night. Yari's zeroeth birthday party was about to become as memorable as Sya's.

It began on the front porch with brothers-in-law Kevin Johnson and Derek Simpson. As the sun began to disappear, so did the beer. With each cold one, nine months of anxiety began shooting through every pore on my body. I turned to them with, "Come on, boys. Drinks are on me." The three of us headed into the night.

By the time we got to the Safari Room, the Skeletons were in high gear. So was the crowd. When the three of us stormed into the place, it became a tornado site. Cigars were passed around, filling the entire place with thick, obnoxious clouds of smoke. Round after round after round of drinks were hoisted. Lloyd Hicks, Lou Whitney, Donnie Thompson, and Nick Sibley were getting after it on stage.

When I joined them, our version of "Surfin' Bird" was so savage that, to this day, people still walk up to tell me they remember the night I became Tornado Man.

I spent Sya's zeroeth birthday party quietly with friends at the Trout Farm. I spent Yari's zeroeth birthday party singing "Surfin' Bird" at the Safari Room.

On the morning of September 12, I called Stan and Jerry with the good news and let them know I was ready to get back to work. One of the first gigs was a taping of the *Midnight Special* to promote *It's Alive*—which was about to come out.

It Shined

With most of the summer scattered, we hadn't been playing much. But that didn't matter. We only had to do two songs, and we figured we could just macho our way through them—like we'd been doing. We flew out to L.A. to tape a segment for the upcoming fall season.

When we walked into Merv Griffin's Vine Street Theater, we were greeted and treated to the sound of the Crusaders filming on an adjacent stage. We were all big fans, as their records were another constant on the Bijou sound system. They were just as funky live.

When they finished, Tucker, Trask, and Charlie readied our stage. Lights and cameras were focused. As the cameras rolled and the audience rose, we began to barrel into "Heaven." With a full head of steam, we rolled into the second verse, just in time for the headphoned director to barge directly on stage, madly wave his arms and yell, "Cut. Cut. Cut. Cut. Cut. Cut. Cut." Proceedings ground to a halt.

After informing everyone that "We have a problem," we were all instructed to "Stand by." Then he suggested that we "might as well take a break and relax. We've got a problem with camera three, blah, blah, blah, blah, blah, blah, blah. We'll resume taping as soon as we can blah, blah, blah …"

The crowd sat down. We headed back to the dressing room. Though our equipment remained ready, the air was definitely let out of the balloon. As the first hour of waiting turned into a second, you can only imagine the damage we did to the liquor on the catering table, as well as the bag of blow someone produced.

We had been in this situation before. A few years earlier, during a taping of the *Filter Furor Show* in Nijmegen, Holland, things went haywire. Fixing a television camera in Hollywood only takes a couple of hours. Fixing a television camera in rural Holland took all night.

Not wanting to just hang around, the entire evening was spent across town at the home of a local Dutch hash merchant. As a friend of a friend of the promoter, his supply of goodies was endless. It was well past midnight when we finally made it back onto the Nassausingel Hall stage.

When the lights finally came up on the *Filter Furor Show*, the repaired camera caught very dark circles under very sunken eyes.

When the lights came back up on the *Midnight Special*, the repaired camera caught us at warp speed.

By the time we were summoned back to the Vine Street Theater stage, we were blasted into smithereens. When we revved up "Heaven" for the second time, Steve started screaming his harp riff through a distorted amp. I began screaming at the home viewing audience, singing into Steve's mic—Mick and Keith style.

That night, what the cameras did not capture was our usual array of instruments. What they got was your basic Southern rock three-guitar lineup, with John, Canway, and the Condor all standing up front. Jerry Mills was no longer present, due to the fact that not only had we decided to discontinue his promotional efforts, our sound no longer required his mandolin. There wasn't one acoustic instrument in sight.

That night, what we lacked in preparation and finesse, we more than made up for in drunken intensity. The second time through, "Heaven" wasn't much more than two minutes long. We all breathed a sigh of relief at the end, when we were informed that there were no technical difficulties.

Then the question of our second song arose. As we mulled it over, we decided to keep the joint jumping. In this same ranting vein, we did "Tough Luck," one of Steve's new ranting songs. Even though we'd only played it a few times, everyone was in a ranting mood. Though we had only a rough sketch of an arrangement, we decided to just take a shot at it. If nothing else, it would be interesting. It was also played at warp speed.

Stan, sitting with Jerry Moss, couldn't believe his ears. When Jerry asked why we were doing a song that wasn't on any of our records, Stan could only throw his palms to the sky.

We blasted into "Tough Luck," arrangement or no arrangement. Steve jumped around the stage like a frog on a hot tin roof. When he forgot the words to the third verse, instead of stopping, he just threw his head back and bellowed, "Aaahhhh" into the air. The rest of us just kept slamming away. "Cut" was not an option.

Giant close-ups of Ruell pounding the piano, and Rune's slide guitar filled the screen. Larry, hidden behind the drums, remained that way, garnering not one shot.

As we neared the end of the extended outro, complete with its Allman Brothersesque twin-guitar figure, we began looking at each other for the final cue. When we stumbled across the finish line to a slopply conclusion, we all had a big laugh and headed back to the bar in the dressing room. Jerry Moss wasn't laughing.

"That's the point, I think, where Jerry was questioning what we were really doing," Larry recalls. "After coming to see us play, the next night in Santa Barbara, he said, 'This isn't what I signed.'"

That fall, when our *Midnight Special* segment aired, we found ourselves on the bill with the Atlanta Rhythm Section, the Climax Blues Band, the Little River Band, and A Taste of Honey. Though we hadn't caught one glimpse of him, there was Wolfman Jack, on the screen, howling, "The Ozark Mountain Daredevils. Ow-oooooh!"

That night, our lack of finesse oozed right through televisions and onto carpets. Both songs were played so fast, neither had much of a groove. When we got to the end of "Tough Luck," the producers kindly faded out the botched ending.

Our, "Let's all just get trashed and have a party" approach may have been going over well at the Fargo Convention Center. It didn't come across very well on TV.

On September 9, when *It's Alive* scraped the bottom of the charts, it attained the lofty position of #179 during its lengthy three-week stay. By the first of October, it had already come and gone. No singles were released.

This brought us to the end of the third phase of our contract. Once again, Jerry had until the end of the year (ninety days) to decide whether to pick up his last option for the final two records of our deal.

That fall, as he mulled over his decision, we embarked on a series of "Dollar Concerts" with label-mate, Joan Armatrading, who was promoting her latest A&M release, *Show Some Emotion*. We were already fans. We'd been listening to her records for some time.

Now, let me clear something up right here. I shouldn't sound so critical of the A&M roster. There were wonderful artists we listened to and enjoyed-like Joan. The Signature jazz series was fabulous, providing us with the wonderful music of Dave Brubeck, Wes Montgomery, Paul Desmond, Charles Lloyd, and Chuck Mangione. As for Gino Vanelli, Rick Wakeman, and the Carpenters ...

Stan recalls, "When Joan Armatrading opened those shows for us, we did them for a dollar and a can of food. We'd seen her in a London club and we all liked her. I said, 'Why don't we do something, like a dollar and a can of food.' It'd be a buck, and a lot of people would come out who might not want to pay five or six bucks to see us—and it would help her, who Glyn was producing."

This also reunited us with her band, which consisted of Fairport veterans Dave Mattacks, Pat Donaldson, and Jerry Donahue, along with a young guitarist by the name of Albert Lee. With A&M giving tour support to not one but two of its acts, we were able to pass along the savings to the crowd. It was a great idea. The food went to a local charity. I don't know where the buck went.

Starting in Milwaukee's Oriental Theater, we visited Chicago's Riviera Theater, Detroit's Royal Oak Theater, and Toronto's Massey Hall. Then, a long swing took us through New England and down the East Coast, before ending at Atlanta's Fox Theater and the Warehouse in New Orleans.

Each night was played to a packed house. (It's easy to fill a concert hall when you only charge a dollar.)

Each night, A&M threw huge parties afterward, packed with media and radio people. (It's easy to fill a party when you give away free booze.)

We were in heaven. How could you not be? With a packed house for the gig and a packed liquor cabinet for the party, both bands blasted into morning after morning after.

As the tour ended, the holiday season began. As the record was fading from sight, we decided to take the time off to be with our families. When the new year rolled in, Jerry, who had been pondering his option, made his decision—by not making one.

After waiting the obligatory 90-day period, we waited 120 days. After 150 days, we thought we'd found a loophole. As it turned out, we hadn't found anything. Jerry knew what he was doing. He hadn't overlooked a thing.

For years, he had listened to how we didn't want to do this or that and how we just wanted to hang around Springfield. After *It's Alive* came and went, he granted us our wish (insert "watch what you wish for" adage here).

When we notified him that he had failed to notify us, he didn't even reply. After six months (180 days), our deal was unceremoniously terminated. Basically, not interested in working with us anymore, Jerry quietly walked away from the great Ozark experiment.

We weren't that broken-hearted. After the first couple of albums, the promotional budget for each subsequent record had declined—and there was no indication this trend was going to change. After six years of having to deal with our crazy shit, we were no longer a priority. Not only did he not pick up our option, he didn't pick up the phone.

If we really just wanted to be a bunch of Springfield guys, hanging around Springfield, he was willing to let us be just that. This is a decision we would come to regret. Not only did A&M sever ties, we acquired the reputation throughout the industry as being stubborn, lazy guys, hanging around Springfield.

In the music business, stubborn and lazy are not assets.

CHAPTER 26

By spring, we were without a record deal for the first time since 1973. Stanley began thumbing through his phone book, while flying out to L.A. and reconnecting with Don Ellis. The jolly, rotund Ellis, whom Stan had known since his days at the Vanguard, now sat as senior A&R man with Columbia Records.

When he expressed interest in the band, arrangements were made for him to fly to Vail, Colorado and meet us for a gig at Studio in the Rockies.

That night, when we hit the stage, the Studio's dry, sterile sound was a bit disconcerting for a cocktail party. But with the help of Old Faithful—also known as our wonderful Colorado fans—we had a great time, filling the place with merriment. Even though we felt that we hadn't played all that well, Ellis, swept up in an avalanche of Rocky Mountain high, was sold.

Afterward, when we all retreated to the hotel for our traditional post-gig high jinks, he informed us that he liked what he heard, felt that the band was still a viable entity, and would get the ball rolling as soon as he returned to his office on Monday.

Everyone shook hands.

Everyone smoked cigars.

Everyone drank cognac.

By late summer, we had hammered out a two-record deal with Columbia (one album, with an option for a second—their option). By late fall, we were headed to Los Angeles, Westlake Studios, and a meeting with veteran producer John Boylan.

The silver-haired Boylan, who began his production career in the '60s working alongside Rick Nelson's Stone Canyon Band, the Dillards, and the Association, noted fresh ideas when, "I realized that the most exciting music for me was rooted in the American folk tradition. Then, I began to think of ways that I could combine those roots with contemporary rock and roll."

A short time later, a chance meeting with Linda Ronstadt at the Troubadour gave him the opportunity to explore some of these ideas. When Linda asked for his help to form a new backup band for her first solo tour, he quickly turned to the extended family of struggling musicians, playing in various configurations at the Troubadour's Monday night, "open mike" concerts.

First to be hired was Detroit transplant Glenn Frey, followed quickly by Texan Don Henley. Both had been pitching their songs, hoping to get Linda to record them. Rounding out the band were ex-Stone Canyon Band bassist Randy Meisner and ex-Burrito Brother Bernie Leadon.

This led to production efforts in the '70s with Commander Cody, Roger McGuinn, Mike & Tom, the Pure Prairie League, and Charlie Daniels. His work with Daniels would win him a Grammy for "The Devil Went Down to Georgia." His work with Mike and Tom (ST-11261) contained Steve Canaday's "Fair Play."

Boylan, with his finger on the pulse, was coming in with not only a good handle on our style of music, but a great track record. It was a nice fit. Unlike Kerschenbaum's un-laid back L.A. style, Boylan came in with his very, very, VERY laid back L.A. style.

While Kerschenbaum drastically rearranged the material, Boylan wanted to drastically rearrange the band. To suit his tastes, Canway, Rune, and Ruell were excluded from the tracking. After the first day of rehearsals, he gathered the rest of us to express his desire to not only use a different guitar player, but a different drummer.

Our jaws hit the floor. Using a different guitarist was one thing. Using a different drummer was another. Luckily, Larry's cool head prevailed.

Long-time Bread drummer Mike Botts was brought in along with old friend and Granny's Bathwater alum Jon R. Goin on guitar. I played bass. Steve played harp. Dillway played guitar. Rune would fly out for a couple of days of overdubs, adding slide guitar to "Lovin' You," a song he had co-written with Dillon, and "Tough Luck," the song we'd been playing at gigs. There were no mandolins, nor any hint of an acoustic sound. There were also no country tunes.

This, as it turns out, was a conscious decision between Boylan and Columbia, wanting to market us to a rock 'n' roll audience, in the same manner A&M had tried years earlier; we didn't mind. Columbia was writing healthy checks that weren't bouncing. We didn't put up much resistance. We were happy to have another shot at another album.

L.A. session veteran Jai Winding was called in to do some keyboard overdubs. Buddy Emmons dropped by with his pedal steel guitar. Singers Venetta Fields, Rosemary Butler, and Paulette Brown were hired to lay in some very nice, very in-tune background vocals. These are all talented musicians—and wonderful people. But they sure made the band sound different.

I quickly meshed with Botts. Even though he played in a very solid and—thank God—un-Bread-like fashion, things just weren't the same without Larry playing drums. Larry's funkiness was replaced with Botts's streamlined techniques. This would turn out to be our slickest-sounding record yet.

As we started with "Take You, Tonight," I was enthused that a harmonica riff was going to start the record. It's a very cool song. We quickly got a very solid track of it, along with a rowdy version of "Tough Luck."

Larry's melodic "Oh, Darlin'" featured another parade of his obtuse chord changes, as well as "Jump at the Chance," with its spry Granny's feel. This wasn't unusual. Jon R. played all the overlapping guitar parts.

The radio-ready "Sailin' Around the World" featured another harp solo in the middle (good sign), along with a "There's Going to Be a Heartache Tonight" handclap breakdown at the end (bad sign).

"Empty Cup" and "Runnin' Out" accurately described our home lives, as well as our collective gas tank.

The former featured a plodding beat and lyrics like "The door is wide and the dogs are calling. Can't keep it shut. The river's dry and the sky is falling. Can't fill 'em up." Not a pleasant sentiment.

The latter received a funky guitar track from Donnie Thompson, in town to do a gig as part of Steve Forbert's traveling band. When he, along with the rest of the Skeletons, stopped by the studio for an afternoon visit, we strapped a guitar on him and told him to just let loose.

Each song came out slim, trim, and muscular—with no excess anything, anywhere. The same could be said for the song list. We recorded no extra material. Ten songs. That was it. This meant I would not have a song on the record. I played a couple of them for Boylan. But he just didn't seem to be interested. This bothered me, but not enough to pitch a fit.

Our collective approach was simple. Maybe we ought to just leave things up to one of the biggest record companies in the world. We decided to let them do what they do and not meddle, like we had at A&M.

When Columbia asked us to do a photo shoot for the album cover with noted photographer Norman Seef, we had no problem with it. I balked, though, when they suggested that I get a haircut.

I couldn't believe my ears. Was this Columbia Records? Weren't they supposed to be hip and happening? Weren't we a rock 'n' roll band? You bet I balked.

I didn't like it when my father told me to cut my hair.

I didn't like it when my high school principal told me to cut my hair.

I wasn't going to let my record company do it either.

I didn't mind that my three partners had all made trips to the barbershop—I mean *salon*. I agreed to a trim, but not before making sure everyone knew MY definition of the word *trim*. I wasn't thrilled with the way this new image thing was shaping up.

On the way to Seef's Hollywood Hills studio, a short detour was made to the salon—I mean barbershop. Once I was in the chair, a very friendly, very attractive woman with very well-displayed cleavage began to work on me. As she snipped away, she made sure I enjoyed the view. Conversation was light and engaging, until she suggested, "Oh, come on. Why don't we just go ahead and cut it all off?" The session abruptly ended.

On my way to Seef's, while thinking about this a little further, I got perturbed. Then I insisted on wearing my hair down for the entire photo session. Maybe in this manner, I could salvage a little bit of "old hip," in this sea of "new slick."

I'm not sure if the rat I smelled was real. I'm not sure whether the stylist's thoughts were an edict from the label. When we got to Seef's and walked out onto his deck to take the shot, with a smoggy L.A. sunset behind us, I made sure my hair was down.

With music blaring, cocktails pouring, and assistants dashing about with cameras, we stood with our backs to the west. As Seef began snapping away, he pointed out that the polluted, L.A. sunsets made for nice, warm orange backgrounds. I found this to be funny and not funny at the same time.

Then he instructed us to throw our arms around each other's shoulders and look directly into the lens with expressions "devoid of emotion." So I looked into the lens with an expression devoid of emotion.

I found this to be quite unnatural. Still, I followed his coaching. He's a brilliant artist who has photographed some of the most famous faces in the world. I had no reason to doubt him. So I didn't. The songs on the album were of a somber nature. Why should the cover shot be any different?

I didn't have a bad time. I just didn't have a very good time. Neither did John. I felt uneasy, scowling at the camera and throwing our arms around each other—like we were having a scowling good time. John wasn't about to put his arm around anyone. That's because he couldn't. If you look at the album cover, you will see him peering over the edge of Seef's deck, his right arm cradled with his left. Let me explain.

Several days before, as we finished our last day of tracking, Tucker began packing our gear out of Westlake, headed for Missouri. As we headed into overdubs, we decided to mark the occasion with one last party at the Oakwood Apartments—where we'd been staying.

Sitting equidistant between Hollywood and the San Fernando Valley, "Oak World" is a world unto itself. The huge complex was filled with musicians, writers, actors, and industry figures, all of whom preferred an apartment atmosphere to that of a hotel. We fell into this category.

At any hour, you could hear music pouring from any of the hundreds of units that made up the place. On the night of December 7, the music poured from our apartment.

As libations flowed, everyone was feeling good. All of the tracks were done and we were giving them one last listen before we started to overdub on them. They sounded great. As the evening progressed, arm-wrestling matches began to break out on the kitchen table.

As Dillon and Tucker squared off, the rest of us began placing side bets. When Charlie began the match by announcing, "Ready, set, go," the huffing and puffing and blowing your house down began.

Dillon picks up the story: "Tucker and I were arm wrestling, and I was determined to at least break even with one of our roadies. All of a sudden, I heard a pop that sounded like a .22 going off, and my wrist banged back against the counter. I said, 'What was that?'

"Right when it snapped, Stanley yelled, 'God damn. What *was* that?' Cash, who was sitting next to me, leaned over and said, 'That was you.'

"My [right] arm wouldn't work. I set it on a chair and tried to get it to come up, but I couldn't get it to do anything. I went into shock … and got extremely hot. I went out and laid on the balcony. When we realized what had happened, Stan took me to the hospital. We got there about nine or ten that night. And it was Saturday night. The place was a zoo. There were people coming in with gunshot wounds. I finally saw a doctor the next morning.

"When the doctor came in, without taking an X-ray or anything, he said, 'Yeah. You've broken your right humerus—a spiral fracture.' He took a pin and began sticking it deep into my hand and all up and down my arm.

"He said, 'Do you feel that?' I said, 'No.' Then he asked, 'What do you do for a living?' I said, 'I'm a guitar player.' He got right up in my face and said, 'Not anymore.'

"When I asked, 'Well, what do you mean?,' he said, 'There's a nerve that circles the humerus. A lot of times, we see this in spiral fractures. That nerve has been severed.'

"They started moving my arm around, and I could feel my bone just flopping around in there. Then I could feel my hand flashing on and off. That was a good thing. The nerve hadn't been severed, but my arm was still really broken. They fixed me up, set my arm in a sling, and sent me off.

"It put a damper on things for me. Luckily, my guitar parts were done, and all I had to do was sing. Tucker felt terrible, but it wasn't his fault.

It just happened. Boylan was scared to death, because—ironically, the other person that he was producing was Charlie Daniels. A couple of days after I broke my right humerus, Charlie broke his. Now Boylan is dealing with two people that he produces, both with broken right arms.

"I should've taken more time to heal, because when we went out to do gigs, Tucker had to come on stage and help me change guitars. I couldn't even plug them in because of my arm.

"It was about that time that I found out Les Paul has his elbow fused purposely in that position so he can use a pick. I figured if he could do it, I could. Then, a few years later, I ran into Charlie Daniels, and we traded war stories about our broken arms—and how pissed off Boylan was about it."

With John's wounded wing, we headed into overdub world. As everyone else went back to Missouri, John, Larry, Steve, Charlie, and I stayed at Oak World. At this point, along with Boylan, engineer Paul Grupp, and his assistant Ed Cherney, things became quite tedious. Not only was the hustle and bustle of a musician-filled studio replaced with the quiet environment overdubbing requires, we were getting frustrated with Boylan's laid-back approach.

Often were the times we would turn to him with a question, only to find him missing in action. "I remember singing my butt off one day," Steve agitatedly recalls. "When I asked him what he thought, he was out in the lobby on the phone. He was on the phone ALL THE TIME." This would've been a bigger distraction, had not the long-haired, mustachioed Grupp stepped up to call the shots we weren't calling for ourselves.

At this point, Dave Concors stopped by the studio. Even though he had relocated from Springfield to Los Angeles ten years earlier, he and I had never lost touch. He had taken a position on the technical staff at Teac. When he stopped by for a visit, I introduced him to the staff at Westlake—a staff that just happened to be looking for a handyman/technician/troubleshooter.

He became all three, flinging himself into the deep end of the rock 'n' roll gene pool, citing "Westlake led to my work with Giorgio Moroder, which led to the Billy Idol days. That was a hazy and warped period of indulgence of everything bad for you." Dave's presence at Westlake enabled the two of us to hang out again, talk about the Days of Sloth Gone By, and the days that lay ahead.

We once again became running and snorting buddies, receiving an invite to a Christmas party at the home of Fleetwood Mac's Bob Welch. When we walked in, the place was your typical party scene from your typical Hollywood movie. The bright lights of L.A. lay just off the balcony, as every dark corner was filled with a dark character. Blow was everywhere.

Blow was also everywhere in the Record Plant, where Boylan would move us to mix the tapes. Here I discovered Raul was just a shout away. All I had to do was pick up the phone in the control room, and in a matter of minutes, a parcel of powder was hand-delivered—its tariff added directly to the recording budget. I kept Raul's number close by.

As the completion of the album was drawing nearer, so was Christmas. When Boylan informed us that we could work up until the twenty-third, but not the twenty-fourth or twenty-fifth, we knew things would be tight. As it became more and more apparent that we weren't going to get done, decisions had to be made.

After a month and a half of running up a large studio tab, flights back to Springfield on the twenty-fourth, along with flights back out on the twenty-sixth were out of the question. After having invested so much time, we just wanted to get done and get the hell out of there. We only had a handful of sessions left.

Should we stay or should we go? The four of us decided to stay until we were done. This meant spending Christmas in Hollywood.

David Trask, who had recently left our road crew to take a similar position as John McVie's personal assistant/house-sitter, stopped by the studio. When he informed us that he was also going to be spending the holidays alone in McVie's vast, empty house, invitations were extended.

The easygoing McVie, remembering us from his pub days in Headley, didn't mind our stay. Though absent, he was still a gracious host. His splendid house was a wonderful respite, as thoughts of spending Christmas at Oak World were very, very depressing.

Phone calls to Springfield were not met with warm receptions. But we were so close to finishing, we had to stay. So we did. We knew the importance of this record. We also knew that we had to follow through and make sure things were right. This time, "good enough" would not be good enough.

On the afternoon of December 24, 1979, the five of us drove up Benedict Canyon, to the House the Penguin Built. Trask greeted us at the door with margaritas, a grill filled with smoking goodies, and McVie's blessings. A dinner plate of cocaine sat on the kitchen table, along with invitations to help ourselves—Fleetwood Mac style. This meant take the straw, stick it into the pile, and snort as much as you could handle. When the pile was gone, you'd just get another.

When we walked through the door, I headed right for the plate. After all, it was my birthday. Charlie was right behind me, as we decided to also celebrate his New Year's Eve birthday. As the evening progressed, holiday spirits flowed freely among the six of us. Songs were sung, but much of the focus remained on the booze in the blender and the plate in the kitchen. The theme of the evening? Merry Christmas to all, happy birthday to me—I mean, me and Charlie.

After a night of holiday cheer, I found myself watching the Christmas morning sunrise from the friendly confines of McVie's outdoor hot tub. With spectacular views of Lynda Carter, Warren Beatty, and Redd Foxx's rooftops below, Christmas Day was spent lolling about McVie's, drinking Bloody Marys, watching football, and getting ready to head back into the studio the next day.

We all missed our families. We also knew what was riding on this record.

On the twenty-sixth, we resumed mixing. We buckled down, knowing we were close and had to get done by the end of the year. So did Boylan and Grupp. We all smelled the finish line, making a mad dash for it. Days were long—fifteen and sixteen hours long. Sleep was short. I kept Raul hopping.

On the morning of the thirty-first, after a very long week, we flew home, tired and spent, arriving just in time to usher in the new decade. As we bid adieu to the '70s, our first album for someone other than A&M was in the can.

During the recording, there hadn't been much contact with our new label. They pretty much left us alone, and we stuck to our non-meddling vow. But what a difference a record company makes!

The short walk from A&M's front gate, up the steps to David Anderle's balcony was replaced with an elevator ride to Columbia's seventh-floor

It Shined

aerie. Here, amid a sea of metal, glass, and fluorescent light, the place resembled an insurance company as much as it did a record company.

Right after the first of the year, Stan made the trek up the elevator to turn in the album to Don Ellis and talk about the pending option. He was informed that Don Ellis no longer worked here. Details were not disclosed. Nor were they important.

What was important was the fact that when Stan walked into Ellis's office, there was a new guy sitting behind the desk. That was a bad sign.

Then, when the new guy asked, "Oh, you guys are on our label?," that was another bad sign.

When he placed our tape on top of a pile of other tapes on his desk, this was a third bad sign.

Then, to think about him picking up any kind of option for a second record seemed pretty slim. Strike Four is always a bad sign.

When bad sign number five appeared, it made a knuckle sandwich and hit me square in the gut.

I ushered in the '80s by learning that our constant traveling had taken its toll on my family. Karen was moving to Florida and she was taking the kids with her. By early spring, I found myself living alone in a big, ten-room house.

I wasn't the only Duck sitting on rough seas, as marital discord had begun to rear its ugly head in several of our households. We all handled it in different ways—some better than others, others louder than others. The same could be said for our wives. Relationships began to crumble before our very eyes. "Smooth sailing" would not describe our personal lives in Springfield.

Two things that do not mix well are a pending divorce and an appetite for cocaine. Both became quite prevalent in my life, on top of a big, empty house. The hustle and bustle of the family that occupied it last year was replaced with the hustle and bustle of a constant party and snowball fight.

Crazy things began to happen; some good, some bad, some ugly. Most lasted for days on end. As the '80s began, I may have lost a wife, but I gained three dogs named Jim, Tom, and Terry. They would help with the volatile period I, as well as the Ducks, were about to head into.

CHAPTER 27

As the new year began to take shape, we readied for the release of our first Columbia album. We did this by just hanging around Springfield. Gigs were played, but not many. Most were around the Midwest, short distances away.

As we reunited with Ruell, Rune, Canway, Charlie, Tucker, his new helper, John Aikin, Dan Mayo, and Rick Redford, the circus began to gear back up. Though it wouldn't really hit high gear until summer, the gigs we did play that spring were treated with the same abandon we'd been using—as much, if not more, attention paid to dinner and drinks than paid to the gig itself. I was one of main culprits.

Because of our various stages of divorce and a shifting of emphasis from the gig to the post-gig gig, the bus began to fill with women. When we hit the road, the thing became a rolling cocktail party from the time we left Springfield until the time we got home.

Through it all, though, the first rule of the road was strictly obeyed: What happens on the bus stays on the bus. Man, did it start to happen.

Many of us were relieved just to get gone and get away from the everyday discord that had begun filling our domestic lives. Though the pissing and moaning about not wanting to be on the road, not being able to sleep on the bus, and the yucky diesel fumes continued, when the bus pulled out of town, most of us were glad to be on it. When it pulled back into town, a substantial amount of the party shifted up into my empty house on Main Street.

Charlie and I became roommates off the road, as well as on. Not only did we share hotel rooms, he moved into one of the empty bedrooms of my house. This may not have been a very smart idea, but …

Born exactly one week apart (me on Christmas Eve, 1950, him on New Year's Eve, 1950), we took the opportunity to combine these two days into one continuous week of abuse. The annual weeklong parties became notorious.

Here, the group of musicians I had been on the bus with was replaced with another group of musicians from across town. When everyone on the bus went home, the guys from across town came over.

Terry Wilson, Tom Whitlock, and Jim Wunderle began stopping by on a regular basis. Here, we quickly formed a band, for the sole purpose of having fun, getting stoned, and playing all our favorite rock 'n' roll songs. Deeming ourselves Dog People (after our collective love of all things canine), after only a couple of rehearsals, we had enough songs to do a gig. We hauled all of our stuff into Humphrey Klinker's, a small pizza joint on the corner of National and Elm.

Things went so well that when we finished, club owner Jeff Nye asked if we could just leave our stuff set up and play again the next night. This posed no problem. After two nights of rock 'n' roll, two hundred songs, and two hundred bottles of beer on the wall, Jeff eagerly asked when we could do it all again.

He got out his calendar and let us know that we could play at any time. I got out my Daredevils' calendar. It didn't have much on it.

I began playing with Jim, Tom, and Terry on a regular basis—not to replace Daredevil gigs, but to occupy the gaps between them. Everyone knew my situation. This I made clear right off the bat. The Dogs would have to adapt their schedule to that of the Ducks. If the Ducks called at the last minute, the Dogs were shit out of luck. No one had a problem with this.

I deemed it a good way to keep my chops up, my instrument in my hands, and my hands out of trouble. When I informed everyone that the Ducks would be out of town from the third through the ninth, the Dogs were booked on the tenth and eleventh.

When the Ducks rolled back into town, Tucker and Aikin would just swing by Klinkers and drop off my amp. The same Alembic amp I used to fill the Omaha Convention Center began to fill this little pizza joint with its low and mighty rumble.

As spring progressed, I spent my days in an empty house and my nights at Klinkers. Larry spent his days and nights in his basement studio. Along with our album, which was soon to be released, Columbia had offered him the chance to make another solo record. He jumped at that chance.

"When they [Columbia] asked if I wanted to do another record," he recalls, "all I could say was, 'Sure.' I was doing a lot of writing, because there was the possibility of making one. I was working up a bunch of the material I had written with Jon R. [Goin] and had been working up with Frank [Westbrook], Ike [Stubblefied], Bill [Jones], and Don [Shipps] in my basement."

As Larry worked up his songs and I played Klinkers, a busy summer began.

On May 24, our first album for someone other than A&M hit the stands. It was stark. It was gray. It was pink. It was L.A. It looked and sounded like all of the above. In contrast to all of our other albums, there was no attempt at any kind of lightheartedness in the music. Nor was there anything resembling a smile on the cover.

As part of the image makeover, the album had no title, just our name scrawled in a stilted pink script above our four scowling faces. Remember those expressions devoid of emotion? Well, there they were—in stunning black and white and grey and pink.

With our arms draped over each other's shoulders and John cradling his broken arm, the back cover featured our best Eagles-like sneers, warmed by the L.A. sunset, glowing orange and brown in the background.

Though the photo did reflect the troubled times that were taking shape at home, I wasn't particularly fond of it. Not only did I think it to be a feeble attempt at trying to be heavy dudes, I knew the folks back home wouldn't buy into it. They didn't. It missed the mark.

The music, though we dug it, also missed the mark. Everyone eagerly anticipated the new album, produced by the guy who had produced Charlie Daniels and the Pure Prairie League. Expectations were high.

Unfortunately, the record sounded more like another of Boylan's recent productions—Boston (the band).

"Man, those guitars are mixed awfully loud," Larry observed.

That spring, *Ozark Mountain Daredevils* was released. On May 24, when it hit the charts, though it stayed one week longer than its predecessor (four weeks, to *It's Alive*'s three), it only reached six positions lower (#170 to #176).

"Take You Tonight" was released as a single, and it sounded great on the radio. Unfortunately, it only stayed around for five weeks, making it to #67. On its heels, Larry's "Oh, Darlin'" was released with even less results. By midsummer, the album had come and gone.

Reviews were not bad. Nor were they good. That's because there weren't any. Columbia (in a major reshuffling)—as well as the entire industry (going through an economic crunch)—was still unaware we were on the label. The record got no publicity. Radio people didn't play it. Newspaper people didn't write about it. It was placed so far on the back burner, you couldn't see it due to the curvature of the Earth. The splash it made was a giant cannonball/belly flop right into the cut-out bins.

Mark Marymont, though, kept Springfield readers informed, writing, "The Daredevils—pared down to its basic nucleus of four—are alive and well, kicking up dust with a new record label, a new album, and a new sound. Of sorts.

"Actually, it's more of a highly polished synthesis of all the old sounds, into a lively LP of mostly rock-flavored tunes that are as clean and catchy as you please.

"Of the new album, Larry Lee says, 'It's a lot more rock 'n' roll than anything we've done before. There's really no acoustic stuff or ballads. We'd been playing and we put a "live" album out, but we haven't done a studio album in three years.'

"A Daredevil concert has always been a delightful exercise in challenging eclecticism," Marymont continues. "They kept you on your toes—if slightly off balance—at all times. It was, above all else, consistently interesting, which is more than can be said of too many bands that sell a lot more records.

"I always thought it was interesting, too," Lee says. A&M, on the other hand, had problems with the diversity of the music, which Lee said, "was understandable, but we didn't want to repeat that same sound for every album."

Lee said the new contract (Columbia) gave the group a chance to re-evaluate their music. "This time we wanted to have a successful album, so we thought about all the criticisms we've had the past six years."

Though the record was slip-sliding away, we hit the road to try to resuscitate it and, more importantly, make a living. When we loaded onto the bus, crazy things started to happen—everywhere we went. There were festivals with the Beach Boys and the Allman Brothers. There were fairs with Waylon and Willie. All were three-ring circuses.

There were clubs crammed with drunken fans.

There were empty football stadiums.

As we began making two-week runs, cocaine became even more prevalent, and Charlie made sure it kept coming. Every afternoon, while Tucker and Aikin set up our gear at the venue, Charlie would stop in to meet the promoter and take care of business.

Some promoters were first rate. Others weren't. Some were cool and tried to help at every turn. Others tried to get away with as little as possible—and pay us with drugs. Others tried to wrangle out of paying us at all.

A chilly rain fell on Calgary's McMahon Stadium. As the sun dismally disappeared over the Canadian Rockies to the west, the country rock festival trudged on. At six o'clock that evening, the 54,000-seat stadium, home of the Calgary Stampeders football team, held fewer than 200 drenched concertgoers, all gathered at the foot of the stage, built on the goal line.

It had been raining all day. As evening rolled in, temperatures dropped. As our scheduled ten o'clock set neared, at nine-thirty, Charlie smelled a rat.

Earlier, when we pulled into the place, the first thing we saw—53,800 empty seats—was not an encouraging sight. The drizzle continued to throw cold water on any prospect of a "walk-up" crowd. The turnstiles weren't turning.

As Tucker and Aikin began setting up our gear, a suspicious Charlie grabbed Cash by the arm and said, "Steve, come with me. This might get weird." The two entered the promoter's office to get paid. His car idled in the parking lot.

Payments for our concert appearances have always come in two installments. Half of the amount is to be submitted a month prior, to be used as expense money to get to the gig. The other half is to be paid, in cash, before we walk on stage. Occasionally, we would fudge a little on the "before we walk on stage" clause. This was not one of those occasions.

As Steve and Charlie stepped into the office, they found themselves sitting across the desk from a sullen promoter, surrounded by a handful of cross-armed, weightlifting, jewelry-bedazzled henchmen.

"Fucking rain. I can't believe it."

"Yeah, man. That's too bad," replied our consoling but cautious road manager.

"God damn it. We didn't sell shit for tickets."

"Yeah. That's too bad, too."

As a nervous silence permeated the festivities, Steve quietly looked on, anticipating anything. As the henchmen maintained their jutting jaws and bloated biceps, the promoter threw the ball into Charlie's court, asking, "I guess you boys wouldn't be interested in cutting us some kind of deal, would you?"

"Nope."

"Ah, c'mon."

"Look, we're a long way from home. We've got to have that money." Taking a deep breath, Charlie finished his thought with, "Plus, we have to have it before we play."

"Well, we ain't got it."

"Then we ain't playing."

"You can't do that."

"Oh, yes we can," reassured Charlie, reaching into his briefcase for his copy of the contract.

Realizing he was painted into a corner, the promoter shot out of his seat, walking briskly to one end of the small room. Turning his attention to his stoic friends, he asked, "You guys said the money was on its way, didn't ya? The money is on its way, isn't it?"

"Yeah, yeah, yeah," they mumbled, to the shuffling of their feet.

"Good. Good. Good," chirped Charlie, sitting back in his chair, slowly lighting a cigarette. "Then we'll wait. Cigarette, anyone?"

"Man, let's just get this shit over with," the promoter continued. "It's fucking raining out there, it's been raining all God damn day, and there's only fifty stupid fucking people out there, standing in it."

"But they're our fans," reminded Charlie, "and we're gonna play. The stage is covered, isn't it?"

After realizing that Charlie meant business, the situation was cut and dried. The conversation continued.

"Okay. How about this? Why don't you guys just go ahead and start and we'll bring you the money as soon as it gets here?"

The bobble-headed goons agreed. The idling on the parking lot continued.

"Nope," Charlie insisted.

"No way?"

"No way."

The air thickened further. After a pregnant, pregnant pause, things came to a head when the promoter finished his thought with a sheepish, "Then, what are we going to do?"

Taking a long, slow drag from his cigarette, allowing the smoke to slowly billow out through his thick moustache, Charlie took the bull by the horns and spoke up. "Is that a Rolex?"

"Yeah."

"Can I see it?"

"Sure."

After giving it the once-over, Charlie turned to one of the other goons and continued. "Let me see yours too."

One by one, each man took off his jewel-encrusted timepiece. When it became apparent what Charlie was about to do, the ball was back in the promoter's court.

After going around the room, gathering gaudy watches, Charlie brought the brief meeting to an end with a cheerful, "Well now. It looks like its 'show time.' You guys come find me when that money gets here. Okay? I'll be right out there on the stage. I won't be hard to find. Man, you guys got nice watches."

With timepieces on their hands, Steve and Charlie stood up, turned, and walked, wide-eyed, out of the office. The rest of us, nervously waiting in the hallway, followed them directly to the stage. That night, we played in the drizzle as our fans danced in the rain.

It Shined

The money finally materialized. Charlie finally got paid. The watches were returned to their rightful owners. As we played, we watched our road manager walk into the football team's office with a fistful of jewelry and walk out with sack full of money. We had to laugh at the wry smile on Sting's face.

Other promoters were great, most of their gigs going without a hitch. They were easy, and a pleasure to deal with. Others were just plain cooked and coked out of their minds. They were not fun to deal with. They were, though, a lot of fun to party with. And party with them we did. On many occasions, Charlie would walk up, whisper, "Do have," and tromp off to the bus for a snort.

Being road manager, the phone rang off the hook in his and, consequently, my hotel room.

Being road manager, he came in contact with promoters, club owners, radio guys, and dope dealers on an everyday basis.

Being road manager, he also had to deal with band members who continuously stopped by for one reason or another. Some came by for cash advances. Others, for a place to hang out, have a cocktail, and do a bump.

Rune was a regular, as his appetite for cocaine became as voracious as his appetite for tobacco, alcohol, and a good party.

It was a quiet afternoon when he stopped by our room. He and Charlie had decided to split a gram for the evening, which Charlie had neatly prepared into two piles atop the TV. Because he had stepped into the shower, at the time of the knock, I answered the door.

Upon entering the room, Rune's eyes lit up. As I returned to the chair in the corner and my book, he quickly began rolling up a dollar bill. When Charlie emerged from the shower, Rune greeted him with a cheerful, "That was a nice line, Charlie." When he was informed that he had just inhaled his entire half of the gram in one fell snort, I had to chuckle.

Happy Hour in our room started around 3:30 in the afternoon. By 4:30, everyone was pretty happy. By 5:00, if we were still in the mood for food, we started looking for dinner. Sound checks were ignored. Nice restaurants were not.

We became especially fond of Japanese food, seeking it out whenever we were in a town big enough to fashion a Japanese restaurant. We liked the sushi. We loved the sake. After one particular meal, Charlie walked back in with his red plaid thermos and instructions to the waitress to "fill 'er up." The rest of the evening—gig included—was washed away in a sea of rice wine. Halfway through the set, when a voice from the crowd bellowed, "Why don't you guys have some more drinks?" we did.

Hey, Skol.

If our room was the epicenter of Happy Hour, Steve and Rune's was definitely the epicenter of the post-gig shenanigans. Each night, Rune transformed into the Condor. Each night became theater of the absurd.

When asked to describe these late-night forays, the large man would humbly explain, "I'm just jazzing around, man." The term "jazz" became our instant moniker for jaunts into Keith Richardsville.

On many "mornings after," Rune would emerge from his room, greeting me with a grin and a, "Supe, did you find any jazz last night?" All responses were met with large laughter, large bear hugs, and large tales of midsummer night's mischief.

All members played in this jazz band. If someone hit a clam onstage, Rune would ask, "Hey, John? Was that jazz you were playing last night?" It was all jazz, all the time. All laughed.

This laughter often carried on stage, as it did the night we rolled into Toronto's famed El Mocambo for a live radio broadcast and a late-night studio interview with Canadian musical icon, Kelly Jay.

Though we agreed to make both appearances, we did not agree to be sober for either. We weren't. After yet another large dinner in another nice restaurant, we arrived at the club well-oiled. This was fine with the crowd, who was also well-oiled—and packed in like sardines.

Just a couple of weeks earlier, the Stones had recorded *Love You, Live* on this same stage, amid the swirling controversy of Ron Wood and Margaret Trudeau. The place was still abuzz with jazz.

When we hit the stage, the disc jockey introduced us and we were off like a house on fire. Steve delivered a screaming "Chicken Train," complete with my chicken squawks that sounded as if the chicken had just come from the sushi bar/crack house on the corner. Rune's guitar licks soared over the top of everything. Ruell viciously pounded all eighty-eight keys.

As we usually did, in the middle of the show, Larry would step from behind the drums to do a couple of his piano tunes. Canway would take off his guitar and assume the drum throne. The show smoothly carried on.

The El Mocambo stage is a small one—especially for a band with seven guys in it. On top of this, because it was being broadcast on the radio, the station cluttered things even further with more piles of their cables. This caused a substantial amount of squeezing by each other during instrument swaps. After delivering "Jackie Blue" and "Oh, Darlin,'" Larry and Canway re-exchanged places.

We were in the home stretch, and the crowd was in the aisles. As Canway's "Horsetrader" was called, he reached for his guitar, not knowing that in the middle of all the shuffling, it had been knocked over and returned to its stand—but not retuned. Larry started the stomping intro.

As the beat began to swell and blast over the airwaves, I informed everyone that "We're going to get ole Canway up here to do the 'Horsetrader.' Here we go." The El Mocambo crowd chimed in on the stomping, along with a healthy dose of just plain "whooping it up." Feet stomped. Hands clapped. Tambourines banged. Cowbells clanged. Spontaneous howls rang through the room. The "Horsetrader" was off to a flying start.

As the beat continued, we waited for Steve to hit the opening lick that would cue us into the song. He turned around and hurried to the microphone—without checking his tuning.

After a stirring thirty-second intro, his first dozen notes were so sour, all we could do, was look around at each other in disbelief. The guitar had been knocked so far out of tune, it was impossible to carry on. Proceedings came to a cringing halt.

Then the crowd in the club, as well as the radio audience, heard the blood-curdling scream. Completely flustered and smashed, Steve began waving his arms in the air, yelling, "EEEAAHH. Hold it, boys. Hold it. HOOOLD IT. There's something real bad wrong here."

The stomping was replaced with laughter that instantly grew from polite chuckles into full-blown guffawing. When Cash-o walked to his microphone to ask, "What's wrong? What are you trying to do to these lovely children?," the entire song broke down into complete rubble.

The laughter carried on for several minutes until Canway could figure out how to get his guitar back in tune. Then the stomping started back up and the song began again. I'm not sure if the hilarity translated well to the listener at home. I don't think so. But everyone in the club was in stitches.

By the time we got to the station that night, our condition went from "stewed" to "completely stewed." This didn't matter to Kelly. As pianist/front man for Canadian rock 'n' roll band Crowbar, he was used to this kind of behavior. He joined right in, quickly catching up.

He asked, "What was so God damn funny over there at the club? It sounded like a bunch of howling banshees."

Rune replied, "Canway was playing some jaaazz."

The interview went well (I guess) and well into the night (I know). No one has any idea what we tried to even talk about, as Kelly didn't have a tape running. I did hear a tape of the gig. It wasn't very good. Very funny. But not very good.

The next afternoon, as everyone nursed hangovers, Tucker and Mayo took the opportunity to stroll through the streets of downtown Toronto. Stumbling upon a sporting goods store, their eyes were caught by the large wood-and-plastic trophy of a Viking in the window, proudly standing amid the array of hockey gear. They could not resist. Thirty minutes later, the two laughing roadies emerged from the store, trophy in hand.

With long, flowing hair cascading from beneath a winged helmet, the twelve-inch plastic warrior—clad in total battle regalia—stood atop a polished wooden base. The freshly engraved plate at his feet read, "THE VILD WIKING JAZZ AWARD FOR CONSPICUOUS CONTRIBUTION TO THE JAZZ SENSIBILITY."

The first recipient of the trophy was Steve "Black Tee" Cash, whose name was etched under the year 1980. Following years were left blank for future honorees. That night, the jazz trophy was awarded for the first time. Everyone laughed—but Rune.

With massive doses of mock resentment, he bombarded Steve with constant barrages of, "Steeeve. Can I see your trophy?", Steeeve. Can I borrow your trophy?" and "Steeeve. Does this mean you're a real Viking?"

"I don't want the stupid, fucking thing," came Steve's emphatic answer. "I didn't have anything to do with it. You can have it. Here, take it."

To which Rune would coyly reply, "No, that's all right, Steve. Maybe I will win it next year."

The bantering went on, day and night, as the jazz trophy became a lightning rod for our very comedic soundtrack—one that included continuous viewings of *Monty Python and the Holy Grail* and continuous listenings to the Statler Brothers' *Lester "Roadhog" Moran and his Cadillac Cowboys, live at the Johnny Mack Brown High School.*

When we saw ugly girls, we yelled, "RUN AWAAAAY."

I introduced many songs with, "All right. Mighty Fine. Kick it off, Wichita."

The next year, even though there were none, Steve was relieved of his "jazz trophy" duties. Taking the honor for his bouts with constant back pain, contorted posture, and a steady diet of painkillers, the 1981 recipient was Steve "Big, Tall, Sideways" Canaday.

The torch was passed. The trophy was taken to the engraver. Steve's name was etched right under Steve's. He began receiving the wrath of the Condor.

I was awarded the thing the third year, as Michael "We're Goin'" Granda was engraved onto the plate under 1982. I took the cake that year for an unbridled enthusiasm for all things sex, drugs, rock 'n' roll, and the St. Louis Cardinals baseball team—who, that fall, won the World Series.

Having recently met pitchers Bruce Sutter, Danny Cox, Jeff Lahti, Joe Magrane, and Springfield native George Frazier on the team's winter caravans, it was great to hang out with these guys when they didn't have anything to do but hang out—and drink beer. I fit right in.

I wanted to talk baseball. They wanted to talk music. So we talked both. When we played in St. Louis, they came to our gigs, drank beer, and chased girls. We were extended invitations to their games at any time. I took them up on their offer—often.

After lanky, John Kendall finished frolicking around in his Fredbird suit, acting like an idiot, he joined us for late-night revelry, where we all acted like idiots. He and I hit it off famously. He came to gigs. I went to games. Afterward, we painted the town Cardinal red.

I became consumed with the team, often attending all six games of a home stand. All I had to do was go to St. Louis for the week and hang out at the ball park in the afternoon. I was generously issued an "all-access" pass.

I watched with interest as the team prepared for its games, the same way a band prepares for a gig. After hanging around the park so much, I began forming my observations of baseball (in general) and the Cardinals (in particular) into essays. As these columns began to get published in magazines and newspapers around the area, I began a love affair with writing them.

I often left my voice in Busch Stadium. After a week of cheering and screaming, I oftentimes brought a shredded throat and no singing voice to a gig. I won the Jazz Trophy that year, by screaming, "WE'RE GOIN.' WE'RE GOIN' TO THE SERIES" seven bazillion times.

In 1982, I suffered the Condor's wrath.

After that, the novelty of the trophy wore off. Rune's diatribes waned and it unceremoniously found its way into a box in my dusty attic. Though Rune's name was never engraved onto the thing, that seven-dollar piece of wood and plastic brought 7 million dollars' worth of laughs.

Because many of our gigs were still being held in college auditoriums, many of our dressing rooms were in adjoining classrooms. If the room happened to contain a chalkboard, Rune instantly filled it with humorous caricatures of band members. No one was safe from his chalk and sense of humor.

One evening found him spontaneously bursting into song. As he quietly strolled among the classroom desks, meekly singing, "Hey Jude. Don't make it bad ..." when he reached the song's grand finale, he morphed into the Condor. When he bellowed, "... to make it better, better, better, better, better, AAHHHH," he screamed the song's patented outro, "Nahh. Nahh. Nahh. Nah, nah, nah, nah. Nah, nah, nah, nah. Hey Jude." As he did, he proceeded to toss all of the desks into a noisy pile in a far corner of the room.

Once the desks were heaped into the corner and the refrain was over, so was the bit. Then he politely untangled them, neatly set them all back up into rows, and started the song over. Eventually, the desks found their way into the corner again.

His antics at the gig were only surpassed by his antics afterward.

One affair spawned a late-night beauty pageant to break out in his Oshkosh Holiday Inn room. One by one, he led female revelers into the bathroom for a bump and a primp. When the gal emerged back into the room, strutting her stuff, thunderous rounds of applause rippled through the audience.

After a handful of contestants, when Rune stepped out of the bathroom, wearing nothing but a shower cap and the slip he'd taken off of one of the previous contestants, he was unanimously voted Miss Wisconsin. His promenade around the room was nothing short of magnificent.

Another night found him and Steve with a burning desire to talk to the king of Norway. They figured out that, due to time zone differences, their 3:00 AM wild hare correlated directly to breakfast time in Oslo. Steve did the dialing. Rune did the talking.

After being put on hold several times, a hush fell over their hotel room. When their call finally found its way to the king's residence, the voice on the other end was that of personal secretary, Mr. Blum.

Blum leerily informed Rune that the king was eating breakfast and was not to be disturbed. No matter how hard Rune tried to convince Blum that the two drunken callers were famous rock 'n' roll guys and he was from Norway and blah, blah, blah, he got nowhere. When Steve took the phone, matters only got worse.

When it became apparent that the king was not going to take the call, the experiment ended. I'm not sure what the two would've talked to the king about, had they gotten through. But the international long-distance phone bill was worth every penny.

The Miss Wisconsin Pageant was a rousing success.

The phone call to the king of Norway wasn't.

Though the nights were long and festive, mornings were not pretty. They became even less pleasant when Charlie would come stomping down the hall, banging on everybody's door. Some were hard to rustle. Rune was the worst.

Cash, who remained the Condor's roommate throughout the mayhem, describes it best, observing, "Rune was the absolute worst to try to wake up. Over the course of the night, he would roll over into that little space between the bed and the wall. That's where he would sleep. He was one big mass of sheets, covers, pillows, and hair, which looked like a million snakes coming out of his head.

"And nothing could wake him. I would try to shake him, but he was dead to the world. I would lean over and yell at the top of my lungs, two inches from his head. But he wouldn't move. I'd have to go get Charlie and we'd literally have to pick him up and carry him to the bus.

"If he just happened to snap to, he would jump up, ask for a cigarette, and start telling jokes. The guy was amazing. I've never seen a man sleep like that. It was more like hibernating."

Amid all of the frivolity, women began finding their way into rooms and bunks throughout the ranks. It was interesting to see who would come down to the coffee shop for breakfast, occasionally having to introduce yourself to the person you were waking up next to.

Once again, there was only one rule you had to adhere to: "You must be responsible for your 'seal'"—another term Rune developed for female guests. If you were going to have your way with them, it was not cool just to abandon them. If you had a seal, you had to be responsible for her.

I began using Rick Redford's assistance to hunt seals. During our shows, he nonchalantly strolled through the crowd. When I spotted a pretty girl, I pointed her out with a subtle nod. He would tap on her shoulder, and a backstage pass was issued. Each night, the backstage area filled up. Each night, hotel rooms did the same.

Gigs became even more important to our financial well-being than ever. We began grabbing all we could. When a good-paying gig came in, we did whatever it took to get there. If it was possible to do two in the same day, we would. This was nothing new. Years ago, we often did two and sometimes three in a day.

That Fourth of July, a scorching early-afternoon set under the arch for St. Louis's VP Fair was followed with a mad dash to the airport and a guerrilla run across the state for an evening gig and fireworks display under the Soldier's Memorial in Kansas City.

What a long, strange weekend this next one was—Friday night at Six Flags in St. Louis, and Saturday night at a biker festival in Prince George, British Columbia. Both gigs offered very healthy paychecks. Flights were booked.

After playing at the amusement park, when we headed to the St. Louis airport the following morning, things were fine. When we landed in Seattle to meet our connecting flight to Prince George, things weren't fine.

Torrential rains had not only engulfed the entire area for days and weeks, but continued to pour in buckets and sheets. The airport became a mess—a mass of frantic, stranded people. Flights were delayed. Others were canceled altogether. When the last connecting flight to our small outpost destination was canceled, we joined the ranks of the stranded.

Bewilderedly sitting in the Seattle airport, it became apparent that the only way we were going to get to the gig was to charter a plane. On such short notice, the only one we could find was a Lear jet. The only problem was, it only held seven passengers. This meant not everyone would be able to make it. Someone would have to stay behind. That someone would be Charlie.

A phone call to Tucker, who was already in Prince George with our gear, came back with reports of nothing but muck. He also told us that the festival was still going on in the muck. We had to make it. The price tag was too high.

(For those of you with inquiring minds, Danny Mayo and Rick Redford helped us pull off the Six Flags gig on rented equipment.)

A second phone call to the promoter explained our situation. He assured us that a bus would be waiting at the airport. If nothing went wrong, we could make it to the gig just in time to walk on stage.

Knowing that the rainy weather would make for a bumpy ride, I hated climbing into that little plane. But though the storm clouds jostled us during takeoff, the plane was so fast, it only took two minutes to pop above them and into calm, clear night air.

As an unexpected bonus, for the next thirty minutes, the Aurora Borealis delivered its spectacular show right before our very eyes. At 12,000 feet, the Northern Lights were spellbinding. When we dove back down through the clouds and landed in Prince George, it was dark and drizzling.

Time was of the essence. We quickly loaded from the Lear jet onto a bus, which took us to the end of the paved road. Here, we jumped into pickup trucks, which took us as far as they could go in the mud. The final leg of the journey was made when we climbed into the front scoop of a giant Caterpillar, which could go anywhere, no matter how much mud.

As we sloshed our way across the field, festival lights and bonfires glimmered in the misty distance. Though not nearly as spectacular as the Northern Lights, we headed right toward them, unable to keep from laughing at our drastic downgrades in transportation.

The mire was ankle deep when we climbed out of the scoop and into the sloppy backstage area. With sheets of plywood strewn atop the muck, nothing was going to deter these mud-caked Canadians. Nor had it deterred Elvin Bishop, who was finishing his set.

Complete lawlessness ruled, as there was no way any kind of authority could even get back into the place—unless they arrived by Caterpillar. Drugs were openly and flagrantly being used everywhere. The female singer from one of the previous bands had been raped earlier in the evening by some of the security guards—the same guys who decided that while we were playing, they were going to stand on the stage, under the warm lights. We were not about to tell them they had to move.

The conditions were horrendous. When we arrived, all Tucker and Aikin could do was shake their heads. By the time they got everything set up, all we wanted to do was play, get paid, and get the hell out of there. Mercifully, all of the above happened without further calamity.

The next morning, as we gathered for breakfast in the coffee shop, we could only laugh at the disparity of our last two gigs—Friday night under the roller coaster at Six Flags and a Saturday night field trip to Sodom and Gomorrah.

Elvin was not laughing. He still hadn't found one of his guitars, which had disappeared into the late-night muck. He was not a happy camper.

We were more than relieved when we headed back to the Prince George airport and boarded our flight back to Seattle. Charlie was a welcome sight, standing at the gate with our boarding passes to St. Louis in his hand. He was speechless as we recanted stories of the night before.

Though the Prince George gig took the surreal cake, others were just plain odd. The Great Northern Music Festival in Mole Lake, Wisconsin became an annual booking. Held on the Mole Lake Indian Reservation, the festival was completely run by members of the tribe. Because it took place on actual reservation land, a different set of laws was in place.

The first law struck from the books was any kind of curfew, noise ordinance, or code of behavior. The second law struck from the books was the banning of the peace pipe. Curfews weren't observed. Pipes were passed.

On our first trip to Mole Lake, we thought we had misread our contract; 1:00 AM seemed a bit late to play. But when we arrived, the grounds were full of folks and no one was the least bit interested in sleep. Plus, there were two bands scheduled to play after us. Time did not matter at Mole Lake. The place was abuzz.

Huge bonfires were maintained and danced around, as people threw everything into the flames they could find. From our onstage vantage, we could see couches and tree trunks ablaze, silhouetted revelers jumping through the flames. Vendors, selling everything from tequila to T-shirts to tattoos to mushrooms, surrounded the area.

When I learned about the festival's chant, "MOLE LAKE. MOLE LAKE. MOLE FUCKING LAKE," I started yelling it throughout our entire show. We became a crowd favorite, returning year after year. With each visit, we began recognizing faces. Fellow Missourian John Hartford was also an annual visitor, delivering his own Mole Lake chant from atop his electrified clogging board.

Anyone who remembers anything about the Great Northern Music Festival remembers the chant and how loud and powerful it could get when chanted by thousands of people. Through the years, we shared the Mole Lake stage with Dwight Yoakam, Charlie Daniels, Doug Kershaw, David Allen Coe, the Band, and Nitty Gritty. Every year was a wild scene. The festival was very well run.

Randy Erwin, who had recently moved his offices from Missoula, Montana to Minneapolis, kept us coming through on a yearly basis. Due to this relocation, he also kept us working through the northern states and Canada. Entire tours wound their way across the large northern fair, festival, and casino circuits.

The long, crazy year ended with a handful of post-Christmas gigs through Kansas, culminating with New Year's Eve at the Uptown. Charlie and I were knee-deep in our weeklong birthday bash. The rolling party rolled merrily, merrily along. That is, until we woke up on the morning of the thirty-first in Hays, Kansas and looked out the window.

By the time we started stirring, Mother Nature had covered everything with a thick blanket of snow. It was beautiful. It was also frightening. Snowstorms in the middle of Kansas are nothing to fool around with.

When you get stuck in one, you are stuck. When you get stuck in one, you are fucked. We wanted nothing to do with either scenario.

Weather forecasts were foreboding, containing nothing but ice and snow, followed by more ice and snow. We had to get gone, as Charlie and Tucker got everyone up very early. We had to beat the elements into Kansas City before sundown. There was no time for breakfast. There was no time for anything. It was a long, deliberate trek across the state.

When we pulled out of the Hays Holiday Inn parking lot, the bus was already starting to slide around on the pavement. If the highway was impassable during the day, it would be impossible by night. Frozen nights, stranded along I-70 in the middle of Kansas are no fun—and nowhere to spend New Year's Eve. Tales of the Frozen Bros. were recounted.

By the time we hit the Missouri line, the afternoon snow had accumulated so much, we were forced to leave the bus at a highway truck stop, simply because it wouldn't be able to handle Kansas City's hilly—and now icy—streets. We found our way to the hotel in cabs.

That afternoon, when we arrived at our rooms, radio stations were calling on a continuous basis, wanting to inform their listeners, many of whom would be traveling long distances—all of whom would be traveling in inclement weather.

First, we had to decide whether anyone could even physically get to the theater through the sheer amount of snow. The gig was still five hours away. This meant four and a half additional hours of snow on top of what was already on the ground.

Then, after midnight, when everyone left—drunk—there would be … Well, you get the picture.

We were already at the hotel, which sat only a couple of blocks from the theater. Tucker also safely made it in and was already setting up the gear. There was no problem with the local PA company, which only had to come from the nearby Westport area. Though conditions were definitely bad enough to warrant canceling, we didn't want to. So we didn't. It was New Year's Eve.

When Rune discovered that there were stoves in our rooms and a grocery and liquor store around the corner, he offered to mix up a batch of Glug. This traditional Norwegian holiday quaff, concocted of red wine, vodka, apples, oranges, cranberries, cloves, and other spices was to be sipped hot. He trudged to the store.

Returning with bags of fruit and liquor, he began pouring the ingredients into a large cauldron atop his stove. By early evening, the whole place filled with wonderful aromas. By mid-evening, after many taste tests, everyone filled with holiday cheer. Charlie and I raised numerous birthday toasts.

Gig time became Glug time—and the cauldron was still half-full. By this time of night, not even cars were able to get around in the snow. This forced us to walk to the theater. But we didn't mind. We were warm from the inside out. Deciding that we hadn't had quite enough, we carried the warm cauldron with us as we stumbled along the snowy street.

When we got to the Uptown, we couldn't believe our eyes. Where we were expecting to see only a handful of people, the place was filled to the rafters—another testimony to how crazy—I mean *loyal*—our fans have always been. They weren't going let a little bad weather keep them from having a happy new year. Glug flowed.

I don't remember the gig.

I do remember the chocolate and banana cream pies Danny Mayo brought back to the hotel afterward.

I do remember the Three Stooges episode that broke out and how thrilled I was to be a participant.

I don't remember who hit me with the first pie. I do remember getting hit with several.

I don't remember who I hit with one of those pies. I do remember throwing several.

I remember the walls, curtains, bedspreads, televisions, and piles of coats in the corner that were unable to get out of the way of the pastry projectiles.

I didn't remember much about the crazy, hazy year that had just flown by.

I do remember ending it, covered with pie and full of Glug.

CHAPTER 28

"We got all that fame shit out of the way early," Cash recalls. "Then we got down to building a fan base."

This is exactly what we began doing in 1981—a year that began with a pie in the face on New Year's Eve in Kansas City and ended with a reunion gig in Kansas City—all sandwiched around real tragedy in Kansas City.

By this time, Rune had been in the country for almost five years, had grown accustomed to the Springfield way of life, and had had more than his share of Americanization. This included a wife, a child, a mortgage, and all the other accoutrements that go along with it.

That spring, he informed us that he would be leaving the band, effective immediately. Terry Wilson became his simple and logical replacement. The two of us had been playing together quite a bit with the Dog People. This would also make it convenient for Tucker and Aikin. When they dropped off my amp in town for a Dog gig, they could drop off Terry's too.

The switch was seamless. We really didn't even consider other guitar players. It was cut and dried. When Rune left, Terry was in. No big announcements. No fanfare. No rehearsals. No promo pictures. No nothing.

The local guitarist had heard us play many times over the years. He knew what we were doing. Not only is he a wonderful guitarist, he's a quick study. He and I ran through the Ducks' set a couple of times at my house after a Dog rehearsal. He was on the bus. We didn't miss a lick.

This upheaval, though, paled miserably to the real tragedy that would soon befall Stan and his family. On April 27, after a long, courageous fight with the neurofibromatosis that had been eating away at his body, eldest son Joey succumbed to the disease. At the age of seventeen years and seventeen days, he passed away.

"You gotta remember, it was at that time, Joey started getting really sick," recalls Stan. "I started losing interest in anything—except taking care of him. But he never lost his positive attitude or his sense of humor."

The optimistic lad with the wonderful ideas (the Little Red Record) never got a chance to flourish into adulthood. It was a dark day, as we all made our way to Kansas City for the small, simple funeral.

"He may have lost his body, but he never lost his mind," recalled his reflective father. "And he looooved this band."

Soon afterward, I received the phone call I had been dreading. My divorce was coming final. Things were crumbling all around me, as I was summoned to the courthouse. Here, I met my attorney, Sandra Skinner. When we came face-to-face with Karen, she had also retained a female lawyer. Then, when we all walked into the courtroom and stood before the bench, it was occupied by a female judge.

There I was, the only guy involved in the entire ordeal. Sandy advised me not to make a scene or waves. I took her advice. Papers were shuffled. Lines were signed. I's were dotted. T's were crossed. Judges were judging. Lawyers were lawyering. Assets were divided. The gavel came down.

The only stipulation I insisted upon was that I not be denied access to my daughters. This was easily granted. All of the other shit—the houses, the cars, the trucks, the farms, the bank accounts—didn't matter. I just wanted that time with my girls.

I was saddened when I realized I wasn't going to be there to do the little Daddy things—like put Band-Aids on their knees when they fell off their bikes, or tell them how pretty they looked when they went to the prom.

It was still mid-morning when I walked out of the courthouse. The sun shined brightly. It was a dark day.

As 1981 unfolded, the band lost a guitar player, I lost a family, Stan lost a son, and we all lost a recording contract. Columbia wasted no time not picking up their option for a second album. Morale was not high. Gigs were sporadic. When they did come in, there was little excitement about playing them. We had already played everywhere—thrice.

Press coverage dwindled to almost nothing, which suited most of us just fine. This left me and Wilson to do interviews, and he had only been in the band for a few months. That left me. I got tired of doing it too. So I didn't.

When the Whatever City Gazette was contacted, their response was an underwhelming, "Oh. You guys again? Weren't you just here not too long ago? Got a new record out? You don't? Well, we'll call you."

We did take the opportunity to do a handful of demos at Larry's. But when we weren't traveling, we weren't together. Because of this, I began spending more and more time playing around Springfield with the Dogs. We had become quite popular, as people began packing in for the nightly chaos.

It was nothing for us to play four sets a night for five straight nights. I looked at this as a good way to keep my instrument in my hands, my hands out of trouble, and my mind off of my divorce. Frustrated energy, channeled into a rock 'n' roll band, can be a powerful as well as productive thing.

Occasionally, Cash-o would stop in for a couple of beers and join us on stage for a couple of songs. His divorce had also recently come final, and Dog People gigs were a great place to get laid. As Tom, Terry, and I began pounding out savage beats, Steve stepped to the microphone, bursting into long, impromptu rants of rhyme.

One particular evening, when we finished, I could not get his ranting—or the groove we'd been playing—out of my noggin. As soon as the gig was over, I headed straight home, where, with a head full of freshly pounded rock 'n' roll meat, I laid down a rough version of the song we'd been flailing away at a mere thirty minutes earlier.

Nor could I get the phrase, "There oughta be a law against it" out of my head. It had been the theme of Steve's rant and was stuck in my head like a dart.

The next morning, when I called, he didn't remember much about the evening either. When I told him I'd put together a rough guitar demo of the song we had played, he didn't remember doing a song. When I asked if he'd like to hear it and work on it, we decided to get together and do just that.

When I stopped by his house, hair of the dog was administered. By the end of the afternoon, "There Oughta Be a Law Against It" was honed from his informal rantings about insidious women, into a formal song about said insidiousness.

The next time we played a gig, I suggested we try to do it. This was easily done. Terry and I already knew it. That night, with minimal instruction to Larry, John, and Canway (Chuck Berry in the key of A), Steve stepped to the mic and we finished the evening with a rowdy version of "There Oughta Be a Law Against It." It worked like a charm. Not only did it add another harmonica song to the show, it got people up and on the dance floor.

Like "Stinghead," "Law" became a nightly staple of our encore.

So inspired, a second song instantly popped into my head. When I came in with the driving, chugging beat of "Gonna Buy Me a Car," it was also inserted into the set.

With more upbeat tunes like this being interjected, Dog chaos began to seep into Duck shows. Consequently, Larry's mellower material began to fall by the wayside—even more than it already had. His influence became less and less.

Though I didn't think Terry's style was that well suited to what the band needed, "Law" and "Car" were going over very well, every night. The *News-Leader*'s Mary Sue Price would observe, "Every time a guitar solo came around, it was Terry Wilson's show. He plays electric guitar with the unaffected grace and abandon of a scruffy kid in tennis shoes, who has no idea how good he is."

We didn't put many restrictions on what, or how, he played—just so long as he hinted at the signature lick. After that, he was on his own. Many of his leads tended to be much heavier than we were accustomed to hearing. It caused many of our older fans to scratch their heads, wondering why they were hearing a hard rock guitar solo in the middle of "Standing on a Rock."

As the summer season kicked in, we began playing more and partying more—a party that would stretch from Seattle to Disney World. This, along with the fact that my divorce was final, sent me off the deep end, in search of every possible extracurricular, mind-numbing activity I could get my hands on.

It was a typical Pacific Northwest morning, as rain beat against the windows of Seattle's Edgewater Inn. For decades, entertainers had been coming here to enjoy the sweet, salty air of the Pacific Ocean, which lapped directly beneath their window—a short hook, line, and sinker drop below. Rods and reels were sold in the gift shop, where Polaroids of celebrities and their catches graced the walls. John Bonham and Bing Crosby fished for sharks here. I woke up in an art gallery full of seals.

There was one in my bed. When I looked over at the other bed, our crew member had two. Over the course of the night, these three women had snuggled in wherever they could find room. Five people. Two beds. It had been a crazy night. It was a foggy morning.

After climbing over bodies and fumbling for the coffee machine, scattered everywhere about the room hung all the artwork that, last night, had hung in the hallways. It was a splendid sight. Our gallery was magnificent. The seals clapped their fins.

After a summer of meandering across the road map, the season ended with a swing of gigs through Florida with the New Riders (which would be great) and a gig at Disney World (which would be downright painful). Small theaters and clubs were booked, which meant in order to make ends meet, both bands would do two shows a night. Neither had a problem with this.

Deciding to sacrifice larger crowds for the warmer acoustics of these theaters, we sounded good. The New Riders sounded good. Songwriter Jack Tempchin, who was opening the shows, sounded good. Crowds were coming out in droves. They sounded good too.

Then we hit Gainesville, a college town that reminded us of Columbia, Lawrence, and Madison—with the addition of easy access to the coast and the boats from Peru. With two nights at the Great American Music

Hall and a Sunday afternoon gig on campus for the college radio station, we parked it here for a few days.

This is where I met—let's just call him "Sonny." After a blazing first set in the Music Hall, the tall, affable Floridian stopped me on my way to the bus. Friendly enough, when he complimented me on the show, I thanked him and shook his hand. When he asked if I'd like to do a bump, I instructed him to follow me.

Before opening the door to the bus, I warned him that there might be a few people inside who would also enjoy a stiff sniff. He reassured me this would be no problem. We climbed aboard with a couple of hours to kill until our second set.

After the shades were pulled, a large pile of powder was poured onto the table. By the time our second show rolled around, our eyes were rolling around in our heads. When we went on stage, Sonny climbed onto the New Riders' bus and pulled the same stunt.

Both buses stayed up all night, carrying on, drinking, snorting, and singing Hank Williams songs. By this time, no one sounded so good. We didn't sound so good. The New Riders didn't sound so good. Jack Tempchin didn't sound so good. Phil, our singing bus driver, didn't sound so good. But we all had a great time, watching the sun rise.

Sunday afternoon was a prototypical Florida day—sun-drenched and hot. Not only had the student body shown up, the entire artistic community gathered in the park. Though the sun beat down on our potato heads, Larry and Terry didn't mind. They had other plans, which included some mushrooms they had found. Not only did the funky fungi take the edge off the night before, it added a funky frolic that afternoon. Everyone danced in the sun.

Afterward, when approached by a student disc jockey for an interview, the two mushroomed Missourians followed him across campus to the station. Those of us who remained on the bus tuned in, just to see what these giggling buffoons were going to do. Whatever it was, we knew it would be funny. We knew how toasted they were. The station was only a building or two away. The interview started in a flash.

When the microphones were turned on, the proceedings began with your typical, "Hi. This is Joe Blow from radio station WRUF-FM, on the campus of the University of Florida. We're sitting here in the studio with Larry Lee and Terry Wilson of the Ozark Mountain Daredevils, who just finished playing a great set. Welcome to Gainesville, guys. How are you doing?"

Then, all we could hear was the incessant giggling. Answers only consisted of three or four words, before bursting into flames of laughter. The bus rolled in the aisles. Long sentences, or any train of thought, were simply not a possibility. Several other questions were asked. But it quickly became apparent that Larry and Terry were just too stoned to talk.

That is, until Terry emphatically piped up with, "You know who I hate?"

"No," replied the DJ, thankful just to get a complete sentence out of these guys.

"I hate that Rupert Holmes guy."

Larry added, "Yeah, and that stupid song, 'Him. Him. Him. What are we going to do about him?'"

An instant bond formed between interviewees and interviewer.

"Oh, God. That song makes me sick too," the DJ replied. "I think we have a copy of it here at the station."

At this point, things started happening.

"You do?" exclaimed our happy, hippie drummer.

"Yeah, I know right where it is."

"Go get it."

"Okay. We'll play another one of your songs while I head to the library."

As "Take You Tonight" played, no one on the bus listened. We were more interested in hearing what these two knuckleheads were going to do with a Rupert Holmes record when they came back on the air.

The interview continued with, "Okay, we're back in the studio with Larry Lee and Terry Wilson of the band, and I've found that Rupert Holmes record."

"Great!" exclaimed Larry, inching closer to the turntable. "Let's play it."

"Sure. It'll take me a second to cue it up. Okay. Okay. We're ready. Here we go."

On the bus, "Him. Him. Him. What are we going to do about him?" began bellowing from the speakers. Then we heard the screeching. Then we heard the scratching.

Larry had reached across the console in the studio, grabbed the arm of the turntable, and started scraping the needle back and forth across the grooves of the record. The racket was horrendous, the laughter maniacal.

An elated Terry burst in with, "Can I do that?"

"Sure," replied the DJ. "Let me cue it back up for you."

This time, when Holmes began spewing pronouns, Terry took his turn at the turntable. Cringing faces filled the bus.

The on-air giggling and laughing turned into outright howling and screaming, as additional assaults were made on the record. When they finished, the interview was obviously over. The station returned to its regularly scheduled program. Larry and Terry returned to the bus.

The next day, when the bus pulled out of Gainesville, Sonny remained on board. After a week of complete insanity, we pulled into the Disney World Hotel for a day of rest and two shows in the park. That is, except for those of us who congregated in my room for the all-night snowball fight. I could only look around and think about how wild it was to see that much cocaine right under Mickey's nose.

The next morning, after being up all night, Charlie decided to head to the pool to catch some sun. After all, we were in Florida. As he stretched his towel across his deck chair, the Mickey Mouse-shaped pool filled with families of excited children.

Once he reclined, it only took him a few minutes to relax—I mean, fall asleep—I mean, completely pass out. Like Rune, when Charlie passed out, he was OUT. That afternoon, by the time I found him, he was cooked like a lobster. Though I rushed him straight to a cold shower in our dark hotel room, the damage was done.

That evening, when we headed to the pavilion to play, he was scorched from head to toe. His large forehead was so pink, it throbbed purple. The tops of his feet were burned so badly, he couldn't put on shoes. The man was in total agony. Luckily, Dr. Sonny kept him well-medicated.

Once at the gig, a crowd gathered and we began to meet the stage crew, who treated us very well. Then we met members of the Disney World staff, who looked at us like we were from the Black Lagoon. After a sleepless week in Florida, we were a scraggly bunch.

Charlie asked about the possibility of having Mickey Mouse join us on stage for the end of our first show—so as to entice people to come back for the second. We were informed that this could easily be done, as, at any given time, there are multiple Mickeys strolling around different parts of the complex. One could be radioed to the stage instantly.

Then, after a suspicious "What are you going to do with him?" Charlie assured the officials that we weren't going to kick him around or pour beer on his head. All we wanted him to do was come out and do a little dance to "Commercial Success."

The visuals would be great. He could jump around. We could all jump around. We hadn't anticipated the exclamation point that was about to be placed onto the end of the song—and the show.

Even though most of us had stayed up all night, we were playing well. By the time we got to "Commercial," the joint was jumping. As we stood there, slugging it out, lights were flashing. A pink and purple Charlie stood at the mixing console, his doctor at his side.

When we started the song, Mickey appeared. The place went nuts. Steve immediately started dancing with him, while delivering his wonderfully un-Disney-like lyrics.

As we crescendoed into our dramatic last note, Mickey spun off into the wings. When Steve spun back around to the rest of the band, he noticed a harp he had dropped earlier. When he bent over to pick it up, the train hit him.

It's a move Terry often used to end the song. By slipping his guitar strap off the bottom of his guitar, gravity would cause the body of the instrument to fall. Holding onto the neck, with the iron grip of an E chord, he would let the guitar drop. Then, with a flick of the wrist, whip it high into the air in a long, sweeping arc. When the guitar re-entered the atmosphere, one last power chord would be strummed. It was a real crowd-pleaser.

Tonight, as the song ended, amid the chaos, Terry reached for the button on his guitar. Steve reached down to pick up his harp. Wilson let her fly.

It was a direct hit—an absolute bone-cruncher. Amid the din, I heard the crack of wood on skull. Then, I saw Steve hit the floor, face-down, right in front of me. Due to all the noise and flashing lights, many of the other people—band members, included—didn't even see what had happened. The crowd loved it, thinking it was just part of the show. I knew it wasn't. Steve had been knocked silly. I ripped off my bass, and in the middle of all the cheering, went to pick him up off of the floor.

Realizing I had to get him off stage, I helped him stand up. When he yelled, "Get me outta here," John and I guided him like a blind man across the darkening stage, dodging microphone stands. Though the blow across the bridge of his nose and forehead didn't break the skin, it raised welts the size of grapes.

Charlie and Sonny, who HAD seen what happened from the soundboard, rushed in. Mickey Mouse was still hanging around, getting ready to head back out into the park. Disney staff members flooded into the room, raving about the show, completely oblivious to what had actually happened.

Steve could only sit in a chair with an ice pack laid across his face—and, we still had a second show to do. When the Disneybots left, Sonny administered the numbing medication, and we headed into another set. By the time we left Florida, we were glad to get gone.

In the middle of all this craziness, Terry and I had been keeping up a hefty Dog schedule around Springfield. As the end of the year rolled around, I started stretching myself thin.

When the idea of one last holiday gig in Springfield came up, it seemed like a good idea. Then, when the idea arose of making it into a bash that would include all past and present members, it seemed like a great idea.

The headline of the *News-Leader* read, "Daredevils Come Home to Clay & Monroe."

In an interview with music editor Mary Sue Price, Larry laid out the groundwork: "See, Hammons Center is built on the same corner (Clay Ave. and Monroe St.) as this little restaurant we used to hang around called the Trilogy. We would play there on Sundays once or twice a month.

"To a lot of people who used to come and see us there—this concert will make a difference. Those people will be at this concert."

When explaining the evening's format, he continues, "I think we'll just come out with the sound as it is right now, then sort of work backwards. As we progress, we'll introduce Randy [Chowning] and Buddy [Brayfield] and do some of those songs that we haven't done for five years.

"We'll do a lot of songs that we haven't done in a long time. As you go on and grow, you start eliminating songs off the older albums—they just get lost."

Price's article also accounted for Buddy and Randy's recent whereabouts with a simple "Brayfield, who started in pre-med at Drury, is finishing up his studies in Kirksville. Randy is pursuing a solo career."

This quiet corner that once housed a cozy, fifty-seat cafe was now home to Hammons Center, the university's cavernous, 7,500-seat basketball arena. Though still relatively new, the place had already seen its share of rock royalty. Elvis had paid a visit on his last tour.

The gig, deemed a reunion, was booked, and wheels were put into motion. Everything about it would have to be special. We would have choirs. We would have grandmothers. What other kind of crazy shit could we do? Would Perry Allen make his first appearance since his vaunted Christmas Parade of Thrills ten years ago?

With the help of a local TV station, we filmed some very funny commercials. It was a brilliant, blue morning, as we gathered downtown in front of the ornate ticket kiosk of the Gillioz Theater. Here we began the festivities by drinking Bloody Marys and donning old women's hats, dresses, shawls, sunglasses, gaudy jewelry, and purses.

Sloppy cherry-red lipstick was applied to bearded and stubbled faces, as we portrayed a gaggle of cranky old maids—in line to buy tickets for the concert.

Larry's interview with Mary Sue continued to point out that, "The most common comment we get about the drag commercial is 'God, you guys are ugly.' Then the person laughs—and that's what its all about."

This group of hideous, hairy old men, dressed up like hideous, hairy old women, began making television audiences laugh throughout the area. While stumbling on our high heels and banging into each other with our purses, we clamored over and over, "We want to see the Grandmothers."

The One Hundred Percent Grandmothers Band, based out of Marshfield, Missouri, has had a revolving membership for generations. Consisting of an informal group of simple—and unhideous—country women, who just loved to sit, knit, gossip, and sing, there was only one stipulation for membership: You had to be a grandmother.

All were really good singers, though they didn't sing very loud. Several played guitars, dulcimers, harmonicas, and jugs. The rest just sang, clapped their hands, and banged on shakers and tambourines.

When approached about participating in our show, their reaction was an enthusiastic "Suuure."

When we asked how long they could play, they replied, "We can only play about thirty minutes, until we get tired."

When asked how many of them would be coming, they replied, "All of us—about fifteen or twenty."

Their name went right onto the poster, as special guests. We thought the Grandmothers Band would be a little more special than Mike and Tom or Danny Cox.

When Ducks, present and past, were approached, all agreed to play. Because some hadn't played in a while, all agreed that a few days of rehearsal would be necessary to pull off some of those old songs we hadn't done in years—as well as some of the new songs we hadn't done ever.

Old friend John Gott cleared out one of the large rooms of his Dynamite Sound warehouse and we set up shop for the week prior to the gig. Plus, because he owned a sound company, it was easy for him to set up a nice PA system.

Integrated into our usual stage plot, we placed an extra amp for Randy, an extra amp for Rune, a twenty-foot grand piano and plenty of other keyboards for Buddy, Ruell, and Larry. Bill Jones set up a station for his horns. A platform was built for Jody Troutman, Beth Spindler, and Connie Canaday Ripley.

For those of you who recognize Connie's middle name, meet Steve's kid sister. Those who know her know that along with her Big Mama Thorntonesque voice comes a big Phyllis Dilleresque sense of humor—two traits that would lead her onto the radio airwaves as an early-morning drive-time comedienne.

Dubbed the Darelicks (Dan Hicks had his Hot Licks. We had our Darelicks), all three women sang around town. All had wonderfully soulful voices, whether they blended or blasted them. Either way, it was sweet to hear. They were hired to handle all of the harmony parts for all the crazy songs our ever-shuffling band was going to attempt.

Rehearsals were a blast, due to the fact that the Darelicks' platform was positioned directly beside my amp. The wisecracking was nonstop. When Happy Hour entered the equation, they became side-splitting.

A schedule was established, as well as a song list—one that included anything anyone wanted to do. Buddy and Randy came by for afternoon sessions. Ruell, Rune, and Canway came by in the evening. Old songs were dusted off. New songs were polished up.

I taught everyone my "Little Tootle-Doo," which featured Ruell's barrelhousing. My ode to how toot'll turn you into Larry, Moe, and Curly was a simple, two-chord song. Ruell and Terry already knew it, having helped me recently record it with the Dogs at Steve Smith's Mau Mau Studios. Charlie had sung the original demo at Pat Shikany's Dungeon Studio. It smoothly worked its way into the show.

Canway offered a couple of new songs, "Pumping Iron" and "Durty Girl." We resurrected "Rescue Me."

Randy would sing "Country Girl," "Leatherwood," "Thin Ice," and "Whipporwill." He and Cash-o would do "Cobblestone Mountain."

The Drury College Choir would do "Chicken Train."

That's right. The Drury Choir would do "Chicken Train."

When John asked the seventy-member choral group from his alma mater if they would like to participate, they jumped on board, right next to the Grandmothers. Plans were made for Steve, Larry, and Bill to visit one of their rehearsals, meet everyone, and teach them the crazy, modal arrangement Bill had written for the one-note song.

After handing out meticulously written sheet music to each section, he began to teach them their parts—much like he taught each of us our parts on "Mr. Powell" years ago in Nashville.

When all of the individual parts were sung in unison, the results were quite weird and very entertaining. With seventy voices, it was also loud. Bill conducted the choir. Larry helped with the harmonies. Steve hung around, drank beer, and listened to his song, sung by a choir.

Though we hadn't used Carlo Sound in a while, they were still the best in the business. Plus, we knew John Logan was just the man to handle all of these crazy ideas we were coming up with. In addition to mixing us, he would have to figure out how to mix two dozen grandmothers on the stage and six dozen choir members from the back of the hall.

He was more than eager and up for the challenge, agreeing to come in from Nashville and hang his big, new PA and light system from the Hammons Center rafters. It was an impressive sight.

When the night finally arrived, the entire town came out. Giant spotlights beamed skyward in front of John Q's latest monument to himself. Smaller spotlights accompanied television trucks from every station, that were covering the gig as *news*. All of our families were there. People came in from out of town. Others came out of the woodwork.

As the 7,500 people began to excitedly file in, the seventy-five robed members of Drury's choir assembled in a downstairs rehearsal room. Twenty-five grandmothers, all dressed in matching floor-length gingham dresses occupied another.

We were going to turn the joint back into the Trilogy—where anything went.

Once everyone had found their way inside, the Grandmothers were introduced. Standing shoulder-to-shoulder, they stretched from one side of the stage to the other. Logan and Tucker set up a handful of microphones in front of their chorus line and they were off like a herd of grandmas.

Beginning with "Keep on the Sunny Side," their repertoire spanned from "Amazing Grace" to "I'll Fly Away" and "You Are My Sunshine." Those who played instruments were placed near the middle. The rest just joined in wherever they could. The crowd loved it.

Price, in her follow-up review, noted, "And play they did. The women, ages 42-76, entertained the crowd with saw solos, harmonica tunes, jigs, whistling, and silly songs—just as grandmothers have entertained children for years."

"Did you see them all flicking their Bics? I thought they were going to set us on fire," claimed Winnie Shelton, president of the group. "We were surprised at their reaction. We thought they were gonna throw rotten eggs at us. We thought they were super—just like our own grandkids."

"Yeah. Loud and noisy," chimed in another grandma from across the room.

If the sight of two dozen grandmothers on stage didn't tickle you, the very fact that there were two dozen grandmothers on stage should have. It took them almost as long to climb on and off stage as it took for them to sing. But sing they did—straight from the heart.

When the house lights came up, Charlie grabbed a microphone and, in his booming voice, good-naturedly informed everyone that "The Grandmothers have left the building." While Tucker and Aikin prepared the stage for our set, the Drury Choir stood in the wings. Each member held a single candle.

When the house lights went down, they began a slow, deliberate procession across the floor to the darkened far end. This took a little while, which gave the audience plenty of time to settle in and wonder what in the hell was going to happen next.

Once the entire choir was in position, a candlelit hush fell over the entire arena. When Bill waved his baton into the air, modal waves of "Chiiicken Traaaaain. Ruuunning all daaaaay. Can't get oooonnn. Can't get oooooff" began wafting through the air. With everyone's attention drawn to the far end of the floor, we quietly sneaked on stage and got ready.

When the choir crescendoed into one final, "Chicken Train. Take your chickens awaaaaaaaaaaaaaaay," Danny Mayo threw up all the stage lights and we barreled right into—you guessed it—"Chicken Train."

Wilson blasted away on his twang bar, which we were now using instead of the mouth bow. Cash started blowing his harp lick, and I started cackling like a mad hen. The place went even more bonkers than it did for the grandmothers.

As we started to wind our way through the program, each song swayed and rolled. As we began to introduce past members, each was greeted with welcoming applause. Buddy and Randy came out, followed by Ruell and Rune. After a couple of hours, Elizabeth joined in for one last rendition of "Beauty in the River" and "It'll Shine When It Shines."

The entire crowd danced in the aisles. The Grandmothers danced in the wings. The Drury Choir, now robeless, danced all over the place. Afterward, when everyone walked out into the holiday night, we all felt fortunate to have heard those songs one more time, on the corner of Clay and Monroe.

Price, in her follow-up review, also noted, "Daredevils, past and present, presented a two-hour show that had the crowd members on their feet most of the time, singing along with the tunes they learned when the Daredevils were just another Springfield bar band.

"Their music comes straight from the heart of the Ozarks. And this concert came straight from the heart of a community where—at least for one evening—the old people are valued, the young people are appreciated, and the music is heard by everyone."

Afterward, we all headed back to the outskirts of town and John Gott's warehouse, which had been drastically cleaned up. Three days ago, it was a rehearsal hall, full of ashtrays and beer cans. Tonight, it played host to an all-night party for family, friends, out-of-towners, who had come to town, and locals who could stumble by. The doors were thrown wide open, as were throttles.

John had set up a small PA in the corner, along with a set of drums and a handful of amps. When we arrived, Terry and I spotted the gear, grabbed Tom and Jim, and began to play. With our ability to do any song at any time, we became the house band for the evening. One by one, people began to join in.

Canway jumped up to do a handful of his old South Side Boys songs. Charlie got up to sing some of the songs he'd been singing around town for years. Local legend Benny Mahan did the same. One by one, the Darelicks did songs by Grace, Aretha, and Janis. Bill pulled out his tenor sax. Steve joined in on harmonica.

The howling went through the night.

The Grandmothers were invited, but none made it.

We would stage a second, much smaller, much less inspired version of the same reunion program in Kansas City on New Year's Eve. It was fun. But it just didn't have the same sizzle. There were no grandmothers. There were no choirs. There were no hideous television commercials.

The year 1981 ended where it began—at the Uptown Theater, though there was no snow on the ground, glug on the stove, or pies in the face.

As '82 began, we would receive some good news and some bad news. Let's start with the good news.

While rehearsing for the Grandmothers gig, Stan had walked in with an offer to do a commercial for Busch beer. Alongside Lynyrd Skynyrd, Wet Willie, Marshall Tucker, and the Allman Brothers, we became part of their Southern rock, "Hell, yeah, we drink beer" campaign.

When we were handed the lyrics, we hit Heaven's groove and began to sing, "Let's head for the mountains. That time is here. Let's head for the mountains. Head for Busch beer. It's smooth, it's got taste and it's just that time of the day. So, let's head for the mountains. Head for Busch beer."

As we raucously played the ditty, over and over, an energy that hadn't been present in a while emerged. We met at Larry's to lay down a demo of the tune. When the brewery heard it, they loved it, flying us to their studio in Chicago to re-record it. We laid down a sixty-second spot and a thirty-second spot that would not only identify Busch as a beer, but us as a band. It was a cool commercial.

While we were cutting the track, if it ran sixty-three—or fifty-seven—seconds, we could simply speed it up—or slow it down—until we hit sixty seconds, right on the nose. The same was done for the thirty-second spot. Then we all gathered around the microphone and gang sang our way through it.

When the ads hit the airwaves, they were a hit—especially around St. Louis (home of the beer) and Springfield (home of the band). It had been quite some time since we'd been on the radio. These sixty-second bursts of guitar and harmonica sounded great, each one fading out with old friend Hoyt Axton bellowing, "Anheuser-Busch. St. Louis, Missouri."

After the first year, because the spots were so popular, when Stanley demanded more money, we easily got it. For the next four years, our contract was automatically renewed. This put a nice jingle in our pockets each January.

After the first year, not only did we receive more money, the ad was expanded for television. Setting the song to stock black-and-white footage of guys with handlebar moustaches and bowler hats, recklessly driving their cars in circles, off cliffs, and into trains and telephone poles, the wacky TV ads were hilarious.

For the next few years, those ads found their way onto the radio. Unfortunately, our records did not.

Now, the bad news.

As 1982 slowly began, Larry—who had continued making trips to Nashville—decided to make the move permanent. His divorce had come final, as he recalls: "I sold the house on Meadowmere to get some money for the divorce. When all of that was over, I just didn't even want to hang around Springfield anymore. We weren't working that much, for whatever reason ...

"I'd been going to Nashville and loving it. I needed the change. Plus, I didn't want to be on the road anymore. I just wanted to spend more time in the studio."

This relocation was not the only reason for his withdrawal from the road. We all saw his ongoing battles with allergies and nagging sinuses. On many nights, we watched him sneeze "Jackie Blue" through a handful of Kleenex. His choices were simple. No one had a problem with them.

When Larry made his move, the rest of us were forced to make some, too. It wouldn't be difficult. But it would mean a downsizing—a drastic downsizing. The first issue was easy. Canway could play drums. No problem. This would eliminate carrying around his amp. Then, when we decided not to carry around a piano, we eliminated the piano player that went with it.

Ruell, who had spent the better part of the last five years with us, knew that if there wasn't going to be a piano around, he was pretty much useless. Spinning off into a successful two-decade residency at local pizzeria, McSalty's with Nick Sibley and Ned "The Band" Wilkinson, the gig has become Springfield folklore.

As the rest of us prepared for the following year, this was as small as the band had ever been—a lean quintet. Besides John, Steve, and me, the only other two guys were Canaday and Wilson. Our setup became less complicated and a lot, lot smaller.

Danny Mayo, who had been a member of our crew since the Cowtown days, stayed on to take over Charlie's road-managing duties. This maintained a closer tie to Kansas City, along with a closer eye on our straining expense reports and Stinghead's thousand-dollar entries for "band entertainment."

Crew member Rick Redford was the next downsizing victim, leaving me without a seal-hunting partner.

One of the biggest side effects of the downsizing, though, was the elimination of the bus. Due to the fact that we were no longer receiving any kind of tour support from a record company, the bus was the first thing to go. Having absolutely no interest in buying one, and less in maintaining one, we traded it in for a couple of large, rented Lincoln

Town Cars. This wasn't nearly as impressive when we rolled into town. But it was a hell of a lot more economical.

Because we had two vehicles, two factions formed within the band— 1) those who wanted to hang around the gig and visit with old friends, and 2) those who didn't want anything to do with anybody. Those who claimed, "I don't want to get there until I have to," were afforded the luxury of, "Let's get the fuck out of this puke hole."

Oftentimes, the first Town Car was gone before the next band hit the stage.

The Ozark Mountain Daredevils hit the road for the festival season of 1982, a smaller—much smaller—entity.

CHAPTER 29

As Larry embarked on his new path to Nashville, the rest of us hit the same old one—the highways of America. The festival season for the next few years found a much leaner Ozark Mountain Daredevils coming to town.

When Canway moved to the drums, because he pounded them harder than Larry, the sound got punchier. With Terry next to him, things really got punchier. Steve began to play his harp with more of an edge, and John stuck more to his electric guitar than his acoustic. We continued to carry a fiddle. But all we used it for was one song—"Homemade Wine." In the middle of all this punchiness, the element Larry took with him—and the one we found hardest to replace—was his voice. It was an essential part of our harmonies and impossible to replace.

The rest of us knew we couldn't even attempt to do "Spaceship Orion," "You Know Like I Know," or "Oh, Darlin.'" I would begin to sing "Homemade Wine," giving it an animated vocal, steering it into comic relief territory. John began to sing "Jackie Blue"—a very hard song to sing in the first place. We did "Wine" to highlight the fiddle. We did "Jackie" because it was our biggest hit. These were the only songs of Larry's we had to do. They were the only two we did.

For the rest of the show, I was usually relegated to one of the high harmony parts. This I was quite unsuited for. This I won by default, due

It Shined

to the fact that, with Larry's departure, the Ozark Mountain Daredevils became a group of guys with average, though distinctive, voices.

Everyone scrambled to cover all of the vocal parts. Some were a real strain to hit. Others weren't even close. If I'd been to Busch Stadium for some Cardinals games, it was hard to even speak—much less sing.

Our background vocals became shakier than ever—as well as the furthest thing from our minds. The band may have shrunk in size, but it was still intent on getting into as much jazz as we could find.

"Background vocals? We'll work on them in the hotel room." Remember that? Well, we didn't work on them then. We didn't work on them now. We went to Happy Hour instead.

What our vocals lacked, we more than made up for in other areas. With a stripped-down lineup of a couple of guitars, a couple of drums, and a harmonica, we began to sound—as well as play—like the Stones. Their background vocals are atrocious.

For the next couple of years, this five-man lineup would remain intact. Gears were shifted into "autopilot," as we plowed through gig after gig after gig—many of which were blurs.

Though Charlie was not around anymore, cocaine continued to flow ... freely. Wherever we went, friends came out of the woodwork on a nightly basis to get the band stoned. Everyone seemed to have it in their pockets. On many occasions, I would have it in mine.

Its blatant use became reckless, as it is wont to do—and I was one of the main culprits. I acquired the reputation of being able to stay at the party for several days. I kept up a hectic, chemically-induced pace, as in between every Duck tour was a nightly three-ring Dog circus. I was one of the ringleaders.

By the mid-'80s, it was getting harder and harder for a band from the '70s to garner any kind of attention. We joked among ourselves that we'd sell more records if one of us were to die in a motorcycle wreck or a drug overdose. No one stepped up to the plate on that one.

After a grueling summer of fair, fair, festival, fair, autumn would provide another drastic set of personnel changes and a new record—sort of.

On August 23, Mark Marymont reported in his *News-Leader* column that, "It's a brand-new album that's thirteen years old."

Though press coverage around the rest of the country had all but disappeared, Marymont continued with his gracious column inches. We may have lost our profile nationally, but in Springfield, we still made headlines. Mark made sure of this, keeping everyone in town informed of what the boys were doing out there.

He continued, "The Lost Cabin Sessions were recorded in 1972 by a then-struggling band, hoping to impress executives at Epic Records. The album was produced by Paul Peterson, who along with Stan Plesser, ran Good Karma Productions.

"'I first heard the tapes in '72,' said Peterson from his Kansas City office. "'These were the songs that never made it onto any of the albums. I just dug them out of the closet and cleaned them up.

"'I told the guys that this would be the easiest album they ever made. None of them were looking over my shoulder when I was working on it. They seem to like it.

"'This music is true to the band's Ozark roots. But I don't know how it will sound between Van Halen and Motley Crue. It's not going to win any new, teen-age fans. But we thought some folks might like it.'"

Marymont gave it a favorable review: "These songs were recorded as demonstration tapes, so the sound quality is hardly stunning. The songs, though, are typically OMD—sometimes obscure lyrics, a neat sense of rhythm and excellent harmonies. It's obvious why the folks at A&M decided to sign them. 'Outside My Country Home' is almost bluegrass, with lots of fiddle. 'Sheriff's Comin',' a Larry Lee song, sounds a lot like 'Crazy Lovin',' written by Dillon and Cash for their *Don't Look Down* album. Lee always wrote the most pop-oriented songs.

"On 'Chains,' Dillon and the rest of the guys rock their socks off. 'Moon Come Up,' 'Sometimes You Earn' and 'Running Away' are all reflective ballads. 'Moon,' another Lee song, would sound really nice with the same, sparkling production touches of the similar-sounding 'Spaceship Orion.'

"Fans usually like this kind of project. The musicians involved usually don't. Past is past, and demos from the distant past are sometimes more of an embarrassment than a reflection of the group's 'roots.'

"The *Lost Cabin Sessions* will hardly be confused with any new material the band may soon release, but there are some good songs here. The band has nothing to be ashamed of."

We didn't even waste our time buying a *Billboard* magazine. We knew there wouldn't be a chart for guys selling hundreds of records. We knew it wasn't going to set the woods on fire. We also knew there would be some people who would enjoy it. Stan and Paul pressed a couple thousand copies on the Sounds Great label and scattered them around stores throughout the area.

Except for Marymont, when the album came out, there was no media coverage. Pretty soon, there would be no band. The grind had become harder and harder, as the distances we had to travel became farther and farther. After a grueling summer, no one wanted to go anywhere. Some of us wouldn't.

CHAPTER 30

As Larry had done the year before, John and Steve decided that they'd also had enough and were removing themselves from the picture. Unlike Larry, who moved away, John and Steve remained in Springfield. Before the dust even began to settle, Stan was in motion.

Having recently severed ties with Mike and Tom, we were the only horse in his stable. He was not about to put it out to pasture. Neither was I.

When he called to talk things over, I asked, "What's the plan, Stan?" He laid out Plan B, which was to reach back into the Good Karma fold for one of our own—Randy Chowning, who, over the years, had maintained a good relationship with Stan and Paul, retaining them as his managers.

When presented with the proposition of putting a band together with him, I had no qualms. Reservations? Yes. Qualms? No.

It would still be the Ozark Mountain Daredevils, and it would still feature two original members. It sounded good to me. All Randy and I had to do was put the music together. Good Karma would take care of the rest.

As we began assembling the band, the two of us were in total agreement about who the drummer HAD to be—Bobby Lloyd Hicks. Not only had Randy used him on his solo album, *Hearts on Fire* years ago, the two had spearheaded the original Skeletons.

Fresh off a two-year stint with Steve Forbert and gigs with local songwriter Keith McCormack (Sugar Shack), Lloyd had a good voice. He had an even better knack for being able to hear and arrange harmony parts.

"And I gotta tell you," he continues, "I was happy as a pig in shit. I wasn't jealous of your success, unlike some other Springfield musicians. I was just envious. I'd wanted to be a Duck for years, and was up for helping make it the best that we could … even offering to sing 'Jackie Blue.' In this case, my falsetto wasn't loud enough. So I thought, 'Hey, I'll sing it full voice.'

Ozarks, 1982 (left to right) me, Joe Terry, Randy Chowning, Bobby Lloyd Hicks, and Gary Smith (photo by Jim Mayfield)

"Good Lord," he concludes. "There isn't enough rum in Jamaica to make that even tolerable."

The three of us set up in the dining room of my Main Street house and began amassing a song list. There were certain tunes we knew we HAD to do. No one had a problem with this. I began singing "Southern Cross," "Chicken Train," and "Standing on the Rock," as well as "Ooh Boys, It's Hot." Randy sang "Walkin' Down the Road" and "Black Sky," as well as "Country Girl" and "Look Away."

Plus, it was Randy's voice—not John's—on the original version of "Heaven." Singing AND clucking "Chicken Train" was a bit rough, but I machoed my way through it. When we played "Standing on the Rock," we crescendoed out of instrumental breaks with "Better get back to the condo." The laughter pealed across the bandstand.

Though we chuckled, the gag was ironic. Steve had recently sold his cabin on the Niangua, as well as his house in town, and had moved into a small basement apartment. John, who had acquired Larry's portion of their Arkansas land, watched as the entire spread was sold on the courthouse steps. He had come to town and began staying in friends' spare bedrooms. I had been living in town for years.

Our young, enthusiastic, "Let's get back to the country" attitude had become a placid, middle-aged, "Aah, let's just go back to the condo."

For a couple of weeks, Randy, Lloyd, and I had a ball, sitting around, thinking up songs, singing 'em, playing music, drinking beer, smoking pot, and laughing. Randy played harmonica on "Chicken Train" and "Heaven." Both sounded good. In no time, everything sounded good—really good.

More importantly, he and I wanted this to be an outlet for new material. He did "Turn It Up," "Hillbilly Baby," and "Jimmy Boy"—a song he'd just written with Steve. I worked up "Car," "Law," "Wassa Matta Whichya, Baby?," and "Well, I Tried"—a song I'd also just written with Steve.

Lloyd unloaded furious beats, doing "Nervous Breakdown," Johnnie Otis's "Crazy Country Hop," Jerry Lee Lewis's "Let's Talk About Us," Jim Lowe's "Green Door," and Lou Whitney's "Trans Am." With him on the drums, we rocked hard—real hard. With the bulk of Duck tunes, a few obscure covers, and a handful of old Skeleton standards, we had no trouble filling out an evening of material.

From here, it was easy to assemble the rest of a very good band. We began inviting friends over to my house to play on a daily basis. Tulsa guitarist Gary Smith, who had just moved to Springfield, dropped in.

"Prior to joining the group," he recalls, "I was working with Mike Brewer, who had just completed a new solo album, produced by Dan Fogelberg, entitled *Beauty Lies*. We formed a group to tour and promote this new release.

"I was doing a lot of sessions around town and had worked with Lloyd in numerous studio settings for years. I was doing some local Springfield gigs with Vicki Self [Ronnie's daughter] and Karen Irish. Lloyd called one day and said you guys were looking for a guitar player. Then, the three of you came out to hear me play."

Not only did the three of us like what we heard, we liked what we saw. Not only did Gary play clean, precise guitar, his trimmed beard and precise hair was a spitting image of John.

This made band pictures funny. Whenever someone pointed a camera at us, Gary would furtively glance off to the side and cradle his right arm with his left.

Once we hit the road, he was mistaken for John on a nightly basis. Though it didn't remain funny to him for very long, the rest of us howled. Some fans actually asked him how his broken arm was mending. Others went through entire evenings without even realizing it wasn't John on stage.

Gary continues, "Then, you guys asked if I might recommend any piano/keyboard players. I suggested Dickie Sims, a friend of mine from Tulsa, who had been keyboardist for Clapton and had cut 'I Shot the Sheriff' and 'You Look Wonderful Tonight' with him. But his main deal was Hammond, and you guys decided we needed more of a piano player."

Sims came to town and we ganged up on his massive Hammond B-3 organ, hauling it up into my house. Once it was in, it was fun. But everything sounded like the Allman Brothers. Though he really knew how to make it jump, it just wasn't what we wanted. We wanted a piano player.

Fellow St. Louisan Joe Terry was asked to drop by. When he did, he filled out the band nicely. He was hired on the spot. His upbeat personality, as well as his electric piano, gave our sound a real swing—the same swing he had been delivering around town with his latest band, the Couch Dancers.

"I was playing in a rockabilly outfit called the Couch Dancers," he cites. "We'd bring a couch to our gigs, set it on stage, and dance with it. The name basically came from our parties, where we would pick up the furniture and dance with it, a la Elvis's 'if you can't find a partner, use a wooden chair.'

"Donnie [Thompson] used to come see us. One evening, he helped us out by actually playing a gig with us. He brought Randy, whom I did not know—but knew who he was. After the gig, he walked up and asked if I'd like to come over to Supe's house and play some music.

"At first, I didn't know I was auditioning to be in a version of the Daredevils. But when I got there, it became obvious. I also remember, at a few of those first rehearsals in your dining room, I got stoned—because you all were. I really didn't smoke pot, so I was forgetting all the chords to the songs constantly and getting nervous that I wasn't cutting the mustard."

But cut the mustard he did. Cut the mustard everyone did. Like I said, it was easy to put together a good band. We put together a very good one.

Once the five-man lineup was intact, we realized we needed more room to stretch out than my dining room allowed. We vacated Main Street, hauling all of our gear downtown to Boonville Street and up to the second floor of local merchant Tom Embry's architectural antique business, Aesthetic Concerns.

The spacious three-story brick building, which once housed a magnificent feed mill and mercantile, was perfect for what we needed. Complete with a heavy-duty freight elevator in the back for our equipment and floor-to-ceiling windows in the front for our viewing pleasure, the space held cool views of the Springfield skyline.

We cleared a large, open space, right inside the windows, laid old rugs across the wooden-planked floor, and set up among stacks of antique doors, windows, chandeliers, light fixtures, sinks, mirrors, wrought iron and stained glass.

Tom only had one request—that we wait until he closed, so as to not disturb his customers below. At the end of the day, when he turned his OPEN sign off, we all headed upstairs. Until then, we were asked to refrain from everything. After that, we refrained from nothing. Anything went.

Tucker and Canway showed up every evening. Larry was to stay on as equipment manager, coming by to familiarize himself with all of the new guys' gear. Steve was to take over Mayo's road-managing duties. He showed up with snacks, itineraries, martinis, and beer. It was Happy Hour on Boonville Street.

Tucker sold the big green truck, replacing it with a diesel pickup and a customized horse trailer. Figuring no one would suspect that a horse

It Shined

trailer actually contained expensive musical equipment, he did nothing to draw any attention to it—other than just letting it get dirty, like any other horse trailer. Another asset of the rig was the fact that, once he got to a gig, if he needed to run an errand, the trailer could easily be unhitched.

When Stan first approached me about all of this, he assured me that everyone everywhere would be compensated. John and Steve received a stipend from each gig for use of the name. I was assured that, because I was the one who was signing on the dotted line for the van and truck loan, the lion's share of the take would be designated to pay for them. With a commitment from everybody to stay on the road for longer stretches of time, we paid off both vehicles within the year.

An extended tour through Wyoming, Montana, Idaho, Oregon, Washington, and British Columbia was booked with America. Though I never was that big a fan of their music, they were a bunch of good guys. As both bands became familiar with each other, the daily routine ran very smoothly. Tucker worked well with their crew. Load-ins and load-outs were a snap. If space was limited, setups were flexible. Gear was readily shared. Canway had no problem working out the everyday logistics with their road manager. It wasn't hard. Rock 'n' roll isn't rocket science.

Though there was a nice camaraderie between the two bands and it looked good on paper, at times, our "hillbillies on whiskey and weed" approach was a little too intense for their laid-back California stylings. Their show may have been a lot tamer than ours, but it was filled with a lot more hits.

Girls swooned on a nightly basis—not only at Gerry and Dewey's boyish good looks, but the tender subjects of their songs. There wasn't much space in our rumpus room for good looks or tender subjects.

Each night, we just attacked our sets.

Each night, they stood in the wings to watch the flailing.

Each night, we left after their first half-dozen ballads.

As the tour neared its end, we accepted their invitation to join them on stage for their traditional, "last-night" extended encore jam of "A Horse with No Name." Members of their road crew would be playing guitar. Come one, come all. Everyone sing, "Nah, nah, nah, nah, nah, nah, nah, nah, nah. Nah. Nah."

This meant we had to hang around for their entire show. This was no big deal. Canway had connected with their road manager, tapped into his powder horn, and invited me in for the reindeer games. By the time we heard the opening strains of "Horse," all three of us were blasted off.

As I ran out the door and onto the stage, I grabbed the first guitar I saw. With flailing arms, their guitar tech frantically began to explain that I had grabbed some kind of weird guitar in some kind of weird tuning. I told him not to even worry about plugging it in, and strolled on stage. The horse was picking up its gait.

When the guitar break rolled around, I turned to their guitarist and yelled, "Cover me." As he turned his back to the audience and blasted into a tasty solo, I walked to the edge of the stage and blasted into a tasteless air-guitar show—complete with facial grimaces and posturings. The crowd went nuts.

Gerry and Dewey could only stand there and chuckle—the same way Mike and Tom laughed at me years ago when I acted up on stage. When the song ended, I approached both Americans to make sure I hadn't stepped on any toes, and if I had—tough shit. They assured me their toes were fine. It was a funny, funny night.

Another swing led us up the Eastern Seaboard, starting at the Lone Star Cafe in New York and landing in Halifax, Nova Scotia, with stops along the way through Portland and Bangor, Maine and St. John and Moncton, New Brunswick. Over the years, we'd played many gigs in Canada. This was the first time, though, that we had ever played east of Toronto. By the time we got to Scotia, the Scotians were ready—good and ready.

All along the way, seafood restaurants and oyster bars were sought out. Arriving in this picturesque setting—which is so far east, it has its own time zone—we spent four days riding ferries around Halifax Harbor, visiting the lighthouses at Peggy's Cove, eating lobsters by the dozen and drinking Guinness by the gallon.

When informed by the club owner that our set times would be eleven thirty and two, we started drinking. We hadn't played this late since Mole Lake. But he knew what he was doing. When we stepped onto the stage at two in the morning, the place was packed.

As we ripped through song after song, the Scotians matched us, blow for blow. By three thirty in the morning, everyone (band included) was completely hammered. They were also not going to let us quit. So we didn't. After doing everything we knew, we began playing songs we kinda knew. We just continued to play—harder and faster and louder. The Scotians matched us step for step, decibel for decibel.

We made sure our contract rider contained plenty of alcohol, and it was Canway's job to make sure its flow to the stage remained constant. He did an excellent job. Night after night, we attacked our shows with a viciousness that none of our previous incarnations had ever attained.

After a year and a half of constant travel and abuse, things came apart as easily as they came together—and they came threefold.

Lloyd was offered a sit-down gig in Springfield with Kerry Cole and the Lefty Brothers. This meant steady work for him, with no travel. For us, it meant a new drummer. Once again, Canway came to the rescue, climbing back onto the drum throne.

Joe received an offer to play with local rockers the Morells, who had just won rave reviews from *Rolling Stone* for their album, *Shake and Push*. Though it was a step back into the Springfield scene, it meant a lot—and I mean, a lot—less travel.

Then, Randy completed the trifecta by coming over to the house to inform me that he was also no longer interested in going on the road, due to his crumbling marriage. That morning, I went into a state of shock. With a full slate of gigs a few weeks away, in the wink of an eye, I had no band.

Then, in another wink, I did.

That morning, Stan called, frantically wondering what we were going to do. That afternoon, Canway came by the house to talk about these same issues—but in a much calmer way. When he mentioned that he thought he could convince John and Steve to re-enter the picture, he was given the green light. This was easily done. After some time off, both John and Steve agreed to climb back into the van, back onto the stage, and back into the "V." All gigs were salvaged. More importantly, the two came on board with new songs.

At this point, the striking resemblance between John and Gary was really funny. For the next few months, we looked like we had Glen

Campbell and John Davidson bookends on guitars. I could literally watch the double takes ripple through the crowd.

Though the sound no longer had that manic edge Joe and Lloyd provided, it did settle back into the comfortable groove our fans had, over the years, grown accustomed to. Another thing that returned was a lighter travel schedule—much lighter.

This erratic, anemic workload would soon take its toll, leading directly to another pair of quick departures.

Gary pointed his focus, as well as his studio gear, south to an exploding Branson scene. He was replaced by local guitarist Jason LeMasters.

Larry Tucker, who had been on board for more than a decade, was also forced to look elsewhere.

"I was still planning on staying. But the band just wasn't working enough," he explained. "We had just played some gigs using Maryland Sound. While talking to their monitor man, he and I agreed a lot about the theory of what sounds good. He had just worked with Kris Kristofferson, who was looking for a monitor man for a ten-week tour. He recommended me to Kristofferson's people. They called and offered me the gig. I had to take it."

Randy, who had discovered that, not being on the road wasn't the key to saving his marriage, stepped back in, to take Jason's spot on guitar. No longer interested in grueling, two-month tours, the lighter workload was also more to his liking.

A ten-day jaunt took us to Alaska, which we were all eager to see. When Canway struck a small deal with Bass Pro Shop owner, Johnny Morris, we headed north, outfitted with new coats, new sweatshirts, new gloves, and new thermal boots. All came free of charge, as long as we wore them with our new Bass Pro Shop hats.

This was no big deal, as we had no problems taking a couple of group shots in front of a couple of Alaskan landmarks—with our new hats on. We got really nice coats and boots out of the deal. It was a fair trade.

When we landed in Anchorage, time was of the essence. We still had to catch a puddle jumper that would take us out to Kodiak Island for our first gig at the Kodiak Cultural Center. Things were running smoothly, until I learned that my luggage had not made it. Luckily, my bass had. Though my suitcase would be arriving on a later flight, we had no time to spare.

After a long day with two long flights, we quickly jumped into a little plane and were treated to spectacular views of the magnificent southern Alaska coastline. When we landed, we were dog tired. The locals, on the other hand, were ready to go—Alaska style.

With Mike and Tom as our opening act, we had an hour or so to gather our thoughts. They had no time at all. They went right from the plane to the van to the stage. We all had to rely on rented gear and were at the mercy of a local sound engineer. The joint was rocking. It may have been cold outside, but inside, everyone worked up a good sweat—especially me, still in my thermal boots. The next morning, right after we flew out to Kenai, my bags made it to Kodiak.

For the next couple of days, I played leapfrog around Alaska with my clothes. After three hot, sweaty gigs, my socks became quite aromatic. When my suitcase finally caught up with me in Fairbanks, I just tossed my socks, along with my shirt and underwear, into the hotel dumpster.

This was the first time we had ever made it to our forty-ninth state, and we fell in love with the place. Not only were the audiences wonderful, the landscapes breathtaking, and the seafood magnificent, but a genuine sense of mischief also permeates the state.

The place is full of mavericks and misfits, as you cannot be sure that the name on their Alaska driver's license is the same name that appeared on their Indiana driver's license the year before. If you ever need to disappear and change your name in order to fend off the wolves, the lawyers, the IRS, or the ex-wife, this is the place. It is still a genuine frontier.

After our gig in Homer, I was approached by a friendly gent with an outstretched hand and a, "Man, it's great to hear you guys again. I'm from Columbia, Missouri, and I saw you at the college, years ago. I've been up here for almost nine years."

When he informed me that he was a salmon packer, asking, "Do you like smoked salmon?" he produced an entire fish. I eagerly nodded my head, panting like a cartoon puppy.

When he asked, "Do you like salmon jerky?" he produced a large sack, filled with pink pieces of fish. The puppy drooled.

Then, when he asked, "Do you like marijuana?" my eyes popped out at the sack he produced. There wasn't one bud any bigger than the end of your thumb. But there were hundreds of them crammed in there.

When I exclaimed, "Thanks!" he walked off, finishing our brief chat with, "Welcome to Alaska."

For the rest of the trip, I rolled joints every morning, freely passing them out to anyone—Mike and Tom included—who wanted some. Then, once we made it to the next hotel, I laid out the salmon. Everyone came up to my room to chow down.

Nothing is close-by in this state. Everything is hundreds of miles apart. Airplanes are an everyday way of life. Though I was thrilled to be in Alaska, I was not thrilled about flying around in those little planes, through snowy mountainous terrain that makes Colorado look like Tinkertoys. Colorado may be big. Alaska is massive.

Though our gigs in Anchorage and Fairbanks were both very good, they were very different. Anchorage, a port city, sits right on the ocean. Filled with people, flavors, smells, and spices from around the world, its influences are many and varied.

Fairbanks might as well be the capital of West Dakota. As hunters, trappers, lumberjacks, and oil-field workers (who had been cooped up on the pipeline for a month) came to town—so did the whores. All were hell-bent on having a good time, and no one was going to stop them—not even the authorities, who just kind of looked off in the other direction for the evening.

Bands didn't come around these parts very often. When they did, these people lit up—big time.

Gigs in Nome and Barrow were canceled, due to the fact that it was too cold to even get there. Then, once we got there, there was the distinct possibility of getting stranded there. This awarded us a few extra days in Ketchikan and Juneau, whose weather has nothing in common with Nome or Barrow. I immediately fell in love with this part of the state and the south trade winds that temper it.

Our downtown hotel sat within walking distance of the Juneau Center for the Arts, where we were to play. Though this is the capital of the largest state in the Union, it has a population that rivals Joplin, Missouri.

Its temperate weather allowed us to relax and meander through the streets for a couple of days—more than enough time to see the town. We became familiar with faces and places. When we met the music director from the local radio station, he invited us to stop by their studios, which sat just a block and a half away from our hotel. I took him up on his offer. Once again, I went alone.

Gone from Juneau was the yay-hoo element of Fairbanks. In its place was a friendly, sophisticated city with a keen sense of heritage, artistic pride, and nice restaurants. The interview was very relaxed, articulate, and a lot of fun. So was dinner.

So was the gig, as the people nestled into the comfortable 800-seat auditorium, which was much more conducive to listening than the honky-tonks and community centers we had been playing. In a nutshell, there was a lot less whiskey consumed and a lot more attention paid.

All that week, we had been playing really well. So were Mike and Tom, who had been coming to Alaska for years. As we received the welcome mat for the first time, they were greeted as returning heroes. The shows were well-paced, ending with a very merry band of very stoned men, singing nightly encores of "It'll Shine" and "Wichi-Ti-To."

Along with "Jackie," "Heaven," and "Chicken," we peppered the sets with not only some of the new songs Randy and I had been doing, but some of the new songs John and Steve had written. The Alaskans, like the Scotians, didn't seem to mind. They dug the new stuff as much as they did the old stuff. It all fit together quite well. I was just thrilled that I no longer had to wear those thermal boots.

Though we continued to play gigs to support ourselves, our focus (which never centered on being "road dogs"), shifted toward Larry and Nashville. It had been almost five years since we had been in a recording studio. We had some new songs and were anxious to get them on tape. We were not anxious to go back to the Sioux Falls Civic Center.

So we loaded up the truck and headed for Nashville—with five original members.

What we didn't take along was Good Karma Productions. With dwindling everything and lingering lethargy, life was pretty much back down to basics. We went, played the gigs, got paid, and came home. That was about it.

With no success drumming up another record deal, the only thing Good Karma was doing was fielding calls from Randy Erwin with gigs. When we figured, "Well, hell, we can do that—and not have to pay a commission," we did just that.

Another aspect, which was also dwindling, was our publishing monies. Royalty checks, which had been sent to Kansas City for years (where another commission would be administered), would now be sent directly to Springfield. With a simple change-of-address form, this was easily done.

Ways were parted as amicably and unceremoniously as they were joined. There was no binding contract, due to the fact that it had expired after the first year—and no one felt the need to draw up another. No one wanted a long, drawn-out legal affair. There was no ugliness or acrimony. We shook hands and walked off—simple as that.

This also meant that license requests for our songs would come directly to us. One of the first came from West Virginia filmmaker Jacob Young, in the middle of shooting episodes for his public television series, *Different Drummer*. One of his unique subjects was a clogging renegade from Boone County, by the name of Jesco White.

Titled, "The Dancing Outlaw," the episode featured White, who tap danced to two songs—"Wildwood Flower" and "If You Want to Get to Heaven." Without these two songs, Jacob knew he had no show. He also had no money. We agreed to let him use the song. We've always been proponents of public television.

The episode is a classic, with copies finding their way onto every country music bus in America. Years later, when I would make my move to Nashville, I received more recognition and enthusiasm for Jesco White than I did for "Jackie Blue."

Soon afterward, Good Karma closed its doors and we all went our separate ways. The real estate at the corner of Forty-third and Main was sold. It has since been razed.

It was the end of an era.

CHAPTER 31

By the mid '80s, though Nashville remained the sleepy town we dreaded coming to in the '70s, the country music industry was anything but. It'd been three years since Larry had left for Tennessee. We thought it might be a good time to pay him a visit. He and all his friends had all their fingers in all the pies.

This burgeoning music scene still centered in the ten-block section of town near the Vanderbilt campus, known as Music Row. It was nice to see the residents of the Row taking pride in refurbishing their buildings—unlike Springfield, which continued to be intent on knocking down their older houses.

The large, unassuming, three-story building at 1030 Sixteenth Avenue was a microcosm of the area—outside, a plain exterior; inside, a beehive of activity. It housed the 1030 Music Group.

Louisiana native Mike Robertson sat in the middle of the hive. "I came to town in '83," he recounts. "I thought Nashville needed another recording studio, so I came and opened the Song Cellar. Then I realized there was a studio on every corner and I was better fitted—and there was more need for—artist management.

"I moved into the 1030 building, which was owned by pop artist Lobo. He didn't have a studio, so I bartered out studio space for studio time. Then, when he moved to Florida, I just bought the building.

"The whole idea of the 1030 Music Group was to be able to have this creative place to work, where we could do all different kinds of music. We weren't doing all of the typical things that were going on on Music Row at the time. If you look at that timeframe, it was the back end of the Urban Cowboy thing. Country music was very slick.

"But it was beginning to go through a change. There were a lot of younger people that had moved here, not because of what was going on on the radio, but what was going on in the clubs around town. People like the Foster & Lloyds, the Roseanne Cashes, the Mary Chapin Carpenters, the Dwight Yoakams, the Vince Gills were yet to come in. For a young person like me, it was the excitement of what was yet to come, rather than what had already happened.

"The older guard was still in charge. But for us, it was this vision of how to make creative music, but not be bound by any major corporate policies. We were all young enough, and [laughing] foolish enough to think we could just do that—and be successful."

Another person who was making music outside the Nashville box was Larry. "When I first came to town, Norbert was running a studio called the Bennett House," he recalls. "I moved into Will Jennings's pool house for a while, and everybody was just hanging out with everybody. Jon R. [Goin] and I had written a bunch of songs. Norbert said that if we wanted to put some things down, we could use the place on the weekends. We started going out there to work with [engineer] Danny Hilley.

"He [Danny] was a younger guy, who had worked with Barbara Mandrell—who, at the time, was a pretty big deal. He just wanted to do some other things. So the three of us just clicked, musically.

"Shortly after that, through Danny, Jon and I started writing for this publishing company, Carlsongs—started by this Norwegian from Minneapolis named Jerome Carlson. He was a great guy, who kept me alive for a couple of years. We got one song cut by the Everly Brothers ['These Shoes']. I wasn't really a studio musician. So I couldn't get into any of that.

"When I got down here, I just wanted to write. Jon and I really got on a roll, and through this publishing company, were able to make really elaborate demos. But they weren't country demos. They were pop demos. I was still trying to get a deal.

"Danny and I went to New York to play our tapes for some guys. Then we went to L.A. and did the same thing. We kept running into the *If you're from Nashville, you can't be too cool*, kind of thing. They just didn't take us very seriously."

Enter Wendy Waldman.

"Then, I met Wendy singing on a Buffett record," Larry continues. "When Buffett went on tour in '86, he had been recording with Tony Brown, who had hired Mac [Macanally] and Josh [Leo] to play guitars. Timothy [B. Schmidt] was bailing and they needed that high voice. Jimmy said yeah and I was in. That's how I got hooked up with Buffett's band."

He fell into a loose-knit group of artists from Los Angeles, commonly referred to as L-Aliens. Wendy, Josh, Bernie Leadon, Jim Photoglo, Vince Melamed, and Harry Stinson had all recently made the move to town in search of not only greener pastures for their music, but nicer pastures for their families.

Mike notes, "It was John Prine who, when asked how to start a record company, said, 'You put your hand on a rock and say, *We're a record company*. Well, we put our hand on a rock and said, *We're a production company*. That's how we started 1030. I was the business guy, managing John Wesley Riles and Jonathan Edwards—who were also making records in our studio. Suddenly, I was in the management business, managing Lee Roy Parnell and Pam Tillis.'"

If Mike was the center of 1030's administrative circles, Wendy Waldman was queen bee, mother hen, and Wonder Woman, rolled into one. The Los Angeles native, whom Mike fondly describes as a "sponge for creative outcasts," came from good musical stock. Her father, composer Fred Steiner, wrote the *Perry Mason* theme, as well as music for episodes of *Star Trek*, *Gunsmoke*, *Rocky & Bullwinkle*, and *The Twilight Zone*.

A definite child of the '60s, when her first solo album, *Love Has Got Me* came out on Warner Brothers in 1973, she was proclaimed by *Rolling Stone* magazine to be the "singer-songwriter debut of the year." She was then the youngest member of the Warner Brothers "brain trust"—a group of artists signed to the label who were known for their innovative, critically acclaimed approaches to music—a group that also included Maria Muldaur, Randy Newman, Ry Cooder, Captain Beefheart, and Van Dyke Parks.

When Larry met Mike and Wendy, the three of them hit it off famously. His stories about the band piqued their interest, prompting them to come to Springfield to see for themselves what was going on, meet us, and hear some music. When they got to town, they found a disheveled group of guys.

"She and I went to Springfield for a rehearsal," Mike recalls. "It was really odd, because Dillon was singing 'Heaven,' even though Randy was there. Larry was, of course, no longer in the band, and you guys weren't even doing 'Jackie Blue.' It was so weird that you had two giant hits and one of them no one else picked up singing, and the other one was sung by another guy. It was all perfectly confusing."

Still, along with Larry, the two thought making a record with the original guys would be a good idea. We thought so too. When Wendy offered to produce the sessions, we headed to Nashville, Music Row, and 1030.

When John, Steve, Steve, Randy, and I got to town, a couple of weeks' worth of studio time was booked, and we moved in. But not before the L-Alien queen, on our first night in town, threw us a welcoming party. As her tribe climbed the steps to her three-room second-floor apartment, beer, wine, covered dishes, and guitars came in tow. After introductions and groceries, instruments were pulled out and tuned up. Though we were tired from traveling, we tuned ourselves up.

Unlike the Nashville scene we had encountered in the '70s, we immediately identified with the Nashville scene of the '80s. Songs began flying everywhere. One by one, along with joint after joint, they were passed around the large circle with Wendy, Larry, Photglo, Josh, Vince, Harry, Kathy Mattea, and Jim Ibbotsen. A bona fide Nashville guitar pull chugged right on into the night.

The Ducks were in town.

Everyone sang. The harmonies were outstanding. We sang our songs. They sang theirs. Then we sang theirs and they sang ours. It was a format we knew well. One of the highlights of the evening was Wendy and Photoglo's "Fishin' in the Dark." When we took it under our wing, John, Larry, and Randy sang it like birds. As they did, you could hear the vocal blend we had been missing for years.

All night, everyone sang out with such assurance and gusto—an approach I enjoyed very much. I pulled up a small amp, plugged in, and thumped along. Though I had never heard any of the songs, I had no trouble keeping up. This spurred several of the L-Aliens to go out of their way to let me know they had noticed my navigational skills and, if I ever wanted to, could probably make a good living here. I play my bass with my ears, as much as I do with my fingers.

Though "Fishin' in the Dark" wasn't one of our songs, it sounded so good, it was immediately placed onto our "must-record" list. We didn't care if we had a hit with someone else's song. A good song is a good song, is what we always contended. Everyone in the hive bought into 1030's "one wins, all win" theory.

Also placed on the "must-do" list was Steve Earle's "Heatin' Up," Russell Smith's "Lonely Knight," Dave Loggins's "Give 'em My Number," and "Heart of the Country," a song co-written by Wendy and frequent 1030 flyer Donny Lowery.

This was the first time we had actually gone out of our way to find outside material. But it was the Nashville way. Several years ago, the L.A. way hadn't worked. We figured we might as well try this one.

That night, we were greeted with a Nashville guitar pull. The next day, we were greeted with a Nashville session in a Nashville studio, complete with some Nashville cats. Wendy slid into the producer's chair and took the helm. John Wiles began twiddling knobs by her side.

Everyone manned their stations, which included Harry Stinson on drums and Michael Chapman on bass. That's right. You heard correctly. There was another Mike on bass. Though this bothered me immensely, I figured that if Rune, Canway, and Larry had been open-minded enough to accept not playing on our last record, I could keep an open mind now. I hated it but held my tongue. Canway and I basically became cheerleaders.

This wasn't sprung on us at the last minute. We knew this was how Wendy wanted to work. She had a core group of musicians who worked very efficiently together—and on an everyday basis. With prepared charts in front of them, they began hammering out track after track in a very assembly-line fashion.

Canway and I did play on Randy's "Turn It Up," which we had been doing for the past couple of years. It only took us a half dozen takes, and that only took half of an afternoon. It sounded great. So did the rest of the songs. All were "L-Alien" slick—every P and Q minded, every ooh and ahh perfectly in pitch, every bell and whistle used. It just didn't sound like the Ozark Mountain Daredevils.

None of Canway's songs and none of my songs were even considered, though they were already worked up. Five years ago, they didn't fit into Boylan's idea of how he thought the band should sound. This time around, they didn't fit into Wendy's.

None of Larry's songs were used either, which was a conscious decision. If someone were to give us a record deal, and we had to go on the road to promote it, Larry wouldn't be there.

John and Steve began recording their stockpiled, "Everywhere She Goes," "I'm Still Dreaming," "Love Is Calling," "True Love" and "Over Again." Years later, the two would take this same batch of songs into a Nashville publisher, who would deem them "too poetic." This was met with tirades of "Too poetic?" and "Fuck them!"

While the Ozark Mountain Daredevils were cutting another batch of mid-tempo songs about dreaming, being in love, and dreaming about being in love, you could count the number of harmonica licks on one hand.

That is, until "Turn It Up"—Randy's song about getting off work and unwinding with a beer and a band in a bar. After this brief three-minute burst of harmonica, we returned to more songs about being lonely knights, having lonely nights, and being all alone on the river.

On the entire record, Steve only sang one song—Steve Earle's "Heatin' Up." As I have said many times, Cash-o is my favorite lyricist and harmonica player on the planet. On this record, his funkiness was missing, drowned in a sea of sweetness. Don't get me wrong; I like Steve Earle. I would rather have heard Steve Cash.

But it was the Nashville way. Though I didn't do much, I had a great time hanging around.

Mike recalls our visits fondly. "You guys would come into town and I was like the starving manager/studio owner. We would always wind up at the L&N Seafood place, and the fact that you guys lived so large. There was always great food and lots of wine. It didn't matter how poor everybody was, it was like a big feast, night in and night out. I also remember laughing until my face hurt."

I really dug the creative community that was unfolding here—human as well as artistic. I felt so good, I didn't even mind losing a bet to Jim

Ibbotesen during the NCAA basketball tournament. As we gathered in the 1030 lobby to watch March Madness, when we learned underdog Villanova was going to be pitted against powerful Georgetown in the championship game, Ibby began obnoxiously singing Nova's praises.

After a while, it was more than Josh and I could stand, telling Ibby to shut up and put his money where his mouth was. Twenty-dollar bets were laid on the table. That Monday, as we watched Georgetown go down to defeat, Ibby happily slid our Jacksons into his pocket. Then we all went for drinks.

As the tracking finished, Canway and I headed home. Neither of us had anything to do. Nor had we done anything—except hang around, be in the band, go out to eat, get drunk, get stoned, and crack a bunch of jokes. We both knew that, with our voices, we weren't going to be included on any of the vocal sessions. We headed back to Missouri.

While John, Steve, and Randy stayed in Nashville with Larry and Wendy, I returned to Springfield with not only a lukewarm feeling for what we had just done, but a burning desire to be in the studio—and actually do something. I called Lou Whitney and booked a session at his Column One Studio.

With Lou at the mixing console and the rest of the Morrells—Joe Terry, Donnie Thompson, and Ron Gremp—at my side, we headed into the small, low-ceilinged building on the quiet south side of town. I had to get this litter of songs, which included "Car" and "Law," out of my head and onto tape. I knew this wasn't going to happen at 1030.

As layers of lush vocals were being heaped on in Nashville, I went into Lou's funky, little Springfield studio with a rock 'n' roll quartet and an icebox full of beer. Laying down "Car" and "Law," along with "Happy Hour," "Jerri Lynn," and "If You Can't See That, You Can't See Nothing," I encouraged everybody to just let it rip—which they did. The Morells are a great band. My songs danced from the speakers.

While I was out there having fun in that warm Springfield sun, dissension reared its ugly head in Nashville. Once again, it came from the same source. Once again, Randy decided to jump ship in the middle of the stream.

This left the L-Aliens in a bind—one that Larry and Wendy dealt with by using a plethora of ruby-throated Tennessee warblers. John replaced

Randy's vocal on "Turn It Up," because it HAD to go on the record. It was the only harmonica song there was.

Then, when it came time for us to go out and play a gig, we had to find a new guitar player. When we learned Phil Pojar, who had taken Tucker's place, would also be leaving to take a gig in Branson, we called on not one but two old friends.

Before we get to this new phase of the band, with these two new/old friends, allow me to finish our Nashville saga. It won't take long. In a nutshell, nobody gave a shit. Then we lost "Fishin' in the Dark."

Mike tells the story. "We pitched the record to every label in town—even the smaller, independent labels. But we were still dealing with the same thing you guys had been dealing with for a long time. One guy sang one hit, another guy who sang another hit, and there was one guy who was no longer in the band. When we mentioned Ozark Mountain Daredevils, everyone asked, 'What is it?' They just couldn't get their arms around it.

"We just couldn't get anybody to bite. We got close at Sony with Steve Buckingham, but just couldn't get a commitment out of them. There were still a lot of the 'older-school' people in those A&R positions. It got better a little later, but …

"When I couldn't drum up any interest for the band, 'Fishin'' lost out by committee to the Dirt Band. You guys cut it first, but you didn't have a deal. They were coming to town on Warner Brothers to get their country career back up, and we had a couple of songwriters in our camp who were trying to make a living.

"It became a career record for them. Radio stations still play it. Years later, when I managed them, it made me think about what could've happened had you guys put this record out—and you had had another round of hits.

"Then, oddly enough, a couple of years later, we got a small, $5,000 advance from Dixie Frog, and the record actually got released [*Heart of the Country*, 1987]. We never put it out over here, but this eclectic little label in France did—with these nice guys who were so passionate about American music. They were also putting out a Tony Joe White record. They offered to just license the tapes and release them.

"By then, it wasn't about the money or the recoupment, but the gratification that it got released somewhere."

When the record came out, the Dixie Frog folks asked if we'd come over to help promote it. No one had a problem with this. But between now and then, we had to put a band together.

Throughout the '80s, Donnie Thompson was, without a doubt, the guitar king of Springfield. Not only had he received nationwide notice for his guitar work on the Morrells,' *Shake and Push* (Borrowed Records, 1982) and the Skeletons' *In the Flesh* and *Rockin' Bones* (Next Big Thing Records, 1985), his self-released, 45-rpm version of "Driving Guitars" on Column One Records garnered him a substantial fan club around the Midwest.

I was one of those fans. We all were.

His ability to play any style of music also endeared him to the parade of clients who came through the Column One doors. If you were in need of a guitar player who could handle any kind of music, Donnie was your man. When I went in to record my songs, he was one of the first guys I called.

In 1971, he had been a frequent visitor to the House of Nutz & Loonies, joining Ruell's band, Spillwater Junction. In 1985, when we asked him to fill in for a few gigs with the Ducks, it led directly to a three-year stay.

His chicken pickin' gave the band more of a country sound than it'd had in some time. Gone was Wilson's bombast, Randy's deliberateness, and Rune's whimsy. In their place was Donnie's red-hot skillet licks—another fine example of the excellent musical gene pool Springfield is blessed with.

In keeping with the side projects I cook up with our guitar players, Donnie and I formed "Ozarkestra, the $6,000,000 Band." With Wunderle singing, Joe Terry on piano, and Ron Gremp on drums, the level of musicianship was very high and very swinging. We had a long song list to choose from—the Dogs, the Symptoms, the Morrells, the Skeletons, and the Couch Dancers.

Plus, these were the same guys who had played on my Column One sessions. They were already acquainted with my songs, which were instantly thrown into the mix. As we began to play around town, I brought in more and more of my tunes. They were also easily worked up and tossed into the festivities. Soon, I had a whole set of rocking, original material worked up.

Local sound technician/percussionist, Rick Davidson also came on board to start hauling our gear around. Not only was the husky man with the husky beard an old friend, he ran a sound company (Down Home Productions) with Mark West out of the garage of his rural Nixa home—a short hike up the hill from the Trout Farm.

As he traveled extensively throughout the area, setting up small sound systems at bluegrass festivals, he knew how to set up a little country band. More importantly, he knew how a little country band was supposed to sound. If you wanted big and boisterous, he didn't know much about it. If you wanted small and funky, he was your man. We called it "'Lumpy" sound—and we liked it.

Deemed "Lumpy" by his boyhood friends, never has a moniker so suited a man. Since playing drums in high school garage bands with Buddy Brayfield and Charlie McCall, he had remained a high-profile and respected member of the music scene. As percussionist for his latest band, the Undergrass Boys, never has a washboard looked so natural than when it hung around his neck. We called his pace "Lumpy" time.

Fresh off a six-year residency at local amusement park Silver Dollar City, where they played all day, every day, the Undergrass Boys were a tight and well-oiled bluegrass machine. Their self-titled, self-released album was a wonderful showcase of acoustic virtuosity.

Their record may have been good, but their gigs were really good. Because I had a friend's washboard at my house, I watched with interest as Rick played his. Then I watched with interest as he played the bones. When he played the spoons, I was caught.

When I approached him for a spoons lesson, it took him all of thirty seconds to show me how to hold them. Then it took me all of thirty seconds to figure out how to play them. I was on it like stink on shit. After a few minutes, I was clacking up a storm. Within the hour, I was sitting in with the band.

Thus, began my impish habit of sneaking up and barging in on people with my spoons. I could really make 'em go. It wasn't long before I felt confident enough to start jumping in with the Dirt Band, the New Grass

Revival, Vassar Clements, and David Grisman. I practiced at home to Spike Jones and Bonzo Dog Band records.

Plus, they're easy to find. Walk into any kitchen and grab two. I carry mine in my guitar case at all times.

The joke is always the same: "It's Supe, on spoons."

With Lumpy and Donnie on board, we hit the road. The first thing we did was sell the van and pickup with the customized horse trailer. Both had served their purpose. Both had several hundred thousand miles on them.

Once again, to avoid paying for all the shit like tags, taxes, and maintenance fees, we returned to rented vehicles. I jumped into a cargo van with Lumpy. John, Steve, Steve, and Donnie jumped into a Town Car.

To alleviate bulk, I bought a much smaller bass amp. For the next couple of years, along with Donnie's small Fender Vibroverb, our setup was tinier than it ever was. While Mike and Wendy continued to pound the pavements of Music Row, we slashed across the highways of America, a two-car family.

Though we played the same string of fairs and festivals, we never bothered to work up the Nashville material. What we did in Nashville, stayed in Nashville. When we played a gig, it was back to our usual set list. On occasion, we attempted to do a couple of those songs. But their delicate natures just weren't fitting in with the biker festivals we were playing.

We did work up "Fishin' in the Dark." Though Canway and I did the best we could to sing it, neither of us could hold a candle to Larry and Harry and Wendy. Then, when the Dirt Band's version hit the airwaves, we were doing a cover song.

We worked up Cash's "Hilltop Girl" instead—which was a lot more fun. With its elongated outro, I was reminded of the times we would blast into the end of "River to the Sun" and stay in the same groove for a long time. Playing "Fishin' in the Dark" just reminded me that I hadn't played on the record. It faded from our repertoire. I wasn't sad to see it go.

When Lumpy—who had spent a lot of time making a lot of money selling Undergrass Boys tapes and T-shirts—asked why we weren't selling tapes and T-shirts, he was greeted with grumpy choruses of "Aaah, we don't want to fuck with that kind of shit."

When, he suggested, "I'll do it", he was given the green light. The t-shirt part was easy. He just went to the same folks, who were printing Undergrass Boys shirts and had them start making Ozark Mountain Daredevils shirts. Each night, when we finished a gig, he rolled out a road case, opened the doors and began hawking shirts.

When, he informed us that the most frequent question he got, was about new music, we went into Column One, cutting versions of "Law," "Car," "Hilltop Girl," and Steve's, "Flame of Laredo." Combined with "I'm Still Dreamin'," "Everywhere She Goes," "Over Again," "Love Is Calling," "True Love," and "The River" from the Nashville sessions, we had enough material to round out a cassette.

The much smaller cassettes were much easier to handle than carrying around a bunch of heavy boxes of records. Though there isn't much room for artwork, we used Elizabeth's amusing sumi portrait of an imposing, authoritative monkey. It looked great. We boldly titled it *Now Hear This* and pressed up a thousand copies.

People snapped them up like hotcakes. After the first thousand, Lumpy ordered another thousand. After a while, he was able to hand out checks as portions of the profit. Even those who didn't want to fuck with this kind of stuff in the first place became converts.

Out on the road, we continued to slug it out. Donnie's red-hot country guitar rides on "Walking Down the Road" and "Gonna Buy Me a Car" garnered double takes from not only the crowd, but the rest of the band. Though our sound was smaller, it packed a much bigger wallop.

Halfway through our sets, when Lumpy sauntered on stage with his washboard, crowds went berserk. As we blasted into our "Bo Diddley"/"Not Fade Away" medley, he walked out front and began banging and clanging away. After his animated solo, I grabbed a pair of drumsticks and started wailing on his cowbells. The old wooden contraption made a lot of racket, was a crowd-pleaser, and on occasion, a babe magnet.

There were gigs to be played all over the place. We played all of 'em—1) Long runs across Canada, 2) a trip to Europe in support of the Dixie Frog record, and 3) a series of annual summer picnics in Springfield. We kept our plate full.

Let's work backwards …

3) The Ozark Mountain Stadium, a brand-new softball complex with a fully stocked bar, was a perfect facility for softball. It was also

set up nicely for a concert. When club manager Kevin Gerschefske approached with the idea of setting up an outdoor gig/picnic with the Ozark Mountain Daredevils at the Ozark Mountain Stadium, we lent each other our names.

Kevin took the picnic by the horns. There was more beer, barbeque, and liquor than you could shake a stick at—and we could invite whoever we wanted to play. We wanted Jerry Jeff. Walker was contacted, and he came up from Austin with his band to be on the bill. It was great to see him and Bob Livingston again.

Subsequent years garnered appearances by Leon Russell and the Rainmakers from Kansas City. Lumpy set up a PA, and people spent summer evenings under the stars, sprawled on blankets, strewn across the freshly mowed outfield grass.

2) Our trips across Canada became longer and more arduous. The longer we stayed, the drearier it got. Summertime in Canada is a kaleidoscope of yellow, green, and blue. Unfortunately, the window is only open for a few months out of the year. The rest of the time is spent in a kaleidoscope of grey, brown, and slush.

We still commanded a nice paycheck up there, but had to start going to Medicine Hat, Moose Jaw, Cold Lake, Red Deer, Prince Albert, Lloydminster, North Battleford, Drumheller, Ft. McMurray, Grande Prairie, and our all-time worst gig ever—Rocky Mountain House—to pick those checks up.

"Sometimes we'd have to set up in a disco," Lumpy glumly recalls. "I had to deal with these club owners, who were trying to tell me how they had a twelve-channel mixer and a sound system, which was just a bunch of disco speakers in the ceiling, right next to the mirror ball. And I had to find a way to make it work."

The cinder-block building in Rocky Mountain House was just that and nothing more. Outside, neglected, white paint flaked off the walls. The inside of those same walls were caked with alcohol, sweat, and nicotine.

A bar sat at one end of the room, adorned with a handful of neon Molson signs. I'd like to say a stage occupied the other side of the room. But there wasn't one. Lumpy just set us up against the far wall. Folding chairs and tables were randomly scattered across the concrete floor.

With not one window in the entire place, there was no way for any kind of sunlight to get in. Nor was there any way for the smell of tobacco and stale beer to get out. *Dismal* doesn't come close to describing the place.

As we drove to the gig—I mean, the cinderblock building—a cold, pouring rain kept our windshield wipers busy. When we pulled up, there was no dressing room of any kind. This meant we either hung out in the crowded, smoky bar or we hung out in the van in the rain. We chose the van.

When it came time to play, we threw our coats over our heads, dashed inside, and started. The mud-caked crowd sat in their folding chairs with blinding indifference—except for one beautiful Indian girl, intent on dancing to every song with every guy in the place.

In a sea of less-than-attractive people, her beauty was stunning. Though she wasn't an excellent dancer, as many eyes were focused on her as were focused on us. Mine were. Two others were those of her irate, drunken Indian boyfriend, being restrained at the front door by a slew of security guards.

With each song, as she twirled around the floor, veins bulged in his neck. He didn't have the money to buy a ticket and was too liquored up to figure anything out. She was literally driving him crazy—firewater crazy.

Time after time, he would barge back in the door. Time after time, he was thrown back out into the rain. With each visit, you could see his needle plunging further into the red. The music was loud enough on stage to keep us from hearing what was going on at the front door. We could, however, see what was going on—and it was not good.

This soap opera lasted until midway through our set, when the power went off. This was no big deal. Rock 'n' roll bands blow fuses all the time. We've had the power go off on numerous occasions. This time, it was different. Not only had all the lights gone off on stage, the Molson signs and beer coolers at the bar were out too. The entire room was plunged into pitch-black darkness.

Not only did the building's lack of windows prevent sunlight from getting in, it also prevented moonlight. Bic lighters began to flicker about the room. The local electrician, who was in attendance (everyone in town was in attendance), stepped outside to check things out. When he re-entered, he could only shrug his shoulders and shake his head.

The dancing girl's boyfriend had decided to put an end to her gallivanting—by shattering the power supply completely off the building with a cinder block. Then, when we learned that the damage was so extensive, it'd be impossible to fix until the morning, the concert was officially deemed *over*.

There was nothing anyone could do. The promoters apologized profusely and paid us immediately. We made a mad dash for the door. Lumpy packed up the gear in minutes flat and made a mad dash for the hotel. The next morning, we all made a mad dash for the next outpost.

Many of these gigs were in the hotel where we were staying—usually the biggest in town. Occasionally, we would play two or three nights in the same hotel. By night, their cabaret rooms were nightclubs, full of fans dancing to "Chicken Train." By day, the same rooms were strip joints, full of strippers dancing to Twisted Sister.

Contrary to what Mike Robertson cited, Canada was not on the tail end of the Urban Cowboy craze. They were still smack-dab in the middle of it. Annual summer jaunts to the Calgary Stampede kept us around town for a week at a time, playing a couple of different clubs, along with a half dozen corporate parties. There were cowgirls and strippers galore.

We spent a lot of time in Calgary, which afforded those of us who were interested the opportunity to wander and explore the city—something I've always been interested in. When it wasn't just ass-bite cold, I really enjoyed strolling around Calgary. Trips to Banff and Lake Louise were breathtaking.

It was a beautiful mid-summer afternoon, as I stepped out of our downtown hotel and into the warm sunshine. The Stampede was in full swing. The streets filled with cowboys and Indians.

With an afternoon to bide, I could hear the indistinct thumping of a distant band. Once again, it was the beat, it was in the air, and I headed toward it like I did on the first page of this book. Stopping along the way to take in the sights and smells of Stampede-mania, the music became clearer and clearer. As the band began to come into view, I began recognizing the song they were playing.

On a tiny side street of Calgary's Eighth Avenue Mall, a country band, clad in fancy Western shirts and big cowboy hats were playing for the pedestrians, also in fancy shirts and hats. As I wandered into the far end of the courtyard, wearing an unfancy shirt and no hat, I heard strains of, "Gonna lay here in the shade and drink another ice-cold beer. Cause, ooh ooh, boys, it's hot."

Even though I was thrilled, I stayed incognito. They didn't know who I was, and I did nothing to draw any attention to myself. To them, I was just another guy standing in the back, eating an ice-cream cone. "Ooh, Boys" just happened to be one of the songs on their song list.

Then they played "Standing on the Rock." Then they played "Homemade Wine." Then they played "Panama Red." Then they played "Amy."

Then I got bored and left. Still, it was nice to hear someone pay respect to one of your songs by singing it. The ice cream was extra good that day.

You'll have to ask the Pure Prairie League guys, but I don't think they ever got asked to play "Jackie Blue" as much as we got asked to play "Amy." We began to assemble a mock song list that included not only "Panama Red" and "Amy," but "Mr. Bojangles," "Hot Rod Lincoln," "Third Rate Romance" and "Ramblin' Man."

The next nagging misconception that followed us around was having to inform people that, "No, Jim Dandy is not here."

When the '88 Winter Olympics were staged in Calgary, we came to town and stayed for ten days, playing corporate parties—some of which started at nine thirty in the morning. It's a chore to rock 'n' roll with a mingling crowd that's still drinking coffee and eating doughnuts.

We were fortunate enough to play the opening ceremonies' after-party for the athletes. Security was extremely tight, just to get into the Olympic Village. On the way in, every road case was opened at every checkpoint, resealed with inspection tape, and sent on to the next set of authorities. The international presence was, as international presence usually is, bizarre and intense.

Once we got started, things were fine. We knew most of these nineteen-year-old athletes from nineteen different countries wouldn't even know who we were. Winning a gold medal was first and foremost on their minds. We were just the band—nothing more than a travel brochure for American country music. This didn't matter to us. The check from the International Olympic Committee was a healthy one.

As the party got rolling, I had a bird's-eye view onto the dance floor. Just like the drunken Indian incident at Rocky Mountain House, because we were playing so hard, I could not hear what was going on right down in front of the stage. I could, though, see the two short Korean male ski jumpers trying to pick up two slender Finnish female figure skaters.

I couldn't wait to see what was going to happen. Just the sight of it was amusing. As we charged into song after song, I continued to watch with interest. As they yelled into each other's ears, it became apparent that the Koreans were asking the Scandinavians to dance. When they finally overcame their language barriers and hit the dance floor, the two statuesque women began to move in long, fluid motions, while the two little guys burst into spastic fits of break dancing.

When we finished the song, the Finns vacated the floor in record time, while the Koreans high-fived each other. I didn't know who any of these kids were. Nor do I know if any of them won a medal. This American judge gave them all 9.7's.

As the week wore on, we received tickets to a hockey game, pitting the United States against Norway. I jumped at the chance, but got waves of indifference from my band mates. I attended the game alone, drank a beer for Rune, drank one for me, drank another one for him, ate a hot dog, and watched the grace of the skating. I didn't care who won. I just wanted to experience the pageantry and spirit of international goodwill. The Americans won 3-1. I cheered for all four goals.

Every one of our trips through Alberta resulted in a gig at Ranchman's, Calgary's legendary honky-tonk. It was Ranchman's where, after a stampeding Saturday night, we assembled at the bar for a quiet nightcap. The gig was over, the tour was over, and the club was emptying. It was our last night in the country, and we were headed home in the morning. We were all feeling good.

Then, Lumpy and I felt a tap on our shoulders. As we turned, a couple of nondescript, clean-cut guys stood there. At first, we thought they were just a couple of fans. They were—sort of. But we'd seen these guys before. Then, when we figured it out, it was a bone-chilling sight.

Ten days earlier, while crossing the border into Alberta, the two young Canadian customs agents took me off by myself into a tiny room. They had gone through one of my bags and found a couple of forgotten roaches lodged in the cluttered bottom. A few minutes later, they led Lumpy in. He had most of a whole joint.

Then, when they opened my shaving kit and tipped it upside down, a pile of dried basil leaves fell onto the table. I could only slap myself on the head, having forgotten that my friend Jerri Lynn had gone into her garden, broken off a sprig of basil, and placed it in there for aromatic purposes. I knew it was there. It had been there for a while. Every time I opened my kit, it smelled like basil. But it sure looked like pot.

As the two of us sat across the table from the two of them, a long, arduous afternoon of answering questions, filling out forms, and wondering what was going to happen next began. Their first question was a simple, "Is this all you have?" We both nodded our heads. Neither one of us was trying to smuggle anything in but a couple of puffs for later.

Then they continued with, "If it is, tell us now. Because if it isn't and we find it, you're in a heap of shit, ay?" The two of us nodded our heads again, as the two of them headed for the van. We knew they weren't going to find anything. We also knew that if they were going to bust us for less than a couple of joints and some dried basil, there was nothing we could do about it.

The clock on the wall ticked loudly. We still had a two-and-a-half-hour drive ahead of us, just to make it to the first gig in Medicine Hat. All afternoon, these guys continued to march in and out of the room. More forms were filled out; more questions asked. By late afternoon, time started becoming critical.

I don't really know what happened behind those closed doors. But when they walked in for the umpteenth time, tossed our keys onto the table, and told us to get lost, we did. They hadn't found anything else in the van.

As we left the building and raced for Medicine Hat, Rick and I could only look at each other and shake our heads in disbelief at what had just happened.

"They [the agents] knew just how long it was going to take us to get to the gig. They kept fucking with us all day to keep us tied up until the very last minute," Rick recalls. "Then, a couple weeks later, they came to the show."

Now, here we were, standing at the Ranchman's bar, staring at the same eyes—this time, dressed in civilian clothes. Their first question was, "Hey, remember us, ay?" My jaw hit the floor. Lumpy's followed.

When they continued with, "We thought we'd come check out your band. You guys are really good. Can we buy you a drink, ay?" the bartender set 'em up. Then they began apologizing for last week's debacle at the border, explaining that it was their job, they had families to feed, and blah, blah, blah. We couldn't believe we were having a drink with the same agents who had busted us the week before.

We quickly downed ours, thanked them, shook their hands, and made a beeline for the door. The next morning, we made a beeline for the border.

1) In the spring of 1988, *Heart of the Country* was released in France on Dixie Frog Records. We were asked to fly over and play a string of clubs and festivals to help promote it. We agreed to, at once. Then, when they asked for a recent photograph of the band, we didn't have one. We had some old ones, but none of the current lineup.

Not only did Dixie Frog want a mug shot for posters, they needed one for the album cover. John, Steve, Steve, Donnie, and I quickly assembled in Springfield to take one. It had been years since we'd done this, never even bothering to take a photo with Terry in it.

As we bunched up, Jim Mayfield began snapping his shutter, occasionally lowering his lens to suggest that Donnie smile, instead of trying to maintain his constant frown—the same frown Randy had insisted on years earlier. You can see it on any Skeletons or Morells record.

Don't get me wrong. Donnie's a great guy and one of the finest guitarists on the planet. But his persona became a source of amusement to the rest of us. Whenever someone pulled out a camera, we watched him transform into a New York punk.

Once again, it was Canway who broke the ice. I don't remember the joke, but when he leaned over and cracked it, it sent shivers of laughter through everyone in the room, Donnie included. Jim snapped the moment. When we looked at the contact sheets, this was the only shot in the whole bunch that had all five of us smiling. We used it.

When *Heart of the Country* hit European shelves, there we were on the front cover, cracking up at Canway's gag. Though I hadn't played on the record, there was my name on the back. Donnie and Canway were in the credits too. Neither had played on it either.

We started the trip with a stop at the Mean Fiddler—London's premier rock 'n' roll showcase club. As a wine-filled dinner in their fine adjacent restaurant was being eaten, the club filled with people, all curious about where we'd been for the past ten years. Dinner was great. So was the gig.

The place was packed with appreciative, knowledgeable fans. When we met the Three Stooges—Shane McGowan and Spider Stacy of the Pogues, along with veteran pub rocker Roy Harper—the hilarity began. We played our asses off. Pipes and pints went down easy.

We blazed through the same set we'd been doing for the past couple of years—but with that little extra "oomph" you always get when you play over here. Canway pounded the shit out of his drums. Donnie's fingers flew. Cash blared his harps, and I acted like a damn idiot. When Lumpy came out with his washboard, the place came unglued.

We treated everyone to a taste of the old, hairy-ass hillbilly shows we used to do. Plus, it was nice to play for an audience who knew Jim Dandy was nowhere in sight and they were not going to hear "Panama Red" or "Amy."

From here, we jumped over to Norway, reuniting with Rune, who had just felt the nasty teeth of American divorce, given up the Springfield ship, and moved back to Bergen. Once again, we were treated like kings in this beautiful city.

I never understood why we never played over here while he was in the band. Still, it was great to see, as well as hear him. The Flying Norwegians, who had reunited upon his return, became our opening act. It was a very cool show, as Condor and his cohorts were given free rein to join in wherever and whenever they wanted. The night ended with a stage full of hillbillies and Vikings.

Each morning, we piled into a little, short bus, barely big enough to snugly hold all of us up front, as well as all of our gear in back. It was immediately deemed the Goob Bus. It was on the Goob Bus where we met Victor, our bus driver. Victor became Wictor, who then became Wictor the Wiking.

We were also introduced to Ziggie. The portly fifty-year-old Bergen native, who had signed on as tour manager, knew his way around the

European circuits, the ropes of European travel, and several languages. He jumped in the bus, not only for our Norwegian stretch, but for our jaunts into Germany, France, Holland, and Spain.

A weeklong swing took us from Bergen, down the coast to Stavanger, around the cape to Kristansand, and up to Oslo. From here, we would cut directly back across the heart of the country for a second night in Bergen. Counting Ziggy and Wictor, there were eight of us crammed into the little wehicle.

Though each day was filled with breathtaking drives along the North Sea, distances were long. As the crow flies, they weren't. But then, a crow doesn't have to drive around massive fjords. When it came time to return to the west coast, there was no other way than to follow the crow cross country.

It's only a couple hundred miles from Oslo to Bergen—the same distance it is from Springfield to St. Louis. Missouri's Route 66, though, does not take you through the Stone Age or Ice Age. As soon as we headed west out of Oslo, we entered a frozen land, so enchanting and medieval, you can almost hear the gods rattling their swords against the mountains.

As we drove, the snow fell. As we neared the middle of nowhere—a middle of nowhere that is more middle-of-nowhere than any middle of nowhere anywhere in North America—the road grew slick. When the sliding began, knuckles whitened. As Wictor began to lose control of the bus, we slowly started drifting toward the ditch on our right.

He wasn't going very fast. He just couldn't stop. When he finally yelled, "Oh, fuck. Here we go!" in Norwegian, we gently slid off the road, tipped over a little bit, and landed face-first against a giant snowbank that not only softened our landing but kept us semi-upright.

We hadn't tipped over. We just sort of ... tilted over. In a matter of seconds, we found ourselves hanging off the side of the road at a forty-five-degree angle. No one was hurt, and we weren't going fast enough to break anything. The bus wasn't damaged. Its rear left wheel dangled three feet off the ground.

When we got out and gathered on the road, it was cold. A hundred yards down the road, a light burned in the window of a small Norwegian cottage. Ziggy trudged toward it in search of a phone. We climbed back on the bus. We could still hang out in it. It was just sitting at a humorously helpless angle.

When the car lights came over the horizon, Wictor jumped out and flagged them down. Remember, this was still the '80s. The cell-phone boom was still years away. But this guy just happened to have one in his car. He called a wrecker service and was on his way in a Norwegian minute. We all headed toward the little house on the glacier.

When we climbed their steps, the older couple who answered the door warmly opened their home to us. We were most interested in the space around their wood stove. We could tell they were startled. But it was nothing a couple of guitars and a couple of songs couldn't fix. Though they spoke no English, the music seemed to ease them. When they pointed to hot tea, we all drank hot tea. It was pure Norwegian Rockwell. The tea was great.

After thirty minutes, the wrecker pulled up. In thirty seconds, he had the bus tipped back up onto all fours and it was "Bergen or Bust." They have a very efficient wrecker service in Norway, as sliding off icy roads is a common occurrence.

As we left Norway, we jumped over for several days in Amsterdam, their coffee shops, and a gig at the famed Paradiso. Once again, we were greeted with chorus after chorus of "Where have you guys been?" and "Would you like to smoke some hash?"

Our hotel, which sat only a few blocks up (or down) the canal, was run by a couple of transplanted Californians who had come to this wonderful city and never bothered to leave. Their inn was a frequent stop for touring bands and artists visiting Amsterdam.

Though it was nothing fancy or modern, it was an oasis. There were no problems with translations. They made sure currency was easily exchanged and readily available. Plus, they made sure their guests were treated to healthy doses of Dutch hash-pitality. This suited the Dutch in me to a T.

The place was not large, but tall and skinny—three tiny rooms to a floor, four floors high, all connected with steep, creaky wooden staircases. As I did at Headley Grange, I headed straight for the top floor and my attic room, which was quite small. I enjoyed it up there, for no other reason than its long view down (or up) the canal.

As the evening of the gig slowly began to roll in, our hoteliers threw a small party for us in the lobby. Inviting the Paradiso staff, as well as their friends in the media, once again, everyone was curious about what we'd been up to for the past ten years. Festivities spilled up the street to the smoke-filled club.

Here, a hazy gig went well into the night, as the people in the front row openly and generously shared with the people on stage. Afterward, all reconvened back in the lobby of our hotel.

Here, things picked up right where they left off. Because it was our last night in the country, when Lumpy turned and asked if I'd mind showing him the red-light district, I snapped to, exclaiming, "Let me get my hat!" It didn't matter that it was already two thirty in the morning.

We were warned not to carry a whole lot of money with us, due to recent troubles in the district. It was a perfect recipe for a couple of stoned goofballs from Missouri to get rolled. Ziggy joined us.

As the three of us jumped out of the cab, Lumpy's eyes got as big as saucers. As we strolled past window after window, cottonmouth led us into the first watering hole we could find. The small, dingy bar at the end of a long alleyway was the only place open. When we walked in, the handful of other patrons didn't even bother to look up.

As we sat, we were joined by a waitress, who not only took our drink orders, but offered a "sexy show" for a fee. Lumpy ponied up, as she began swirling around him like the genie from a magic lamp. The sexy show may have only cost five dollars, but each round of drinks cost thirty-five.

In no time, both Lumpy and I had spent all of our money—ALL of it. Somewhere along the way, Ziggy had mysteriously vanished. This left the two of us with no money for blowjobs. More importantly, it left us with no money for cab fare. As we got up to leave, Lumpy headed for the bathroom. I headed up the alley and out to the street. All I had in my pocket was a matchbook with the address of the hotel on it and a handful of leftover Krones.

As I stood in the misty morning, not one cab came by. This was fine, due to the fact that Lumpy still hadn't made it out of the bar. As I waited, I started to get concerned. Then I started to get mad. Then I stomped back down the alley, muttering under my breath, "God damn it, Lumpy. It's four o'clock in the morning. Why can't you ever just leave somewhere?"

When I walked back in the door, I had to sit down, due to the fact that I witnessed one of the funniest sights I had ever seen. I'll try my best to describe it.

On his way out, our waitress/sexy dancer—who had taken a liking to him—grabbed him and pulled him onto the small, dimly lit stage in the corner of the room. By the time I walked back in, the two were involved in a freeform tango/ballet to Rod Stewart's "Do You Think I'm Sexy?," which blasted over the sound system. I'm not sure how her underwear got on his head. But there they were.

When the song ended, I gasped to catch my breath. When she realized he didn't have any more money, we were gone. As the two of us walked out of the bar, its din was replaced by the eerie silence of the streets of Amsterdam. By now, it was after four in the morning, we still had to get home, and we had no money.

When the taxi finally pulled around the corner, we flagged it down and jumped in. I handed the driver my matchbook. Then I continued in my best broken English to explain, "Now, here's our problem. We don't have any money. But if you get us to this address, we'll be able to pay you. We're in a band, and we're staying at that hotel, and ..."

In perfect English, the driver cut me off with, "Sit back. I see guys like you all the time. I know the two who own the place. I know right where it is. Don't worry."

So we didn't. We followed his instructions, sitting back with giant sighs of relief. When we pulled up to the front door, the party inside was still a-roar. The cabbie turned his car off, came in to get paid, and stayed for the festivities.

German festivals in Hamburg, Bonn, Frankfurt, and Munich with Willie Nelson were a downright blast. The Germans ate us up. Beer flowed like wine.

When we crossed from Germany into France, wine flowed like beer. Here, we met the folks from Dixie Frog, who had booked a small string of gigs around the country, which took us from not only the hustle and bustle of Paris, but through the wine region of Bordeaux and into the remote village of Pau in the French Pyrenees.

Each day was filled with scenic drives through the French countryside (we were still in the Goob Bus), wonderful French meals (we ate like kings), and wonderful local wines (we drank like fish). Each evening was filled with wonderfully festive scenes. When Dixie Frog's Guy and Philippe asked why we weren't playing songs from *Heart of the Country*, we stuck "Fishin'," "I'm Still Dreaming," and "Turn It Up" into the set. We were at it again—confusing another record label.

After playing Pau, we headed south to Barcelona and an appearance on *The Angel Casas Show*—the Johnny Carson of Spain. Sharing the bill with Janis Ian, a dance troupe, and a young, voluptuous Spanish actress, we spent the day rehearsing and hanging out in a television studio full of Spaniards.

That evening, when the cameras came on, Angel Casas burst into the spotlight, a handsome mass of jet-black hair and straight, white teeth.

When the cameras came on, he and the beautiful actress began talking in rapid Spanish. I tried to catch a word or two. But my Spanish had become quite rusty.

When the cameras came on, Janis Ian brought me to tears with a gorgeous rendition of her 1975 hit, "At Seventeen." It had been several years now since I had lived with my daughters, and I missed them terribly. My eyes moistened, as Janis's lyrics hit me right in the heart. When I let her know how much her song had moved me, she meekly smiled and nodded her head.

When the cameras came on, we blasted into "If You Want to Get to Heaven," as Angel, Janis, the actress, a studio audience of fifty, and a nation of millions watched. I yelled, *"Gracias,"* and *"Buenas noches."*

Afterward, we all headed into the Barcelona night for a bite. The place was still jumping. Europeans don't eat until late—a custom I've acquired and maintain to this day. We kept wave after wave of tapas and Spanish wine coming to our table. The next day was spent touring the city in our little bus, marveling at the works of Antonio Gaudi.

Then, it was back to Paris, back to Chicago, and back to Springfield. Two weeks later, it was back to Kansas, back to Iowa, back to Nebraska, and back to explaining why we weren't going to play "Amy."

When we returned home, it was Canway's turn to leave the V. Not only had he had enough of the rigors, he was burdened with a crumbling, melodramatic marriage, some shady financial dealings, and some shoddy book work that directly affected all of us.

Mike Robertson describes the scene: "There was just nobody doing anything. Canway was your road manager, just getting you guys from point A to point B, and doing the books, and having a relation with a banker and a hairdresser. Even in the weirdest situations, he was always happy. He was the 'King of the Scam.'"

On occasion, in order to keep up his facade of affluence, he dipped into our coffers. On occasion, paychecks bounced. He had been the bookkeeper since we parted ways with Stanley. Though we eventually recouped the money, when he informed us that he was moving to Nashville, the books were in complete shambles.

Mike describes what happened next: "He was here [Nashville], just trying to get away from Springfield. Lee Roy [Parnell] was just starting to have hits, and I knew that Steve had road managed for the band. In typical Canway fashion, even though he wasn't the most organized guy to be tour manager, everybody just loved him. It was more like an artist, tour managing an artist. The grown-ups back in the office would have to call and say, 'Okay. Now, don't forget. You've gotta be here by such and such …'"

"When Steve and I first met," recalls the sandy-haired Parnell, "within fifteen minutes, it was like I'd known the guy all my life. We were spot on as to the music we liked—and just things in general. Plus, we both had motorcycle fever."

The Austin, Texas native, fresh off a stint as Kinky Freidman's guitar player, continued, "So I hired him to be my road manager. He was kind of quiet and liked to read a lot. He took care of, and paid attention to, the things that mattered. He had an innate sense of how to deal with people—a real 'people person.' The way he treated people, he left them feeling good about themselves.

"A lot of the other guys in the band just wanted to lay around in their hotel rooms and watch TV. But not Steve and I. We'd always rent a car and just head out to see anything—and everything—there was to see. We called ourselves the 'Kings of Useless Information.' If there's something you don't need to know about, we'll tell you everything there is to tell you about it.

"Plus, restaurants were also big on our priority list. Wherever we went, no matter what city, he knew good restaurants to hit—mainly because you guys had already been there before."

Our next step was easy, though short-lived. Lumpy was a drummer. He just started loading up his drums and playing them. He already knew the songs. He'd been listening to them from the sound board for a couple of years. This meant that he would, now not only set up the gear, but play the show. Then he'd start selling T-shirts and tapes.

Fortunately, he was willing to take on the extra workloads. Unfortunately, this scenario wouldn't last long. When the lure of a steady paycheck reared its ugly head, he informed us that he had been offered the job as house sound mixer at Ray Stevens's theater in Branson.

It was a perfect gig for him. His Nixa home wasn't far from Ray's theater. He replaced twenty-hour drives to and from Canada with a thirty-minute drive from his house to a beautiful theater, equipped with state-of-the-art equipment. On top of this, Ray was going to pay him a lot more than we could. We all knew he had to go. He went with blessings.

At the same time, Donnie—who had also grown weary of the road—put in his resignation, opting to re-form the Skeletons with Lou, Lloyd, Joe, and keyboardist Kelly Brown. He also left with blessings.

This brought to an end a very good and very fun version of the band. As the '80s drew nigh, John, Steve, and I once again had to find a drummer and a guitar player. Once again, we dipped into the Springfield gene pool, filling the holes with a couple of Sandwiches.

CHAPTER 32

Over the past year, as Rick and Donnie had begun phasing themselves out of the band, I began phasing in yet another new side band. Once again, I realized that if I wanted to play something other than the same twenty-two songs we'd been playing for the past seventeen years, I would have to put together another project. Thus, Supe & the Sandwiches.

I was tired of playing those old songs too. I was saddened at the lack of any interest to get together and work up some new ones. I had a whole briefcase full of new ones—and I was excited about them. More importantly, I still had the desire to get together with a bunch of guys and make a bunch of rock 'n' roll noise.

With Don Shipps on bass, Mark Wilhoit on harp, Bill Brown on guitar, and Jerry Revella on drums, we headed downtown and into local entrepreneur Buddy Freeman's empty warehouse. Here, we began making sandwiches—late, late, late into the night.

Along with our gear, we brought massive amounts of drugs and alcohol. Rehearsals lasted for hours on end, as we worked up four sets of my nasal-manic material in no time. All the songs were at peppy, danceable tempos and peppered with large doses of humor. Each week, I'd bring in my notebook and we'd work up a dozen of the songs in it. The laughter from this combination of goofballs literally never stopped. Neither did the rocking—or the rolling.

I wanted Don to play bass, so I could play rhythm guitar. It's much easier to teach someone a song with a guitar in your hand. If I wasn't going to play bass, I wanted his funky Granny's presence. He was one of the only guys in town I trusted with the grooves. This freed me up front to lead the mayhem.

I chose Mark Wilhoit for his dirty Junior Wells style of playing.

I chose Bill and Jerry because of the younger rock 'n' roll sensibilities of their band, the Misstakes.

As we worked up song after song after song after song, I was stubbornly intent on keeping our repertoire filled with nothing but original material. I was also intent not to be a total song Nazi. If it was a cool song, written by one of us or one of our friends, it was thrown into the mix.

We worked up great versions of Randy's "Hillbilly Baby," Dillway's "A Little Further Up the Road," Wunderle's "Crawling Back to Me," Dean Billingsley's "Styrofoam," and Cash-o's "Jenine," along with a few other songs Steve and I had written—"King & Queen," "City Limits," and "Reach in My Pocket." All fit nicely alongside "Car," "Law," and "Well, I Tried."

I had no problem sharing the microphone either. When I passed it to Don, I pleaded with him to do "Harmony Grits" or "If You Blow It, I'll Know It," a couple of his staples. People loved those songs when he played them with Granny's. They loved them when he played them with the Sandwiches. I loved them as much as anyone.

When I passed the microphone to Bill, he and Don became John, Paul, George, AND Ringo. Both were Beatles scholars who could rip through any song from any Beatles songbook. This gave me the opportunity to catch my breath, head to the bathroom, take a leak, step outside, do a bump, head to the bar, grab some shots of tequila, and make it back to the bandstand. I only missed a couple of numbers.

We debuted on Thanksgiving 1988 at the Regency Showcase. After everyone around town had finished their dinner, they curiously stopped by to hear what in the hell I was up to this time. What they heard was a heaping helping of new songs. What they saw was me, eating my Thanksgiving dinner.

Halfway through the evening, when I passed the microphone to Bill and Don, I'd made arrangements for a plate of turkey and dressing and mashed potatoes and beans to be delivered to the stage. Here, I'd set up a little table for one, complete with a checkered tablecloth. I strictly instructed club owner Gary Thomas to deliver a glass of red wine—in a real wine glass. As Bill and Don began a long Beatles medley, consisting of "Tell Me Why," "Slow Down," and "Do You Want to Know a Secret?" the dance floor filled. I calmly sat center stage and ate dinner.

By the time they had finished their medley, I had finished my meal. I stood up from the table, wiped my mouth, downed the remaining contents of my wine glass, picked up my guitar, and we ripped into "Lord of the Shuffleboard," "I'm Going Down to the River," "Pasta Man," and "If Your Phone Don't Ring, You'll Know It's Me."

Deemed by local legend Benny Mahan as "the best fucking dance band in the world," we began playing four sets a night for five nights in a row at the River Rock, a rowdy nightclub nestled on a quiet back street on the south side of town. I continued to fill the gaping holes in the Ducks' schedule by making sandwiches at the Rock.

Run by songwriter Mark Denny, the place courageously presented live music every night of the week. Fronting his own band, the Coconut Brothers, he also remained focused on his outrageously funny original material. When he and I got together, we became Siamese twins joined at the humerus bone. We began writing songs by the peck.

In no time, the Sandwiches and the Coconut Brothers became wacky bands with interchangeable lead singers. After all, he and I wrote most of their repertoires. Whenever I was around, I had an open invitation to be a Coconut Brother. He had the same invitation to be a Sandwich. We began invading each other's space on a regular basis.

On quieter nights, we got out our acoustic guitars, I broke out my mandolin, and we played our songs in a quieter, but no less festive, fashion. Many of them were even funnier in this acoustic format, which placed more emphasis on lyrics and punch lines than on a pounding beat. People who knew how silly we were began showing up to hear the Mark & Mike Show. I know some funny people. Mark Denny is, without a doubt, the funniest of them all. We are serious about our silliness.

Still, the main focus of my interest was the raw power of the Sandwiches. With plenty of chemical enhancement, we played at breakneck speeds for hours on end to crowds that matched us every sweaty step of the way.

With the lineup we had, I enjoyed the cross section of people we drew. Not only did we draw curious Ducks fans, we drew Granny's fans who wanted to hear Don. Then we drew younger fans, who just wanted to watch Bill thrash about on his guitar.

Supe & the Sandwiches gigs at the Rock became spicy stew pots of social, economic, cultural, and racial diversity. Lawyers sat next to bikers. Natty bankers sat next to shaggy artists. Long-haired college kids (who were there to get drunk and get laid) sat next to their balding professors (who were there to listen to the lyrics—then get drunk and get laid). Blacks sat next to whites. Champagne glasses sat next to bottles of beer. Cigar smoke mingled with clove cigarettes. Some arrived in BMWs. Others rode their Schwinns. All came to hear the "best fucking dance band in the world."

When Donnie told John, Steve, and me that he was leaving the Ducks, I had the logical replacement. Just as Terry Wilson had done ten years before, Bill Brown made the jump from one of my side bands into my main band.

If Donnie was the local king of surf guitar, Bill was, without a doubt, the king of rock. The Springfield native had spent the last five years playing with local glam rockers the Misstakes. With a self-released album, an insatiable appetite for a party, and the reputation of trying to take every miss home, the mascaraed quartet had been a favorite on the local scene, as well as among small Midwest circles.

The focus of the band was Bill, a perpetual whirling dervish of flailing hair, dangling cigarettes, and volume. After Donnie's precision, Bill's guitar histrionics and embarrassingly clichéd rock posturing made us all laugh. The only problem was, he wasn't trying to be funny.

While his influence helped my manic Sandwich songs, it didn't do much to help the Ducks. On several occasions, I would take him aside and suggest, "Look, Bill, you're not getting paid by the note. Tonight, why don't you try playing more like Chuck Berry and less like Van Halen."

He would enthusiastically shake his head with, "Yeah. Right. Okay. Chuck Berry. No problem." But when it came time for his first solo, he reverted right back into hair-flinging stardom, while stomping on the myriad of effects pedals he kept at his feet.

Being much younger than the rest of us, he was the first Duck more connected to the younger generation of the '90s than he was to our throwback shit of the '70s. When we were making our records, he had been in grade school. On occasion, actual generation gaps would form.

He would get excited when Slash came on the tube. The rest of us couldn't reach the remote in time. He knew every word to every REO Speedwagon song and every guitar lick to everything by Rush (two of his major influences). He was very good at it. The rest of us couldn't stomach REO or Rush.

Though he was a very good guitarist, a quick study, and a great hang, he knew no other way. Among this pack of old dogs, he was a feisty puppy, eager to please and with all the desire in the world.

When he also agreed to set up the equipment, he was hired. At the beginning of the '90s, Bill Brown jumped into the van.

Once again, we dipped into the Morells/Skeletons clan for a drummer. There is only one difference between the two—that's the drummer. If the Skeletons got a gig, Lloyd played drums. If the Morells got the gig, the drummer was Ron Gremp. Simple as that.

Years ago, when Lloyd was on the road with us, the Morells flourished at home. Now that Donnie had left the Ducks to re-form the Skeletons, this put Lloyd on the drum stool and Rongo on ice.

Rongo took to our band like a duck takes to water. He and I had worked together on numerous gigs and studio projects over the years. I always looked forward to playing alongside the guy. Not only did we both like to play, a majority of the time was spent laughing at each other.

Had we known each other in grade school, Gremp and Granda would've sat right next to each other in class—a scary thought. I'm afraid the two Polish kids from St. Louis would have found their fair share of Polish mischief—another scary thought.

It wasn't the only thing we had in common. Generations ago, my great-grandfather, wishing to change his family's image by changing its surname, altered Grenda into Granda. Rongo's grandfather shortened Grempczynski to Gremp.

After stints with Eric Ambel as part of Roscoe's Gang, and several tours around the Midwest with old friend Doug Sahm, Rongo was already road savvy. He already knew what it entailed.

Ambel, who had come to town in the '80s with his band, the Del Lords, to record parts of *Lovers Who Wander* and *Get Tough* with Lou Whitney, stayed behind to form Roscoe's Gang. Eventually, he would end up recording *Roscoe's Gang* (Enigma, 1988), using the Morells as his band. He chose Rongo as his drummer.

Not only had I known Doug Sahm from our days at the Armadillo World Headquarters, I knew I could always count on him to show up at my house around October or November—harvest season—in his long, silver Cadillac and stay for a couple of days.

Then, I knew I could count on him to go somewhere else and stay there for a couple of days.

Then, we all knew we could count on him to hang around town, smoke everybody's pot, and fuck everybody's girlfriend.

Most of all, I knew I could count on him to come to town and play some music. When he didn't bring a band with him, he called me, and I'd scramble to fill out a combo. Then we'd all head to Commercial Street, pile into Bruce Rader's club, Lindberg's, and have absolutely rip-roaring times.

Occasionally, Doug would stay in town a little longer, assemble a little touring band, base out of Springfield, and travel around the Midwest. He chose Rongo as his drummer.

Rongo and I quickly found a nice, simple, solid, and infectious groove—one that was impossible to sit still to. This also meant that the Ducks now had a complete Polish rhythm section.

When I asked Rongo to replace Jerry Revella, he became a Sandwich. We played a lot, and I mean a lot. I kept up a hectic pace. Bill and Rongo matched me step for step.

In 1989, the Ducks played ninety-four gigs. The Sandwiches played sixty.

In 1990, the Ducks played 103 gigs. The Sandwiches played sixty-eight.

In 1991, the Ducks played thirty.

That July, we played the Swiss Villa Amphitheater in Lampe, Missouri and went our separate ways.

Ozarks, 1991 (left to right) John, Bill Brown, Steve, Ron Gremp, and me (photo by Jim Mayfield)

But not before a myriad of odd gigs.

The headline of the *News-Leader* informed its readership of the death of Clarence Jones. I was contacted to help coordinate a benefit gig for Roscoe, who had the complete sympathies of everyone in the area. He also had no money or wherewithal to fend for himself in the real world.

The entire community gathered in the Nixa High School gym for Clarence's wake, with all the proceeds going toward helping relocate Roscoe into an assisted-living facility.

Over the years, we'd made a conscious effort not to play a lot of benefits, choosing to shy away from organizations with agendas, politicians with rallies, and corporations with mall openings. This would've opened the flood gates to everyone in town who wanted us to play their benefit. It would have also pissed off those whose particular benefit we chose not to play. When we played, we usually liked it to be for our benefit. That night, we all felt it appropriate to play for Roscoe's.

We spent ten days in Springfield, Illinois, playing the Illinois State Fair. Of course, we weren't on the main stage, which featured Lee Greenwood, Kenny Rogers, Barbara Mandrell, and Foreigner. We played in the Budweiser tent.

It Shined

We spent two weeks in St. Paul, Minnesota, playing the Minnesota State Fair with Doug Kershaw, Danny Davis & the Nashville Brass, and Williams & Ree. As the four of us alternated sets throughout the day (starting at 9 AM), we had our evenings free. This allowed us to visit Springfield native George Frazier, who had become a pitcher for the Minnesota Twins.

When he invited us down to games, we went. When the Twins asked if we'd be interested in singing the National Anthem, we looked at each other and reluctantly said, "What?." We were relieved, when we were informed that due to the serious slapback echo of the Metrodome, no performer was allowed to sing the song live. All were required to go into a studio and record the song, which would then be played over the stadium's public address system, while the artist stood on the field and lip-synched.

Several weeks prior, Canway, Dillway, and Nick Sibley had gone into Nick's studio to sing the song. After one pass, they sang it again, which created the effect of a six-man glee club. With plenty of reverb, it sounded great.

We walked out to third base, as the public-address announcer announced, "Ladies and gentlemen, please rise and direct your attention to the third-base area, where we'll be led in the singing of our National Anthem by international recording artists, the Ozark Mountain Daredevils."

When we heard the first strains of the song booming from the speakers in the ceiling, we began moving our lips accordingly. Not only was I scared to death to be doing this in the first place, I was even more frightened that there would be a malfunction in the tape player. There was none. The crowd cheered. The Twins took the field. Afterward, George invited us into the clubhouse to meet Gary Gaetti and Kent Hrbek. We went to the games by night. They came to the state fair by day.

There was the obligatory stop at Mole Lake, where we united with the Band, joining them onstage for a 3:30 AM rendition of "I Shall Be Released."

There was the annual long jaunt across Canada, where we seemed to find even more outposts than we had last time.

There was a week at Harrah's in Lake Tahoe, where we once again were not on the main stage, but playing two shows a night in the lounge.

There was the college gymnasium in Rolla, where our warm-up act was Calvert DeForest, better known as Larry "Bud" Melman. A fan favorite from David Letterman's *Late Night*, the old guy was making some extra spending money on weekends, playing college campuses. He was so funny, our set seemed anti-climactic.

Then, there was an ill-fated four-day stint in Branson.

Let me take a minute here and talk about Branson—or what Springfield musicians refer to as "the B-word." Hopefully, this will answer those of you who, over all the years, have asked, "Why don't you guys just go to Branson?"

In the early '50s, when the Army Corps of Engineers decided to dam the James River and form Table Rock Lake, the tiny town of Branson watched as the water level rose right up to its back door. Lucky residents became instant owners of lakefront property. The scenery was breathtaking; the fishing, magnificent.

In the mid '50s, Ozark Jubilee regular Bob White came to town, hired the Presleys as the band, and opened Presley's Theater—the oldest music hall in the Branson area.

As we all know, if there's one thing country musicians like to do, it's fish. Bob invited them all down. They all came. They all fished. At night, because they were all musicians, they all looked for a place to play.

By the late '50s, as the Ozark Jubilee was packing up its tent and moving to Nashville, many of the musicians did not want to leave Missouri. Many didn't. Many wonderful musicians stayed put, right there in the Ozarks. When they were unable to find enough work in Springfield, many headed south to Branson.

The fishing business on Table Rock Lake was booming. When the Baldknobbers opened a second theater, right across the street from the Presleys, to handle the overflow of music lovers, the music community began to boom. Fishing holes. Country stars.

Though Springfield and Branson sit only forty miles apart, there is very little interaction between the two musical communities, as well as few similarities in their approaches to music. The same can be said for Springfield and Joplin, which only sit seventy miles apart.

Every week in Branson, you have a new batch of fishermen and their families coming to you. Every week, you have a different crowd walking into your theater. You don't have to go anywhere. You can set up camp, sit tight, and play the same show over and over and over and over and over.

For years, when the Jubilee cameras came on at 7:00, the home viewing audience didn't care why you were late. At 7:00, you were expected to be in your position, with a smile on your face. When the curtain goes up at 7:00 in Branson, you are expected to be at your post and on your best behavior—all with a smile on your face. If you can't do these things, you are fired and easily replaced with someone who can.

Punctuality is not mandatory for Springfield musicians, who have a relaxed approach to the down beat. Occasionally, a Branson musician, wanting to break away from the monotony of his gig, will venture up to town to loosen up and sit in. Springfield musicians don't venture down to Branson.

Late in the summer of 1989, we were hired to test the Branson waters, with a four-night stand in Freddy Fender's old theater. Freddy had already come and gone. He came. He saw. He said, "Get me the hell out of here." He was not alone. Willie Nelson and Johnny Cash had both recently shared this same B-town experience.

But there we were, competing with the Presleys, the Baldknobbers, Wayne Newton, Roy Clark, Jim Stafford, Ray Stevens, a Japanese violinist named Shoji Tabuchi, and a dozen smaller theaters, all featuring rousing nightly versions of "I'm Proud to Be an American." We came in a distant, unbedazzling last place.

When Freddy's curtain came up at 7:00, Bill was still plugging stuff in, Rongo was still adjusting his drums, Steve had gone out to his car to get something, and John was still in the bathroom. I don't even know where I was. When we finally assembled onstage at ten after, there wasn't one sequin in sight—another direct contrast to the star-spangled entertainers on Branson's Highway 76—better known as "the Strip."

After four nights, playing to crowds of forty, fifty, sixty, and sixty-two people, the great Branson experiment was—mercifully—over. The promoter took a bath. We drove back to Springfield. In coming years, on occasion, we would try to play here. Each venture ended with the same dismal results.

Our fans didn't want to go to Branson. So they didn't—and I can't blame them. We all like going to the lake. We just don't want to have to put up with the endless string of Winnebagos clogging the artery of the Strip. Our fans don't like it there. We don't like it there either.

I have one last thought on the topic. Then I'll get off my soapbox. If someone wants to come to Branson from Hollywood, Vegas, or Tokyo, do a million shows and make a million dollars, that's fine. If you want to work extra hard and make two million dollars, that's fine too. Just don't throw your shit in the lake. I don't care about your elaborate stage show, or how proud you are to be an American. I do care about the lake.

That fall, I took the Sandwiches into Column One to record some of the songs we'd been doing. We were well rehearsed, tight as a drum, and hitting on all cylinders. In no time at all, with Lou at the board, we laid down versions of "Makin' a Living, Not a Killing," "Rockin' Chair," "Ode to Mel Bay," "Born with a Beard," "Pasta Man," "Secret Weapon" and Gord Ross's "Chains of Misery."

All were favorites at the River Rock. All were assembled onto a cassette, entitled *Supe & the Sandwiches, Greatest Hits, Vol. III*. I watched with interest as Lumpy sold shitloads of *Now Hear This*. I pressed up a thousand copies of the *Greatest Hits* and sold them all by the end of the year.

1990 was a carbon copy of 1989, complete with a couple more visits to our neighbors to the north, another shorter—but no more successful—two-day visit to Branson, a foray into the political arena, and a New Year's Eve gig in Springfield.

In place of our summer picnics, we began a string of New Year's Eve parties. Like those warm, summer gigs, December 31 became the hottest ticket in town. Everyone showed up in the downtown Holiday Inn ballroom, where they proceeded to get completely obliterated before just having to stumble upstairs to their rooms. It was a great idea. You can't get a DUI on an elevator.

They were nice gigs, and the paycheck was a welcome sight on January 2—the start of the slowest time of the year.

For those of you who were paying attention a few paragraphs ago and are still wondering about the political foray I mentioned, let me explain. It was a stormy, stormy night.

Actually, it was a steamy, steamy night as the Sandwiches blasted through another evening of debauchery. Earlier that morning, everyone in town had witnessed fellow Springfieldian (and state representative)

Jean Dixon on NBC's *Today Show*, ranting and raving about her new "cause"—censorship of music. We also saw the flaunting of her newfound celebrity go directly to her head, causing her hat size to swell six sizes.

This first stage of her Warholian fifteen minutes was as tasteless and obnoxious as it gets. As she raged over network airwaves about how Ozzy Osbourne was killing our children, she made us—her constituents—look like a tribe of Jethro Bodines.

She was my neighbor. I lived in her district.

She was coming up for re-election.

We all saw her screaming on television that morning. That night, I started screaming into a microphone too.

As the Sandwiches got faster and louder, so did my ranting. When I yelled, "You know what I ought to do? I ought to run against her," laughter rattled the rafters. I thought nothing of it, turning to call the next song.

At the end of the night, the three gentlemen at the back table didn't leave. As the lights came on and the place emptied, they approached with outstretched hands.

Remember earlier, when I was describing how diverse Sandwich crowds were? This night, we had drawn a couple of local politicians, who just wanted to drink beer and laugh at my silly songs.

They were as smashed as I was. When I invited them to join me at the bar, they informed me that my idea of running against Dixon may not be such a bad one. After agreeing that we were all too blasted to talk about it, we all agreed to meet at their office the next afternoon.

The rain continued to pour the next day, as I walked into their office. A secretary led me down the hallway, where I took a seat at the conference table. This wouldn't take long.

After pleasantries, they laid out a simple plan. If I wanted, I could really raise a ruckus in the community, by placing my name on the ballot for the upcoming Republican primary elections. Along with my high profile around town, it just might make a difference. These guys detested Dixon as much as I did. They just couldn't scream their disgust into a loud rock 'n' roll microphone. I could.

I drove to Jefferson City, where all I had to do to become a candidate for the Missouri House of Representatives from the 135th District was prove I was a resident and give them fifty bucks. My name was placed on the ballot for the upcoming election. It was that simple. When I did it, the flood gates opened.

The next morning, when "Rock Star Throws Hat into Ring for Dixon's Seat" hit the front page of the *News-Leader*, my phone rang off the wall. Everyone wanted to know how I was going to unseat my unpopular neighbor, or if this was all just a Pat Paulson skit. I let everyone know that I was going to do whatever I could to help, even if it took being an obnoxious asshole musician for the summer.

When noted surgeon Dr. H.B. Ivy called, I took his call. With an invitation to lunch, we met at a quiet local restaurant on Park Central Square. When he sat down, his resemblance to Colonel Sanders was uncanny. As I looked across the table, I saw me in thirty years.

We hit it off immediately. He was just a crazy old man and I was just a crazy middle-aged man. He let me know that he thought what I was doing was well intended. Then he let me know about a third candidate on the ticket—who also detested Dixon as much as I did.

Then he explained the theory of "voter pool dilution"—recently made popular by Ralph Nader and the Y2K coup d' etat of the White House. If I siphoned off a couple hundred votes, allowing Dixon to gain re-election by a hundred fifty, I would have a giant hole in my foot. I wanted nothing to do with the Ralph Nader role. I knew what had to be done.

Knowing I was going to eventually withdraw my name from the ballot, I kept a high profile, speaking at lectures, clubs, and meetings. My platform was simple—the more young people we could get to the voter registration booths in the summer, the better chance we had at the polls in the fall.

That was all I was suggesting, as Dixon started up her gaudy campaign wagon. I continued to talk to media people, attending Republican functions and asking everyone to just chill out and do their part by registering to vote. Then I let them know that Ozzy really wasn't killing our kids.

Several Republicans discreetly took me aside to let me know that they were embarrassed by Dixon too. Along with her inner circle of uber-Republicans, they hated me. They especially hated me when I showed up at Republican functions dressed like Abe Lincoln—complete with a three-piece blue suit, white shirt, red tie, trimmed beard, and top hat.

I had a committee, which just consisted of a handful of friends who liked to get together, talk politics, smoke pot, and watch baseball. I had no overblown aspirations of winning an election. Still, checks began to come in the mail from prominent people in the community—who all hated Dixon's audacity.

This made for a summer's worth of crazy, crazy gigs. I felt a huge sense of relief when the Ducks went out of town to play for people who had no idea what was going on back in Springfield.

Local Sandwich gigs, with the added influx of politics, got very intense—VERY intense. As we played to packed houses, I started to get nervous in the spotlight and in the alley, when I left the club.

When noted music journalist and activist Dave Marsh caught wind of what I was doing, he called from New York to find out what was going on. When I explained my strategies, he asked if I'd chronicle them into an essay for his book, *50 Ways to Fight Censorship* (Thunder Mouth Press, 1991).

My strategy was simple—keep a loud profile through the summer and get as many people to the registration booth as possible. Then, at the eleventh hour, hold a press conference at the courthouse, announce my withdrawal from the race, instruct all of my supporters to shift their support to Doc's friend, and drive back to Jefferson City to remove my name from the ballot.

Doc picked me up at the courthouse in his Cadillac and we cruised through a summer afternoon to the capital. Here I went through the proper channels to remove my name from the ballot. After three of the craziest months of my life, I was very relieved to be out of that limelight. If you think rock stars are in love with their mirrors, they don't hold a candle to politicians.

When the election results came in that November, Connie Wible successfully unseated Dixon. With an invite to the "watch party," I walked tall into the lobby, just as Dixon conceded defeat and stormed out of the building. She said nothing as she gruffed by. I tipped my top hat as she passed.

I was very relieved when the whole ordeal was over, though now I could include "politician" on my résumé along with baseball scribe, professional comedian, and obstetrician.

I was glad to see 1990 end. When 1991 rolled in, the Ducks began taking on water and losing steam. Our gigs were not only further into the boondocks, they were further out of the spotlight. We were no longer visiting cities of any size. Media coverage was next to nil in Boone, Iowa and Chadron, Nebraska.

We agreed to take the first half of '91, maintain a healthy touring schedule, take the money, and throw in the towel. Let me clarify that. We all didn't agree on the "towel" thing. At this point, I started getting outvoted two to one on a regular basis.

I didn't think doubling our price, so we only had to play half as much, was sound thinking. The vote was two to one.

I knew that finding something else to do in Springfield was just that—something else to do. I knew what I wanted to do. It was the same thing I'd been wanting to do since I was fourteen. The vote was two to one.

That Fourth of July, after playing Alton, Illinois's Festival on the River, the plug was pulled. The vote was two to one.

My next thought was, if the plug was really getting pulled, I had no desire to find something to do around Springfield and be a "local king." I enjoyed making seventy-five bucks a night playing smoky clubs. I also knew that, ten years from now, I would still be making seventy-five bucks a night in those same places.

Plus, I had had my fill of cocaine. After years of fun in the sun and frolicking through the night, it became less and less of a good time. Everywhere I went, people were offering it to me in substantial amounts. I couldn't say no. I wanted to. I just couldn't. If there was a little line on the table, I would do it. If there was a big pile, I would sit there until it was all gone—even if it took three days.

At one time, these binges were fun. They no longer were. It felt like a good time to exit, stage left.

My phone to call to Larry in Nashville was brief.

"Larry, do you think there's room down there for one more guy to make a living?"

"Everyone seems to be doing it."

On July 22, 1991, I packed my bags, put the Sandwiches on ice and headed for Nashville with my guitar, a box of crazy songs, a ton of persistence, and the desire to continue making music.

Over the years, we had shared many stages with singer/songwriter Gene Cotton. Our gigs together were always cool. His sets were fun and uplifting—and our fans always seemed to enjoy him. I dug his affable nature, as well as his constant offer of a place to stay if I ever wanted to come to Nashville.

When I arrived in Tennessee, I took him up on it, sleeping on a futon in his studio for the week. His beautiful thirty-acre mountaintop home in Leipers Fork was only a thirty-minute drive from Music Row.

As a twenty-year veteran of the Nashville music community, the healthy royalties he had received over the years from writing "Let Your Love Flow" not only helped him afford his mountain home but also the wonderful studio he had built.

I was generously given a key to the place, with its spectacular views of the surrounding hills. I informed Gene and his wife Marni of my intentions: stay for a week, make a decision. Then make—or not make—the move.

It only took me a couple of days to realize that I had found a new home. As I spent every day pounding the streets of Music Row with my songs, I spent every evening climbing onto stages, participating in every jam session and writer's night I could find.

At week's end, I returned to Springfield, hooked a trailer onto the back of my truck, backed it up to my storage locker, cleared everything out of it, and headed back to Tennessee.

I had a wad of money in my pocket from the first six months of Duck gigs to pay for the last six months of rent. I immersed myself completely in writing, singing, playing, and collaborating on an everyday basis with a myriad of Nashville artists and writers.

I'll admit it. I was scared shitless.

There are two reactions people have when they first move to Nashville. You either see the extremely high level of musicianship, get intimidated, and head back to your small pond with your fin between your legs. Or you flourish, choose to raise the level of your work, and jump into the big pond with both fins.

I found myself solidly lodged in the latter category. By the end of the year, I had made a name for myself around town as a writer of silly songs. I thought they were a welcome respite to the sea of sappy love ballads that seemed to be flooding the market.

When I walked into publishers' offices, they listened to a couple of verses of a couple of songs, before they chuckled, sat back in their chair, and said, "Yeah. That's funny. But have you got any relationship songs?" In the early '90s, funny wasn't selling.

I did not want to be Weird Al Yankovic funny.

I did not want to be Cledus T. Judd funny.

I *did* want to be Roger Miller and Cowboy Jack Clement funny.

As country music was booming across America, rugged, handsome cowboys were looking for sensitivity and schlock. I had neither. But I didn't let this bother or hinder me. I knew I had some cool songs, and someone somewhere would like my brand of "funny." I bought a small four-track cassette recorder and a drum machine. For the rest of the year, I holed up in a tiny one-bedroom apartment with my nose to the grindstone.

From the moment I woke until the moment I slept, I demoed not only old songs I had brought from Springfield, but the slew of new songs I was writing on a daily basis.

The rest of year quietly passed, ending with a very rowdy Dog People weekend at the Ozark Mountain Stadium. When the holiday season was over, I couldn't wait to get back to a sober Nashville.

When I did, I found fellow "funny" lovers David Rhodes Brown and Tommy Riggs. I began making a new batch of Sandwiches at once.

Cincinnati guitarist Brown had also just relocated to town. He fell in love with not only the silly subjects of my songs, but my rock 'n' roll grooves, which fit in perfectly with his rockabilly guitar style.

When he mentioned that Lonnie Mack's drummer, Maxwell Schauff, would also love them, the three of us began meeting in Brown's upstairs apartment. We thrashed through "Pasta Man," "Ode to Mel Bay," "Monday, Tuesday, Wednesday, Thursday, Friday, Saturday Night" and "City Limits" with the same fervor I did in Springfield.

When Maxwell, who was spending much of his time on the road with the Sweethearts of the Rodeo, mentioned that their piano player, Rick "Pickle" Gerkin, might also be interested in playing, the lineup was solidified. I used the same gonzo presentation as I did in Springfield, only with a pounding piano instead of a wailing harp.

Writer's nights are fun and all, but I had me a rock 'n' roll band—and a damn good one. As 1992 began, we played the Ace of Clubs with NRBQ,

It Shined

which helped me reach a community of folks who would appreciate my brand of funny. I was in heaven. It was a very cool club with a very good PA system, a very good sound man (Howie Tipton), very good acoustics, very cold beer, and a very hip and famous clientele.

When Boardwalk Cafe owner Rick Moore—who is also blessed with an engorged sense of humor—caught my act, he hired us on the spot to play his south side club on a weekly basis. Here we began drawing large crowds with large senses of humor.

One of the largest was Tommy Riggs—your prototypical jolly fat guy. Weighing in at well over 300 pounds, he was a renowned entertainer around town, fronting the house band at Buddy Killen's legendary steakhouse/nightclub, the Stockyard,

But on nights the Sandwiches played, he came to the Boardwalk, waddled in, took a seat, and sat there all night, eating, drinking, heckling, and laughing his fat ass off. When he invited me to come downtown and sing with his Stockyard band, I jumped at the chance. They easily followed me as I led them through the simple, twelve-bar progression of "Monday, Tuesday, Wednesday, etc.." I began making the Stockyard crowds laugh too.

When Riggs offered to pay for a recording session, I jumped at the chance. Working at a relaxed but determined pace, it only took us a couple of weeks to make an entire album.

After recording eleven tracks, I began inviting local luminaries into the studio. Bobby Keys, who had begun sitting in with us at the Boardwalk, stopped in. When he wailed at the club, the place came unglued. When he wailed in the studio on "I Don't Do Lunch" and "Monday, Tuesday, Wednesday," I could not believe that a Rolling Stone was playing on my record.

Local mandolin wizard Sam Bush was invited to play. After laying down wonderful mandolin and fiddle tracks on "Ode to Mel Bay," the Kentucky native's fee was tickets to some St. Louis Cardinal baseball games. That spring, he and I drove to Cincinnati for opening day with our beloved Redbirds, as equipment manager (and dear friend) Buddy Bates set us up with tickets to Riverfront Stadium.

When all the recording was finished, I agreed to give Tommy and his partner, publisher Ken Jenkins, one year to find a record deal. If, in that amount of time, they failed to produce one, I retained control of the master tapes and more importantly, control of my publishing rights. Then I would have a batch of nice recordings with Bobby Keys and Sam Bush on them.

Ken and Tommy began pounding the Music Row pavement. I told them that I hadn't had much luck with my "funny" down there. But if they did, I would gladly split the money with them. I always wanted to laugh all of the way to the bank.

That May, as I continued my assault around town, I received a phone call from friend—and fellow bassist—Manny Yannes, who was playing in the most recent version of Michael Clarke's Byrds. When I picked up the phone, his voice on the other end inquired, "Supe, what are you doing Saturday?"

When I replied that I didn't have anything going, he asked if I could find my way to Louisville, Kentucky and cover his Byrds gig for him. When he told me that the gig paid a couple hundred dollars, I told him my truck was full of gas. When he offered to get me a tape of the songs, I told him that wouldn't be necessary. All of those songs were already indelibly etched into my mind.

Directions to the Louisville Holiday Inn were jotted down. Bright and early that Saturday, I was off. Here I met Michael, who I'd known since his days in Colorado with Firefall, along with twelve-string guitarist Jerry Sorn and lead vocalist Terry Jones Rogers. When we met in the hotel lobby, Mike and I met as old friends. When we headed to the gig, we met as new bandmates.

Having recently purchased the rights to the name, he and Gene Clark had spent the past couple of years traveling the world as the Byrds. After Gene's untimely death, Mike, Terry, and Jerry continued to keep the music alive. I felt honored to be part of the legacy.

I dug the gig. I didn't have to bring anything but my bass. Rented gear would be provided and in place. All I had to do was walk in and plug in.

When we began with "I Feel a Whole Lot Better," I couldn't believe I was doing a gig with the Byrds. When we came to "Eight Miles High," I couldn't believe I had to do a bass solo. I'd never done a bass solo in my life. Still, when the time came, I just started flipping and flopping around in the key of E.

As we ran through song after wonderful song, the crowd danced and sang along, just like they did when the Ducks played "Jackie Blue" and "Chicken Train."

When we finished, Mike and Terry asked if I'd be interested in joining them the following week for a five-day run of gigs from New York to Boston. I asked about Manny, who played great bass solos. I was informed that he had just been replaced. I agreed to meet everyone in New York. The week after that, I joined them in Texas. Just like that, I was in the band.

Terry, who took care of the logistics—as well as being Michael's babysitter—informed me that a package of plane tickets would be in the mail. That spring, I made a five-day trip to the Chicago area, a five-day trip to the Denver area, a five-day trip to the Pacific Northwest, and a five-day trip through Florida.

I fit into this old hippie band quite well. If the Ducks were beginning to feel they were getting old, along with their fans, fans of the Byrds really *were* old. I got mistaken for bassist Skip Battin on a regular basis. But I didn't want to make a scene. I chuckled to myself, as I scribbled "Supe" to look like "Skip" on their album covers. No one cared. Everyone laughed.

When I called St. Louis to let my mother know what I was up to, she asked, "Who are the Byrds?" When I explained their place in history, she headed to the record store to buy a copy of their greatest hits. A couple weeks later, I had to chuckle when she informed me that her favorite song was "Eight Miles High."

It was a very good band. Terry and Jerry sang well together, along with Jerry's superb twelve-string work. Michael, on the other hand, was either really good or really bad. The man was a very solid rock 'n' roll drummer—until he got drunk. Then he turned into a stumble bum. When he rocked, we rocked. When he didn't, I exercised my right as the stoned-out bass player to linger in the shadows all night.

This was his gig. I was just the side man. On most nights, though, I loved strolling to the microphone to add a third, "Turn, turn, turn."

That June, when my phone rang, it was Steve, asking if I'd be interested in playing a Fourth of July gig in Alton. We had just played there last year, as part of our "last hoorah." The Altonians had such a good time, they insisted on having us again. When Randy Erwin informed them that we had doubled our price, they didn't flinch. The gig was booked.

On the third of July, I headed to Alton. Here I met John, Steve, Bill, and Rongo on stage, and we ran through a rusty show. I had been playing eight-mile-high bass solos on a nightly basis. Some of the others hadn't touched their instruments since last summer.

When we went on stage, our St. Louis area crowd rose to their feet, raised their Budweiser cans into the air, and cheered with holiday glee. We sounded like hell. But no one seemed to mind. We took the money and ran, agreeing to do it again—if it entailed our doubled price.

Then, when I explained how the Byrds never carried any gear, this also became part of our contract. Now, not only had we doubled our price, we didn't have to bring anything with us but our guitars. If it was good enough for the Byrds, it was good enough for the Ducks.

For the remainder of 1992, we played nine of these gigs. All were good-paying. All were big festivals on big stages. All were big fun. Most didn't sound too good, which became easier for me to swallow. I figured if everyone else was just going to go through the motions, all I had to do was show up and act like a chicken for a couple of hours. No problem.

For the rest of the year, it was easy to juggle the two schedules. The Ducks played nine gigs. The Byrds played forty. When New Year's Eve rolled around, I headed back to Springfield, back into John Q's ballroom, and back into an avalanche. It still didn't sound very good. But it was fun. Once again, we took the money and ran.

In 1993, we played thirty-one of these gigs—enough to make a nice living.

As 1994 began, after a fifteen-year absence, we received a phone call from an old friend—Jerry Moss.

He wasn't calling to chitchat. He wasn't calling to offer us a record deal. He was, though, calling to offer us a publishing deal. He and Herb had just sold A&M to mega-conglomerate Universal Records for a mega-check with mega-zeroes on it. While reprioritizing his life, one of the things he always wanted—but never was able to have—was the publishing rights to our songs. He laid an offer on the table we couldn't refuse.

Publishing company buyouts happen every day. Traditionally, they're based on the following formula: Earnings for the past three years are totaled. That's the price tag. Simple as that. When Jerry offered ten years, our ears perked up. This would put a substantial amount of money into each of our pockets, Randy and Buddy included. This would also mean boarding up the doors of Lost Cabin Music. The vote was 6-0.

When Jerry cast his line into the water, we bit. On May 16, 1994, he wrote us a very generous check. He's a generous man. Like we always had, we split the money on the spot and scattered. Once again, this gave us a reason not to work very hard on the road. That year, we played nineteen gigs.

By this time, I was really glad I lived in Nashville, where I could work all the time.

Before I began just spending this money on thangs, I plunked it all down on a modest house on the east side of town, near the airport. I'd been here for almost three years and intended to stay. I figured if I was going to continue to fly in and out of town—which I intended to do—I might as well live near the airport. I was elated when I moved out of that tiny apartment and into an actual house. Thanks, Mr. Moss.

After having retained our publishing royalties for more than twenty years, the checks no longer passed through Springfield. From now on, they would pass through Jerry's hands.

After cruising through 1994 on Jerry's money, in 1995, we would make two records—one we're very proud of, and one we were not.

Read on, my friend. We're almost done.

CHAPTER 33

After the dissolution of Good Karma in 1984, both Stan and Paul had sporadically kept in touch—Plesser from the same modest suburban Kansas City home he had occupied since his Cowtown days, Peterson from his modest third-floor apartment, two blocks from the front door of Hollywood's famed Whiskey A Go Go.

Though things remained cordial, contact had waned. When Paul called in the fall of '94, the deal was simple. It had only been six months since we had sold Lost Cabin. When he was contacted by Eclipse Records, asking if the Ozark Mountain Daredevils would be interested in making a record, he called us with this same question.

Happy, happy, joy, joy? Not so fast.

1) The deal? Simple.
2) The amount of money? Substantial.
3) The amount of recording time? Ridiculous.

Of these options, the first two interested us greatly. The third caused us to scratch our heads. Due to the first two, though, we listened to all three.

Even though it is done on an everyday basis, licensing original master tapes can be quite expensive—especially hit records. Both, "Jackie" and "Heaven" had been licensed numerous times, finding their way onto "Hits of the '70s" compilations.

It Shined

This was not Eclipse's cup of tea. It was cheaper for them to pay us a lump sum of money to come to Nashville and re-record enough of our old songs to fill out a new record.

Once the new versions were recorded, we would receive our check and relinquish control of the master tapes. From here, we would have no further say-so about their fates or their journeys. We would, however, have a chunk of change in the bank.

They housed us at the historic Hermitage Hotel in downtown Nashville. Recording time at the futuristic Iliad Studios—smack dab in the heart of Nashville's bustling Second Avenue District—was booked.

We all agreed on the songs—"Black Sky," "Homemade Wine," "It'll Shine When It Shines," "Fly Away Home," "Country Girl," "You Made It Right," "Walkin' Down the Road," "Chicken Train," "Jackie," and "Heaven."

It'd be a piece of cake. We'd been playing these songs for twenty-three years. Now all we had to was play them in three days.

Not three days to cut tracks.

Not three days for three songs.

Three days to do everything—play, sing, AND overdub. Then we would leave, and the tapes would be mixed—which we also had no control over. Eventually they would be released.

Publishing money would, of course, go to Jerry. But Universal would have no control over these new recordings. Option number two was substantial. This would insure that there would be no need or desire for extensive touring that year. We played twenty gigs.

We agreed that the best way to do ten songs in three days was to set up in the studio as if we were doing a live gig. To ready ourselves, we went out and played a handful of fairs to re-acquaint ourselves with the songs. Then it was off to Tennessee.

I was already in Tennessee. As the rest of the guys checked into this glorious old Southern hotel, I was handed a key to a room. I didn't need it. Why would I want to stay in a hotel when all I had to do was drive home? I turned it back in.

When I called Larry to ask if he had ever heard of Iliad Studios, the conversation was brief:

"Larry, have you ever heard of Iliad Studios?"

"No."

We both knew right where it was—because of the address. I'd only been in a few studios around town. Larry had been in almost all of them. When we asked if he'd like to join us when it came time to sing, he agreed. Vocals were only going to take one day. Plus, he was curious to see the place.

Presiding over the Cumberland River, Nashville's Second Avenue is a bustling four-block stretch of cobblestone, lampposts, cowboys, cowgirls, restaurants, souvenir shops, and history, lined with the sturdy, handsome brick buildings that once housed the city's everyday river commerce. When you walk down the street, you are offered a quaint, old feel.

When you walked through the heavy, wrought-iron doors and descended into the bowels of Iliad, things became anything but quaint or old.

When the elevator opened onto the basement complex, it wasn't a step back in time. It was a step directly into the future. With a massive recording console that resembled the Starship *Enterprise*, there were more knobs, faders, blinking lights, computer screens, and monitors than you could shake ten sticks at.

Outside, horse-drawn carriages may have clacked along the stone walks. Inside, a state-of-the-art studio quietly hummed.

Here we met producer/engineer Bob Wright, who told us he was used to making these "three-day" records. A massive studio sprawled throughout the entire basement of this hulking building, and we set up in a very small portion of it.

Because we were playing well, and because we were well acquainted with the songs, by the end of the first day, all ten tracks were cut. Some had a wart or two. But none really sucked. John brought his mouth bow and we tried to recreate the original sound of "Chicken Train," which, for the past fifteen years, had sported a Bo Diddley beat. Though weak, we did the best we could. Plus, Bob couldn't record the mouth bow like Glyn could.

Throughout it all, focus remained on the big picture—the pot at the end of the rainbow.

The next day, we added vocals. Besides Steve singing "Black Sky" and me singing "Homemade Wine," John sang the rest of the songs. When Bob requested that Larry not sing a lead vocal if he wasn't going to be in the band, no one had a problem with it. John sang "Jackie."

The third day, using a "strength in numbers" approach, we all gathered around a pair of microphones to sing backgrounds. Larry and Canway dropped by to sweeten things up, which Bob didn't have a problem with. We had a great time singing and laughing all day. Then we all went out for sushi and sake.

Afterward, things were tidied up and percussion added. By the end of that third day, we were done. On the fourth day, everyone was on their way to Missouri. On the fourth day, I was on my way to the bank.

The next week, I returned to add some mandolin tracks. When I played "Homemade Wine," I found that Bob had had a Nashville fiddler come in to redo John's fiddle part. This didn't matter. When the record came out, other than the title—"Jackie Blue" by the Ozark Mountain Daredevils, featuring Michael Granda, John Dillon, and Steve Cash—there was absolutely no information on it.

The packaging was horrendous—a poorly colorized copy of our Phelps Grove park bench photo. Luckily, John, Steve, and I were sitting next to each other. Larry was simply chopped off one side of the picture, Buddy and Randy off the other.

The marketing budget was nothing. Retail price was not $11.95 at Tower Records. This was because you could not find it at Tower Records. You could, though, buy it for five bucks at the Tower Truck Stop in Flagstaff, Arizona. It was made cheaply so it could be sold cheaply.

We knew we'd be joining the ranks of Chuck Berry, Little Richard, Patsy Cline, Slim Whitman, Johnny Paycheck, B.J. Thomas and Engelbert Humperdinck, who all sported low-budget discs on the shelves—I mean truck stops—of America.

Over the years, the long, strange trip of these recordings has turned in small, incestuous circles. Several years later, after Eclipse had pressed up and peddled a couple thousand copies, they sold the rights to another company, who repackaged the same tracks under a different title. A few years after that, the same thing took place again, and yet another company released them. These same recordings of these same ten songs can be found under almost a dozen different titles. We recommend none of them.

Benny Smith had been a fan, as well as a friend of the band for some time. "John [Dillon] had my father, Dr. Sam Smith, as a college professor," he recalls. "Dad was a theology professor at Drury. That's where I first heard John's music."

Since his school days in the '60s, when he walked down the hallways of Parkview High School and burned up the dance floor of the Half-a-Hill Club, he'd found his way from Southern Missouri to Southern California. Here, he settled and began raising a family, claiming, "I got invited out to California by a girl. I went for one weekend and stayed for five years."

Through it all, he never failed to keep many of his Ozark ways. One of those things was his love of our music. "I had heard about what was going on with you guys. One day, while listening to the radio in Southern California—a weird radio, at that—I heard 'If You Want to Get to Heaven.' There was just something about the sound that day that made me say, 'I know this.' When the disc jockey said, 'That was the Ozark Mountain Daredevils,' I was glad to see friends from Springfield doing something."

He may not have been in the crowd when we played the Bijou or the Landers. But he was in the crowd on that November '74 day, when we played the Santa Monica Civic Center with the Burritos. He arrived with bells on and a whole slew of friends in tow.

The late '70s found him relocating his family back to a simpler life in the Ozarks and into the cattle and hay business. One of his neighbors was Steve Cash. "I'd see him at the grocery store—Wood's Market in Buffalo—and we began talking about our farms."

In the early '80s, he took up another of his interests. "In 1981, I was invited by a friend who was interested in stock car racing—like me—to take a look at this used race car. The guy made me a heck of a deal. So I bought it and went racing. It was a big block Dodge with a highway patrol motor, and it was ready to go."

Painted white with green and yellow stripes, "Benny Smith in the #12 car," got sponsorships from John Deere and McCurry's Farm Supply for tires, fuel, and fenders.

"The first day out in my race car, I won the race at the Bolivar Speedway. Then I was just addicted and began running two or three nights a week, following the race circuit around Southwest Missouri—the Lebanon Speedway, the Branson Speedway, the Monett Speedway, and the Airport

Speedway in Springfield. We reached speeds of maybe ninety miles an hour—sideways.

"In 1988, as a direct result of my divorce, I ceased racing. You know, if you won the race, you only got forty or fifty bucks. You spent more than that just getting there. The expense of racing was no longer something I could handle."

He sadly finishes, "I also had to get rid of the farm."

In the early '90s, when his family returned to California, Benny was forced to move into Springfield. One of the first things he wanted to do was refamiliarize himself with the local music scene, arriving just in time to watch me eat Thanksgiving dinner on stage at the Regency. He instantly identified with the freewheeling. Having been friends with Don for years, he immediately started hanging out with my band, falling in love with our music and our crowd, many of whom were old friends.

Though he had been gone for years, Benny quickly and easily reverted back into being a Springfield guy—a phenomenon that occurs with many people who move away from the place. As he helped the Sandwiches get from set to set—and shot to shot—he became an honorary member. We dubbed him our Ambassador of Goodwill.

Soon, Benny's assistance would transfer right over, as he began tagging along to help out the Ducks the same way he did with the Sandwiches.

On top of all this, he had a nice, big van that could comfortably accommodate everyone, claiming, "I just tried to help with the caravan of people and vehicles that were trying to get places." This meant we no longer had to deal with Hertz and Avis. As quickly as he became a Sandwich, he became a Duck.

During a quiet moment on one of our multi-hundred-mile treks, John, Steve, and I mulled about how unfulfilling our Iliad experience had been—and how we'd really like to make a new tape with new tunes. We all thought this was a great idea. When we contacted Larry, he thought so too. When Randy was invited to participate, he also agreed to come in. There wouldn't be a whole lot of overhead. We all decided to take a stab at it.

Though we all had become quite adept in the studio, Larry agreed to take on the lion's share of the production duties. After all, he had a pretty good track record when it came to making records.

Unlike what we had done many times over the years, instead of trying to do too much at once, we would concentrate on six songs, finish them, and not leave behind a bushel basket of rags and remnants.

Lastly, and most importantly, we all agreed that things were to remain fun. If we ever lost this sense, the plug would be pulled.

Larry and I made the drive from Nashville, as we all convened at Nick Sibley's Ozark Sound Studios on the corner of Walnut and Campbell in downtown Springfield. The band would consist of five original members, John, Larry, Steve, Randy, and me, along with Bill and Rongo. A week of studio time was blocked and booked.

Embedded in an old building that once housed a garment store, we were a mere two blocks from the town square and three blocks from the Landers Theater. Nick's large room, used primarily for his jingle business, was reminiscent of Olympic. With its high ceilings, brick walls, and wooden-planked floors, there was plenty of room to stretch out, hang out, and move around.

The recording console, on the other hand, was the complete antithesis of the console we had just used in Nashville. In place of Iliad's Starship *Enterprise* was Nick's S.S. *Minnow*, complete with vintage recording gear strewn everywhere about the room. He knew his equipment, as well as its many, many idiosyncrasies. This frustrated Larry—who would soon take over engineering duties—to no end.

We set up in the big room, just like we had at Olympic—all in a semicircle, facing each other, so as to play off each other. With Bill, Ron, and I providing a funky, chunky track, John sat with his guitar, Larry sat with his, Randy sat with a mandolin, and Steve wandered in and out with his harps.

We had the best of both worlds—Bill, Rongo, and I providing a solid sandwich foundation, with Randy and Larry re-instituted on top of it. The sound was nice and full—a sound much more suited for Tower Records than the Tower Truck Stop.

When Nick hit the red button, we were off. When he did, we began singing, playing, drinking beer, cracking jokes, and having a good time.

Because we didn't want to use Mike Robertson's versions of "I'm Still Dreaming," "Everywhere She Goes," "Over Again," and "Love Is Calling," new versions were easily cut.

It Shined

When Larry offered his song, "Where Are We?" it was thrown into the mix. Bill took to the song's Beatlesque arrangement like crazy. Larry's smooth vocal added his essential spice.

Bill's running gag was, whenever someone mentioned the title of the song, he would answer, "I don't know." We also heartily laughed, retelling the story of Rune, misunderstanding the opening doo-wop vocal line to "I Only Have Eyes for You." From then on, the running gag between Rongo, Bill (who went ballistic when he heard Rune's tale), and me was to continually ask each other if they'd washed their butt. Our Ambassador of Goodwill sat in the back of the room, taking the occasional photograph.

When I offered "Standing on the Corner of Live & Learn," one of the new tunes I had written in Nashville, everyone jumped right on it. In an instant, it turned into a Neil Youngish, electric/acoustic country song. Bill added the chunky baritone guitar part I hummed to him, as Randy strummed on the mandolin. Steve wailed the harp solos.

When it was suggested that Randy try singing it, I led him to the microphone and led him through the melody. His textured, country voice laid down a wonderful vocal track. When he, John, and Larry sang the choruses, they sounded like a million bucks. By the end of the day, the song sounded like ten million.

By the end of the week, we were all juiced up. A second session was booked for later that spring. Until then, we had a tape with the original guys on it. Hopefully, this time around, we could get a record label to listen to it. We garnered less interest than Mike and Wendy had.

"Since that [label interest] did not happen," Benny continues, "I remember thinking, 'This shouldn't just stay on the shelf, getting dusty.' I went to the primary members of the band, made an offer to form a label, borrow the money to finish the project, manufacture them, and at least take them to shows."

We carried on. After having had a month to listen to what we'd done, when we reconvened at Nick's, we all eagerly came to the table with opinions about what we thought we needed to make a well-rounded record. The first thing we had to deal with was Randy, who had decided not to participate any further.

When he requested that all of his parts be erased, this was met with outbursts of "What?" and "Aaawww. Not again." We started hitting the erase button. There was no time to waste. Nor was there any desire to try to talk him out of it. The consensus was, "We've been through all this shit before. If he doesn't want to be here …"

The rest of us got down to the task at hand—having a good time making music. This meant I would have to re-sing "Standing on the Corner of Live & Learn." Though the vocal blend wasn't as smooth, it's still a cool song, becoming a solid part of our live shows—what few we were doing.

John and Steve did the bouncy, acoustic "Dream-O." It immediately took its place as the opening track. "Bar Hoppin,'" their ode to this time-tested American tradition, would end the disc.

Larry offered his mellow "If It's True," I offered "In the Day, in the Night," and John offered "Tear in the Rain"—all tunes that had been finished with Steve's lyrical help.

Steve blasted into "Bad Road," a driving harmonica tune, and "New York," a muscular beat poem, filled with colorful street scenes from the Big Apple. Both were very up tempo. I dug it.

This time, we decided to go ahead and cut all of the tracks, even if by the end of the week they were in various stages of completion. An additional week in July was booked to finish them. Benny footed the bill. He was serious about putting this record out.

Plus, Larry and I had had enough of Springfield. It had been almost five years since I had relocated to Nashville, and it was almost fifteen years for him. Both of us love Springfield, Missouri, but our homes were now in Tennessee—and we'd been away from home for a time.

He had projects on his plate, and so did I. In addition to playing gigs with Vassar Clements, Wanda Jackson, and the Brooklyn Cowboys, a hippie amalgamate that featured Vassar, Buddy Cage, Walter Egan, Joy Lynn White, Michael Webb, and Fred Perry, I began a very productive writing relationship with Rockpile's Billy Bremner.

When Billy and I met, we hit it off instantly—a couple of geezer rock 'n' rollers. In addition to writing a bunch of songs, we put a small combo together, which was a perfect blend of our bands. When we played, we sounded like Ozark Mountain Rockpile. Our very un-Nashville-like songs, "Green with Envy," "Wheel of Misfortune," and "Road to Love," would find their way onto his solo albums with his Swedish backup band, the Refreshments.

Along with all this, I had auditioned for and gotten the role of a drug dealer in Collin Raye's 1996 video, "I Think about You." The morning audition was easy. So was the evening of filming. All I had to do was hang around in a leather jacket and pretend I was a stoned goofball in a smoky apartment. Piece of cake. The video would go on to win the Country Music Association's 1996 video of the year.

Over the course of the summer, I would land parts in a couple of other videos—a biker, getting beaten up by his biker girlfriend in BR-549's "Cherokee Boogie," and Trisha Yearwood's shrink in "Everybody Knows."

That July, a few days before Larry and I returned to Springfield to put the final touches on the album, I retrieved a phone message that made me listen thrice, to make sure it wasn't one of my friends playing a trick on me.

Message machine: BEEEEP.

Voice: "Yeah. This is Chet Atkins and I'm interested in finding the person that wrote 'Ode to Mel Bay.' You might be the person, or you might know who did it. I've written some new words to it and everything, and I'd like to talk to you about that. I'm at 329-0401. We'll be here until about 6:30. You can leave a message on our phone service, if you would. Thanks a lot."

After a second listening, it was clearly him. The first thing I did the next morning was call the number. His secretary put me right through. Chet had already cut the song and had simply called the number on the demo tape. That number was mine.

I remembered when a young, clean-cut man approached me after an animated Sandwich show at the Boardwalk. He shook my hand with a friendly, "Hello. My name's John Burns. Do you have a copy of that Mel Bay song? Mr. Bay and my father [Jethro Burns] put out several mandolin books together."

After gladly giving him the Nashville handshake, I thought nothing further of it. That is, until he played the song for his Uncle Chet, who recorded it on the spot.

When I heard his version, I couldn't believe my ears. Not only was he doing my song—which was the utmost compliment—he included my musical joke—a sophomoric "Red River Valley" guitar solo. My cap acquired not one but two very large feathers.

For five years, I had been playing that song for every country artist in Nashville, confident that one of them would want to pay homage to Mr. Bay. But every one of them was stuck in the muck of relationship songs. Completely disgusted and discouraged, I'd given up on pitching it to anybody. As soon as I did this, the silly thing found its own way into Chet Atkins's hands and onto his 1996 Columbia album, *The Day Finger Pickers Took Over the World*, with Australian guitar wizard Tommy Emmanuel.

When Chet asked who owned the publishing rights, I informed him that I did. Realizing how lucrative Lost Cabin had been over the years, I took the same approach with Missouri Mule Music. Shunning writing deals with Music Row's cookie-cutter publishing houses, I stuck to my guns and my publishing. I was willing to eat tuna until my ship came in with a big, juicy steak on it.

"Good!" he exclaimed. "We won't have to deal with a bunch of lawyers. You can have the royalties. I don't need royalties. I just love the song. I think it's very clever, and I want my name on it. Here's how we should credit it: 'written by Michael Granda and Mark Denny, with additional lyrics by Chet Atkins.'"

All I could mutter was, "Uh. Yes, sir."

Though by this time, he was starting to feeble, every time we met, he would ask with a sparkle in his eye, "Are you still doing our song in your shows?" When I assured him that I was, I asked him the same question. When he assured me he was, we both had a nice chuckle.

When "Finger Pickers" was released, he and Tommy appeared on the Nashville Network's nightly cable show, *Nashville NOW*. I attended the taping. When Chet and I met in the hallway, he asked if we could speak in private. I knew something was up.

"I gotta admit something to you," he confided. "I didn't write that third verse. Shel Silverstein did. He's a friend of mine and he owed me a couple of favors. I decided to call one of 'em in. I sang him the song over the phone and he called me back about twenty minutes later with the words."

It Shined

> On Page 21, you taught us how to play a G.
> On Page 22, you taught us how to play a D.
> But Lordy, oh Lordy, we never learned to play an E.
> Cause some guy in the outhouse stole Page 23.

Now I really couldn't believe my ears. It was pure Shel, and as plain as the Polish nose on my face. To hell with all of those new, young country-singer guys, their hats, their attitudes, the horse they rode in on—AND their relationship songs. Mr. Atkins was doing one of my funny tunes, Mr. Silverstein had written a verse, and Mr. Bay, we surely would've never, ever learned how to play. I thank thee three.

A few days later, when Larry and I headed back to Springfield, I was beside myself. I'd just gotten my first cut. Needless to say, the week at Nick's was a spirited one. We got back down to work, as each song received its final touches.

This didn't happen, though, without a major effort from Larry, who on several occasions, would turn to me and say, "Where the hell is everyone?" As the Springfield guys came and went—when there were kids to be picked up, dinner to be eaten, or something on TV—Larry and I remained in the captains' chairs.

By the end of the week, when everything was done, he and I were quite frazzled. As he left for Nashville, I stayed in Springfield to make a run of gigs around the Midwest. All I wanted to do was get back to Nashville and hear Chet sing "Mel Bay." In the meantime, I sang "Homemade Wine" and "Live & Learn" at the Cotillion Ballroom in Wichita, Kansas, the Buffalo Rose in Golden, Colorado, and the Trempeleau Hotel in Trempeleau, Wisconsin.

On top of everything, Larry had had it with Nick's rickety gear—which continued to be in a constant state of discombobulation. We knew the nice, full mixes these songs deserved would not be possible here. That August, John and Steve came to Nashville for four days of mixing time at Recording Arts, a quiet, unassuming house in a quiet, unassuming neighborhood in the shadows of Nashville's famed Parthenon.

Owned by Rhode Island native Carl Tatz, he recalls, "When we walked in, Larry and I really dug what they'd done with the place, with all the skylights. So, we bought it, moved our gear in, and named it Leche Sound. Plus, we needed somewhere to put Larry's grand piano."

When we first met Carl in '75, while making *Car Over the Lake*, he was the wickedly funny maitre d' at Julian's. Over the years, he and Larry had remained in auditory as well as culinary touch, recalling, "Larry and Norbert spent a lot of time and money at Julian's.

"After a couple years, [Larry] wanted to build his house, so I bought him out of the studio, and changed the name to Recording Arts. He still continued to work here all the time. We were there for eighteen years."

The two became acclaimed producers. Larry used the room to mix several of Alabama's platinum records. Carl used it to mix Jack Jones's 2000 Grammy-nominated *Tribute to Tony Bennett*. The place had a wide variety of clients.

Though Alan Jackson's *Don't Rock the Jukebox* came from the place, it became known as a place where Johnny Paycheck and his Muddy Cowboys wouldn't feel very comfortable. Hugh Padgett did, though. So did Levon Helm, Mark Knopfler, and Don Was, who used the place to produce Felix Cavaliere's 1994 *Dreams in Motion*. Did I mention a wide variety of clients?

We fit right in. Carl gave us a "brother-in-law" deal.

Twenty years ago, we all sat around, laughing, at Julian's. Now we were all sitting around, laughing, at Carl's. The place more than compensated for all of the scraped knuckles we put up with at Nick's. This was one instance where we really were actually going to be able to "fix it in the mix."

One by one, each song got a good polishing. By the end of August, we handed them off to Benny. When he asked if we had any artwork, we got right to work. Actually, this had been happening while we were mixing—which became one continuous, "name the album" cocktail party.

Steve pulled out an old postcard he had kept in the back of his desk—as well as the back of his mind—for years, depicting five mountain climbers, just about to reach the snow-capped peak of a jagged mountain ridge. It was perfect. We all fell in love with it.

The first thing we did was run through the song titles, to see if any would fit as an album title. None seemed to, though I thought "Over Again" did on a few levels. I felt the lyrics, "Here we go. Over again. Feel that sail filling up with the wind," carried the appropriate message. The climbers on the cover were about to go over the mountain. We were about to put out our first record in a long time. Essentially, we WERE starting over again.

This, as well as all other ideas, was quickly squelched, as Steve began to emphatically insist on *13*. As the rest of us scratched our heads, wondering what in the world that number had to do with this wonderful photograph, his rationale was: 1) There were thirteen songs on it (correct); 2) it was our first album in thirteen years (It was actually fifteen years); and 3) thirteen was his lucky number (a luck none of us was that anxious to obtain).

As each subsequent suggestion emerged, he kept coming back and harping on *13*. Each time, the harping grew louder and more adamant. Eventually, the rest of us wore down, caving in with, "Okay. Okay. Okay. We'll call it *13*."

In June 1997, *13* hit the streets of Springfield. I would say it hit the streets of America, but it didn't. It was Benny's first attempt at selling records. Though he kept the record stores in town stocked, stacks of discs remained in his garage. "New Era had lots of inventory," he chuckles.

I would often remind him, "Herb and Jerry started A&M out of their garage in Hollywood. You can start New Era out of yours in Springfield."

"New Era's mission is dedicated to the preservation of the Ozark Mountain Daredevils music catalog," Benny decrees. "I began thinking if there was just some way to help these guys. Seeing the band in the '90s, floundering at fairground shows, small bars, and so on, I thought there just had to be more at this stage of things. It was just, 'Go do the gig. Go home.' That was about the excitement level of it. The band was just getting lost out there. This band has a track record that should not just dissolve into nothing.

"Then, one of our best fans in the world approached me. Kansas City native Dennis Pratt had a home-designed Web site dedicated to the band and their music. It was already up and running. It had the history, a discography, and a schedule of gigs. But it didn't have a sales page on it. We met and opened a store. This was a good way to access this new music directly from the band."

This garnered some sales, but the woods weren't exactly being set on fire. Having spent all of his money on manufacturing, there wasn't much left for promotion. Tom and Pam Pierson offered to sell *13* in

Kaleidoscope. At one time, they ordered our albums by the thousands. This time, they ordered our disc in boxes of thirty.

Though it didn't make a pebble ring on the *Billboard* charts, those loyal fans who found it were able to enjoy our first new music in more than fifteen—I mean, thirteen—years.

Benny asked to use our most recent publicity photo of the band (John, Steve, Bill, Rongo, and myself) for the back cover. This would help him sell discs at gigs. When we finished playing, like Lumpy, he would quickly set up a small mercantile and begin hawking T-shirts and discs. This he did very well. (Insert "sell an icemaker to an Eskimo" adage here.)

As he talked tirelessly with the fans, he pleaded tirelessly with the band, asking for its cooperation to help get his endeavor off the ground. When he suggested that if we played a few more gigs, we would sell a few more discs, he met a stone wall. The vote was two to one.

I had been making this same suggestion unsuccessfully for years. Benny didn't stand much of a chance today. I warned him about it right from the start. In 1997, to support our new record, we played thirty gigs. Wherever we went, people ate it up. We just didn't go many places. The following year, we played twenty.

In quieter moments, he frustratedly confided in me about the lack of input he was getting. All I could say was, "Sorry, man. I warned you." Still, he remained determined to keep New Era afloat and the music of the Ozark Mountain Daredevils alive—even if the Ozark Mountain Daredevils didn't seem to care.

Bill, even more frustrated with the prevailing winds, began to refer to an ever-dwindling schedule as our "Lack of Interest Tour." All he (and I) could do was shrug our shoulders at the talented local musicians we continued to work with on a regular basis. These wonderful players (who would've given their left nut to trade places), as well as our friends (who knew who was and wasn't doing what), knew which way the wind was blowing.

While people who heard 13 were digging it, one of their other main concerns was the fact that none of our older music was available on disc. Not only had they worn the grooves off their vinyl, many no longer even owned a turntable. The format had definitely switched over to CD, and we were being left in the dust. Phone calls to Universal on the topic garnered exactly as much interest as phone calls to A&M had—ZERO.

"Benny, you'll talk to anybody," Bill would often bellow. His second phone call to Hollywood was met with the same indifference as his first. His two hundredth found its way in. Once he was in, he was in like Flynn.

While A&M had expressed no interest in releasing those albums, Universal did. There wouldn't be any recording costs. All they had to do was dig out the old tapes, dust them off, and remaster them. If that was too much to ask, Benny proposed Plan B.

Universal became quite interested in Benny's Plan B—license the tapes himself and carry the ball from Springfield. When he asked about the licensing fee for *It'll Shine*, it was too high—due to the fact that the album included a hit song. Such was the case with the quilt album. When Benny asked about *Car Over the Lake*, the price was much more reasonable. Along with the assistance of local banker, Jim Huff, New Era got a much-needed financial shot in the arm. Wheels were put into motion.

Over the past twenty years, while we were rising through the ranks of the music industry, Huff—an old friend and avid fan of the band—had been climbing the rungs of the banking ladder. Sitting at the head of the board for the People's Bank of Nixa, he approved loans for local farmers in need of tractors, trucks, and chicken feed. When we were in need of amps and trucks and personal loans, a handshake was all that was needed to obtain one.

When Benny walked into Jim's office, explaining how he wanted to start releasing our music on disc, he received no resistance. In conjunction with the People's Bank, when New Era Productions called Universal Records, wheels were greased.

Realizing that this goofy guy from Missouri, who incessantly kept calling, just might be on to something, Universal agreed to license *Car*. Along with this, they put out a greatest hits package.

"Their catalog research man, Mike Ragogna, contacted me and said, 'We're getting ready to take a look at the Daredevils and some of the other artists in A&M history,'" Benny recalls. "'We heard you may have some information about the band.'"

In time for the Christmas holiday season of 2000, *Time Warp, the Greatest Hits of the Ozark Mountain Daredevils* hit the shelves. Complete with a tasteful twelve-page booklet, the twenty-one-song retrospective was a much better representation than the feeble package A&M had put out as a contractual obligation two decades ago.

Benny continues, "*Time Warp* was a nice success for them [Universal]. But they said, 'We may do another compilation, but we won't do entire albums.' That following spring, New Era released *The Car Over the Lake Album*. I had to order 5,000 copies. So I went to Jim. He made it possible to get the series of reissues started. Each license was actually for 10,000 copies—5,000 on the first pressing, and another 5,000 over a three-year period."

This time, after large amounts of blood, sweat, and tenacity, Benny had a much easier time selling copies of *Car Over the Lake Album* than he did selling copies of *13*. That fall, he and Jimmy went through the process again. *Men from Earth* was released.

Our music benefited greatly from this new format. You could clearly hear all the sounds and subtleties we'd put into each song. Rolled into the deal, Benny included extra songs that hadn't made it onto any album.

Car Over the Lake Album contained the three songs from the Little Red Record: "Establish Yourself," "Time Warp," and "Journey to the Center of Your Heart."

Men from Earth contained my "Roscoe's Rule" from Caribou, Steve's "Dollar's Worth of Regular" from Nashville, and Randy's "Better Days" from Ruedi Valley.

Our fans were ecstatic. Not only were they finally getting to play our music in their CD players, they were hearing songs they'd never heard before. I was also ecstatic. Several of the songs that would see the light of day for the first time were mine.

With a more cooperative Universal and an ever cooperative People's Bank, New Era was up and running. One by one, the rest of our albums began to get released, with the proceeds from one being funneled directly into the creation of the next. By 2004, every album we ever made was available to the public—thanks to Benny Smith and Jim Huff.

Unfortunately, Benny was still dealing with a band that, in 2001, with three new albums on the shelves, played thirteen gigs. In 2002, we played five. In 2003, we played two. In 2004, we played for the last time. The vote was two to one.

As record after record began to come to life, Duck after Duck began to lose theirs.

It was a beautiful Saturday morning when my phone began ringing off the hook, each call casting a shadow thick enough to blot out the most magnificent of suns. The headlines of the September 26, 1999 *Nashville Banner* (the morning after) read, "Former Ozark Mountain Daredevil Dies in Plane Crash."

Brian Mansfield wrote, "Former Ozark Mountain Daredevils member, Stephen Canaday was killed Saturday (Sept. 25) when the vintage airplane in which he was riding crashed into a vacant house in Nashville.

"Canaday, 55, joined the Ozark Mountain Daredevils in 1977. More recently, he had worked at a Nashville photographic supply store and as a tour manager for country singer Lee Roy Parnell and Nashville folk-rocker, Marshall Chapman."

The *Tennesseean*'s Jay Orr elaborated. "Several Germantown residents poured out of their homes and businesses yesterday and tried to help two men whose vintage airplane crashed through the treetops, skidded across a lawn and smacked against an unoccupied triplex on Fifth Avenue North. Both men died.

"No one on the ground was injured. As of last night, the cause was still undetermined. Officials were trying to determine who was piloting the North American SNJ-5 World War II-era, single-engine trainer plane. Startled witnesses watched on the clear day as the plane took a right turn over Bicentennial Capitol Mall, dipped in a spiral, pulled up and then nose-dived into the historic neighborhood.

"The plane may have turned originally to allow photographs. 'The pilot had a photographer and was doing some low-level work,' said Keith Stem, Federal Aviation Administration investigator." While Loudermilk was signed on as the pilot, officials last night said that type of plane could be flown from the back or front seat and they weren't certain who had control at the time.

"One neighbor had praise for the pilot. 'If he hadn't of pulled out of that spiral, he would have taken out two of my neighbors' houses and ours.'"

Lee Roy recalls the night before. "The night before it happened, he [Steve] met us at the bus, as we pulled out at midnight—just to see us off. He came by and sat for thirty or forty minutes and began to talk about this adventure he was going on the next day. That next morning, phones started ringing all over the bus. They came back and got me and said, 'Man, I've got some bad, bad news.'"

On a brighter note, Lee Roy points out, "At least he was doing two of the things he loved to do—flying airplanes and photography."

If shockwaves reverberated through Nashville, Springfield was devastated. Before we made the lonesome trek back, we had to make the lonesome trek into Steve's house to retrieve his things. "That was real hard," sighs Mike Robertson.

Though it was a sad day, it was a high-profile funeral—in direct contrast to Rusty's several years earlier. When Rusty left the V, he headed further into the Ozark woods and a reclusive life. When Canway left the V, he stayed in the big-city spotlight. These two men were essential to the early DNA of the band. Now, both were gone.

A couple of years later, after a long, arduous battle with lung cancer, Charlie McCall finally succumbed. The *News-Leader* reported, "McCall had a great passion for music, working as road manager for Granny's Bathwater and the Ozark Mountain Daredevils in the late 1970s, and through the '80s. He was currently working for Silver Dollar City as the stage manager for Echo Hollow."

The following spring, Roscoe Jones died. Over the years, we had often invited him to join us on stage. Lumpy would set up an extra microphone and hand him a harmonica in the correct key. As we all sang "It'll Shine," the diminutive man would stand right in the middle of us and play along—just as he had at the Trout Farm, twenty years earlier. He was a crowd favorite.

On July 23, 2004, we got hit with a double whammy. The *News-Leader*'s Michael Brothers described the scene: "What was supposed to be a big show featuring the Titanic Blues Band at the Outland on Friday night turned into a memorial of love and remembrance for Bill Brown and Don Shipps, who were killed earlier that morning in a house fire.

"The two local music icons died when they failed to escape from their burning duplex on Springfield's east side. The blaze, which started shortly after 4 a.m. Friday, took place in the 800 block of South Link Avenue and heavily damaged the duplex, said assistant fire chief, Bill Arrington.

"'The fire started around a chair in the living room and was consistent with fires started by smoking materials,' Arrington said. 'There were no smoke detectors in the unit. If there would've been, their chances (for survival) are 80 percent better.'

"Don's band, which Bill had recently joined, was scheduled to hold a live recording session with producer Lou Whitney Friday at the Outland. Instead, the time slot turned into a memorial in the heart of Springfield's music scene. The only thing more powerful than the music Bill Brown and Don Shipps played were their personalities and love for others."

When I learned of the news, shivers ran through my entire body. The scene was all too familiar to me. For years, Bill and I had been roommates on the road. I'd worried about him and seen him fall asleep/pass out with a lit cigarette in his fingers many times. As this horrible news came in, visions of smoldering furniture danced in my head. I was deeply saddened, but not overly surprised.

By now, Bill had become completely disgusted with the lack of Duck activity and had teamed up with Don for the first time since the two were Sandwiches. On my way to Springfield, in the midst of all the sorrow came the redeeming thankfulness to have known them—personally, as well as musically. They were a match made in heaven.

As the wakes and funerals took place, plans for a benefit concert were already in the works. "The original idea was Howie's," recalls Benny. "But when things started rolling, I knew I had to be a part of it."

Both Bill and Don had children. Neither man had a pot to piss in. Everyone in town started lining up to play. The gig could've gone on without us, but if John and Steve were serious about not wanting to play anymore, it would've looked pretty weird if … well, you know.

The Concert for Bill and Don was scheduled for that October. Because both were so well revered and respected around town, local businesses and organizations, as well as musicians, came out of the woodwork to donate their time and services. When the stage of the 3,000-seat Shrine Mosque was offered, the show had a home.

With a lineup that included many friends, the main draw was still the Ducks. We hadn't played but once in the past year—a thirty-minute acoustic set in the pleasant afternoon sun on the parking lot of the People's Bank. As the day for Bill and Don drew near, a strange feeling began to wash over me. This could be the last time. I don't know.

We'd threatened everyone—as well each other—with this many times over the years. But things just seemed to find a way to keep on keepin' on. This time, though, things were different. Interest was completely gone, as Bill often told the story of opening John's guitar case to find a string, still broken from the last gig months ago.

Big-money local gigs were disregarded. When officials from Springfield's Ozark Empire Fair called, offering a mouth-watering sum to help commemorate their hundredth anniversary, the two denials were, "Steve doesn't want to do it because …" and "John won't do it because …"

Both had veered completely off the musical path and into non-music endeavors—Steve, in the midst of writing his first novel, *The Meq* and John, in the midst of starting an advertising agency.

One way to not embarrass yourself in public—especially in front of friends—is to not play in public. The dissolve to nothingness was nearing completion.

The Concert to Celebrate Bill and Don was a sad but cleansing affair. Though the healing process had begun, this gig would bring closure to a lot of things, for a lot of people.

There was no way I was not going to participate, immediately agreeing to do a set with the Sandwiches, whether John and Steve played or not. Both agreed to a thirty-minute set, early in the evening. Everyone in town was thrilled.

When the night of the gig rolled in, Springfield put on its finest face. Benny observed, "There was a real nice, mellow feeling in the crowd. Everyone was there to have one last good time for the boys."

As the six-hour concert progressed, the crowd gathered in front of the stage in anticipation of our Duck set. I was scheduled to play right before, so as to already be set for the changeover. Inviting Granny's alums Bill Jones and Benny Mahan to join in, as well as Howie's Hillcats, we blasted through a very spirited six-song set.

When the Ducks were introduced, the place went bonkers. When we blasted into "Heaven," we invited all of the guitar players who had ever played with us to join in. When Terry Wilson came out to play, Joe Terry joined in on piano. When Donnie Thompson came out to play, Bill Jones wailed on his sax. Dave Painter, who was filling Bill's shoes, was already there. With each turnaround, the Mosque lifted further and further off its foundation. The roar was absolutely deafening—a genuine purging.

After catching our collective breath, we began the finale, "It'll Shine." One by one, all of the musicians began to wander on stage, buddy up to a microphone, and sing. When the song's loping middle section came around, we just allowed it to roll over and over and over again. A mass of red-eyed musicians huddled on stage in harmony, sorrow, and embrace.

When the song softly landed and folks started to wander off, I could not move. I stood silent, motionless in the middle of the stage for several minutes. Friends, arm in arm, and families with weary heads on each other's shoulders, were beginning their recovery with the medicine of music.

Not only was my heart heavy for Bill and Don, I had an eerie feeling in my heart that this very possibly might be the last time the Ducks would play. (That is, unless some rich cat somewhere ponied up the only thing that seemed to mean anything, anymore—lots of money.)

As equipment started to be shuffled around for the Misstakes, I quietly headed for a far dressing room. I did not feel like joining the party that was gearing up down the hall, or partaking in the drugs and alcohol that were going along with it.

I didn't want to talk to anyone. I didn't want to see anyone.

I just wanted to unceremoniously fade off into the distance—like my band seemed to be doing.

As the next band of merry men began to rambunctiously assemble on stage, I slipped my bass into its case, headed for a side door, and slipped into the quiet night. As the festivities inside kicked back into gear, I could hear that loud, joyous noise wafting through the air over my shoulder.

It was the beat.

EPILOGUE

The '60s were exciting, memorable times. Everyone remembers right where they were on November 23, 1963, when they heard the news of John Kennedy's assassination. Everyone remembers right where they were on July 20, 1969, when man stepped foot onto the moon for the first time. Everyone also remembers right where they were on February 9, 1964, when John, Paul, George, and Ringo stepped onto the stage of the *Ed Sullivan Show*.

I remember right where I was—in front of our black-and-white TV—just like millions of other Americans. The British Invasion was underway. I was immediately obsessed.

Along with classmate, Rick Tenting, the two of us retreated into the cocoon of a Beatles songbook. We set the book right in front of us. He already knew how to play guitar. He strummed. I sang and turned the pages. The racket we made—in the words of our fathers—was reminiscent of a "scalded cat." The joy that washed over me was reminiscent of a fat cat lying in the sun, solely content with being fat.

After the first evening, it quickly became apparent that just singing and turning pages was not going to be enough. When I noticed that not only the Beatles but every band had a bass player, a trip was made to the neighborhood music store, and information gathered about bass lessons.

With a head full of steam, my Dutch persistence, and the *Mel Bay Electric Bass Instruction Book #1* under my arm, I headed to the woodshed.

There wasn't an actual woodshed and, come to think of it, there wasn't an actual bass. Only being able to afford the eight dollars it took to rent an acoustic guitar, I tuned the top four strings to the match the corresponding strings of a bass. The woodshed was our family basement, which my father had remodeled into a Dean Martinesque rathskeller. Here, I would spend the next five years of my life with my guitar, my record collection, and tunnel vision.

Lesson one was the ingestion of the entire Mel Bay book in a matter of days. Lesson two consisted of learning "Wooly Bully," "Louie, Louie," "Do You Love Me?" and "No Particular Place to Go." I became a musical sponge, listening to anything and everything I could get my hands on.

Except for my grandfather, Theouphlis Grenda, who had been known to get his accordion out as he tended bar in his south St. Louis tavern, no one else in my family played a musical instrument. Oftentimes, the jolly man—nicknamed "Tabby"—consumed as much beer as he served.

"I hate the accordion," his wife, my dear grandmother Ethel, would cite. As she quietly bided her evenings in their second-floor apartment, directly above the noisy tavern, she recalls, "That meant Tabby had broken out the whiskey. That also meant that, when he closed the bar, he and all of his friends would be coming upstairs. I'd have to head back to the bedroom and pretend I was asleep. They wouldn't bother me or anything. But they would sit up and drink and sing all night long. I HATE the sound of the accordion."

Though no one else in my family was musically inclined, there was always music in our house, thanks to my father and his monolithic Philco hi-fi record player. While the cool big-band sounds of Louis Armstrong, Frank Sinatra, Tony Bennett, Benny Goodman, and Johnny Mathis wafted down from above, Chuck Berry, the Stones, and the Beatles blared from my little record player in the basement.

When family members gathered at our house for Sunday barbecues, many brought records with them. Vinyl discs spun all day long. But with a back-beat-infested mind, I paid little attention to the smooth soundtrack of the family fete.

That is, until one day, my favorite uncle Don brought a couple of records by Fats Domino and a bald guy named Professor Longhair.

When he put these records on the turntable, the party seemed to perk right up. When he played Spike Jones, everyone laughed—me, more than anyone.

I enjoyed my uncle's music much more than my father's. A frequent Mardi Gras reveler, I never failed to ask Don to bring those records with him. Here I learned that our St. Louis parties were being injected with a healthy dose of New Orleans rock 'n' roll. One afternoon, I asked if I could borrow his records for the week. They were immediately inserted into my play list.

My thirst for them was insatiable, as was my taste for the phonetically endowed, "Purple People Eater," "Alley Oop," "Itsy-Bitsy Teeny-Weeny Yellow Polka Dot Bikini," "Rubber Biscuit," "See Ya Later, Alligator" and "Papa-Oom-Mow-Mow." I fell in love with silly, wacky songs—the sillier and wackier the better. As I played Louis Jordan and Little Richard records over and over, I discovered they used the same progressions the Stones used.

(Note to reader: If you ever want to inject life into a sagging party, play any Rolling Stones or Fats Domino record. Watch what happens on the dance floor. It never fails.)

My thirst for music lessons was insatiable. As my instructor lopingly strummed along, I had no problem, using my knack for mathematics to read the notes of the bass clef. When the lesson was over and I'd successfully played "Red River Valley" and "Michael, Row the Boat Ashore," I would show him how I'd also learned to play "Shake, Rattle and Roll" and "Get Off My Cloud."

This ability to read music paid off immediately, affording me the ability to re-enter the Beatle book and figure out Paul McCartney's remarkable bass lines, note for note. In no time, I became well acquainted with the way he played.

My structured lesson plan was simple, consisting of a ten-week course, followed by an evaluation. If enough progress had been made, the next level of lessons would be installed. If interest wasn't being held (as is often the case in a young person's life), so be it. At this point, it became obvious who was going to sink and who was going to swim. I acquired fins and gills.

It only took a handful of lessons before my instructor advised me to stop paying for them, noting that I was learning much more on my own than I was from him.

This only threw fuel onto the fire. Rick and I recruited Bruce Crowe to play drums, and we had an instant band. Practices were no problem, as we all lived within shouting distance of each other. They usually took place on Sunday afternoons at Bruce's, because every Saturday, the three of us would head to the bus stop and catch the bus into downtown St. Louis.

Here we would spend the entire day watching a battle of the bands, sponsored by KXOK radio. On the way home, we talked about what we would do if we could ever get into one of those battles. Then we'd light into our instruments on Sunday, three suburban kids from the south side, wanting to be part of the urban musical landscape.

Like my father, Bruce's dad also had a nice hi-fi. But unlike my father, Bruce's had tape recorders, radios, tubes, soldering guns, wire, and antennae strewn all over the place. He helped us plug our only microphone into a tape recorder. Then, while simultaneously pushing the pause and record buttons, he plugged the tape recorder into his hi-fi. Ta-da. Instant PA.

I saved up enough money from a job at a neighborhood laundromat to buy a brand new Kingston bass with two pickups. Rick had the only amp—a Gibson he had bought because it was the loudest one he could find. It was perfect. It had two input jacks—one for his guitar, one for my bass.

Here, the Coachmen formed, slowly accumulating a song list made up of Chuck Berry, John Lennon, and Keith Richards songs. While all the other guys were down at the Steak 'n' Shake, idling away the hours under the hoods of their cars, the three of us spent ours listening to records and trying to figure out how to play them.

When our first gig came in, we practiced even harder. The local junior high was having their annual chili festival in the gymnasium, and the Coachmen were hired to provide the afternoon's entertainment.

Because Mr. Crowe wasn't too keen on us hauling his hi-fi around, we were forced to use the PA system that was already installed in the gym ceiling—the same one used by the principal to make his daily announcements. Though it had the tonal qualities of a nasally gymnasium PA, it was there.

As we set up in a corner, the room filled with booths and balloons, cake walks and bingo. When show time arrived, we blasted into the hits of the day. The thrill was immediate, and completely rearranged my DNA.

As the evening wound down, an older gentleman approached, a saxophone case in his hand. Looking old enough to be one of our teachers, he asked if he could sit in and play along. In the middle of my rock 'n' roll daze, I thought it was a great idea. I turned to my band mates, who had expressions of terror on their faces. We'd never had to deal with anything like this before. It had always just been the three of us—and this was our very first gig. Though they felt more comfortable sticking to the songs we had worked up, I was swinging for the fences.

Taking matters into my own hands, I turned back around with a "Sure. Come on up." I couldn't wait to see what was going to happen. To this day, I still enjoy what happens when unexpected musicians get thrown into the fray. Plus, I knew how sweet the saxophone could sound.

After climbing onto the stage—I mean, the corner of the room—came the topic of what to play. Our repertoire wasn't very extensive. Neither were our collective abilities. We had rehearsed maybe a dozen times, and only knew a couple dozen songs.

But when he turned to ask, "Do you know the *Batman* theme?" he got a unanimous nod from the Coachmen. We didn't really know how to play the song. But Adam West's *Batman* was a popular TV show of the day and we could probably fake it.

When we started, we immediately figured out how simple the song was. Then we had a great time just whooping up on it. When the sax began to wail, the popular show's theme song brought the house—I mean *gym*—down. When we finished, the audience demanded we play it again. So we did. It was back-to-back Batman at the very first gig.

The hook had been set. This is where I acquired the one-track mind that would rule and sometimes haunt the rest of my life. It became the only thing that mattered to me.

We played as many dances, parties, sock hops, and skating rinks as we could, becoming celebrities of the eighth grade. After one of our gigs, we were approached in the hallways by Terry Zwick, who said he liked our band and asked if we would be interested in becoming a quartet.

It Shined

The Coachmen Four, St. Louis, 1967 (left to right) Rick Tenting, Bruce Crowe, me, and Terry Zwick (photo by Ellen Granda)

With the addition of his Farfisa organ, it meant we would be able to expand our repertoire to include the Animals, ? & the Mysterians, and Booker T & the MG's. All were favorites. The Coachmen, unanimously voted to add a fourth member.

With the organ filling out the sound, we got more energetic. More importantly, we got louder. When the topic of changing the name of the band came up, we were faced with the first professional decision of our career. Half of us thought it wasn't such a good idea to change our name, since we had already played a number of gigs. The other half thought a name change may be a good thing.

When a compromise was struck, the Coachmen became the Carnaby Streetesque Coachmen Four. We weren't fab, but we were funky.

Terry's father was also a fine organist, whose main gig was playing all the functions held at Kiel Auditorium—current home to the St. Louis Hawks of the National Basketball Association. Occasionally, he would allow us to tag along to Hawks games and sit with him at the organ bench. Occasionally, he would let Terry play a song. I was instructed not to touch anything, which was fine with me. I had no problem keeping my hands to myself.

I was still as big a sports nut as I was a music nut, jumping at the chance to see my Hawks play. It was a double whammy for me. As I watched Mr. Zwick play music, I watched Bob Pettit play basketball. In those days, the organist was the only entertainment in the place. During time-outs and breaks in the action, he would burst into song.

I observed how he interacted and played to the crowd. When things were getting exciting and he wanted them to stand up and clap their hands, he played "Beer Barrel Polka." When he wanted them to sit back and relax, he played a soothing waltz. On the organ bench in Kiel Auditorium, I learned as much about psychology as I did about music.

With the addition of someone who had some actual musical training, Terry raised our level of playing considerably. With this, we got better gigs, playing to more people. We bought matching blue sport coats with ascots and epaulets. The act was growing and looking sporty.

Bruce, though, had other things on his mind. Standing six feet two by the ninth grade, he was being courted by the basketball coach. When instructed that, if he continued to be in a long-haired rock 'n' roll band, he would no longer be welcome on the basketball team, he succumbed to the pressure. I was just a scrawny little white kid with absolutely no aspirations of playing basketball. The Coachmen were drummerless.

Terry called young drummer, Danny David, whose father was a bandleader of renown in the area. While the Russ David Orchestra entertained the older crowds around St. Louis, Danny replaced Bruce as our drummer. Not only was he younger than we were, he also went to a different school. This meant not only were we able to play gigs at our high school, we could play gigs at his. The Coachmen Four were conquering the world one school district at a time.

One big night on Gaslight Square put a nice punctuation mark onto the end of the Coachman Four. We were just seventeen- and eighteen-year-old kids—not even old enough to drink in the club. But somehow, strings were pulled and we managed to get the gig. Then, we managed to sneak in a few drinks. This was not hard, nor was it a big deal. My grandfather had owned a tavern. I'd been drinking beer since I was four.

Though Gaslight was definitely in the twilight of its glorious reign, the party people of St. Louis saw the writing on the wall, making sure they were there to the very last note of the very last chorus, soaking up every last drop being poured.

The Coachmen Four walked right in, partaking of all the adult fun that was offered, while using Mr. Zwick's psychology of playing to the crowd. We blasted our young asses off. The result: a filled dance floor. During our breaks, the regulars would take us aside to let us know how much they liked our band, while offering nips from the flasks in their pockets. Then, everyone stepped out back.

Rick and I were able to walk a couple hundred feet up the alley and right into the back door of an adjacent club. Here we came face to face with Chuck Berry, quietly sitting at a table, having cocktails with friends. We were too stunned and starstruck to even approach the man. But when we returned to our gig, we played his songs as hard and fast as we could. Everybody rocked.

This is where I had my first taste of marijuana. Amid a gaggle of people—including a couple of waitresses and the bartender—when the joint got handed to me, I took a long drag like I knew what I was doing. Then, after coughing my ass off, it was back inside for another set.

As the lights flashed and the music began, I felt like a human pinball machine. It seemed that the harder we played, the crazier the dancing got, and the crazier the dancing got, the harder we played. As one seemed to feed off the other, we acquired a healthy dose of "get up and go." I was gone, out of my gourd.

I've always felt that the element of fun plays a very important role in this music thang. With the additional element of pot thrown into the mix, things got even more fun than they already were. On Gaslight Square, anything went—an attitude I still carry in my guitar case. On Gaslight Square, we canceled our subscriptions to *Boys' Life*.

Between my junior and senior year, the "Summer of Love" burst wide open and began to trickle into town. As the media began to cover the innovative lifestyles of Greenwich Village and Haight Ashbury, KSHE and KDNA began to expose St. Louis to the music coming from the two coasts.

Records by the Grateful Dead, the Mothers of Invention, and the Fugs began to find their way onto my turntable and into my life. I really dug the crazy pasta these guys were throwing at the rock 'n' roll wall.

Most of the summer of 1968 was spent hanging around the University City apartment of classmate and singer Ruthie Jamison, playing music and ingesting Kesey, Kerouac, Ginsberg, Zappa, Kupferberg, Sanders, herb, mushrooms, and cacti.

Needless to say, the Coachmen Four bit the dust, as neither Danny nor Terry found these new musical influences to be very interesting. The sheen had worn off our matching blue suits. I traded mine in for sandals, tie-dyed shirts, headbands, American flag bell bottoms, and hair as long as Lindbergh High School would allow.

Rick and I recruited classmates Garen Knobloch to play guitar, Roger Bogguss to play drums, and Jamison to sing. Dubbing ourselves the Illicit Affair, we acquired a much more guitar-driven line-up. Garen, with his thick, hollow-bodied Gretsch guitar, brought a fat, funky sound to the band. We introduced Jimmy Reed and Muddy Waters into our repertoire.

The smoky-voiced Jamison gave us a versatility we never had before. Now we were able to expand our song list to include Aretha, Grace, and Janis. At this point, we traded in "Louie, Louie" for "Respect," and "Wooly Bully" for "Ball and Chain."

Psychedelia became our drug of choice. As we watched our alcohol-laced classmates get drunk, get into fist fights, and throw up all over each other, we felt much more comfortable in mellower environs. This came with a drastic backlash. While we kept one eye on the newspaper for music passing through St. Louis, we kept the other on our classmates from sneaking up from behind in a scissors ambush.

This only caused us to withdraw even more. We stopped attending dances in the gym, opting to head across town to Rainy Days and the Castaway Club—two venues that featured long-haired bands and a long-haired clientele.

Gigs became fewer and farther between, as none of our old friends seemed to want to hear this new music, made by these new bands with these weird names. The chasm grew. While they still flocked to see bands in matching blue sport coats, we flocked to hear Taj Mahal, Traffic, and Cream.

Jamison, a year older than the rest of us, introduced us to her friend Wolfy. The large man cut an imposing figure with his big boots, big beard, and long, long hair. Under the gruff exterior, though, he was a good guy who loved to have a good time. When his friend, Grateful Dead drummer Bill Kreutzman came to town, we all headed to their gigs.

Living in a large three-story house on McPherson Avenue in St. Louis's Central West End—a section of town known as a haven for artists, beatniks, and other assorted oddball characters—he allowed us to rehearse on the third floor.

Basically a glorified attic, we cleaned it up, hung black-light posters, tuned in, turned on, and turned up. Incense burned. Lava Lamps lavaed. Electric Kool-Aid gulped. The kaleidoscoped parties went through the night and well into the morning light.

I felt much more comfortable hanging around the urban Central West End than I did hanging around the suburban shopping malls. By this time, none of our folks wanted anything to do with any of us, and were scared to death of our scraggly new friends. Band practice in their ranch-style homes was no longer an option. They didn't want us there, and we didn't want to be there.

So, it was into the city for the Illicit Affair. We hauled our gear into Wolfy's and blasted away. The summer of '68 was spent in a purple haze.

Concerts were attended, as we never missed the opportunity to see who was passing through town. Many trips of many kinds were made to Kiel Auditorium, the Fox Theater, and across the river to Edwardsville, Illinois, home of the Mississippi River Festival. Sunday afternoons in Forest Park were a must.

School became a cold dish on the back burner. Though I had shrunk my circle of friends down to a mere handful, I caught the eye of Madelyn Harris and Mary Gotting—heads of the speech and theater department.

The two knew I played guitar. (By this time, I had learned what those other two strings were for.) When they asked if I'd be interested in participating in the all-school play, *Dark of the Moon*, I was intrigued. When I read the script, I saw the challenge. I had never done anything like this before, agreeing to a small role as the wise, old man who stayed on the fringes and played his guitar. A handful of songs, to be sung by the lead characters, were learned.

I was handed a rehearsal schedule that wasn't too demanding, and in the middle of a hostile environment called *high school*, was made to feel like an important part of a creative environment called *the theater department*. Rehearsals went smoothly. More importantly, they were fun. Since then, I've always felt comfortable hanging with creative people, as well as being part of a creative team.

Those in the cast who thought I was nothing but a wacko before they got to know me became nice friends. During the day, I was considered an outcast by the student body. But after the bell rang, I was considered an important part of the cast. I poured myself into my little role, the music and the teamwork a production like this requires.

Opening night was exciting. I was well prepared. I put a new set of strings on my guitar and was set. The production was simple, the entire stage stark, painted flat black, and shrouded with thick black curtains. There was no scenery, but for a handful of benches and stools. The entire cast was clad totally in black, with long-sleeve black shirts placing all focus on hands and faces. My hands were wrapped around my guitar.

Opening night, as the audience began to trickle into the theater, I quietly sat alone to one side of the darkened stage. Oblivious to the seating process going on, I began gently strumming a mellow, unobtrusive guitar piece I'd made up. When everyone finally settled into their seats, I faded out my strumming, the lights came up, and the cast began to assemble.

When the female lead lamented to the moon, I accompanied her with a haunting song in a minor key. When the revival scene broke out, I put it into overdrive, strumming as fast and furious as I could. The all-school play was a hit, as we sang and acted like it was Broadway. It is still in existence.

After *Dark of the Moon*, I was asked to participate in a series of melodramatic short stories, which I really dug. I enjoyed wearing funny white suits with ridiculously large cardboard bow ties. I enjoyed acting like a cartoon. The sillier the content, the more I liked it. I felt like I had found a home and a haven in the theater department.

Unfortunately, this happened right as I was preparing to leave.

Music and theater became oases in a turbulent final year of school. Times were tense. Viet Nam was raging, and I was getting ready to graduate—a ripe plum. Nerves were being struck on a daily basis. The entire sociology of America was changing. I, along with every other young male in the country, was faced with heavy decisions.

The thought of any war—of any kind, anywhere, at any time, for any reason—was totally against every fiber of my being. The very sight of Nixon—the crook—made me physically ill. I was not about to let him send me overseas. Staying out of Viet Nam didn't become one of my priorities. It became my *only* priority.

At this point, two people emerged to help with these decisions.

The first was a sympathetic draft counselor, which at the time was an honorable occupation. His advice was simple: Go to college, stay in college, stall for time, and wait for sanity to be restored to the world stage. This became my strategy.

The second was history teacher Mike Mitchell. Though I didn't really like history that much, I did like him and the way he taught. Not only was he from the small town of Springfield, Missouri, he had gone to college in Springfield and attained his diploma in Springfield. His first teaching gig was in St. Louis.

In a sea of Sergeant Carter-esque teachers, principals, and football coaches, Mitchell held after-school discussion groups for those of us who weren't interested in talking about carburetors or cheerleaders.

This exchange of ideas provided an outlet that wasn't readily available during any other part of the school day. It also provided a target for suspicious minds, who just knew we were plotting Communist takeovers from the lunchroom.

Mitchell informed his male students about Springfield. Stuck off down in the Ozarks, the little, nondescript town was an ideal place to lay low. Jesse James laid low there, as did Bonnie and Clyde.

Here we could easily keep our student deferments.

Here we could stay in Southwest Missouri, instead of going to Southeast Asia.

That was enough to convince me. Plus, this small college was renowned for its speech and theater departments. It seemed ideal. A course of action was taken. An application form was filled out. I looked forward to going to Springfield, Missouri.

Printed in the United States
124146LV00002B/2/P